Karon Oliver and Louise Ellerby-Jones

PSYCHOLOGY
& Everyday Life

SECOND EDITION

Hodder & Stoughton

A MEMBER OF THE HODDER HEADLINE GROUP

Dedication

For Chris, with love and thanks for his continued support this time, not only with lots of cups of tea, but also with help keeping my ever-growing menagerie in order.

Karon

Thanks, Nige, for the love and support, but more importantly for the chocolate and Shiraz.

Louise

Orders: please contact Bookpoint Ltd, 130 Milton Park, Abingdon, Oxon OX14 4SB. Telephone: +44 (0)1235 827720. Fax: (44) 01235 400454. Lines are open from 9.00–6.00, Monday to Saturday, with a 24-hour message answering service. You can also order through our website www.hodderheadline.co.uk.

British Library Cataloguing in Publication Data
A catalogue record for this title is available from the British Library

ISBN 0 340 81625 2

This edition published 2004
Impression number   10 9 8 7 6 5 4 3 2
Year   2007 2006 2005 2004

Typeset by Dorchester Typesetting Group Ltd
Printed in Great Britain for Hodder & Stoughton Educational, a division of Hodder Headline, 338 Euston Road, London NW1 3BH by Martins The Printers, Berwick Upon Tweed

Hodder Headline's policy is to use papers that are natural, renewable and recyclable products and made from wood grown in sustainable forests. The logging and manufacturing processes are expected to conform to the environmental regulations of the country of origin.

Contents

Introduction

Although this book is intended primarily for students who are studying the OCR syllabus, hopefully it will provide a good introduction to other students of psychology who have very little prior knowledge of the research which has shaped our understanding of the way human beings think and behave. For this reason, we have included some examples of situations which relate to everyday life. We have also described in some detail, 20 of the most well-known studies in psychology, which, although they may be dated, are still considered very important within the discipline.

The book begins with an overview of research methods, has five further chapters, each containing four key studies, and ends with a chapter on ways to revise for the OCR AS examination. Each 'key studies' chapter gives an initial introduction to the area and puts each study in context. We have also pointed out the different perspectives people have on psychology, as well as addressing evaluative issues and providing a conclusion to each of the studies which we hope will provoke further discussion.

When you start to study the subject, you may feel that it is quite disconcerting to discover that some areas of psychology are still open to discussion, because sometimes it seems much nicer to know that what you are learning is all undisputed truth. Although there are some theories which *are* undisputed, other areas are open to further speculation and this, in itself, can be a source of excitement. It means that everyone has the potential to contribute to further understanding of the way we work.

We hope this book gives you a taste for psychology and that you will enjoy your studies. Who knows? One day it might be you who helps us answer some of our, as yet, unanswered questions about human behaviour and experience.

Acknowledgements

The authors and publisher would like to thank the following for permission to use images: page 107, BFI Films; page 142, BFI Films; page 192, Novosti/Science Photo Library; page 205, Albert Bandura, Stanford University; page 253, Eye of Science/Science Photo Library; page 279, Philippe Plailly/Science Photo Library; page 306 (a), James Holmes/Science Photo Library; (b), GCa/Science Photo Library; (c) Mehau Kulyk/Science Photo Library; (d), Tim Beddow/Science Photo Library.

The publisher would like to thank the following for permission to base key study material on the following studies: Academic Press Inc. for E.F. Loftus and J.J. Palmer (1974) Reconstruction of automobile destruction: an example of the interaction between language and memory, *Journal of Verbal Learning and Verbal Behavior*, 13; the American Psychological Association for A. Bandura, D. Ross and S.A. Ross (1961) Transmission of aggression through imitation of aggressive models, *Journal of Abnormal and Social Psychology*, 63; W. Dement and N. Kleitman (1957) The relation of eye movements during sleep to dream activity: an objective method for the study of dreaming, *Journal of Experimental Psychology*, 53; J. Hraba and G. Grant (1970) Black is beautiful: a re-examination of racial preference and identification, *Journal of Personality and Social Psychology*, 16; I.M. Piliavin, J.A. Rodin and J. Piliavin (1969) Good Samaritanism: an underground phenomenon, *Journal of Personality and Social Psychology*, 13; S. Schachter and J. Singer (1962) Cognitive, social and physiological determinants of emotional state, *Psychological Review*, 69; R.W. Sperry (1968) Hemisphere deconnection and unity in conscious awareness, *American Psychologist*, 23; and C. Thigpen and H. Cleckley (1954) A case of multiple personality, *Journal of Abnormal and Social Psychology*, 49; Elsevier Science for S. Baron-Cohen, A.M. Leslie and U. Frith (1985) Does the autistic child have a 'theory of mind'? *Cognition*, 21; Mrs A. Milgram for S. Milgram (1963) Behavioural study of obedience, *Journal of Abnormal and Social Psychology*, 67; W.W. Norton & Co. for S.J. Gould (1981) A nation of morons, in *The Mismeasure of Man*; Pergamon Press for J. Hodges and B. Tizard (1989) Social and family relationships of ex-institutional adolescents,

Journal of Child Psychology and Psychiatry, 30; and J. Samuel and P. Bryant (1984) Asking only on question in the conservation experiment, *Journal of Child Psychology and Psychiatry*, 23 (2); *Science* for R.A. Gardner and B.T. Gardner (1969) Teaching sign language to a chimpanzee, *Science*, 165 (3894); and D.L. Rosenhan (1973) On being sane in insane places, *Science*, 179; *Scientific American* Inc. for J.B. Deregowski (1972) Pictorial perception and culture, *Scientific American*, 227; and H. Tajfel (1970) Experiments in intergroup discrimination, *Scientific American*, 223; Sigmund Freud Copyrights Ltd, the Institute of Psychoanalysis and the Hogarth Press for S. Freud, Analysis of a phobia in a five-year-old boy, in J. Strachey (ed. and trans.) *The Standard Edition of the Complete Works of Sigmund Freud*; A. Raine, M. Buchsbaum and L. LaCasse (1997) Brain Abnormalities in Murderers Indicated by Positron Emission Tomography, *Biological Psychiatry*, 42, 495–508 reprinted with permission from the Society of Biological Psychiatry (*Biological Psychiatry*, 1997, 42, 495–508); US Naval Institute for C. Haney, C. Banks and P. Zimbardo (1973) A study of prisoners and guards in a simulated prison, *Naval Research Reviews*, 30.

Every effort has been made to obtain necessary permission with reference to copyright material. The publishers apologise if inadvertently any sources remain unacknowledged and will be glad to make the necessary arrangements at the earliest opportunity.

Investigating people

You have decided you want to know more about the subject of psychology. You want to understand how people function, both physically and mentally and, what makes them behave the way they do. Even if you were to be given all the information we currently have about psychological theories and research, there is no way for you to be 100% sure that they are all true. The reason for this is that we can never actually get inside people's heads to find out, and this provides perhaps the biggest dilemma when studying psychology. However, it doesn't mean that we should just give up. What we need to do is to try as best we can to continue researching people using the most effective methodology, with the intention of increasing our knowledge of how people really 'work'.

We could start by looking at the methods used by past researchers to understand these complex creatures called human beings, but how can we ever be sure that the people who were under investigation were actually being natural in their behaviour when they were in front of the researchers, or whether they accurately answered the questions posed to them? Even if we decide to question our own motives and use this as a kind of insight into understanding human behaviour, this may not bring us closer to understanding because we frequently fool ourselves or make excuses as to why we do things. This kind of introspection has a place in psychology, but as you will probably realise, the results are going to be quite subjective.

So when you study a subject like psychology, you must learn to question and evaluate the research that has been done and make your own decisions as to whether you accept the findings of past researchers. You also have to be fair about it, because it is very easy to say it is all rubbish! However, unless you can come up with an alternative explanation, you really have to take seriously what others have found.

You have to remember that *you* are probably going to be biased in some way too, and this may be due to your age. If a researcher is 60 years old, you will probably think he's a bit out of date in his thoughts and beliefs, and this may mean that he interprets what he finds in a different way from someone who is much younger. As we get older, though, 60 doesn't seem *so* old and it makes us look at the researcher in a slightly different way. In fact, if we are honest, the maturity and experience this 60-year-old researcher will bring to his work may actually allow him to be more open and objective in his views, and less driven by the passion of youth!

There is also something known as 'gender bias'. If we are female, then of course we know that females are far superior to males, more intelligent, more able to do lots of tasks at the same time, more sympathetic and so on. However, if we are male, then we argue that women are much weaker than men, burst out crying too often, become totally irrational around the same time every month and all the other stereotypical characteristics attributed to women.

We can take all these factors into the research situation with us if we are not careful. Therefore, in order to try to study people who will also have these biases and prejudices, we have to make sure that we are as objective and scientific as we can possibly be. Even then, we can't remove the hidden biases – things we aren't actually aware of doing – like fluttering our eyelashes (if we are female) at attractive male subjects (or the vice-versa equivalent), or being extremely negative to the older subject who smells of mothballs and has bad breath.

In order to counteract these types of situations, or at least keep to a minimum the influence they have, there are a number of different methodologies we can use. We also have statistical tests which are used to remove the 'extra bits' of bias mathematically and tell us if our results are really relevant or just due to chance. Consider the following:

Alison is going to take her GCSEs next summer and she is already wondering where to go to college to study A levels. She has decided that she has had enough of school. Yeah, okay, the school's not that bad, but she really doesn't fancy having to wear 'sensible' clothes for another two years, and all the boys at the college down the road are so cute!

It's open day at the college and she decides to go and see what it is really like, and she hasn't really made up her mind what subjects she wants to study. Well, some of these weird subjects that she hasn't done before look quite interesting, especially psychology. That's the one that is all about people and why they do what they do, and body language and aggression and mental illness and stuff – isn't it?

When she gets to the college, along with lots of other students from all different schools, she feels quite nervous. Then she sees Sally, her best mate and this makes it much better. The college has arranged a day where you can go and do sample lessons and find out a bit more about the subjects. Along she goes to the psychology department with Sally and quite a few others to hear what the teachers have to say. She is about quarter of an hour early, but she isn't worried because she has a lot of catching up to do with Sally who went to a party with her new boyfriend last weekend. Just as they are about to go into the classroom, two boys come up to them. At first Alison thinks their luck has changed when one of them says, 'Hello, we are psychology students here and we wondered if you would mind taking part in an experiment as part of our coursework?'

Alison looks at Sally, and Sally looks at Alison and they both giggle.

Sally says, 'How long will it take?'

'About ten minutes,' says the dark-haired one, who has such gorgeous eyes.

'Will it hurt?' says Alison, fluttering her eyelashes and showing off her cleavage.

The student grins, 'Not this time'.

How do you think the girls feel about the situation? Do you think they have expectations about what they are going to be asked to do? Do you think they could be nervous? What about the male students?

This is a classic example of how people who agree to become subjects in psychological research may actually enter the experiment with expectations or concerns which, in turn, will affect the way they behave (or perform).

Imagine the same situation with the students asking two boys to take part. They would behave in a completely different way. They may be defiant or act as if they have no fear. Now imagine the situation if the researcher were a middle-aged man in a white coat and the location was a prestigious university.

By now I hope you will be able to see that psychologists must carefully consider ways of investigating people if they want their results to have any value at all. Unfortunately, they don't always get it right, but hopefully you can see that designing effective research is not as easy as it seems. Whenever you criticise research, you should try to work out how it should have been done and whether there was actually an alternative method that could have been used which would not have caused even more problems.

So where do we start? First of all, we want to try to find out why people behave as they do or why certain things occur. In order to investigate this, we must aim to use a process which is objective and reliable and will produce results which are hopefully relevant to everyone and not just the small group of people we are interested in. However, there are always occasions when we might be interested in investigating just a small group of people in a specific situation, and this is quite acceptable as long as the researchers make it clear that the results will probably apply only to the people under investigation. An example would be people in a specific job or institution, such as a prison or a school.

The way that psychologists investigate the things that interest them is by using what is known as 'the scientific method'. This method is really no different to the techniques taught in science at school where you can investigate any question, from 'do plants grow without light?' to 'do pH levels affect the rate of enzyme-controlled reactions within cells?'

The scientific method actually has four parts to it, and these are things that you will probably have touched on at school but may not necessarily be aware of.

The scientific method

1. You must make objective observations of the phenomena that you are interested in, for example differences in gender behaviour or the effects of caffeine on memory.
2. From these observations you will have a good idea of what you want to study. In order to do this you should work out a testable hypothesis on the basis of these observations. A hypothesis is really an educated guess about why people are behaving or reacting in a certain way.
3. You then have to devise a method to test this hypothesis and carry out the research.
4. You should then make both the methods you used and your results available to the public so that others can assess them, replicate them or even extend your findings.

One of the reasons for this is because people can make wild claims which may have a huge effect on our society. A striking example of this was the work of Sir Cyril Burt. He was responsible for the supposed research that resulted in the setting up of the eleven-plus exam (an examination used to decide whether schoolchildren should be sent to grammar school or secondary modern school). Grammar schools were very academic and secondary moderns were intended to teach practical skills to those students who were less academically able. After the eleven-plus had been in place for a number of years, another researcher started to ask questions about Burt's research. He was interested in why Burt believed it was valid to test eleven-year-old schoolchildren and decide their future.

Sir Cyril Burt was supposed to have carried out a great deal of research about the eleven-plus and the fact that your IQ level was supposed to remain the same from age 11 to the end of your life, and that this level was inherited and so would never vary. His argument was that if it was always going to be the same, testing people at 11 was the best time to fit them into an educational system that would best suit them, rather than trying to push them to achieve more than they were capable of. But what had happened was that Cyril Burt believed so strongly that this was true that he made up the evidence to prove it. When this was discovered, the eleven-plus was phased out. If it had been possible to give his evidence to the world, he would not have been discredited and millions of children would not have been disadvantaged.

RESEARCH METHODS

There are a number of methods of investigation which come under the umbrella of the scientific method and these are:

1. Experiments
2. Observations
3. Case studies
4. Surveys/questionnaires/interviews
5. Neurophysiological measurements
6. Correlations (worth mentioning although they are really more of a statistical technique than a method).

All these techniques will be covered in this book. Each one has advantages and disadvantages and each one is suited to specific types of investigations. The problem lies in the fact that sometimes researchers get it wrong. Perhaps they have designed their study poorly and the participants are not representative of the population as a whole. Perhaps the sample is biased in terms of culture – can you generalise from white, middle-class American undergraduate students to the population as a whole? Perhaps the sample just guessed what the study was about and acted accordingly. You also need to consider if the studies have any real value in today's society.

In order to have some idea of the good and bad parts to each methodology it will be useful to go through them, so that when you read the method of each key study you will already have an awareness of the aims of the person undertaking the investigation and what could have gone wrong with their design. We will start with experiments because they are the method everyone always associates with science, and then go through the other techniques in this chapter. The last one, neurophysiological measurements, is detailed in the section on biopsychology.

Although the next section may seem a little simplistic, you will have to forgive the examples used. It is only intended to make what could be a relatively complex (and possibly boring) section easier to understand by using examples that you will be familiar with. The example for describing a simple type of experiment actually has nothing to do with psychology, although our past experiences and beliefs may influence the results, but it is a good idea to start with something simple in order to look at the possible problems that can arise.

The problem we are going to start with is one that faces us every time we go into the supermarket: what kind of chocolate chip cookies should we buy? After all, there are so many different types of cookie and some seem to be really nice whilst others are dry and have fewer lumps of chocolate. However, we do know that there are two main contenders for the title of Chocolate Chip Cookie of the Year.

Therefore, what we need to do is conduct research to decide whether there is a difference in the 'yumminess' of the two main types of chocolate chip cookies and whether one really is much better than the other. The way we could do this is to conduct an experiment into the yumminess factor of each chocolate chip cookie.

Experiments

Let's try using an experiment to work out which is the most yummy cookie. With an experiment it is important to be able to compare two things in order to see if one has a greater effect or influence than the other. But what do we mean by influence? Influence on what? In this case the influence would have to be on different people, and these people will be the subjects (otherwise known as participants) in our research. In fact all experiments need participants, so we will discuss the issue of human participants in our description of this particular kind of research although they are relevant in all methodologies.

FOCUS ON PAST RESEARCH – subjects vs. participants

It is worth mentioning here that some people use the term participants and others use the term subjects to describe the people who take part. In the past people who took part in psychological research were *always* called subjects and in this book we will usually refer to participants as subjects because that was what they were called in the studies we will be describing. We do understand that some people feel the word subject implies that those taking part are 'subjected' to something and can be considered objects to be manipulated at the researcher's will, whereas the term participants suggests that there is a partnership between the participant and the researcher. We accept that this should not be the case and we hope you don't find it offensive for us to follow the title used by the researchers who undertook the core studies. However, for the remainder of this chapter, we will use the term participants in order for you to see that the terms are really interchangeable.

So far we have decided that in this particular study what we will be comparing are the two main brands of chocolate chip cookie and how they are rated for yumminess by the participants. We must also consider at this point, how are we going to measure yumminess?

It is always important to make sure that the phenomenon you are investigating is measurable in some way and this can sometimes be extremely difficult. In this particular study we are going to have to work out what we actually mean by yumminess. Do we mean preference, or do we mean ratings on a scale of one to ten, or do we mean how full these cookies make us? On the other hand, perhaps we mean how chocolatey or how crunchy they are. This would have to be decided before the start of the study because the researchers need to ensure that all the participants are rating these cookies in the same way. The problem with some studies is that the chosen measurement of the effects is sometimes a little worrying, so make sure when you are designing and evaluating studies that you take into account whether the results are actually measuring these effects or something completely different, such as appearance.

Types of data

There are, in fact, a number of different ways of measuring participant responses. If we chose a simple study such as how fast people could run in two minutes, we could then compare the distance. This data would be called *interval data* because there is the same interval between one measure and the next – the distance between one metre and the next is the same no matter how far the participant managed to run. Other examples of interval data would be how many words people could remember from a list they had to learn or how many sums they got correct.

Another type of data is called *ordinal data* or ranked data, and this is where we rank one thing either alone or in comparison with another thing. If we had ten different types of cookies, we could put them in order of preference and therefore we would be ranking them. With our two types of cookies, we could ask participants to rate both of them on a five-point scale where 5 is equivalent to 'the best cookie I have ever tasted' whilst 1 is 'so revolting I would put it in the bin rather than eat it'. We would then add up the scores from all the participants for each cookie and get an idea of which one was rated or ranked better than the other. (This is the kind of score we get from attitude surveys where people are asked to rate liking or preference for different things on a scale.) Actually, these types of scales, which are known as Likert scales, are usually four- or five-point scales. If you have a five-point scale it means you can choose the 'neither good nor bad' score of 3 – and if you can't be bothered to take the study seriously this is the score you would usually choose. On the other hand, a four-point scale means that you have to come down on one side or the other, either favouring or not, but can't choose the middle option as there isn't one!

Alternatively, we could ask participants to rank only one cookie on a five-point scale, where 5 means 'I would always buy this cookie in the future' and 1 means 'I will never buy this cookie in the future'.

The last type of data is known as *nominal data* or categorical data. This is where you have to categorise the cookie by ticking the box marked, 'Yes, I'd buy it again', or the box marked, 'No, I would not buy it again'. There are no half measures with categorical data – the data or response goes in one box or the other.

For our study, it is probably most useful to use ordinal or ranked data, where people have to rank their feelings for the yumminess of cookies they are tasting by using a five-point Likert scale similar to the one described above. Therefore, we will have two conditions:

People who try 'Chokkie-chippy' and people who try 'Lots-o-Choc'.

- One variable (thing that changes) is the different type of cookie.
- The other variable (thing that changes) may be the difference in your 'I'd buy again' rating, from before eating to after eating the aforementioned cookie.

(These are known as the *independent variable* – the variable that is being changed or manipulated by the researchers, i.e. the cookie – and the *dependent variable*, i.e. the result.)

It may be that participants' 'I'd buy again' rating will not be any different before and after eating because they don't care or just don't like cookies, but in order to decide whether this is going to be the case, they need to tuck in!

First of all, we must ensure that the appearance of the cookie packets will not influence the participants. If one of the packets is brightly coloured with pictures of rich milk chocolate and the other is a kind of dirty grey colour with no writing or pictures on it, it's quite likely that this would have some influence on their expectations and set up some kind of bias. In fact, this expectancy bias can have quite an influence on any results. In order to get over this the researchers would have to ensure that all they see are cookies coming from packets which look the same. It is also a possibility that the cookies themselves may differ in appearance and therefore they may actually be required to wear a blindfold if they are to try both types of cookie.

It is quite likely that they may have an idea what the experiment is about – and even if they are wrong they may well try to guess. If they are asked to try one cookie from one packet and then another cookie from another packet they will probably realise that the study may be something to do with taste. It may be to do with amount of chocolate per cookie, or lightness or something similar. Whatever conclusion they come to, it will probably influence the results because they will no longer be eating cookies in the way they would normally. They may be savouring every mouthful, searching with their tongues for chocolate pieces and so on. In fact, they may try to help the experimenter by choosing one cookie over the other if they believe the researcher is trying to promote one particular brand. On the other hand, they may decide to deliberately sabotage the study by saying they taste the same, even if they think they don't, because they think the study is simply another way of biscuit companies making money. These extra influences on the results are called *demand characteristics* and can actually ruin the results of a study.

Examples of how demand characteristics can influence the results of research were demonstrated by studies conducted by Orne. He was interested in the fact that people behave very differently in a psychological study to the way they behave in everyday life. In one study he asked a number of people whether they would carry out five push-ups as a personal favour and, not surprisingly, they all refused. However, when he played the role of research psychologist, they all became very obliging and willing to help. Although the behaviour was the same, and the reasons for asking were the same (to see how people would behave), the responses were totally different.

The most amusing of Orne's studies was carried out in 1962 when he was trying find out whether participants who were hypnotised were more obedient. He never did find out whether or not they were because he became more fascinated by the fact that people act in a totally different way if they think they are taking part in a psychological experiment.

Before Orne started the study, he took away their watches. He then asked his participants to add up rows of numbers on sheets filled with numbers that had been randomly generated. Each subject was given 2,000 sheets and each sheet meant they would have to make 224 calculations. He told them to continue to work and that he was leaving the room but would be back later. After 5½ hours they were still working, which he found extraordinary. They must have believed that the study was worthwhile, otherwise they wouldn't have continued, but he wondered if there was another reason for the way they continued to work. He wondered if they were simply being obedient.

In order to get round this, he decided to make the task so ridiculous that he felt they couldn't possibly agree to go on. He told them that once they had finished a sheet, they had to pick a card up from a pile which would tell them what to do next. The card they had to pick up said: 'You are to tear up the sheet of paper which you have just completed into a minimum of 32 pieces and go on to the next sheet of paper and continue working as you did before. When you have completed this piece of paper, pick up the next card which will instruct you further. Work as accurately and rapidly as you can.' How long would it take you to realise that the whole episode was simply a waste of time? Probably not very long – but that is because you are not taking part. If you had been there, you would have been trying to work out the purpose of such a study. Well, presumably Orne's participants did the same, because they all carried on, adding up numbers and tearing up the sheets, just as they had been instructed!

There is one further problem that could influence the results which is worth mentioning here, and this is that the experimenter can have an influence on how they turn out. Imagine that the packets of cookies the researchers were using for the study were actually different in both taste and quality, it is quite likely that they will have decided beforehand that one is better than the other. Chokkie-chippy biscuits are light and crunchy and have lots of lumps of rich chocolate in them, whilst Lots-o-Choc are soggier and have less chocolate in microscopic pieces. Their knowledge and opinion may be inadvertently transmitted to you by the way they talk to you. 'Try these Chokkie-chippy biscuits' they may say with smiles on their faces. Then they hand the Lots-o-Choc with no comment and no smile. Participants would already have an expectation of the best biscuit, wouldn't they? This influence, known as an *experimenter effect*, may also totally influence the results even though it is unconscious.

If the researchers have managed to control these problems, the next question crops up: who are the researchers going to choose to be their participants?

Some people love chocolate, others dislike it. Others have a savoury tooth and prefer to eat crisps. Some people like biscuits, and some people like biscuits but every time they eat them they feel guilty because they are on a diet and this affects their enjoyment, and other people are allergic to wheat and therefore become ill when they eat biscuits. Think about your own feelings towards cookies: you may well like cookies, but supposing you had just eaten a giant bar of chocolate – the thought of eating cookies would probably make you feel sick. Alternatively, if you are absolutely starving, cookies may be the best food in the world, even if they aren't a particularly tasty brand.

Now think about this in terms of participants for any kind of experiment rather than simply the biscuit study. No two people are the same, are they? Not only are people not the same in terms of what they look like, but they will not have had the same experiences as each other, they will not necessarily be as intelligent as each other, they may not be the same age or gender, or they may have come from different parts of the country. Some may have had normal family lives and some may have been in institutions. Some may have broken bones, or may have suffered with illness. Some may get migraines while others may never have had an ache or pain in their lives. Some may come from one cultural group while others may have totally different codes of behaviour.

What an experimental nightmare! No, the researchers won't give up at this point and go home – they will try to do the best they can. There are three possible options.

Matched pairs

They can either try to match the participants so that the ones in each group are as similar as possible. Obviously, the ideal way is to use clones, but as clones are not readily available to researchers at the moment, identical twins are the next best option. The only problem is that there aren't that many available identical twins around. So what they will do is to match the pairs as far as possible for the factors they are interested in. For this experiment it might be necessary to ensure that no one is on a diet, no one is starving and no one is allergic to wheat. It may then be necessary to match participants for gender (as women generally like chocolate more than men). Perhaps their participants will consist of two groups, with equal numbers of men and women in each, because age and intelligence are unlikely to influence cookie preference. In real psychological experiments, they would match the two groups as far as possible for the factors they are interested in, which, again, could be gender and age, but might also be IQ or background.

CORE STUDY LINK – the study by Hodges and Tizard (p. 219) gives a good example of matched pairs.

Repeated measures

Perhaps the researchers could make the participants try both types of cookie and rate each one. The trouble is that by eating the first cookie, the palate might become dull and therefore the second cookie won't taste any where near as good. Therefore they may have one cookie one day and the other cookie the next day, but they may have had a very strong curry in between and this may affect their taste buds. One way round this would be for half the participants to try Chokkie-chippy biscuits first and Lots-o-Choc second, whilst the other half try them the other way round. This would at least give us a slightly better idea as to which cookie is really the best.

Effects like these can happen when any person has to do different things as part of a study. They may use the experience of the first trial as a kind of practice for the second trial – known as *practice effects*. The things they do between the trials may also influence the results. They may simply be tired the second time, which may affect how well they do (this is known as *fatigue effects*). If you read about studies where participants have to do more than one thing, bear this in mind.

Independent subjects

Another alternative is where our researchers decided to go for a huge number of participants who would then be randomly divided into two groups. Using this method, it is hoped that the differences in participants in the two groups would balance each other out – which is likely when there are a large number of people. After all, if there are enough of them it would seem likely that there would be people of all types in both groups, wouldn't it? I don't need to tell you that logistically, if we are to make this work, we would need a lot of people, and this is one disadvantage of this method.

Each of the designs has problems – but it is the researcher's choice as to which method he uses. You should always look out for the type of design used for research and consider the participants, the way they were chosen and whether or not they represent the population as a whole.

Sampling

Choosing people for any kind of research should not really be that difficult, except that lots of people don't like the idea of taking part in research, whereas others think it's great fun. This should make you aware that even this small difference can mean we have two different groups of people. I'm sure some of you avoid questionnaires like the plague, whereas others are quite happy to take part in surveys.

If people are willing to take part in research and volunteer their services, they would be considered to be a volunteer or *self-selecting sample*. Perhaps there is something about the type of people who volunteer to take part which will have an influence on the responses they may give. Many undergraduate psychology students have the opportunity to participate in research in order to gain 'Brownie points' with their tutors. These kind of self-selecting samples are likely to produce different responses to research than their non-psychology counterparts.

> **CORE STUDY LINK** – the Milgram study (p. 29) uses a self-selecting sample. Do you think this may have influenced the results? Other studies have also enticed their participants with promises of either money or credits on psychology courses – look out for the study by Schachter and Singer (p. 266). In this study the student participants got points towards their exams for taking part.

Ideally, the best kind of sample is a random sample, taken from the population of people you are interested in investigating. A random sample means that every person has an equal chance of being selected. The ideal way is to put everyone's name in a hat and draw out the relevant number of names.

In the cookie experiment, the population the researchers are interested in anyone and everyone, because cookie eating is not targeted at any particular group of people. However, if the company decided it should be for teenagers, the sampling frame would be teenagers and the sample would be taken from all the teenagers there were. In most research there would be a more limited sampling frame like all the teenagers in a certain area, but here it is obvious that that area might not be the same as another area, so we would have to bear that in mind. *Stratified samples* are where you take the same proportion of people in your sample as there are in the population. If we return to the cookie experiment and decide that we need to have people of different ages (in case age makes a difference to cookie appreciation), we would make the decision perhaps to start with children over the age of ten, because children under the age of ten may just like any sweet biscuit, not having had the time or opportunity to develop their gourmet skills. We also conclude that people over the age of 100 probably don't care. This leaves us with a chosen population of people between the ages of ten and say 100.

If the researchers then discover that 20% of the population are between the ages of ten and 30, 35% fall between the ages of 31 and 50, 25% fall between the ages of 51 and 70, and the remaining 20% are aged between 71 and 100, the sample would have to contain the same proportions. If they wanted a sample size of 100, 20 would be between ten and 30 years of age, 35 between 31 and 50, 25 between 51 and 70, and 20 between the ages of 71 and 100.

Quota samples are a bit like stratified samples. You identify the different types of people, but simply have the same number of each, e.g. 25 of each age group to make up a sample of 100.

Snowball samples are used when it is helpful to get a lot of information about a situation or organisation. Key people may be selected for interview and they may suggest interviewing others who would be able to provide more information.

The last type of sample is the one used by most psychology students when carrying out their research, and this is a convenience or *opportunity sample*. This means that you grab anyone available to take part, but the weaknesses of this kind of sample are fairly obvious – do you think the people you come into contact with every day are representative of the population as a whole?

Whatever design is chosen and whatever sample is decided upon, it must be remembered that where the experiment is carried out will also influence the participants, and they will have expectations of what is going to happen from their past experiences. Sometimes you can help to get over this by doing a field experiment – not an experiment in a field but one that takes place in the usual environment for the participants, e.g. an office or school or even a shopping centre. What sort of environment would qualify as a field setting for a study into cookie preference – a supermarket, a café, or perhaps our own kitchens?

Observations

Perhaps an observational study would be preferable. Here the researchers may have decided that they could simply watch the behaviour of the participant during the eating of the cookie, or their behaviour immediately after they have taken the last mouthful. They would have to work out what sort of categories of behaviour cookie eating is likely to fall into before they conducted their study. Will they chew vigorously (and if they do, does this imply that they like what they are eating?) or will they suck and then gently allow the cookie to float effortlessly down their throat (and how will they know that this is what is happening?).

Obviously when a study is designed, the type of study will influence whether to watch the behaviours or calculate the results in some other way. If it is a study looking at the effects of something on behaviour, then observing that behaviour is essential. For other studies, observations would be totally inappropriate, such as a study on memory (watching people remembering lists of words would not be very helpful).

Observations are used for studies of things like aggressive behaviour or behaviour between individuals and groups of people. They can be done by observing the behaviour of participants either overtly or covertly; and occasionally research has been done using a method called participant observation. The observation can take place in a laboratory or in the field.

Overt observation

Participants know they are being observed, but this can be a problem as it may change behaviour. Usually participants get used to being watched after a while and it is said that they have habituated to the researcher. Think of 'fly-on-the-wall' documentaries as an example of how people habituate to situations. You may say that you could never behave as people do in these documentaries if they were being filmed, but after a while the people cease noticing that the camera is there.

Covert observation

This is where people hide in trees or behind walls or one-way mirrors, so they can't be seen. They could also secretly video the people they are watching.

Participant observation

This is where the person observing actually becomes part of the group of people they want to watch. A famous example of one such study was undertaken by Whyte (1943), who joined an Italian street gang in Chicago. It was obvious that he was not a normal gang member, but he used the cover that he was writing a book. The study is most famous because of his statement, 'I began as a non-participating observer. As I became accepted into the community, I found myself becoming almost a non-observing participant.'

If an observational study is undertaken, there are some things that must be taken into consideration whilst designing the observation schedule. Researchers must make sure that the behaviours they are expecting to see actually exist, and that there aren't so many of them that they spend more time trying to work out where to tick on the chart and miss world war three going on in front of them. They must also make sure that the observation schedules use objective criteria, rather than criteria they want to see, whilst ignoring other possible behaviours. An example of this would be research looking at whether boys are more aggressive than girls using an observation schedule which only includes physical aggression but misses out verbal aggression, which is far more common in girls. Having more than one objective observer and then checking that they agree with each other's scores – known as inter-observer or inter-rater reliability – can sort out the problem of remaining objective.

Finally, researchers must make sure that when observing, they don't get so bored that they fall asleep. The boredom factor can be solved by something known as time sampling, where they watch for five minutes, for example, and then rest for five and so on. The other thing to remember is that researchers should never observe someone in a place where they would not normally be on public display unless they have permission.

Case studies

Perhaps we should carry out a case study. Here our intrepid experimenters decide that they will look at someone's biscuit eating over a period of time and document in graphic detail every possible piece of information. They would then be able to look at any strange or unusual phenomena which may occur as a result of the different types of cookie chosen.

Case studies do actually have a specific purpose in psychology. They are generally carried out over a long period of time and involve looking in detail at either one or possibly a couple of participants. They are usually used to look at interesting and unusual phenomena or to develop hypotheses about the cause of a specific type of behaviour prior to carrying out more extensive research. The main problem is that they can be quite subjective. If you get to know someone really well over a period of time, they are going to behave in a slightly different way towards you compared with other people, and you will perhaps be less objective about their behaviour as you would have been at the onset of the study.

CORE STUDY LINK – Freud's study of Little Hans (p. 240) is a case study. When you read the study, think of the problem of subjectivity.

Surveys, questionnaires and interviews

Perhaps we could simply go for a survey, questionnaire or interview. These methods are frequently used in psychology, often to accompany other research. In the cookie study, the researchers could certainly ask the participants how satisfied they feel after eating one or other of the cookies, and this would give them quite a lot of valuable information to work on. The trouble is that in any kind of questioning people aren't always honest and they may report that the cookie they had just eaten was excellent when they actually spat it out.

There are two different types of questions used in these methods: *open* and *closed questions*. Open questions require the participant to answer the questions in as much or as little detail as they like. Open questions are really difficult to analyse but can give lots of very interesting information. After all, some people go on and on about all sorts of things when asked certain questions, whilst others produce great insights into causes and effects.

Closed questions require yes or no answers or perhaps a fixed choice of three or four alternatives, so the amount of information gathered may be less but is easier to score. These methods are often used as they give the opportunity of finding out information from a large number of people (questionnaires or surveys) or allow interviewers to focus on one particular area in much greater detail (interviews with open questions). Whatever happens, the questions must be understandable. Have you ever been given a questionnaire which is really difficult to answer and seems to be totally meaningless or you just don't understand the questions? Another problem is using what is known as 'an answer set' where you always tick 'a' or 'b'. The other really annoying fact is that some questionnaires are so obvious that you can work out what the right answer is and can mark it accordingly to try and make yourself seem 'very popular', or 'a good sport,' and so on.

Neurophysiological measurements

Perhaps the only way it is to measure the participants' brains. This is where researchers actually measure people's responses or behaviours using instruments.

The problem here is that this type of measure is unlikely to be of much use in the cookie study.

CORE STUDY LINK – look at the study by Raine (p. 313) and the study by Dement and Kleitman (p. 283) in order to understand the way physiological measurements of the brain are made.

All methods of neurophysiological measurement use specialised equipment. The idea is that the equipment cannot lie, so that if there is something different about a person's responses it can be objectively measured.

Examples are EEGs, which measure the changes in electrical activity in different areas of the brain. CT scans are useful to see structural abnormalities. MRI scans are similar to CAT scans but are more accurate because they can pick up smaller details. PET scans allow researchers to examine the relationship between brain activity and mental processes. You will find more information about these types of measurement and how they are carried out in the section on physiology.

Correlations

Maybe the only thing left to do is a correlation. Correlations are not really a design, but more of a statistical procedure. They look for a relationship between two variables such as watching TV and aggression. For example, does watching TV affect the amount of aggressive behaviour children display?

Unfortunately correlations cannot actually prove anything because there could always have been another variable which was not taken into account. Our child may well watch lots of violent TV programmes and may demonstrate huge amounts of aggressive behaviour, but the poor child was beaten regularly by its father throughout its life and we haven't taken that into account because it is not one of the variables we are concerned with. Therefore the relationship exists but the TV is probably not the cause. You can see from this how dangerous it is to accept a correlation as being a factual cause.

There are lots of other examples which could be used to make the point here, such as the relationship between hot weather and aggressive behaviour, which is a topic covered in environmental psychology. The problem is that when it is hot, we often drink more, and that drink may well be lots of ice-cold lager, which can lead to people getting aggressive because they are under the influence of alcohol.

Correlations aren't all bad and actually raise a number of potential research questions in psychology. If you find a relationship between two variables, you can then go on to investigate that relationship further. They are also used to check the reliability of psychometric tests (see below) or to compare scores on different types of tests such as how life-stress test scores relate to illness.

Positive and negative correlations

There are two different types of correlation, positive and negative. A positive correlation shows that as one thing goes up, so does another. Supposing we wanted to investigate whether eating lots of steak makes you run faster, we would have to look at the speed of running of athletes and see if there was a relationship between their speed and the number of large rump steaks they ate every week. This could be done by drawing a scattergram.

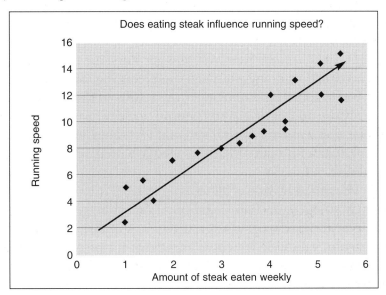

Can you see from the generalised direction that the more steak people eat the faster they seem to run? This would indicate that there is a positive relationship between the amount of steak you eat and your speed of running.

On the other hand, supposing we looked at the number of plates of chips you eat and the speed you can run. We would expect the opposite relationship here, with speed slowing in relation to the number of bowls of chips you eat.

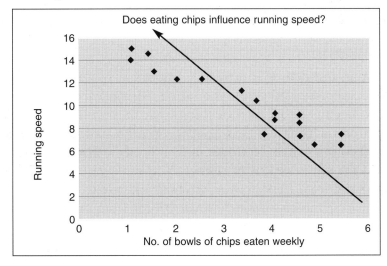

If the amount of food you ate had no bearing at all on your speed of running, the scattergram would show no pattern at all.

Can you see from these examples that we are assuming that the food influences running speed, but we haven't taken into account the athlete's build, or the amount of training they do? These could be far more relevant to the overall performance of the athlete; the food could have very little relevance.

WHAT ABOUT RELIABILITY AND VALIDITY?

One of the things you will hear a lot about in psychology is reliability and validity. Reliability means: is the test going to give consistent results? If you measure people one day and then again a week later, will you get the same set of results?

Reliability is checked by doing a test and then retesting some time later (making sure that your participants can't remember the results of the first test!).

For a test to have validity, it has to measure what we want it to measure. For example, if I gave you a passage to read and said I was measuring your intelligence, would you think that a bit odd? What the passage would actually be measuring is your reading ability.

Validity can be assured by first of all looking to see if it looks like it is measuring what we want it to measure (face validity). We could get experts to check it (content validity) or check it against a test that is supposed to be measuring the same thing (criterion validity). We could also check for predictive validity – is the test a valid predictor of future outcomes? An example here would be whether GCSEs are a valid predictor of A level results.

In order to explain the concepts further, here is a practical example of reliability and validity. Imagine if you were to measure the circumference of your head with a tape measure because you had been told that intelligence and head circumference were related to each other (the bigger the circumference, the more the brain). Obviously this is untrue, after all, Einstein didn't have a particularly large brain, but he was very intelligent. Therefore the test would be a reliable test because your head circumference would not vary from year to year (test/retest), but it bears no relationship to intelligence, therefore it is not a valid test of intelligence.

ETHICAL CONSIDERATIONS

When conducting research, it is extremely important to consider the feelings of the people who are participants in that research. After all, it is not really ethical to make your participants do all sorts of things that they would find unpleasant or embarrassing. You can't shave their hair off in order to analyse them without their prior consent. You can't stick electrodes in their heads whilst pinning them down, even if it is for the advancement of science. You can't push your best friend out into oncoming traffic to look at whether men or women drivers have quicker reaction times. You mustn't wrench small babies from mothers to investigate children's development, and you can't frighten people by throwing buckets of spiders over them, just to see what the effects of over-arousal are. However, people have not always conducted research that followed the accepted ethical guidelines, as you will see from the key studies. In order to be able to evaluate these studies, you must have an idea of what the ethical guidelines are, and if you are in a position to carry out psychological research you *must* follow them.

The British Psychological Society issued revised principles in June 1990 and these are the ones that we use to evaluate our studies and to guide further research. Although there are actually ten principles, they can be reduced to the following most important points (adapted from OCR psychology syllabus, 2000):

Consent

- Have the participants given their informed consent to take part? This means, have they agreed, knowing what the study is about?
- Have the parents of child participants given informed consent to the research procedures?
- Have payments been used to induce risk-taking behaviour?

Deception

- Have the participants been deceived about the nature of the study?
- Was there any way to carry out the study other than by using deception?
- Have the procedures been approved by other psychologists?

Welfare

- Has the physical and psychological welfare of the participants been maintained throughout the whole study?
- Have they left the research in the same condition they arrived?

Debriefing

Have the participants been effectively debriefed?

Back to the cookies! So now the researchers have decided what design they are going to use for their cookie study. They have looked at whether there were any ethical considerations that needed to be taken into account, and they can now get their participants to do what is required. They need to try to make sure that all their participants have not eaten prior to the beginning of the study, so that they will all (hopefully) appreciate the delight that is a chocolate cookie. The trouble is, there will be some things they cannot account for, like the fact that some of the participants went out the previous night to a friend's 21st birthday party and drank far too much punch. They also cannot account for the fact that some of the participants had a horrific journey getting to the place where the research is being conducted, or perhaps just had an argument with someone in the car park who stole their parking place. These things that cannot be accounted for are called *extraneous variables* or rather, extra variables that the researchers don't know about, which can affect the results. Extraneous variables are very similar to confounding variables and sometimes the terms are used interchangeably. Confounding variables are so called because they might confound or confuse the results. In this case, they may make the researchers think that the taste of the cookie is causing the feeling of well-being whereas it was really due to the temperature of the chocolate chips which have gone hard because the place where the research is being conducted is cold inside.

Statistical tests are used to remove mathematically the effects of some of these unwanted variables. How they work is not really of great importance, unless you are extremely interested in statistics! The main thing you need to remember about statistical tests is that they are able to show whether, for example, any differences in the results between two sets of scores are significant differences. It's like saying that one group scored 36 at a test and another group scored 37, but that one score difference may have simply been a fluke – it was not a difference that had any real significance. In order for a statistical test to show a significant difference or relationship, we have to be 95% sure that the results are due to what we have done. We can cope with 5% being due to chance, but any more than that makes the odds too high. In the cookie experiment we would be looking for participants to have rated one cookie to be *significantly* more yummy than the other – significantly more than could be put down to chance.

We hope this romp through the methodology used in psychological research has given you some insight into the kinds of problems that can be experienced. It should also help you to understand the studies in the book. Many of the key studies that you will read about were well designed, whilst some leave a lot to be desired. Samples were not always representative, or were relatively small, and this certainly influenced many of the results. Look at when the studies were done, as many of them were carried out some years ago now, and perhaps the result would be different nowadays. Ethics, too, were not always a prime consideration.

At least you have a basis on which to evaluate these studies and an understanding of how they could, perhaps, have been improved.

Further Reading:

- Lintern, F., Williams, L. and Hill, A. (2003), *Psychology AS for OCR*, Oxford: Heinemann.
- Oliver, K. (2001), *Applying Skills to Psychology*, London: Hodder & Stoughton.
- Russell, J. and Roberts, C. (2001), *Angles on Psychological Research*, Cheltenham: Nelson Thornes.
- Searle, A. (1999), *Introducing Research and Data in Psychology*, London: Routledge.
- The 1994 film *ID* (18), directed by Philip Davis, is excellent to show the effects of being a participant observer on behaviour.

Social psychology

Relationships are one of the most important aspects of our lives, often having more effect on us than anything else, and this is why we are starting with the four social psychology studies. As psychologists are interested in understanding human beings, it makes sense that they would be interested in the types of relationships we have with other human beings, how these relationships work and the way they impact on our thoughts and behaviour. Even more interesting is the fact that we don't always behave rationally when it comes to other people; hopefully, the reasons for this will become more obvious as you go through this chapter.

Humans are innately social creatures who actually *need* to interact with other people. Past research has indicated that one of the cruellest types of punishment is to keep someone in solitary confinement. This is not only because we like the company of others, but also it seems we are biologically programmed to be social creatures. Deprivation studies have shown that if we are kept apart from other people our brain 'manufactures' them in the form of dreams or hallucinations (many of the main psychology textbooks give information about sensory deprivation studies). You may argue that some people actually choose to live a life of social isolation, avoiding any kind of unnecessary interaction, but even people who are anti-social still have to have contact with others for work or shopping, for example, in order to survive.

You will probably have realised by now that if humans need to interact with each other, then this will guide their behaviour. If you need something enough, you will sometimes do things which go against what you actually feel or believe in order to get what you want. This is the basis of much of our social interaction – we need something from others and will do what is necessary to get it.

The topic of social psychology is divided into two subareas. *Social interaction* is concerned with how we interact with each other and how our position in society has a strong effect on the type of behaviour, we demonstrate. It also takes into account the factors which affect this behaviour, such as our past experiences and our perceived vulnerability. You always thought that the way you behave is entirely unique to you, but the trouble is that we all tend to follow certain patterns of behaviour and, in some cases, these patterns are entirely predictable. The two studies which focus on this area of psychology are the study by Milgram, which investigates obedience, and the study undertaken by Zimbardo, who looked at how roles have such a dramatic influence on our behaviour.

Social cognition involves how we think and feel about current social experiences and how we try to make sense of them, much of which is affected by past memories. It also considers how we use stored information to predict the course of interactions and their possible outcomes. The two studies which relate to social cognition are the Piliavin study, which looks at the factors which make us willing to help another person, and the Tajfel study, which looked at how simply being put in a group influences our negative feelings towards others who are not part of that group.

How does all this fit into real life? Part of being a social animal is that our lives involve numerous social relationships. Many of these relationships follow consistent patterns or are predictable, but what if we don't know the person very well or someone close to us behaves in a way which is unexpected or out of character? We are then left feeling confused or anxious and consequently devote much of our time to thinking about these relationships and trying to work out why certain things have happened. In fact, one of the reasons people give when explaining why they have chosen to study psychology is to help them understand their own and other people's behaviour. To explain the point further, here is an example of a situation you may have experienced in some form:

On one particular day my best friend was absolutely foul to me. I was really hurt and spent some time trying to work out why she had been so horrible, because it wasn't like her. It turned out that her boyfriend had dumped her that day and she was extremely upset and just couldn't bear to talk about it, so she snapped at me, almost as a way of making me leave her alone. The trouble was that I didn't know this at the time and I was concerned about the cause of her behaviour. Had she turned into a monster or was there another reason for her being so snappy?

The knowledge that social behaviour usually has a cause, even if it is not easily identifiable, is the basis of social understanding (or social cognition). The situation above would be analysed in terms of trying to work out why my best friend reacted like this. Here I would have to refer to my memory of what she was like normally and think about what had happened recently, using the two factors to interpret the current situation. Another question might be whether I had done anything wrong; this could only be assessed by going back over my own behaviour and trying to work out if I had been nasty to her or forgotten her birthday or given her some kind of just cause to be so horrible.

It appears that we need to have answers to the questions we may pose, because if we cannot come up with a reasonable answer it causes us anxiety. This means that our biological arousal levels increase, and increased arousal tends to lead to anxiety. People hate anxiety. In fact, we tend to do anything rather than allow ourselves to remain anxious for a long period of time. This means that one of the needs we have to satisfy is that of reducing the level of arousal we experience, and we shall see how the study by Piliavin (p. 50) uses arousal reduction as an explanation of our motivation in deciding whether to help or not in emergency situations. Just notice in the future, if you find yourself in a situation where you feel uncomfortable, you will do something to change that situation. The problem is that we don't always behave in the most logical way and we don't always behave according to our feelings.

My best friend hates Joan. She thinks she is the most boring and opinionated person she has ever met. In fact, she has just spent half an hour telling me why she dislikes her so much. Suddenly, Joan comes round the corner.

'Hullo sweetie, how are you? We have missed you and were wondering when we would see you again,' says my friend in the most annoying way.

Why is she saying this when she hates Joan? The obvious reason is that she is two-faced. Well, yes she is, but there is a reason for her behaviour. Is it because she does not want to hurt Joan's feelings? Is it because she wants something from Joan? Or is it simply because she has been socialised to behave in a polite way and not to indicate how she feels?

We will now look in more detail at the often unconscious reasoning which influences our behaviour.

Conformity and obedience

The first study in this section focuses on obedience, but we are going to consider the topics of conformity and obedience. The two topics are very closely interlinked and we often use one term when we really mean the other. Let's begin by considering what we mean by conformity.

During your childhood, there will have been some kind of craze which affected all the people in your school. It may have been to do with a particular toy or possibly a must-have item of clothing. It may have been something as simple as a type of pen or as expensive as an electronic games console.

Such crazes are often linked to toys, such as Transformers, Trolls, My Little Pony, Barbie, Pokemon or Harry Potter memorabilia. Fashion designers, toy manufacturers and anyone else involved in the retail trade, love conformity. Set up a craze, especially in the young, and everyone will go for it. In fact, it's an ideal way to sell huge quantities of merchandise. The levels of conformity in consumerism are phenomenal. When you actually stand back from it and realise how easily we are convinced that having one of these items is the only way we can ensure peace of mind, you see what an important concept conformity is.

Conformity has been described as 'yielding to group pressure' (Crutchfield, 1962). However, this implies that other people put pressure on us to make us conform and this is not always the case. After all, how many people pressurised you into buying whatever it was you bought that seemed at the time to be a must-have item? A better definition is given by Aronson (1976), who said it was a 'change in a person's behaviour or opinions as a result of real or imagined pressure from a person or group of people.' This would make more sense, as often the pressure we feel is imagined. The person or group he refers to would have to be important to the person at the time, irrelevant of their status.

There has been considerable research on conformity. One of the first studies looked at the answers people gave when asked to estimate the number of beans in a bottle (Jennes, 1932). If you have ever entered a 'guess the number' competition, you probably looked at the previous estimates made and based your judgement on what other people had guessed. This is more or less what happened in the Jennes study. First of all, he asked the students to give their own estimates, and then he asked them to decide a group estimate Finally he asked them alone again and discovered that they had stayed with the group answer.

Probably the most famous study on conformity was undertaken by Asch (1951), when he created a situation where many of his subjects gave answers which were blatantly untrue, rather than contradict the people they were with. He did this by getting his subject to sit round a table with six stooges (confederates of the experimenter) so that the subject was the second to last. He then showed them a large card which had three lines of different lengths drawn on it, labelled A, B and C, and a card with a single line, and asked them to say which line length matched that on the original card.

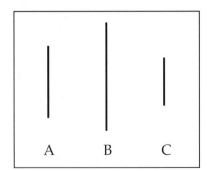 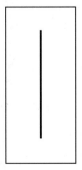

Examples of cards

The stooges gave blatantly incorrect responses in a number of the trials and the subjects were left in the situation where they either reported what they saw with their own eyes or conformed to the norm of the group. When the results were assessed, Asch found that in one out of every three trials where the wrong answer was given, the subject gave the same wrong answer as the stooges. This led to an average level of conformity of 32%, although 75% of subjects conformed to the wrong answer at least once.

Asch interviewed his subjects after the trials to try to find out why they conformed to an answer which was so blatantly wrong. Most of them said that they did not want to cause problems within the group, although they also reported that when they did give wrong answers it made them feel very anxious. We all know that having some moral support makes it easier to tell the truth and Asch found that when there was just one other person present who did not go along with the majority, no matter how many others there were, it was sufficient to make the subject give the right answer.

Each one of us is under different pressures, both actual and perceived, and each one of us varies from day to day in how confident we feel, depending on the situation we are in, and this can influence our behaviour. So on one occasion you might conform to the group, even if you believe they are wrong (especially if you feel threatened by them), and on another occasion you would speak out against the group consensus (usually if you feel relatively secure). The nature of the disagreement and the actual consequences of disagreeing may also sway your decision. Some people feel confident most of the time, and it is these people, people with high self-esteem, who feel that they do not have to go along with the majority. They are confident enough in their judgement to go against the rest without feeling threatened or uncomfortable (Stang, 1973).

So why is it that we have to conform? Kelman (1953) outlined three processes which can explain social conformity.

1. Compliance

Where subjects go along with the crowd to prevent any in-group hostility or bad feeling and to maintain group harmony. However, they do not change their own private belief.

2. Internalisation

Where subjects come to internalise the view of the group and see its view as the more valid one. They may be able to do this, for example, by convincing themselves that their eyesight is poor.

3. Identification

Where subjects actually seem to change their beliefs because they want to become more like their heroes. If they really want to become part of an in-group, they will start to identify with that group and take on the group's values and beliefs, even if they are different to their own original values and beliefs. This can also happen if they want to become more like a person they respect or admire – they will change their attitudes to become more like them. This frequently happens with teenagers who want to become more like a peer group in order to be accepted, and suddenly seem to go against all the values and beliefs of their parents.

If we relate these back to the Asch study, we can begin to see what was happening for the subjects. Asch's subjects were simply complying with the demands of the experimental situation but hadn't actually internalised the group's norms. They agreed in public, but dissented in private.

Having looked at conformity, we are now going to look at obedience. Both of these topics seem to involve people renouncing their personal responsibility in a given situation. With conformity, we give up our individual responsibility when we go along with others in order to be accepted by the group. With obedience, we give up our personal responsibility to make decisions and go along with the decisions of others as to how we should act and what we should do. However, there are a number of reasons why we are obedient.

First, obedience may be a form of self-preservation, especially if the authority figure who is telling us what to do has some kind of power. In such situations we do not necessarily have to see the authority figure as being legitimate (although it helps), because no matter what we feel, we are looking after our own welfare. This can be taken to extremes. In the army, soldiers may be court-martialled if they don't do as they are told. At home, if we don't do as we are told by our parents, we may face being grounded or having our allowance stopped.

The second reason that we are inclined to obey is that we have been taught to be obedient. We have been socialised to tow the line, and it is more acceptable for us to be obedient than to go against the orders or rules, especially from someone perceived as being a legitimate authority figure.

Imagine you are sitting in the classroom in a psychology lesson. The lesson has been going for 10 minutes, and will go on for another 50 minutes. You are bored out of your brain. So why don't you leave? You've finished your compulsory education so you don't have to be there; you could just get up and walk out of the door. How easy do you think this would be? What is there to stop you from leaving? How might you feel? Who has the authority in this situation?

When we are really little, we are trained from a very early age, by both our parents and our schools, to be obedient and we are also taught that these forms of authority are legitimate and have our best interests at heart. We can all remember our parents saying to us, on many occasions, 'Do as you are told.' This will often have been backed up with threats if you were naughty, and praise if you were obedient. What happens is that we internalise the need for obedience and therefore become conditioned to obey voluntarily in most situations (we will talk more about the process of conditioning in the chapter on children's development). This seems to become set as a default position, and this means that eventually disobeying becomes the difficult action. Obedience therefore becomes the norm, and to be defiant or disobedient is perceived as abnormal, drawing the disapproval of others.

Psychology teachers have been known to demonstrate how this works by picking on a particular student and asking them to do something like standing up or going and standing outside the door for no apparent reason. Even though they may question why, the likelihood is that the student will obey the teacher's command. One particular student who obeyed just such a command talked about his experience. He seemed quite shocked that he had obeyed and had thought the order was unfair. He said that he knew the teacher couldn't really do anything to harm him, but teachers tell students to do things, and so he did as he was told.

What we must remember is that most of the time there is nothing wrong with being obedient. Obedience fulfils an important function for us. It is necessary to maintain social harmony, for without some form of obedience to an authority we would end up with a state of anarchy. Stanley Milgram wrote, 'it must not be thought all obedience entails acts of aggression against others. Obedience serves numerous productive functions… Obedience may be ennobling and educative and refer to acts of charity and kindness as well as to destruction' (1963).

On the other hand, we also have to remember that blind obedience is an undesirable state and can result in acts of destruction and damage to others. This brings us to why obedience has been studied by psychologists. What kind of person could obey orders or instructions that would lead to the injury or death of innocent people? Examples often cited are the Holocaust and the Vietnam War, where innocent civilians were slaughtered as a result of orders given by authority figures. However, research has suggested that the people who committed these atrocities were not always amoral monsters.

Eichmann was perhaps one of the worst offenders in the Second World War. He was responsible for arranging the transportation of six million Jews to their deaths. Following the war he escaped to Buenos Aires but was caught in 1961 and sent to trial for his part in the killing of millions of Jews. While the case was being prepared he was interrogated for a total of 275 hours, as it was believed he must have been some kind of monster to have allowed this genocide to occur. Captain Avner W. Less, who interrogated Eichmann for the duration of the 275 hours, wrote:

'My first reaction when the prisoner finally stood facing us in the khaki shirt and trousers and open sandals was one of disappointment. I no longer know what I had expected – probably the sort of Nazi you see in the movies: tall, blonde, with piercing blue eyes and brutal features expressive of domineering arrogance. Whereas this rather thin, balding man not much taller than myself looked utterly ordinary.'

Von Lang and Sibyll (eds), 1983, in R. Brown (1986), p. 3

In fact, Hannah Arendt (1965), who reported on the trial of Eichmann, concluded that he was simply a commonplace bureaucrat like any other, who obeyed orders given to him without question.

The other frequently cited evidence of how obedience to authority can be destructive was the case of Lieutenant William Calley's part in the My Lai massacre during the Vietnam War in 1970. Calley was the commander of a platoon of American soldiers when he received orders to round up all the inhabitants of a village called My Lai. He was told that there were Vietcong in the village, and that the soldiers should round up all the members of the village and 'waste them' (shoot them dead). The inhabitants were mainly women, old men and children and yet they were all wiped out.

Again, the nature of the man who was at fault was questioned. How could a normal person agree to order their men to shoot obviously innocent children? However, he had shown no criminal tendencies before My Lai, and after his sentence he continued to live quietly as an average American civilian. In 1972 a survey was carried out in America to gauge the reaction of the public to Calley's trial. The results were that 51% of the sample said they would follow the same orders by killing the inhabitants of the village if that is what they had been ordered to do, because the orders were coming from a legitimate authority.

Whether we agree with Eichmann's or Calley's actions, the reasons for their obedience are perhaps easy to understand. First, the consequences of disobedience were perhaps too high – court martial and imprisonment or execution. Everyone else was also obeying orders at the time so they were conforming to group norms. It should therefore be evident that there is more than one simple reason why people are obedient and often the reasons involve conformity too.

Milgram (1963), Behavioural Study of Obedience,
Journal of Abnormal & Social Psychology, 67, 371–8

Background

Is the type of person who is seemingly blindly obedient really very different to the rest of the population, representing perhaps a few in every thousand? Perhaps there is just a sadistic minority who get drawn into situations which enable them to gratify their impulses to injure others? Or is it possible that in certain circumstances it is in fact the majority of us who would obey orders, behaving in cruel ways which we would normally like to believe we were incapable of?

Stanley Milgram is the author of the core study which focuses on obedience. Milgram began his career working at Princeton University as a research assistant to Asch, and moved on to Yale University where he took up his first teaching position. Having studied conformity with Asch, Milgram became interested in obedience to authority. One question he considered was that perhaps there was something unique about certain members of the German nation who were prepared to commit what could be seen as mass murders during the Holocaust. If this were the case, maybe other members of society like William Calley, shared the same characteristics. On the other hand, Milgram points out that the inhumane policies of the Nazis 'could only be carried out on a massive scale if a very large number of persons obeyed orders', so perhaps the unquestioning obedience to authority of the thousands who took part in administering the policies may have demonstrated what most ordinary people would do when subjected to extraordinary social influences.

FOCUS ON THEMES – individual and situational explanations of behaviour and determinism

Is it the characteristics of individuals that make them behave the way they do, or is it the situation in which they find themselves that influences their behaviour? This is an important question in social psychology. Its origins lie in philosophy and the question of determinism: how far our behaviour is a result of our own free will and how far it is outside our control, being governed, or determined, by outside forces, such as society and culture, or by internal forces, such as our genes and personality.

Milgram's study attempts to show whether there is an 'obedient type', someone who follows orders to be cruel to others, or whether this type of obedience is something of which we are all capable in certain circumstances, therefore contributing to the individual vs. situation explanations debate.

Aim

The aim of the study was to investigate what level of obedience would be shown when subjects were told by an authority figure to administer electric shocks to another person.

Method

Design

The study was carried out in the laboratory, using observation to collect data. The data consisted of a record of the maximum level of shock the subject administered to the 'victim', together with recordings of the sessions, occasional photographs through a one-way mirror and notes of any unusual behaviour.

Subjects

The subjects who took part in Milgram's study were 40 males between the ages of 20 and 50, who came from the New Haven area of America, from a range of occupations and educational backgrounds. They were recruited by a newspaper article and direct mail advertising which asked for volunteers to take part in a study of memory and learning at Yale University. This was, therefore, a volunteer or self-selected sample. They were to be paid $4.50 and were told this was for simply turning up at the University, theirs to keep whatever happened.

FOCUS ON RESEARCH METHODS – subjects/participants and samples

Remember, 'subject' means a person whose behaviour is being studied. The standard abbreviation is S, and Ss for the plural, 'subjects'. You will also see 'participant' (P) and 'participants' (Ps). These terms are interchangeable.

'Sample' refers to the whole group of Ss being studied. A sample should be selected so that it is representative of the group, or target population, from which it has been drawn. If a sample is biased, e.g. all-male or all-female, represents only a narrow age range, is very small or represents only one culture or group (that is, has an ethnocentric bias), then this limits the ability of the researchers to generalise the findings from the study. There are various ways of selecting a sample and we shall come across some of these as we go through the core studies.

FOCUS ON RESEARCH METHODS – volunteer or self-selected samples

As its name suggests, this type of sample is formed when Ss are asked to volunteer themselves to take part in the study. Typical ways of getting such a sample include putting an advert in a newspaper or a notice on a noticeboard, and sending out postal questionnaires. Those who respond to the ad or notice and those who fill in and return the questionnaires are volunteering to take part in the study.

This can be a cost-effective and convenient way for researchers to obtain Ss to take part in their research, but the drawback is that since the vast majority of people do not volunteer (for example, the return rate for a postal questionnaire is only about 30%), then the sample is fundamentally biased. It is only representative of those people who do volunteer, and since they are atypical, this limits the usefulness of findings of studies which use self-selected samples.

Apparatus

Two rooms were used within Yale University. One room contained what looked like an electric-shock generator, which had a row of 30 switches which ranged from 15 to 450 volts in 15-volt increments. There were also descriptions about the type of shocks, e.g. slight shock, strong shock, intense shock, danger: severe shock and, finally, the last switches were marked XXX. In the other room was a chair with restraining straps where the learner was to receive the shocks via his wrist. There was also a tape recording of responses which were played according to which switch was depressed, ensuring that all subjects heard the same responses in the same order from the learner.

Two male confederates took part in the study:
(i) The experimenter (standard abbreviation: E) – a 31-year-old 'stern' biology teacher who wore a grey lab technician's coat.
(ii) The learner – a 47-year-old accountant who appeared mild-mannered and likeable.

Procedure

The subject was introduced to the learner and told the cover story that the study was about the effects of punishment on learning. The subject and the confederate 'drew lots' to see who was to be teacher or learner, although the situation was rigged: both slips of paper said 'teacher'. The teacher then saw the learner taken to the other room and strapped into the chair, and his wrist attached to the equipment that would deliver the shocks. At this point the learner explained that he had a slight heart condition and asked if the shocks were dangerous. He was told by the experimenter that although the shocks could be extremely painful, they caused no permanent tissue damage.

The teacher and experimenter returned to the first room and the teacher sat at the desk with the shock generator before him. He was told that the learner had to learn word pairs such as 'fat neck', 'blue box' and 'nice day'. The teacher had to read out the first word of the word pair and another 4 words, one of which was correct and the subject had to choose the correct word. The way the learner would indicate the correct answer to the teacher was by pressing one of four switches in front of him, which lit up one of four corresponding lights on the top of the shock generator. If the subject got the answer wrong, the teacher was told to give the subject an electric shock by flicking a switch on the shock generator.

The teacher was then told that for each mistake the shocks would increase and in order to do this 'the subject is instructed to "move one level higher on the shock generator each time the learner flashes a wrong answer"'(Milgram, 1963, p. 374). Although there were actually no shocks given to the learner, the teacher was always given a 'test shock' of 45 volts (switch 3). A battery was installed in the shock generator for this purpose – it wasn't really plugged in to the electrical supply! This added to the authenticity of the study and made the teacher believe the learner was truly being given shocks. As the teacher administered the 'shocks', the tape recording gave pre-recorded responses at each level to ensure that all subjects experienced the same feedback from the 'learner'.

These recordings began with 'Ouch', went on to, 'Ugh! I can't stand the pain, let me out of here', and then, 'Ugh! Experimenter, get me out of here, I told you I had heart trouble. My heart's starting to bother me now. Get me out of here, please. My heart's staring to bother me. I refuse to go on. Let me out'. At 300 volts the victim kicked on the wall and ceased to give answers to the teacher's questions, saying (after an agonised scream), 'I absolutely refuse to answer anymore. Get me out of here. You can't hold me here. I told you I refuse to answer. I'm no longer part of this experiment'.

After 315 volts the learner fell silent. This was disconcerting for the teacher, as the learner had seemingly cried out in pain at much lower voltages, and would lead the teacher to fear that something terrible had happened to the learner.

In response to the learner's cries of pain and comments, the teacher would question the experimenter and ask if he could look in on the learner to see if he was all right. The teacher would protest that he did not want to continue if the learner was being hurt. Meanwhile it was the the experimenter's task to instruct the teacher to carry on. He used 4 verbal 'prods' to pressurise the subject to continue with the experiment. If the subject disobeyed all 4 prods then the experiment was ended.

Prods used by experimenter

Prod 1: Please continue/Please go on.

Prod 2: The experiment requires that you continue.

Prod 3: It is absolutely essential that you continue.

Prod 4: You have no other choice, you must go on.

FOCUS ON RESEARCH METHODS – standardising instructions and procedures

Standardisation means keeping the test conditions the same for every subject. It is a method of controlling situational variables, or environmental factors, which might have an influence on the Ss' behaviour. If Ss were treated differently, this would mean that fair comparisons between their responses could not be made. Standardisation of the instructions, the learner's taped responses and the sequence of prods used by the E are examples of how Milgram controlled situational variables in this study.

33

Further prods used by the experimenter if the subject questioned the welfare of the learner were: 'Although the shocks may be painful, there is no permanent tissue damage, so please go on', and, 'Whether the learner likes it or not, you must go on until he has learned all the words correctly. So please go on'.

At the end of the study, the teacher was reunited with the learner, assured that no shocks had been given, and was thoroughly debriefed about the true nature and purpose of the experiment. Milgram also interviewed the subjects using open-ended questions, projective measures (which are tests intended to predict whether the experience may result in any possible long-term consequences) and attitude scales to ensure (as far as possible) that the subject left the laboratory 'in a state of well-being'.

Results

The dependent variable being measured in this study was obedience. This was measured quantitatively by recording how far the S was prepared to go on the shock generator.

FOCUS ON THEMES – quantitative and qualitative data

When we think of measurement, we tend to assume that this means that numbers will be used to tell us how much or how many of something there was. This is precisely what you get with quantitative data. An advantage of using numbers to measure variables is that it allows for easy comparisons to be made between Ss, e.g. on a memory test, subject one scored ten out of 100 and subject two scored 90. We can also summarise quantitative data easily, using averages or percentages. For example, Milgram found that 65% of his Ss went up to 450 volts.

Another advantage of quantitative data is that it allows for inferential statistics to be used and hypotheses to be tested, as you will see when you are doing your practical folder. It is also easier to establish the reliability of results when quantitative data is collected, as you can repeat the test to see if the findings are replicable or not.

Quantitative data alone can be quite narrow, however, and can also lack ecological validity. For example, if you ask someone, 'How are things with you?' they are more likely to say, 'Pretty good, thanks', than, 'On a scale of 0 to 100, where 0 is terrible and 100 is unqualified bliss, I'd say today was scoring 65'.

In order to increase the level of detail and the validity of findings, qualitative data can be gathered. This usually consists of descriptions in words of what was observed. For example, Milgram tells us subjects were seen 'to sweat, tremble, stutter, bite their lips...[and] these were characteristic rather than exceptional responses to the experiment' (Milgram, 1969, p. 375). This tells us a lot more about the experience of Ss in the experiment than just the fact that 65% of Ss went to the end on the shock generator.

Qualitative data can also be reports of interviews, responses to open questions in questionnaires and reports of what subjects said and did during a study. Using this type of information gives a richness and detail to the findings and is more valid. However, it is harder to make comparisons between Ss' responses or to summarise qualitative data.

Prior to the commencement of the study, Milgram had questioned a number of psychology students, adults and psychiatrists as to how many people would give people fatal electric shocks as part of a psychology experiment, and the estimate from all groups was 0% to 3% of subjects (mean 1.2%). In the context of these predictions, Milgram's results were surprising. This illustrates well that what we think we might do is not what we do when faced with a situation.

All 40 subjects gave shocks up to 300 volts, with five refusing to go beyond this point. Between 315 volts and 375 volts a further nine Ss stopped obeying. This meant that 26/40, a staggering 65% of Ss tested, went all the way up to 450 volts.

In addition to these statistics, Milgram had invited objective observers to record what they observed during the study. Their reports provide qualitative data. He reported that although 26 of the Ss had been odedient to the experimenter's authority right up to 450 volts, they displayed signs of extreme stress. Ss sweated, trembled, stuttered in their speech, bit their lips, groaned, dug their fingernails into their hands or appeared to be crying; many laughed, not in amusement, but as a nervous reaction; three subjects had violent convulsions. Milgram says that the results were also surprising to the observers, who expressed disbelief at the behaviour of the subjects. Milgram quotes one observer:

'I observed a mature and initially poised businessman enter the laboratory smiling and confident. Within 20 minutes he was reduced to a twitching, stuttering wreck, who was rapidly approaching a point of collapse. He constantly pulled on his earlobe and twisted his hands. At one point he pushed his fist into his forehead and muttered "Oh God, let's stop it'. And yet he continued to respond to every word of the experimenter, and obeyed to the end.'

(Milgram, 1969, p. 377)

• Discussion

The level of obedience was totally unexpected. Apparently normal men had obeyed to the point where they believed they might have seriously injured a man just like themselves, the power of obedience outweighing their personal moral beliefs that it was wrong to injure others.

Milgram suggested a number of reasons to explain why the obedience rate was so high in these circumstances:

- The fact that the study was carried out in a prestigious university influenced Ss as to the worthiness of the study and the competence of the experimenter.
- The S believed that the learner had also volunteered and that the allocation of roles was due to chance.
- The subject has agreed to an implicit social contract by agreeing to take part and being paid for his participation and he therefore felt obliged to continue.
- The subjects were told that the shocks were not harmful.
- The situation was entirely new for the subject so he had no past experience to guide his behaviour.
- There was no obvious point at which the subjects could stop administering shocks, because each shock was only a small amount more than the previous shock.
- The subjects who did withdraw from the study did so when the 'natural break' occurred – when the subject ceased to reply.

Milgram suggested that the Ss in his study faced a number of conflicts. First, the conflict which arose from being asked to meet the competing demands of the experimenter and the learner. To meet the demands of one was to fail to meet the demands of the other. The teacher was forced into making a decision, to stop or continue, and this put him in a public conflict with no satisfactory solution.

More generally, there is the conflict the S experiences internally: which of two ingrained behaviour dispositions should he respond to? Should he respond to his belief that one shouldn't harm others and therefore refuse to go on with the study, or respond to his equally ingrained tendency to obey authority figures, and therefore continue?

- **Commentary**

Is the study ecologically valid?

> ## FOCUS ON THEMES – ecological validity
>
> Is the behaviour that the Ss are being asked to perform in the study comparable with behaviours that people might carry out in the course of their everyday life? In other words, how realistic is the study? If the behaviour in a study is very like real-life behaviours then the study is said to be high in ecological validity.
>
> If the behaviours asked of subjects in a study are not like real-life behaviours then the study is low in ecological validity and this limits its usefulness.

Since people tend to behave differently in a lab when they know they are being tested, and due to the artificial nature of the laboratory environment itself, studies carried out in the lab tend to be low in ecological validity.

This study took place in a laboratory, and this was essential to convince subjects that it was a valid piece of research. However, this may mean that the Ss' behaviour was only typical of the behaviour they would display in a laboratory, so the study lacks ecological validity on this count.

> ## FOCUS ON THEMES – validity
>
> Besides ecological validity, there is another type of validity which rests more on the actual design of the research rather than how comparable the behaviours are to real life. In order to ensure that a study has validity, we need to be sure that the study looks realistic and is measuring what we want it to measure (has face validity). For more information of different types of design validity, see p. 18 in Chapter 1.

Is this study valid? Did the Ss really believe they were administering shocks? It has been claimed that Ss were not really deceived by the study and did not really believe that they were administering electric shocks to another person, that their behaviour was simply a response to demand characteristics present in the study (see below). However, when Milgram asked his subjects whether they believed they were administering real shocks in the questionnaire they completed a year after the study, only 2.4% claimed to be 'certain' the learner was not receiving shocks. Unless they were all talented actors, the signs of tension shown by the teachers suggested they really did believe in the study at the time. Also, if they did not believe shocks were really being given, why did some of the teachers feel it necessary to stop before they reached 450 volts?

FOCUS ON RESEARCH METHODS – demand characteristics

Demand characterisitics are the clues or cues given consciously or unconsciously by the researcher, or elements in the procedure of the study that reveal the purpose of the study. If Ss can work out what the researcher is trying to investigate, it is possible for them to falsify their results to please the researcher, to make sure that the study 'works'. Alternatively, Ss may adopt the 'sabotage' approach, making sure they do not behave in the way they believe they are expected to, thus spoiling the study.

If results have been affected by Ss responding to demand characteristics, this will mean they are not valid, that is, they have not tested what they intended to test, and this reduces the value and usefulness of the research.

In social psychological studies researchers can often justify the use of deception, telling Ss a cover story to hide the true purpose of the study, as this is essential in order to avoid demand characteristics from influencing Ss' responses. Imagine how Milgram's results would have differed if he had told subjects that he was trying to see how far the E could coerce them into going on the shock generator.

Is the study ethical?

Milgram's study has been one of the most highly criticised in the whole of psychological research and provoked an investigation after it was published, during which time Milgram's membership of the American Psychological Association was suspended.

Milgram justified his work by saying that he had not anticipated his results. Although Ss were deceived by the cover story, and therefore informed consent was not obtained, this was necessary in order for the study to be carried out. He argued that although the study did encourage the subjects to continue, as that was its purpose, the fact that some Ss could and did withdraw illustrates that this was always a choice for those taking part. Milgram denied that his Ss had been harmed by the study, either by the stress they experienced at the time, or as a result of any self-knowledge that they had gained as a result of their participation in the study. This second point was confirmed by an independent psychiatrist who followed up with Ss a year after the study.

Milgram thoroughly debriefed his subjects at the end of the study, introducing them to the learner and telling the 'obedient' ones that their behaviour was normal. All subjects received a report on the findings of this and subsequent studies and 92% responded to a questionnaire regarding their feelings about having taken part. Less than 2% said they were sorry to have taken part, with 84% saying they were glad to have been involved. Milgram himself saw this point as a key defence. If those who had taken part in the study were glad to have done so and felt it was worthwhile, then this justified the study on ethical grounds. However the participants' enthusiasm for the study may simply have been a way of reducing their cognitive dissonance. *Cognitive dissonance* is a state of discomfort or anxiety, caused by holding two opposing attitudes or beliefs about a situation, e.g. I smoke and smoking is bad for me, or, I am giving electric shocks and I shouldn't be giving another person electric shocks for something as silly as a memory test. To claim that they had learned something of personal significance from the study and that it had high scientific value would have reduced Ss' dissonance.

In the end, Milgram's work was deemed to be ethical and it is regarded as one of the most significant pieces of social psychological research to date.

What does the study illustrate about the social approach?

In terms of the influences on our behaviour, Milgram's study shows us that we do not always act in the way we might predict. He argues that obedience 'comes easily and often', and that if we are in a situation where obedience is demanded of us by a legitimate authority, we can be encouraged by that authority to act in a way that may harm another, even though this means acting in opposition to our personal morality.

In terms of individual and situational explanations of behaviour, Milgram's study demonstrates how it can be the situation you are in that influences your behaviour, and that we abdicate control when we are in the 'agentic state'. We are socialised to obey, but this does not mean that another holocaust is inevitable. In terms of politics, we have the power to choose whom we obey. Good people are easily integrated into a malevolent system, and therefore it is up to us to ensure that such a system is not put into place. Use your vote wisely!

Key Questions

1. Identify one quantitative finding and one qualitative finding from Milgram's study.
2. Could this study be carried out in strict accordance with the ethical guidelines currently laid down by the BPS and APA?
3. How might demand characteristics have affected the findings of this study?
4. What, if anything, do you think would be different if the study had been carried out with female subjects? Or those over 60, or under 20?
5. Would you like to have been a S in this experiment?

Example Answers are on page 450

Further Reading

- Aronson, E. (1994), *The Social Animal*, New York: W.H. Freeman & Co., 7th edition.
- http://designweb.otago.ac.nz/grant/psyc/OBEDIANCE.HTML

Ignore the spelling error – this is a good website for obedience.
- http://sociology.about.com/science/sociology/cs/milgramstanley/index.htm will give you information about Milgram and the classic experiment.
- Milgram, S. (1974), *Obedience to Authority: An Experimental View*, New York: Harper and Row.
- Wren, K. (1999) *Social Influences*. London: Routledge. Chapters 1 and 2.

Altruism

The definition of altruism is when you do something for someone else without gaining anything for yourself. But do you think we ever do anything to help another person without getting back something for ourselves? If you think about it honestly, how many times have you actually done something for another person without thinking that it might be to your benefit in the future?

A. You go and have tea with your grandma who is a bit crotchety and smells of moth balls when you would rather go out with your mates.
B. You wash up and clean the house while your mum is out.
C. You help your friend with his/her homework.
D. You help to decorate a friend's bedroom/house.
E. You collect money for a charity.
F. You help your teacher on open evenings at college.
G. You volunteer to stay behind at work to finish something, even though you aren't getting paid for it.

All these activities are possible acts of altruism, but even though it may appear at first glance that they are being done for someone else, all of them may have ulterior motives.

A. Grandma may appreciate the visit so much that:
- she may give you a small amount of money when you leave or leave you a huge amount in her will
- maybe it will stop your mum from moaning at you for never visiting (the pay-off here is lack of moaning)
- it might make you feel good because you have brought some joy into her life, in which case you are rewarding yourself.
B. Mother won't nag you and will probably let you stay out for longer or give you extra pocket money.
C. Your friend may help you in the future when you are stuck with your homework.

D. He/she may help you with your decorating at some time in the future.
E. You no longer feel guilty about all the charity boxes you didn't contribute to in the past (and if you are a student it will look good on a UCAS statement or CV for an interview).
F. Your help on open evenings is rewarded by a better reference from your college.
G. Your boss bears you in mind for promotion, or finishing the tasks makes life easier for you the next day.

This should give you some idea as to how acts of human altruism are often really selfish acts.

Research into animal behaviour has also shown that apparent acts of altruism are also basically extremely selfish and have more to do with the transmission of genes from one generation to the next. If we think of the example of the rabbit who thumps his foot to warn all other rabbits of impending danger, it appears that this rabbit is putting itself at risk for the sake of the rest of the group, but what it is doing is allowing others from its 'family' to survive and carry the family genes into the next generation.

Returning to human altruism, we cannot be quite so objective, because many seemingly altruistic acts have no relationship to genes although they still have a selfish element. An example of this is where adoptive parents are as protective of their children as biological parents – what would it cost them in terms of pain and misery if they weren't protective? After all, the 'cost' of adoption in terms of time, emotion and organisation means that they have a vested interest in the welfare of that adopted child. However, other evidence shows that kin selection does operate in human beings. Burnstein, Crandall and Kitayama (1994) discovered that people claimed that they would help others most closely related to them if the situation was life threatening, but also said that if it was less serious they would help anyone.

Let's return to having tea with Grandma. There are two ways we can be rewarded for giving up our time: one is extrinsically (or externally), that is, we get praised and shown gratitude either verbally or by being left her entire fortune; the other is intrinsically (or internally), by having a degree of self-satisfaction or, in effect, rewarding ourselves.

At this point, you may have started to think that perhaps altruism does not exist and that is quite a reasonable belief. There are others, however, who strongly believe that altruism does exist, such as Daniel Batson (1991). He agrees that often people help for selfish reasons, but suggests that at other times they are willing to do something for someone else with no apparent gain for themselves, but this is usually because we feel empathy for the person in need of help. This means that we identify with the person and can almost feel the pain and heartache they are feeling.

Penny's coursework was finally completed. Everything had gone wrong for her, from the college computer being shut down with a virus, to her supervising teacher going off on long-term sickness. Penny braced herself against the rain as she ran over the yard to finally hand in the finished work. Just before she got to the door, she tripped and fell over, dropping the folder and spreading its contents over the wet ground.

If Batson is correct, we would probably run to help her, despite the rain, as most of us could identify with how devastated she would feel.

The debate surrounding the existence of altruism alone would be sufficient to provoke research into the area, but perhaps a greater provocation occurred in America in 1964, with the murder of a 28-year-old woman called Kitty Genovese.

Kitty was attacked on three separate occasions, within a 35-minute period, by a man carrying a knife, although it was not until the third attack that he actually succeeded in killing her. What made it worse was that 38 people actually saw the killer from the windows of their homes, but none of them reported the incident to the police. No one was prepared to come forward and help, either by intervening or by telephoning the police until, finally, one man got a neighbour to call after phoning a friend in a different county for advice.

The incident was reported in the *New York Times* in March 1964 and contained the following condensed extracts:

Twice the sound of their voices and the sudden glow of their bedroom lights interrupted him and frightened him off. Each time he returned, sought her out and stabbed her again. Not one person telephoned the police during the assault; one witness called after the woman was dead.

Kitty Genovese was returning home from her job as manager of a bar in Hollis. She parked her red Fiat in a lot adjacent to the Kew Gardens Long Island Rail Road Station... She turned off the lights of her car, locked the door and started to walk the 100 feet to the entrance of her apartment... She got as far as a street light in front of a bookstore before the man grabbed her. She screamed. Lights went on in the ten-storey apartment house... Windows slid open and voices punctured the early morning stillness.

Miss Genovese screamed: 'Oh, my God, he stabbed me! Please help me! Please help me!'

From one of the upper windows in the apartment house, a man called down: 'Let that girl alone!'

The assailant looked up at him, shrugged and walked down Austin Street toward a white sedan parked a short distance away. Miss Genovese struggled to her feet.

Lights went out. The killer returned to Miss Genovese, now trying to make her way around the side of the building by the parking lot to get to her apartment. The assailant grabbed her again. 'I'm dying!' she shrieked. 'I'm dying!'

Windows opened again, and lights went on in many apartments. The assailant got into his car and drove away. Miss Genovese staggered to her feet...

The assailant returned. By then, Miss Genovese had crawled to the back of the building where the freshly painted brown doors to the apartment house held out hope of safety. The killer tried the first door; she wasn't there. At the second door... he saw her slumped on the floor at the foot of the stairs. He stabbed her a third time – fatally.

... the police received their first call from a man who was a neighbour of Miss Genovese. In two minutes they were at the scene... The man explained... 'I didn't want to get involved.'

How many times have you heard a child screaming in the street and simply assumed that the child is playing? How many times have you rationalised the situation to yourself and decided that you should not get involved? In fact, if you think about many of the criminal activities that go on in our world, it makes you realise that it is probably almost normal not to get involved. The case of two-year-old Jamie Bulger being abducted by two ten-year-old boys was seen as horrendous. But imagine how you would have interpreted the situation if you had seen two ten-year-old boys marching a small child out of a shopping centre. You would probably think that they were the child's older brothers rather than murderers. You would justify your lack of involvement by seeing the situation as nothing untoward.

Imagine that you saw a mother screaming at a small tearful child, possibly even hitting it. Would you go up to the mother and stick up for the small child? If not, why not?

Now imagine you are walking along a street. You turn the corner and see a man holding on to a woman's arm and shouting at her while she screams back at him and looks as if she is pulling away. Would you feel that you could 'interfere' in this situation?

If we decided to intervene, we would have to consider the situation carefully because both of these are ambiguous – that is, we have no idea what is really happening here because we don't have all the facts. We would therefore have to make attributions about the nature of the situation and decide who was to blame (if anyone) or whether or not the person actually needed help.

This is the basis of what is known as 'attribution theory', a theory which helps to explain how people attribute causes to their own and other people's behaviour. Although we are really concerned with altruistic behaviour, attribution theory is relevant here because it is part of the basis on which we decide to intervene or not intervene in different situations. If we believe that it is someone's fault that they have got themselves into a situation, then we may be less likely to help than if we attribute the situation to an accident. For example, if a man were drunk and therefore fell over in the snow, we would perhaps be less likely to help him up than if it were a little old lady. We would make the attribution that it was his own fault that he fell over and he shouldn't have drunk so much, whereas being old isn't the little old lady's fault.

We should also be aware of what might happen if we got our interpretation wrong in the situations mentioned above. The mother would be furious and tell us to mind our own business. The man and woman might do the same. The cost of getting involved might far outweigh the benefits and so we would decide not to risk it.

Considerations such as these, together with the Kitty Genovese incident, have resulted in researchers becoming interested in investigating the existence of altruism. We have already considered some of the factors which might influence a person's likelihood of becoming involved, but let us now put them into some kind of framework:

1. The nature of the situation

If you were in a dark street in the middle of the night, you would be less likely to go to the aid of someone lying in the gutter than if you were in the middle of a street on a summer's day and found someone who had seemingly collapsed. If there were lots of other people around, would that make you more or less likely to help? If everyone else was ignoring the situation would you feel it wasn't critical?

2. The nature of the potential or actual helper

If you were a doctor would this make you more willing to help than if you had no medical training? If there were people watching and you didn't think you were very competent, would this affect whether or not you intervened?

3. The cost of helping

If you were on your way to an interview for a job that you really wanted, would this make you more or less likely to stop and help?

4. The nature of the victim

If the person who had collapsed was drunk, would this make you more or less likely to help than if the person was sober?

THE NATURE OF THE SITUATION

Latané and Darley (1968) were social psychologists, teaching in New York at the time of the Kitty Genovese incident. They were interested in whether the presence of other people affected helping behaviour. Using the Kitty Genovese incident as a stimulus, they decided to look at the idea of the 'unresponsive bystander'. They thought that it was because there were so many witnesses to her murder that she wasn't helped.

Latané and Darley asked male college students to sit in a waiting room and fill in a questionnaire before taking part in a study of people's attitudes toward the problems of urban life. They were sitting either alone or in groups of three. The researchers arranged for smoke to pour through a small ventilation grille and secretly watched their behaviour over the next six minutes.

You would expect that the moment smoke came through the vent they would feel very uncomfortable and start to become concerned that the building was on fire. When they were on their own, this was what happened, with 50% of cases reporting the smoke within two minutes of it starting and 75% within the six-minute period. However, what happened with the subjects waiting together was quite different. Only 12% of these subjects reported the smoke within two minutes and only 38% reported the smoke within the six-minute time limit, which meant that the other 62% carried on working for the full six minutes, even though the room was completely full of smoke.

The subjects later explained their actions. The ones who were waiting together had looked to each other for guidance as to how to behave. As none of them knew what to do, and no one moved, they redefined the situation as harmless. Latané and Darley called this redefinition *pluralistic ignorance*, although this situation can only occur when people are not actually aware of *all* the facts of a situation.

Another possible explanation of why the effects occurred was that none of the subjects wanted to look like a wimp in front of the others. Latané and Rodin (1969) decided to investigate the 'macho' ingredient by having subjects wait outside a room. They suddenly heard a female researcher cry out for help after apparently falling in the next room. Obviously it wouldn't affect the 'street cred' of our potential helpers this time, but again the subjects appeared to be suffering from some kind of problem. This time 70% of subjects waiting on their own went to help the woman, but only 40% of the subjects waiting with other people bothered to help. This was an improvement, but still suggested that the presence of others was having a considerable influence. Subjects again showed that they had redefined the situation as not being serious. They had also been influenced by each other's apparent calmness, producing another situation of pluralistic ignorance.

Another factor which influences whether others are prepared to help or not is when *diffusion of responsibility* occurs. Diffusion of responsibility is where the responsibility for the situation is actually spread or diffused amongst the people present. This means that the person's lack of action is actually not so bad because everyone else isn't doing anything to help either, so all are equally to blame.

Here is an example of how this works:

Okay Class 4B, I know that some of you wrote those obscenities on the board. I want the culprits to own up or the whole class will stay in after school tonight.

Doesn't feel so bad when you are part of the group, does it? You have shared the responsibility amongst all of you, rather than just one single person taking the blame.

Darley and Latané (1968) thought that if there were lots of people present this might decrease the likelihood of helping behaviour. They decided to investigate this by again manipulating the size of a group. In this case, however, none of the group could see each other, yet all were apparently aware of exactly what was happening.

They recruited their subjects from a group of students and told them they were to take part in a discussion group where college students were to talk about the kinds of personal problems they were experiencing. They were told that the way they would be assured of anonymity was to stay in separate cubicles and talk over a kind of intercom. It was also explained that this was to ensure that they could talk openly without embarrassment.

At the beginning of the discussion students were led to believe that they were taking part in the discussion with either five other students, three other students or one other student. They were also told that they would each have a chance to speak for two minutes and that the other members of the group would then have a turn each to make a comment on what the student had just said. The reason for this was in fact because there was only one subject per group, and all the other 'subjects' were actually pre-recorded voices. Suddenly one of the fake members of the discussion group was heard to made a series of noises and gasps for help, crying out that they were having a seizure and were about to die.

Darley and Latané noted the number of subjects who actually left their cubicle to find out what was happening to the victim or to find someone to help.

- When they believed they were the only ones present, 85 per cent helped within 60 seconds, and by 2½ minutes everyone had sought assistance.
- When they thought there was one other person besides themselves, the speed of response was slower and only 62% helped within 60 seconds. Even after the full six minutes allowed by the researchers, only about 84% finally helped.
- When the subjects thought there were four other students besides themselves and the seizure victim, only 31% helped in the first 60 seconds, and after six minutes only 62% had tried to help.

The conclusion was that the likelihood of people helping in an emergency situation will go down as the number of people who witness the situation goes up. This is the bystander effect, where the responsibility is diffused amongst the people present and the more people there are, the less responsibility each one takes. But is this really diffusion of responsibility?

Piliavin *et al.* (1981) said that we should clarify what is meant by diffusion of responsibility. Diffusion is where everyone knows what is going on but all the people present share the responsibility for the event. He claims that it is often confused with dissolution of responsibility, which is where we know there are other witnesses but their behaviour cannot be observed, and so we can rationalise that someone else will have done something. This is probably what happened in the Darley and Latané 1968 study above.

Other research looking at the effects of being assessed either as an individual or as part of a crowd have confirmed these findings. Ringelmann (1913) discovered that a group of men pulling on a rope exerted less individual effort than when they did it on their own. This lack of effort made when we are part of a group is known as *social loafing*, which is another way of stating that when a number of people are performing an action an individual will put less effort into it than if acting alone. It seems, however, that social loafing only occurs when people feel that their individual performances can't be evaluated. If they are in a situation where it could be assessed, this phenomenon doesn't occur.

ACTIVITY

In gymnasiums you can find weights used for muscle development. If you can get a member of the gym to supervise you, it might be worth finding out whether one person will lift a greater weight when alone than with two other people. This would be done by noting the weight lifted by the individual and the total weight lifted by three people at the same time. The total weight lifted by the three individuals should then be divided by three to give an average lifted weight.

THE NATURE OF THE POTENTIAL OR ACTUAL HELPER

As we mentioned earlier, the type of person who is on hand to help will have to make the decision as to whether they are competent or confident enough to help. There are a number of factors which will decide whether or not they will intervene.

According to Eagly and Crowley (1986) in their review of more than 170 studies, if you are a male and the situation requires some kind of heroic deed, you are more likely to help than if you are female. This is especially evident in Western cultures, where men are socialised to be chivalrous and heroic. Although there are only a few studies looking at gender differences in situations that require more caring and nurturing or involving a longer time commitment, it has been found that women in such situations are more willing to help. This is supported by the fact that the majority of carers of elderly parents in the UK are women.

Perceived competence also plays a part. If you think you are experienced at dealing with a situation you will be far more willing to intervene than if you feel you don't really know what you are doing. Huston *et al.* (1981) investigated what sort of people helped in an emergency situation and discovered that people who are most likely to assist would be those who have the relevant skills such as first-aid knowledge or life-saving skills. This is even more likely to be the case if you are being watched. If you think that someone is there, assessing your performance (even if they aren't), you will be far less likely to help if you don't feel very competent, but if you feel confident in your ability you won't mind being observed.

THE COST OF HELPING

Have you ever been in a car and witnessed an accident? Did you stop and offer to be a witness and, if not, why not?

'I saw a dreadful smash-up on the way to work this morning. The bloke driving the lorry was on the phone and he just ploughed into this car. It was a real mess. I felt so sorry for the little old lady in the car.'
'Was she all right?'
'I don't know. I didn't stop.'
'Why on earth not?'
'Because I would have been late for work'.

People who witness accidents often admit that they didn't stop because it would have taken time and they would have had to fill in lengthy forms or even go to court. It seems that everyone weighs up the cost of helping, often unconsciously, and usually instantaneously, and this will have a huge influence on whether they are willing to get involved.

This cost/benefit analysis is known as 'Social Exchange Theory' and was proposed by Thibaut and Kelley in 1959. This theory can be used to interpret studies of bystander intervention. What it is stating is that we may decide to help if there is some kind of profit in the situation for us. We calculate this profit by looking at the rewards minus the cost of helping. Rewards could be things like feeling good about ourselves, not worrying, striking up a new relationship or gaining some kind of money. Costs could be things like being late to an appointment, looking a complete idiot in front of other people, getting dirty, catching something or being in danger, especially if the person is drunk or the area is one with a high crime rate. Remember here, too, that women may perceive themselves as being in greater danger than men, even though they are in the same situation – this may also help to explain some of the differences in helping behaviours between the genders.

So, according to Social Exchange Theory, we only get involved in some kind of

47

pro-social behaviour as the likelihood of making a profit increases. Where there is too much to lose and very little to gain we would decide not to help. Basically, this points to the fact that acts may look altruistic but are not really altruistic after all.

THE NATURE OF THE VICTIM

If you saw a really unpleasant-looking, smelly, dirty, old tramp trip over something in front of you, would you immediately rush up to him and try to help him up? What about the fact that it might be a frail old lady, who smelt of lavender and had a walking stick in her hand – would that make a difference? It seems that the nature of the victim has a huge effect on whether or not we are willing to act in an altruistic way.

First of all, as you know, we have to make attributions about the type of situation we are in. We have to decide, on the basis of the available information, whether or not the person really needs help. Kelley (1973) devised the Causal Schemata Model, which is one of several models that help to explain how we frequently make attributions about a situation (and why these attributions are often wrong). Let me explain how this model works with an example.

Ruth is walking down the road when she comes across a man lying in the gutter. He stinks of alcohol and he is holding a paper bag containing what is left of a broken bottle. Her initial thought is what a state for a drunk to get into and she passes by on the other side of the road.

What she doesn't know is that he is a priest who is extremely fond of his elderly mother. He also suffers with high cholesterol levels and has been told that he has to take things easy as he has a weak heart. It is his mother's eightieth birthday and he decided that he would buy her a bottle of her favourite spirit as a birthday present. He was just on his way to the off-licence to get the bottle when he was stopped by a parishioner who seemed to have a crush on him. Consequently he was late and was extremely concerned that the off-licence would close, so he had hurried all the way there and was now on his way to buy her a card. Because he had become so anxious, and because he had put his heart under such pressure when running, he had had a heart attack and had fallen down, in the gutter, and the bottle had smashed as he hit the ground.

What a mistake for Ruth to make!

What is happening here is that we are actually using information we have stored in our memories from previous experiences to help us make sense of the situation (you will learn more about schemas in the next chapter which considers the nature of memory). Experience would suggest that if someone has collapsed and smells of alcohol it is the alcohol that is responsible and the likelihood is that it is their fault. We will therefore take the 'obvious' explanation for the situation without considering other possible causes. We seem to use what is known as the 'discounting principle' which means that we discount other possible explanations in favour of what to us, is a more familiar explanation. In fact, what we are using is a kind of 'causal shorthand' (Fiske and Taylor, 1991) to explain behaviour quickly.

Darley and Latané (1970) illustrated how this happens with a study looking at how many people would be willing to give money to someone in the street, and whether the person's reason for asking affected the amount of giving. In the first condition the actor asked for some money for no reason, and in this case 34% of people gave money. I suppose they figured that there must have been a good reason for him to ask in the first place! In the second condition he said it was to make a telephone call and this resulted in 64% of people giving money. In the third condition the man said his wallet had been stolen (a more worthy cause?) and in this condition 70% of people helped. It seems that the perceived nature of the victim's need influenced helping behaviour.

**Irving M. Piliavin, Judith A. Rodin and Jane Allyn Piliavin (1969),
'Good Samaritanism, an Underground Phenomenon?'**
Journal of Personality & Social Psychology, 13, 289–99

Background

The consequence of much of the past research suggested that there were a number of factors which would influence the likelihood of helping behaviour occurring. However, many of the past studies had confounding factors which may have influenced the results, such as ambiguity or a lack of ecological validity. Piliavin *et al.* (1969) designed their study to take place in a natural environment where the ambiguity of the situation was reduced to a minimum so that pluralistic ignorance should not enter the equation.

Aims

The aims of the study were to see, in a face-to-face situation in a real-life setting, from which there would be no clear escape route:

- whether an ill person would get more help than a drunk person.
- whether there would be ethnocentric behaviour in helping – people would help someone of their own race more than someone of another race.
- whether the intervention of a model, a confederate of the experimenters who would step in and offer help, would influence others' helping behaviour.

Method

Design

A field experiment was carried out using participant observation techniques to gather data.

Piliavin *et al.* engaged 16 General Studies students from the University of Columbia to carry out the study and gather the data. These 16 were split into four teams of researchers, giving four members in each team, two of whom were female. Each team member was given a role, they always performed the same role in each trial, and they always worked together in the same teams.

FOCUS ON RESEARCH METHODS – laboratory vs. field experiments

The following table gives a breakdown of the strengths and weaknesses of each approach.

location	☺ strengths	☹ weaknesses
LABORATORY	• In the controlled environment of the lab it is easier to isolate the IV as a causal factor and keep all extraneous variables constant or controlled. • In the lab, technical equipment can be used to measure variables (e.g. EEG machine).	• One problem with the lab setting is that Ss have consented to attend and be studied. This means that all lab studies can be affected by subject reactivity, with Ss responding to demand characteristics. This leads us to question the internal validity of lab-based studies. • Since the lab setting is often constrained and unlike real-life settings, lab studies also tend to lack ecological validity.
FIELD (natural or real-life setting)	• By carrying out a study in a real-life setting, the ecological validity of a study can be improved. (NB Be careful not to assume that all studies carried out in a real-life setting are ecologically valid. For example, if the study involved 300 clowns riding bikes through a supermarket to see how people react this would still not be ecologically valid as the experience of Ss would not be realistic!)	• In the field it is harder to isolate the IV as a causal factor and keep all extraneous variables constant or controlled, so the possibility of other variables affecting the DV, becoming confounding variables, is higher in the field. • It can be harder to transport and set up sensitive technical equipment in the field.

Below is a description of the roles played by the team members:

Team member:	Role, appearance and behaviour
Victim	The victims were standardised in their appearance and behaviour across the four teams. They were always male, between the ages of 26 and 35. Their dress was identical: Eisenhower jacket, old slacks, no tie. They got on the train and went to stand near the pole in the centre of the carriage (critical area), waited 70 seconds then staggered forward and collapsed on the floor, looking up at the ceiling. In order to operationalise the IV 'drunk' or 'ill', the victim played these two roles on alternate days. On the drunk day he smelled of liquor and carried a liquor bottle in a brown paper bag. On the ill days he carried a black cane (walking stick). In order to test whether same-race helping occurred, one of the models was black and three were white (the only black male student who had volunteered to carry out the study was allocated to the role of victim).
Observer 1 and Observer 2	These were female, and appeared to be just ordinary passengers on the train. They would get on with the other team members and make their way to be as close to their allotted position in the adjacent areas as possible. Observer one would then observe and record: the race, sex and location of passengers in the critical area, the total number of passengers in the whole carriage and the total number of helpers who assisted the victim, and their race, sex and original position in the carriage. Observer two would observe and record: the race, sex and location of passengers in the critical area, the total number of passengers in the whole carriage and the total number of helpers who assisted the victim. She also measured how long it took for the first helper to arrive and, in the model conditions, how long it took for a subsequent helper to arrive. Both spoke to the person immediately next to them after the event took place, noting down what they responded and also making a note of any other spontaneous comments made by passengers.
Model	Since laboratory studies had suggested that people did not help, a further team member was used who was to step in and help to

see if his actions would bring in others to help. The model was always male, aged 24–29 and casually dressed. The model was to help by getting the victim to a seated position and staying with him until the train arrived at the next stop.

To see if the model had any effect, and whether which side of the carriage he was in or how long it took him to help would affect others' helping, 5 model conditions were devised:

- Critical area, early help (i.e. he stood in the critical area when he got on the train and helped after approx. 70 seconds after the victim fell).
- Critical area, late help (late meant after approx 150 seconds).
- Adjacent area, early help.
- Adjacent area, late help (for both of these two conditions he would have to cross the carriage to help).
- No model: this was to act as a control condition to see what would happen with no model intervention.

Apparatus

The study took place in the New York subway, between 59th and 125th Street stations on the 8th Avenue line. This particular run of track was selected as there was a non-stop ride of 7½ minutes, giving enough time for the procedure to be carried out. The trials took place between April and June 1968, and between the hours of 11 a.m. and 3 p.m. The teams only selected the old-style trains with two-seater seats.

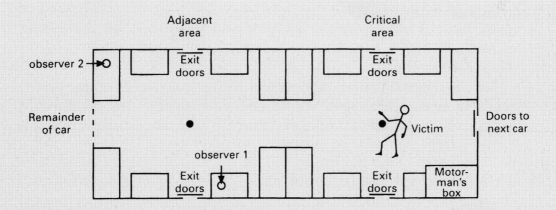

Sample/Subjects

Over the 3-month period approximately 4,450 unsolicited Ss were observed over the trials. The racial mix was about 55% white and 45% black, and the mean number of people present in the whole carriage was 43, with a mean of 8.5 for the critical area where the incident took place.

Variables

There were three independent variables:
- whether the victim appeared drunk or ill
- whether the victim was black or white
- the manipulation of the actions of the model (the effect of the presence or absence of the model, manipulations in the time delay before the model helped and which side of the carriage the model was originally standing in).

The dependent variables measured included:
- the number of helpers and the speed at which they offered help
- the race and gender of helpers
- if anyone moved out of the critical area
- the comments made by passengers during the incident.

Procedure

The teams entered the train through different doors and the victim enacted his 'collapse' after 70 seconds. By consulting a random number table drawn up before the trials, the model would have worked out which condition he was in and he would stand on the appropriate side of the carriage and time himself ready to step in. The observers made their recordings as unobtrusively as possible. They were participant observers.

> ## FOCUS ON RESEARCH METHODS – observation as a data-gathering technique
>
> In the first chapter we discussed using observation as a data-gathering technique. First, observation can be carried out either covertly, that is, undercover and without the knowledge of those being observed, or overtly, where Ss are either aware of or have been informed of the fact that they are being observed.
>
> The advantage of covert observation is that you are sampling 'real' behaviour, uncontaminated by the Ss' desire to respond to demand characteristics. Some researchers believe that the only valid way to sample typical human behaviour is by covert observation in a field setting, the method used by Piliavin *et al.* in this study.
>
> Observation can also be carried out as participant or non-participant observation. This means that the researcher is either a part of the setting/event he or she is observing (participant), or is outside of the setting (non-participant). The advantage of being a participant, as in the Piliavin *et al.* study, is that you get an insight into the experience yourself, and also you have a good vantage point for your observations. However, your mere presence may change the course of the events you are observing. It could be that the inactivity of some potential helpers in the adjacent area in the trials

was because of the inactivity of the two observers; we can't know for sure.

It is also possible that if you are observing as a participant for a longer period of time, you may become too involved in the setting to be objective about your observations.

At the end of the 'no model' trials the model was to get the victim to his feet and get him off the train. The four team members would get off at the next stop and then cross over to the opposite platform and carry out another trial, this time in the other direction.

The teams were supposed to alternate the victim condition daily (drunk or ill), but the victim for Team two did not like doing the drunk condition, and this means that the ill condition was carried out more often. A total of 103 trials were recorded, 65 in the ill condition and 38 in the drunk condition.

Results

One of the main findings was that, unlike the studies carried out under laboratory conditions, people generally helped and were quick to help. So for 79% of the trials the model was not required, and the amount of trials where the model was required was too small to fully analyse the effects of his original location or speed of helping.

The nature of the victim influenced levels of helping. The ill victim received spontaneous help from a fellow passenger before 70 seconds had elapsed after his collapse on 62 out of 65 trials and the drunk victim on 19 out of 38 trials. This confirmed that someone who appears ill is more likely to receive help than someone who appears drunk. Not only was there more help for the ill victim, but help also came more quickly (a median of five seconds rather then 109 for the drunk condition).

Of the 81 first helpers 90% were males (even though the gender breakdown for the critical area was 60% male and 40% female); this leads to the conclusion that men were more likely to help in this sort of scenario than women.

No one left the compartment during any of the trials, but in 21 of the 103 trials, 34 people moved from the critical area to the adjacent area, with more leaving in the drunk than the ill trials.

No significant tendency for same-race helping was seen, although there was a slight tendency for same-race helping to occur more in the drunk than the ill condition.

There was no evidence of diffusion of responsibility. Remember, this was the hypothesis derived from laboratory studies, that the more people present the less help would be offered. This was supposed to be because each person would feel less personally responsible the more people there were available to share the responsibility. In the Piliavin study, a slight trend was shown in the opposite direction, in fact, with the fuller the carriage, the more help being offered.

Results for the ill condition, no model (help came spontaneously before 70 seconds after the victim collapsed), showing the help received by black and white victims:

	Number of trials	Number of times helped	Overall % of helping
White victim	54	54	100%
Black victim	8	8	100%

Results for the ill condition, with model, showing the help received by black and white victims:

	Number of trials	Number of times helped	Overall % of helping
White victim	3	3	100%
Black victim	0	0	N/a

Results for the drunk condition, no model, (help came spontaneously before 70 seconds after the victim collapsed), showing the help received by black and white victims:

	Number of trials	Number of times helped	Overall % of helping
White victim	11	11	100%
Black victim	11	8	73%

Results for the drunk condition, with model, showing the help received by black and white victims:

	Number of trials	Number of times helped	Overall % of helping
White victim	13	10	77%
Black victim	3	2	66%

Discussion

What explanation do Piliavin et al. *offer for the findings?*

Piliavin *et al.* propose a model of helping that included the assumptions that observation of an emergency creates an emotional state in the bystander, that is, it induces a state of arousal, interpreted negatively in this instance as either disgust, fear or sympathy, and that we are motivated to reduce this negative arousal. This can be achieved by the following actions:

- helping directly
- going to get help
- leaving
- not offering help because you have decided the victim does not deserve it.

Additionally, the action we choose in order to reduce arousal will depend on us carrying out a cost/benefit analysis. This means we will carry out the action that we assess as giving us the greatest benefit and least cost. Costs of helping include effort, disgust and embarrassment, and there are also the costs of not-helping to weigh up, such as self-blame and our worry that others will think we are bad if we don't help. Benefits might include self-praise or the praise of others.

Piliavin *et al.* suggest that this model is consistent with all their findings. For example, the drunk is helped less because the costs of helping are higher – he may get angry, over-friendly or may even vomit! – and the costs of not helping are lower, as we may feel less guilt for not helping as we believe he has at least partially put himself in the position he is in.

Women help less in this study because the costs of helping, effort, are high and the costs of not helping are low, as it is not a woman's place to help in such a situation she will feel less self-blame or fear less judgement by others.

Why was no diffusion of responsibility recorded in this study?

Piliavin *et al.* suggest that this may be because the subjects on the train were face to face with the victim and could not either conclude that there was no emergency, or, if no helper came along, that the emergency was over. These are two possible assumptions that may have led the subjects in the earlier lab-based studies not to offer help.

Perhaps the reason why diffusion of responsibility was not evident was because there were more potential helpers present than in laboratory experiments. All past research had involved the use of only one subject, with the rest being stooges of the experimenter. Therefore, there was only one potential helper and that potential helper may have been looking to everyone else to guide them as to what they should do. Bearing in mind that all the other people 'taking part' did nothing as part of the study, perhaps the phenomenon of pluralistic ignorance could explain the results of past research in this area. In this subway study, there were large numbers of potential helpers and this may have resulted in more helping behaviour rather than less, and as the group size increased, the potential number of helpers increased.

It may therefore be that diffusion of responsibilty is only an artefact of laboratory-based studies with one potential helper, the naïve subject.

Commentary

Does the study raise any ethical concerns?

There is a problem with carrying out the study using covert observation techniques. An unsolicited subject cannot be briefed about the nature of the study and give their informed consent. Nor is it always possible for the S to be debriefed and later asked for permission to use their data. This means that this study raises ethical concerns about consent and about invading people's privacy. Don't we have the right to go about our daily business without being monitored for the purposes of scientific research without our knowledge?

Also, deception is used in the study. The victim is not really in need of help, just play-acting a role for the purposes of the study. Seeing someone fall and the anxiety such an event can arouse may have upset some of the passengers on the train, who would never know that this was not a real collapse. They may also have to confront their conscience about their lack of willingness to help, and this self-knowledge may also have caused distress to some Ss.

Is the study ecologically valid?

Given that the study took place on a real train in a real setting and that the behaviour enacted by the victim, although uncommon, is a possible scenario people may encounter, the study is high in ecological validity. The internal validity of the study is also increased by the fact that the Ss were unaware they were being observed, and this would suggest that their behaviour was as it would have been if the event was in fact real and not part of a psychological investigation.

Is the study useful?

The study offers a useful model where helping behaviour is described in terms of the emotional and cognitive processes which a person responds to in making a decision to offer assistance. The study is also useful in that it shows the care that must be taken when trying to generalise findings from the social psychology laboratory to real-life settings.

Even though the study does contradict the earlier laboratory studies, and shows a much higher level of helping than the laboratory studies would have predicted, there is still no suggestion that people act out of pure altruistic motives. Piliavin *et al.* see them as acting out of 'a selfish desire to rid oneself of an unpleasant emotional state'.

Key questions

1. In this study the researchers gathered their data covertly using participant observation techniques. Give one advantage and one disadvantage of covert observation techniques. Do you think the observers had an easy job in this study?

2. Explain what is meant by the term 'independent variable' and identify the 3 IVs in this study.

3. Identify one piece of qualitative evidence and one piece of quantitative evidence recorded by the observers.

4. Do you think the findings would be different if the study was carried out in a large shopping centre in one of the major UK cities today?

Example Answers are on page 450.

Further reading:

- Aronson, E., Wilson, T.D. and Akert, R.M. (1997), *Social Psychology*, New York: Longman, 3rd edition.
- Pennington, D.C. (2000) *Social Cognition*. London: Routledge. Chapters two and three give a good explanation of attribution theory.
- If you go to http://www.lihistory.com/8/hs81a.htm you can read the story of the killing of Kitty Genovese in grisly detail.

Roles

We have considered so far the social influence that can be exerted by one person on another in the form of obedience to authority. We have mentioned, too, that conformity also affects the behaviour of others because they will adjust their behaviour in order to fit in with the desired person or group in order to be accepted by that group.

Social influence also comes into play when we take on one of the many roles that are part of our daily lives: daughter or son, student, grandchild, employee. Your behaviour is influenced by the role you adopt, and the role may also change the status your have in relation to others. In fact, a role does not exist unless it involves some kind of interaction with others. You can't be a nurse unless you have a patient, or a teacher unless you have a student.

A role is usually defined as 'the behaviours expected of a person occupying a certain position in a group'. These behaviours are expected by people seeing you in that position – you would be considered very strange if you dressed in a nurse's uniform and then went out and started directing the traffic.

Think of the roles you have to undertake and the fact that each of those roles requires a slightly different type of behaviour. You would not act with your grandparents in the same way as you would with a group of friends, so the two roles are completely different and involve different norms of behaviour. One important psychological effect of taking on a role is that your individual identity may be replaced by a group or role identity which could offer you a different status and also, perhaps, anonymity.

The following story illustrates this point:

George had just completed his initial training for the police and it was his first day on the beat. He was standing by the entrance to Tesco's car park when he saw a car driving out in which the driver had not put on his seat belt. Here goes, he thought and he could feel the butterflies in his stomach. He raised his hand, indicating to the driver to pull over, thinking to himself, I wonder if he will stop. What will I do if he doesn't? This seems really mean – he was only just leaving the car park, but then if I don't stop him, I would not to be doing my duty.

As he walked up to the car, the driver wound down the window.

'Excuse me, sir, but I have had to stop you as you weren't wearing your seat belt.'

'But I'm only just coming out of the car park,' said the driver, looking both shocked and annoyed.

'I know, sir, but you have just joined a public highway and it's my duty to stop you as you are in breach of the law.' George got out his pad to issue a ticket to the driver. 'I am afraid I will have to ask you to take your documents to the local police station and you will be fined £30.'

The role George had taken dictated that he exert his authority in a situation where he was obviously in slight conflict about what he was doing. You can also imagine that as an individual he would probably find his behaviour a little over-the-top and would have been just as angry if someone else had done this to him. George stopped being George and instead became a policeman, which in turn affected the usual constraints on his behaviour and led to him losing some of his individuality. This phenomenon is known as 'deindividuation'?

There may have been times when you have been in a role that has had a specific influence on your behaviour. If you work in a shop, for example, you take on a different authority over the customers than another customer. You can ask people to move, or tell them to go to the checkout, for example. Imagine doing this with a uniform on; at least here it is harder to be identified as an individual, which increases the feeling of anonymity, and this may make your behaviour more extreme.

One of the topics which inspired the theory of deindividuation was that of 'mob psychology'. This was an idea proposed by Le Bon (1895) when he suggested that crowds were dangerous and he suggested that when a crowd gathered it would behave in a primitive and totally irrational way. He maintained that the members of the crowd would become over-aroused and therefore the normal social constraints which controlled their behaviour as individuals would no longer apply. He actually called this social contagion the law of mental unity.

It is very interesting that he should develop this theory around the time when the government was trying to justify the suppression of demonstrations, and in fact there is very little evidence for this process actually occurring. However, we all know that crowds can behave in a totally different way to individuals.

Let's say you decide that you want a cup of coffee or a soft drink and so decide to go into a pub. Although you have gone into the pub, you are actually quite self-conscious, so you are quiet and probably sit somewhere where you can view what is going on, rather than having your back to the crowd.

In this instance you are behaving according to your own code of behaviour, but there is a certain amount of social influence as to how you conduct yourself. You would feel ostentatious if you started laughing out loud to yourself, or if you put your feet on another chair, or even talked to yourself. Now picture the same situation with a friend.

You and your friend go to the pub and sit yourselves in a position where you can either both see the contents of the pub or you are directly opposite each other, because what you want to talk about is very private/interesting/personal. You may find yourself laughing out loud, moving about, but generally feeling much more comfortable.

Now imagine the same situation with a group of friends, say 10 in total. You will be more raucous, loud and laugh and move about far more, feeling less obvious than you would as an individual. Your friends will, in fact, give you confidence.

Now take this one stage further. Imagine you are all in the pub and you all have fancy dress on, so, in effect, you can't be identified. What will the behaviour be like now?

As a result of Le Bon's work, Festinger *et al.* (1952) first introduced the concept of deindividuation, which he defined as 'a state of affairs in a group where members do not pay attention to other individuals as individuals and, correspondingly, the members do not feel they are being singled out by others.'

Groups give us a sense of identity and belonging and they also reduce our sense of individuality, where we become identified as a part of a whole, rather than the whole itself.

In 1969 Zimbardo brought the two ideas of deindividuation (loss of personal identity) and identification with the mob together, and explained that the result of this process was that people were no longer governed by their individual consciences and would therefore act in a different way to the way they would as an autonomous individual. He claimed that if people believe that they can be identified and therefore be held responsible for their behaviour, they will control their aggressive impulses: the larger the group, the less likelihood of being recognised, and therefore the more extreme the behaviour. So we have an interaction here between behaviour and anonymity, provided either by numbers of people or outfits.

Consider why certain cultures painted their warriors' faces and bodies before they went into battle. The answer should be apparent. Robert Watson (1973) studied 24 different cultures which decorated their warriors in this way and found that they were significantly more likely to commit acts of brutality against prisoners than non-decorated warriors. If you take this one stage further, do the uniforms that any soldiers wear increase their savagery?

Even children are affected by deindividuation. Diener *et al.* (1976) observed 1,300 children trick or treating on Halloween night. Some of the children wore costumes which hid their identity, whilst others were identifiable. When they were completely anonymous they were more willing to steal money and sweets than the identifiable children.

Interestingly, however, the story of deindividuation does not simply imply that if we are in a group and lose our sense of identity to the group we will behave in a violent and aggressive manner. Not all groups are violent, and not all roles incite violent behaviour. A study undertaken by Zimbardo in 1970 found that women were more likely to give higher voltage electric shocks to another woman when they were deindividuated (by wearing bulky lab coats and hoods, and not being referred to by name) than when they were identifiable (wearing normal clothes and being referred to by name). However, another study by Johnson and Downing (1979) showed that the nature of the uniform itself seemed to affect the level of shocks rather than the deindividuation. They suggested that the outfit worn by the women in the Zimbardo study was very like the outfits worn by the Ku Klux Klan and that this may have affected the levels of aggression shown by the participants. They therefore replicated the study but had another group dressed as nurses, and they found that although the nurses were wearing identical uniforms and therefore lacked individuality, they actually gave fewer and less severe shocks. So this gives us some indication that the role is interacting with the means of deindividuation, and that deindividuation can have positive as well as negative effects on behaviour.

These examples of research should help to explain how prisons manage to deindividuate their inmates. Their identity is removed because they wear uniforms and have their hair cut in a similar way. Members of the police and also prison officers are also deindividuated because they wear uniforms which hide their individual identity. This gives them anonymity when they deal with others, but it also makes them anonymous to a crowd where they may be perceived as being less human and therefore targets of aggression. We have also established that this deindividuation process, together with membership of a crowd, is likely to affect the types of behaviour demonstrated and this may result in an increase in aggression. Finally we have also shown that the role played by the people wearing uniforms will affect the way they behave. All this theory has a direct relationship to one of the most famous pieces of social psychological research, undertaken by Haney, Banks and Zimbardo (1973) and known as the prison simulation experiment.

C. Haney, C. Banks and P. Zimbardo (1973), 'A study of prisoners and guards in a simulated prison',
Naval Research Reviews, 30 (9), 4–17

Background

If you take a punitive view of prison, you might think that it is desirable for the experience of those incarcerated to be brutal and harsh, teaching them a lesson. However, Zimbardo *et al.'s* research in prisons, talking to current and ex-inmates and to those working as guards, showed that the system went beyond brutal but fair and into the realms of the inhumane, rife with both sexual and physical abuse. This has an impact on prisoners on their release:

'The experience of prison creates undeniably almost to the point of cliché, an intense hatred and disrespect in most inmates for the authority and the established order of society into which they will eventually return…' (Haney, 1973, p. two).

Even if we are to see prison as a punitive experience, we have to consider that prisoners will be released, and if they have experienced a penal system both brutal and unfair, what is to stop them paying back society like with like?

What led to the 'deplorable state' (Haney, 1973) of the US penal system?

Prisons were clearly not deterrents, with recidivism (reoffending) levels, both then and now, at rates of 75% and higher; nor did they rehabilitate offenders for reintegration into society.

Zimbardo *et al.* then set about trying to answer the question: What causes the inhumane conditions in prisons? Haney says that the prevalent view is the 'dispositional hypothesis' – the theory that the brutality in prisons is due to the 'nature' of those who administer it, or the 'nature' of people who populate prisons, or both. That is, the prisoners and guards are 'brutal types', the guards needing to be so to deal with the brutality of the inmates. This fits in with our stereotypes: guards are seen as sadistic and prisoners as sociopathic.

Haney points out that this is an attractive explanation since it directs attention away from the social, economic and political forces that combine to make prisons what they are. If such forces were to be seen to be to blame for the situation, to bring about change would require complex, expensive and revolutionary actions. Authorities instead favour the dispositional theory which allows the prison status quo to be observed: they do nothing, as people's natures cannot be changed, they can only be contained or dealt with.

A second theory, however, is that it is the way that prisons are organised and operated, that leads to their brutality.

The present study was therefore designed to find out which of these two explanations was correct. It was not possible to research this in a natural, real prison setting. Since both the structure of the prison setting and the nature of those involved were variables already present, they would confound each other and it would not be possible to answer the question of which was leading to the brutality.

The method chosen was to simulate a prison environment as closely as ethically and practically possible and populate it with 'normal, average' types.

If no brutal behaviour was observed, then this would suggest the dispositional hypothesis was correct. However, if brutality was observed in these hitherto 'normal-average' types, then the prison environment and structure could be considered as the causal factor.

The participants in the study would therefore be adopting a role, either as guard or prisoner, and this study illustrates how roles affect behaviour.

Although it was not intended (not possible) to create a realistic prison situation, the experimenters tried to incorporate the psychological effects they had noted as aspects of real prison life into the mock prison:

Guards experienced:	Prison inmates experienced:
Power	Powerlessness
Control	Oppression
Satisfaction	Frustration
Arbitrary rule	Resistance to authority
Status	Anonymity
Machismo	Emasculation

Aim

The purpose of the study was to investigate the effects of a simulated prison environment on a group of students, and to see if the roles they were randomly assigned to play would significantly influence their behaviour. The researchers predicted that the allocation of the role of guard or prisoner would dictate behaviour, not the personal dispositions or personalities of those taking part.

Method

Design

The researchers used an experimental simulation of a prison environment. Using an independent groups design, subjects were randomly allocated to the role of either guard or prisoner.

FOCUS ON RESEARCH ISSUES – randomisation

Randomisation, or random allocation, is where Ss are allocated to experimental conditions on a chance basis, by drawing lots or tossing a coin for example. This is done to control extraneous variables. In this study it was done to avoid experimenter bias in the selection of guards or prisoners. The study would have been spoiled if Zimbardo *et al.* could have been accused of simply picking the biggest of the 24 Ss to be the guards.

Data was gathered by audio and videotape and by direct observation. Also, a number of self-report measures were used:
- questionnaires measured individual reactions
- mood inventories
- personality tests
- daily guard shift reports and post-experimental interviews.

Subjects

A newspaper advertisement was placed asking for male volunteers to take part in a study of 'prison life', for $15 a day, for up to two weeks: 75 potential subjects volunteered and completed questionnaires about family background, physical/mental health history, involvement in crime, etc.

Each potential subject was also interviewed by one of two experimenters.

Finally, 24 were selected who were judged to be most stable (physically and mentally), most mature, and least involved in antisocial behaviours. In other words, the most 'normal, average' 24 were selected.

Ss were Caucasian, except for one Oriental, and were all normal, healthy college students who were in the Stanford area for the summer, and all were largely of middle-class socio-economic status.

Ss were initially strangers to each other, for ethical and practical reasons:
- ethical – to prevent damage being caused to participants' existing friendships
- practical – to prevent existing patterns of behaviour or relationships from interfering with the experimental situation.

Of the three prisoners on 'standby' at home, in case they were needed, two were not called, and one 'standby' guard decided not to participate just prior to the beginning of the experiment, so the experimenters' results were based on 10 prisoners and 11 guards.

Apparatus

A basement corridor in the Psychology Building at Stanford University was converted into a mock prison, containing three small cells (6' x 9'), with black-painted steel-barred doors and no furniture besides three beds with mattresses, sheets and pillows. There were three prisoners in each cell. The rest of the accommodation consisted of an unlit broom cupboard used as a solitary confinement area, a recreation 'yard' which had an observation window, and several rooms nearby for the guards to change into their uniforms and take their breaks in.

Uniforms were used to increase the feelings of anonymity in all Ss and to emphasise their roles. The uniforms were to enhance group identity and reduce individual uniqueness.

- Prisoners wore loose-fitting smocks with identification numbers, a nylon stocking on their heads to cover their hair, no underwear, rubber sandals and a light lock and chain around the ankle. They were issued washing gear and bed linen but were not allowed any personal possessions.
- Guards wore khaki shirts and trousers, reflective sunglasses and carried a nightstick (a long truncheon) and whistle.

The uniforms were also intended to visit on the Ss the psychological effects that had been observed in real prisons. The nightstick and whistle were symbols of control and power. The khakis suggested a military attitude – powerful and macho.

The uniform for the prisoners was a dress, which was both humiliating and emasculating (as only girls wear dresses!) and their lack of underwear made them adopt female poses, again emphasising the emasculating nature of the prison experience. The ankle chain was a symbol of oppression. The use of numbers rather than names and stocking caps to prevent any individuality being expressed through hairstyle contributed to the loss of personal identity in the prisoners.

Procedure

Prior to the start of the study, Ss were told they would be randomly assigned to either the guard or prisoner role. All had agreed to play either role for a period of 14 days and nights, for a payment of $15 a day. All had signed a contract (drawn up with legal advice) which made it clear that 'prisoners' would be under surveillance (and would therefore have little or no privacy) and should expect to have some of their civil rights suspended during the study (excluding physical abuse). Prisoners were to remain in the prison 24 hours a day for the duration of the study.

Once the roles had been allocated, 'prisoners' were instructed to wait at home on a given Sunday, when the study would begin.

'Guards' were invited in on the day before the start of the study for an orientation day. They were introduced to the 'superintendent' (Zimbardo) and the 'warden' (one of the other researchers) and were told about the shifts they would operate – eight-hour three-man shifts – and about the work assignments prisoners would carry out for their $15 a day.

The 'guards' were told that their assigned task was to ensure that the prisoners did not escape and to 'maintain the reasonable degree of order within the prison necessary for its effective functioning'. They were deliberately given minimal guidelines about their guard role, but an explicit and categorical prohibition against the use of physical punishment was emphasised by the experimenters.

The 'guards' and 'warden' drew up a list of prison rules and prisoners' rights. Along with their identification number, prisoners were to learn these by heart. Prisoners would get:

- three bland meals a day
- three supervised toilet visits
- two hours daily for reading/letter-writing privileges
- two visiting times a week and movie rights and exercise periods.

Prisoners would be expected to carry out work assignments to earn their $15 a day, and comply when, three times a day, prisoners were lined up for a count (one per shift of guards).

On the Sunday the study started, 'prisoners' were arrested from their homes by the Palo Alto police. They were taken to the local police department and charged with suspicion of burglary or armed robbery, fingerprinted and put in the police cell. The police refused to confirm that this was part of the experiment. They were then collected by the 'warden' and one of the 'guards' and driven blindfold to the mock prison. This must have been a very disturbing and disorienting experience for the 'prisoner'.

Once at the 'prison' they were stripped, deloused (actually they were sprayed with a harmless deodorant!), and left standing naked in the 'yard' for a while. They were then photographed and given a prisoner's uniform and allocated their number, read the rules of the prison, taken to their cell and told to wait in silence. From this moment onwards, they were referred to by number only and had to use the title 'Mr Correctional Officer' when addressing one of the 'guards'.

Results

The study was stopped after six days because of the zeal of the 'guards' and the deterioration of some of the 'prisoners'. After an initial revolt on day two, which was quickly put down by the 'guards', as the days went on the behaviour of the 'prisoners' was that of model prisoners: passivity, dependence and flattened mood.

In terms of the interaction between 'guards' and 'prisoners', 'guards' were verbally abusive to 'prisoners', with commands being the most common form of verbal behaviour. 'Prisoner'–'prisoner' interaction revealed that the 'prisoners' had internalised the 'prison', it had become real for them. Monitored conversations showed that they talked about the 'prison' 90% of the time, even when they were alone in their cells and could be getting to know one another or talking about things to take their minds off the situation they were in.

Although it has to be noted that half the 'prisoners' had coped in the oppressive atmosphere, the other half had demonstrated such disturbing behaviours that the study was cut short: five 'prisoners' had had to be 'released' because of extreme emotional depression, crying, rage and acute anxiety. The pattern of symptoms was similar in four of them and began as early as day two. The researchers referred to this as *pathological prisoner syndrome.* The fifth S developed a psychosomatic rash on his body and was subsequently 'released'.

At this point the remaining 'prisoners' were asked if they would they be willing to forfeit the money they had earned so far and be 'paroled' (set free)? Only two were not willing, and this was surprising given that the money had been a prime motivator for them taking part in the first place. When the 'superintendent' said he'd have to consider this, the 'prisoners' went meekly back to their cells, showing how tied in to their roles they had become. This is further evidence that the 'prisoners' had internalised the 'prison' (come to believe in it).

Reactions of the Ss when the experiment was over

'Prisoners' were delighted, but in contrast, 'guards' seemed distressed at the decision to stop the study. We have seen how the 'prisoners' had internalised the 'prison'; had the 'guards' also come to believe in it?

There is evidence that this was indeed the case:
- none of the guards had failed to turn up on time for their shift
- on several occasions guards stayed on duty, voluntarily and uncomplaining, for several hours and without additional pay
- on one occasion a guard (who did not know he was being observed) paced the yard, vigorously pounding his nightstick into his hand while he 'kept watch'.

Zimbardo *et al.* suggest that the distress shown by the 'guards' at the termination of the study demonstrated 'that they now enjoyed their extreme control and power … and were reluctant to give it up'. However, they point out that, as with the 'prisoners', not all 'guards' reacted in the same way. Some were tough but fair, some were passive and let the other 'guards' exert control, while others engaged in 'creative cruelty and harassment'.

Discussion

Zimbardo *et al.* claim that power led to the deterioration in the behaviour of the 'guards', and he described this as the *pathology of power* (the syndrome of oppressive behaviour that develops in people given the opportunity to exert power over others). For some 'guards' being given free reign to exert power over others was intoxicating and they enjoyed the absolute control they had over the 'prisoners'.

A number of factors contributed to the deterioration of the 'prisoners', including:
- The loss of personal identity: the lack of individuality of appearance, and the fact that to draw attention to yourself was avoided because of the consequences it could provoke, led to loss of initiative and compliance.
- The arbitrary control exerted by the guards: 'guards' quickly reinterpreted

rights, including food and toilet visits, as privileges from day one. Reasonable requests such as to be taken to the toilet, may or may not be acceded to. A 'prisoner' may incur the same penalty from the 'guard' if he smiled at a joke made by a 'guard' as if he did not. Thus the 'guards' exerted arbitrary rule over the 'prisoners'. The unpredictability of the system and the fact that their requests would likely as not be unheeded led to what Zimbardo *et al.* refer to as 'zombie-like' behaviours, initiating no interaction and passively responding to orders. This can be described as learned helplessness, where the actor believes that nothing he or she can do can change the situation, and this results in giving up and doing nothing to try to affect the situation.

- Dependency and emasculation: being dependent on the 'guards' for food, toilet visits, in fact, everything, led to both helplessness and emasculation. In order to get anything, 'prisoners' had to show good behaviour, which might include doing foolish things or behaving with unquestioning obedience to the 'guards'. The uniforms' emasculating effects allowed the 'guards' to refer to the 'prisoners' as 'girlies' or 'sissies'. The 'prisoners' were emasculated and this may explain why they obeyed even when they outnumbered the 'guards' on the counts 9:3.

Conclusions

The study shows how social roles (which are environmental factors) influence behaviour. The conclusions of the researchers were that the structure of prisons and not the nature of those who inhabit them is the source of brutality. They suggest their work be used to contribute to developing training methods for guards.

Commentary

Is the study ecologically valid?

The study lacked ecological validity because it was not a prison and the people involved were not prisoners or guards. Prisons are not situated in the basement of universities and they usually contain some element of physical violence, racism and homosexuality, whereas Zimbardo's did not. In fact, what was happening in this study was that the subjects were playing the role of what they thought prison life was like. This in itself makes the study valid, and whether that role was accurate or not is not really that important. The study set out to show that an environment results in behaviour rather than the nature of the people involved, and this is exactly what happened. The people were randomly assigned to their roles and undertook them to the extreme.

If subjects believe in the study and take it seriously then it is high in experimental realism. This increases the validity of the study. Evidence for this is the fact that both guards and prisoners internalised the prison experience. It is also clear that for some of the prisoners the experience of being in a prison was all too real and they had to be 'released'.

Is the study ethical?

The study produced strong ethical objections. However, in its defence, Zimbardo *et al.* sought and received firm approval beforehand from the Office of Naval Research, the Psychology Department at Stanford and the University Committee of Human Experimentation. The subjects had all signed informed consent documents, which made it clear that there would be some breaches of civil rights. The study was cut short when it was clear that subjects were suffering, ending on day six when it was planned to run for 14 days.

Finally, the subjects were debriefed and assessed weeks, months and years afterwards to try to ensure no long-term effects.

Despite this, however, there are still some strong ethical criticisms. 'Prisoners' were not informed that they would be arrested at home by real police or taken to a real police station. The experiences of the 'prisoners' were harsher than anyone, including the researchers, might have predicted. The question arises as to whether or not the study was cut short soon enough. For example, the rebellion on day two when the 'prisoners' ripped off their numbers was put down brutally by the 'guards', who took away clothing and beds and left the 'prisoners' naked in their cells. It was clear from very early on in the study that the 'guards' were taking their role too far. Zimbardo himself argued that one of the major ethical problems was his own role in the study. He lost his objectivity by being the 'Superintendent', and this may explain why the study continued as long as it did.

● Key questions

1. Why was this study not carried out in a real prison?
2. What effects were the uniforms intended to have on Ss?
3. On what grounds can the ethics of the study be defended?
4. Does this study tell us anything about why real prisons are brutal places?
5. What if the sample were different? What if 24 postal delivery workers, or teachers or doctors over the age of 40 were tested? What if the subjects were female? Would the results be different?

Example Answers are on page 451.

● Postscript

What we must remember is that there are instances of deindividuation which do not produce antisocial behaviour; in fact, the behaviour that deindividuation can produce could be described as liberating.

Chrissie is having a party and you are there advising her what sort of music to have and what drinks to provide. You have a discussion about how the furniture should be arranged and whether you should make room for dancing. Both of you have had all afternoon to get the place ready, and you are now dressed up and ready with Chrissie for the first guests to arrive. The music is playing and you are really excited. Chrissie says she is so nervous as to how the party is going to go. Is it going to be good? Will many people turn up?

Two hours later, the party is going reasonably well, but people are still a little stand-offish and not mixing as well as you had hoped they would. There seem to be small groups of people in different places, and the atmosphere definitely leaves something to be desired. Suddenly all the lights go out. There is a power cut. A couple of lighters light up, but there is lots of giggling and people actually start talking to each other. They are no longer so self-aware and feel much more confident to talk to each other.

The lights are out for about half an hour. Although there is no music, it doesn't seem to matter because everyone is talking and joking and seem to be enjoying themselves. Suddenly the power comes back on again. Within a very short space of time, the magical atmosphere has diminished. People have become self-aware and identifiable again.

This process was described in an experiment done in 1973 by Gergen *et al.*, known as the Black Room Experiment. Gergen had two groups of subjects who spent an hour together. One group of subjects were in a completely darkened room and the other group in a normally lit room. In the dark room, the subjects were far more friendly, chatting to total strangers, exploring the room and some even beginning to discuss far more serious matters. Even more amazing was that 90% of the subjects actually became involved intentionally in physical contact with each other, 50% hugging each other and 80% admitting to being sexually aroused. In contrast to this, the control subjects talked politely in the light for the whole hour.

Further reading:
- Aronson, E., Wilson, T.D. and Akert, R.M. (1997), *Social Psychology*, New York: Longman, 3rd edition.
- http://www.prisonexp.org is a website on the Zimbardo *et al.* prison simulation study, with a slide show describing the experiences of the 'prisoners' and the 'guards'.

Ethnocentrism or in-group/out-group preferences

Have you ever thought about your group of friends and compared them to other groups of people that you know? The expectation would be that you would rate your friends more highly than other groups of people. Similarly, if you rated your psychology class in comparison to other classes, it is more than likely that you would believe yours to be the best.

You must have come across people who, no matter what it is, always seem to have one better or bigger than yours. Well, this kind of group thinking is very similar, where the belief is that the group to which we belong is 'bigger and/or better' than everyone else's. We also tend to think that our group is the 'norm' and therefore everyone else will be judged by our standards which, of course, are the best. It's almost like being egocentric about your group, and this kind of group self-centredness is known as *ethnocentrism*. Another way of looking at ethnocentrism is to think of it as being centred on our ethnic group (but exchange the word ethnic for social group).

Ethnocentrism seems to occur the minute people are divided into groups. It doesn't matter what that group is, or on what basis it was formed, but what happens is that we perceive the group we belong to as being superior to other groups and we develop an 'in-group bias' (we are biased in favour of the group we are in with). This bias is demonstrated by consistently rating the abilities and characteristics of the group we belong to as much higher than those of other people, even when this is not the case.

Ethnocentricity is linked to the process of stereotyping which involves grouping people – other than us – on the basis (usually) of some superficial physical characteristic such as colour, and then attributing the same characteristics to all the group members. In this section we are going to focus on ethnocentricity rather than stereotyping, although often the results are the same because they may both lead to a kind of discrimination.

According to Tajfel (1982), the process of trying to give ourselves some kind of positive self-identity seems to explain why people have an in-group bias. If we are assigned to a group, any group, either by birth, colour, gender or design, we immediately seem to feel a kind of innate automatic preference for that group over any other group and somehow elevate the group to a higher status than any other. This in-group preference is really a tactic to increase our self-esteem, and even if the reasons why the groups have been formed are minimal, if our group wins over the other group, it will strengthen our feelings of pride in belonging to the winning group and consequently increase our self-esteem still further.

This process was described by Tajfel and Turner (1986) in what is known as *social identity theory.* This theory states that people actually get their identity from the group to which they perceive they belong. However, to gain an identity, we need to make comparisons between our group and other groups, and in order for our identity to be positive we need to see our group as being superior to other groups. If a group believes it is less worthy than other groups, it will be much more likely to accept any discrimination and disadvantage shown towards it without complaint, because it will believe that the discrimination is probably justified. This will result in the group being very unwilling to fight for its cause.

THE ROBBERS CAVE STUDY

Probably one of the most famous pieces of research looking at in-group preferences (or ethnocentrism) was a field study conducted by Sherif in 1956. This involved taking 22 white, middle-class boys aged between 11 and 12, who were considered well adjusted, and dividing them into two groups which were roughly matched in terms of sporting ability, camping experience and general popularity. Their parents were told that they were going to a three-week summer camp to see how well they would work alongside other boys when put into different teams. The parents were also told that they would not be allowed to be visited during that time, but would be able to go home if they wanted to. It was intended that the data for the study would be collected by participant observers. The first step was the creation of the groups, which took place over the first week. At first, neither set of boys knew of the existence of the other set. They were taken to their respective campsites, which were located on a 200-acre, densely wooded area in Robbers Cave State Park, Oklahoma. The campsites had swimming and boating facilities alongside the cabins where they were to stay for the 3-week period. This first week was spent doing a variety of activities where the boys worked together, such as pitching tents and cooking, and they also took part in a treasure hunt.

During this week the two groups seemed to develop different group norms, one group being more 'tough' than the other group, where two boys went home early as they were homesick. They were given caps and t-shirts and gave themselves the names of the 'Eagles' and the 'Rattlers' (the Rattlers being the tougher group).

At the end of the first week they became aware of each other's existence by finding litter left by the other group or overhearing voices. Sherif noticed that already the groups started to refer to the other group as 'them' and their group as 'us'. This was the beginning of part two of the experiment. The groups were told that they were going to take part in a 'Grand Tournament' which involved 10 different sporting events and they were shown the prizes for winning which included a trophy, medals and penknives, which they all found very attractive. The tournament was also to include in the final scores points which would be awarded for other activities, such as how tidy the cabins were kept. These scores were displayed on big scoreboards in what now became a joint mess hall where the two groups now ate their meals at the same time. This was necessary so the two groups would think they were on almost equal scores in the time leading up to the final tournament and would increase the sense of competition. Needless to say, these scores were manipulated by the experimenters.

In order to check how high the levels of ethnocentrism were in the groups, a number of tasks were set up which involved the groups rating their own members and members of the other group. Each time group members rated the boys in their own group much better at the tasks than the other boys, even though there was no real difference between them. An example of this was when they were asked to pick up as many beans as they could in one minute and afterwards the teams were asked to look at the number of beans and guess how many each person had managed to pick up. The researchers manipulated the situation and always showed the boys the same number of beans, but on every occasion the respective groups rated their team members as having collected more than the opposing team. They were also asked to rate all others in terms of how desirable they were as friends and 93 per cent of friendship preferences were in-group preferences. As we mentioned earlier, part of the process of ethnocentrism is the belief that our group is better than the other groups, which is shown by the consistency in the direction of the ratings towards the in-group. The perceived inequalities were increased by the fact that all the boys wanted the prizes but there weren't enough to go round. They all wanted their group to win, so they would each get a prize. If they had all agreed to the fairness of the situation, the competition would not have led to the feelings of hostility that arose within the boys. Each group believed that their group was better and more worthy than the other group, and the team-building exercises they had taken part in at the beginning reinforced this idea. So now, whoever won the prizes, the other group would feel the final result was unjust. Perhaps if the competition was objectively measurable it would have been seen as less unfair, but because the leaders were the ones deciding the scores for the non-competitive activities, it may well have been perceived as unfair (which in fact it was).

When the tournament started, the first competitive game was baseball. The Eagles lost the game (they were the non-tough group who had lost two of their members) and claimed that they had only lost because the Rattlers were older and bigger than they were. This provoked them to go and burn a flag the Rattlers had put at the backstop. The Rattlers were furious, and when the Eagles admitted what they had done, a fight broke out which was broken up by the experimenters. The Eagles won the next ball game and were accused of cheating in the tug-of-war. This resulted in visits by both groups to each other's cabins over the course of the next 24 hours where, unbeknown to the other group, they ripped the mosquito nets, turned over the beds and generally made a mess. The Eagles devised a new weapon in the conflict which consisted of 'rocks in socks' – but these were removed.

The Eagles won the tournament (although not surprisingly with some help from the experimenters), and this resulted in the Rattlers raiding their cabin and stealing the knives and medals and telling the Eagles that the only way they would get them back would be to crawl on their stomachs and beg for them. It was time for Sherif to try to reduce the conflict.

Research has suggested that the two best ways to reduce group conflict is by non-competitive contact, with the groups having equal status and a common goal for them to work towards. This was exactly what Sherif engineered. There were actually seven situations organised which gave the groups equal status contact; these were things like having meals together, watching films together, or having a firework display for the fourth of July. The meals resulted in food fights, the films and fireworks were enjoyed by both groups sitting totally apart from each other. The other method where the groups had to work for common goals had a much better outcome.

The water for the camps came from a storage tank about a mile from the sites and the water supply was cut off. The groups volunteered to help find what they thought might be a leak, although the stretches of pipe were inspected by members of either one group or the other. It turned out that the problem stemmed from a valve by the storage tank and all the boys met there and cheered together when the problem was sorted. The Eagles were allowed to drink first because they were the most thirsty and the groups mixed for the first time with a lack of hostility on the way back to the camps. However, they had another food fight that night at dinner.

The second common goal they aimed for involved trying to raise the money to go to see the film *Treasure Island* and they agreed to join forces to raise the money to go to see it. Even though there were more Rattlers than Eagles, they agreed to split the money required in half. They were therefore co-operating, though the group mentality was still evident.

The final common goal was a visit by truck to Cedar Lake to camp there before the end of the holiday. They were required to get involved with meal preparation and tent pitching together. Although they both travelled in separate trucks, one of the trucks became stuck and all the boys joined in, using one of the tug-of-war ropes to help move it. At this point the group boundaries were beginning to disappear. On the final day, when they were due to return home, they themselves suggested that they travel in one bus and sat in friendship groups rather than as Eagles and Rattlers.

This study was important for a number of reasons. First, Sherif succeeded in setting up a situation where ethnocentrism flourished. The amount of hostility that developed between the two groups of boys was much greater than anticipated, and the results that occurred in such a short space of time were stunning. But we have to remember that the extreme results of Sherif were produced by not only the two groups, but also the perceived unequal status of the groups. There was a conflict of interests between the boys and they perceived inequalities in their situations, some of which were true. The Eagles believed the Rattlers were physically bigger, although they weren't, but they did have two more members in their group. The groups even believed that one group was getting better and more plentiful food than the other group, which consequently increased this feeling of inequality.

Second, the findings of the Sherif study have been mentioned over and over again as the way to remove ethnocentrism and prejudice. Equal status contact and the pursuit of common goals with the support of the people in charge worked for the children at Robbers Cave. The trouble is, it is not that easy in the real world, where there is a much greater history involved in the divisions between the two groups, which may have been present for decades or even centuries. To add to the situation there may also be other pressures from external forces which will help to maintain the segregation, such as pressure from other members of the family or from society, laws which prevent equal status contact, living environments being separated, job discrimination and so on.

H. Tajfel (1970) 'Experiments in intergroup discrimination',
Scientific American, 223, 96–102

Background

Was Sherif right though? Do we need conflict for ethnocentrism to occur? Tajfel claims not, and that simply being in a group and being aware of the existence of another group is sufficient for the development of some kind of prejudice. Consequently discrimination in favour of the in-group will occur. He said this would happen in the absence of hostility between the groups.

In order to test this, he divided up groups on a totally arbitrary basis and discovered that even if they did not know who else was in their group, ethnocentric bias seemed to lead to the group members favouring their own group to the detriment of the other group.

Tajfel suggests that this happens because we need to get positive esteem from membership of 'our' group, so we favour our in-group. Tajfel, therefore, sees discrimination as a side effect, or fallout, from the process of gaining esteem from our group identity – the intention is not malevolent; it is not intended to disadvantage the out-group. However, the result of favouring your own group is inevitably discrimination against the other group (the out group), whether intended maliciously or not.

Tajfel argued that our patterns of behaviour when we are faced with an 'us and them' situation are socialised (learned), and are so ingrained that they will be triggered regardless of how the groups are created. He believed that this would happen even when group members had no idea who the other members of their group were, so behaviour could not be attributed to any personal interest or negative attitudes that may have existed before the study.

Would subjects discriminate in favour of a group to which they had been assigned on only a spurious basis, a group whose other members were not identified?

Definitions

In-group – a group you belong to, or aspire to belong to. Out-group – a group you do not belong to or do not want to describe yourself as belonging to.

Aim

The aim of the study was to provide evidence that merely belonging to one group and being aware that another group existed would lead to discriminatory behaviour in favour of your own group. Tajfel preferred to investigate 'discrimination', a behaviour, rather then 'prejudice', a belief or attitude. This is because discrimination is observable and therefore easier to measure objectively.

Discrimination was also preferred as a variable since the relationship between attitudes and behaviour is weak – we may say one thing but do another.

The study was carried out using two laboratory experiments.

● **Study 1**

Method

Design

The experimental method was used, employing an independent groups design.

FOCUS ON RESEARCH METHODS – the experimental method

The experimental method, or the scientific method as it is also known, is the only research method that can establish causal relationships between variables. A hypothesis is formulated to predict the effect of one variable, known as the independent variable, on another variable, known as the dependent variable. Usually two conditions are operated, with one testing Ss in the experimental condition, where the IV is introduced, and one testing Ss in the control condition. The control condition is used for comparison to see if the IV has made a difference to Ss' behaviour in the experimental condition.

Experiments are set either in the laboratory, or in the field (in a natural setting). You also need to know about quasi or 'natural' experiments. This is where the IV already occurs and, instead of manipulating it, the researcher simply observes it. Examples might be gender or age, which clearly cannot be manipulated for an experiment. An example from the core studies would be the Baron-Cohen study (see the chapter on cognitive psychology), in which whether the S had autism, was 'normal' or had Down's syndrome was the IV being tested.

Subjects

The sample was 64 schoolboys, aged between 14 and 15, from a state school in Bristol, UK. The boys from each group knew each other because they were from the same house in the same form at school. The boys came to the laboratory in groups of eight.

Apparatus

A screen was used to flash 40 pictures of clusters of dots. There were also booklets containing a number of matrices which were used for the boys to allocate rewards and penalties to members of their own group or other groups (never to themselves). The booklets contained 18 pages and on each page there was one matrix.

Procedure

The boys were brought into a laboratory and told that the study was about visual judgements and they were then asked to estimate the number of dots in each cluster that was shown on the screen. In order to be categorised the boys had to participate in two conditions. The first condition involved the boys being told that people consistently overestimated or underestimated the number of dots. In the second condition, they were told that some people are always more accurate than others.

In the meantime the boys then had to undertake the estimation task. When they had finished the task they were told that the researchers were going to take advantage of their presence to investigate other types of decision making and that they were put into groups on the basis of their visual judgements in the 'dot' task.

The boys were taken into another room individually and told which of the 4 groups they were in (over-estimator/under-estimator/accurate/inaccurate), but were not told the identity of anyone else in that group. In fact, the boys had been allocated on a purely random basis. This was to make sure that there was no real difference between the two sets of boys that might confound the study.

 FOCUS ON RESEARCH METHODS – extraneous and confounding variables

For an experiment to establish that it is the IV causing any observed change in the DV, all other variables, known as extraneous variables, need to be controlled or kept constant. The E has to make sure the subjects are not too dissimilar from each other, and has to control situational variables by, for example, standardising procedures and instructions.

Variables which are not controlled operate alongside the IV, making it impossible to establish whether the IV or this second variable, which has become a confounding variable, has caused any change in the DV.

They were then asked to allocate rewards of money to members of their own and/or the other group by making choices from the booklets containing the matrices. They were told that when they had finished each boy would get the amount of money the others had awarded him (they were told each point was worth a tenth of a penny). It was emphasised that at no time would the boys be allocating rewards or penalties to themselves, and they would not know the identity of the person being rewarded as all boys were to be given a code number.

This is an example of a matrix (points table) used in the study. The numbers represented rewards (positive numbers) and penalties (negative numbers). The subject would be required to allocate the amount in the top box to one person and the amount in the bottom box to someone else.

Rewards/penalties for member no. .... of your group	17	14	11	8	5	2	-1	-2	-3	-4	-5	-6	-7	-8
Rewards/penalties for member no. .... of the other group	-8	-7	-6	-5	-4	-3	-2	-1	2	5	8	11	14	17

They had to make three types of choices:
• In-group – when both choices on the matrix were for members of the boy's own group
• Out-group – when both choices were for members of the other group
• Inter-group – when one choice was for a member of the boy's own group and the other for a member of the other group. It was these inter-group choices where discrimination in favour of the in-group and against the out-group was to be observed (this is the type of choice illustrated in the example matrix).

Variables

The independent variable was group categorisation, whether the S was told they were an under- or over-estimator, accurate or inaccurate.

The dependent variable was the allocation of points they made in the inter-group choices.

Results

The results showed that boys were fair when making in-group and out-group choices. In the example above, fairness would be achieved by choosing the pair '-one,-two'.

The difference came when making the inter-group choices. Here, a statistically significant majority of the subjects from all groups gave more money to members of their own group rather than those of the other group. There are a number of pairs that would illustrate this in the example matrix, but since fairness *also* had an influence on the boys' allocation of points, perhaps the best example is the pair 'five, -four'. Here, the in-group member is getting the higher reward of the two boys. Tajfel concludes that in order to bring about this discriminatory behaviour, all the researchers needed to do was to emphasise 'your group' and the 'other group' on top of the Ss' allocation to a group on the basis of their judgement of dots on a screen.

Study 2

The second study was carried out to provide further evidence that allocation to groups on a meaningless (minimal) basis would lead to discriminatory behaviour, and also to investigate which strategies were being used by the boys in their choices.

Method

Design

The experimental method was used, employing an independent groups design.

Subjects

The sample for the second study was made up of 48 schoolboys from the same school. They came to the laboratory in groups of 16.

Apparatus

A projector was used to show 12 slides. The slides were six pictures by Paul Klee and six by Wassily Kandinsky, but there was no indication on the pictures as to the artist (no signature). There were also different matrices which were used for the boys to allocate rewards of points. Again the points represented money.

Variables

The independent variable was again group allocation. This time boys were led to believe that they were in either the Klee group or the Kandinsky group. The DV, discrimination, was measured by allocation of points.

Procedure

This time the boys were tested in groups of 16. They were asked to rate the paintings and were supposedly grouped according to which artist they preferred. Of course, the grouping was randomly manufactured by the researchers into two groups: the 'Klee' group and the 'Kandinsky' group.

These boys were also taken into another room on their own, given their group identity and asked to allocate rewards. Again, different matrices asked them to make choices for two boys in their 'own' group (in-group choices) or two boys in the 'other' group (out-group choices), or for one boy in their 'own' group and one boy in the 'other' group (inter-group choices).

Tajfel looked for three possible strategies the Ss could adopt when making their allocation of points:

- Maximum in-group profit – here the boy would be choosing the highest gain for his own group, regardless of what this would mean the other group got. This would mean the other group might get more than their own group.
- Maximum joint profit – this choice represents a logical strategy. Here the boy would ignore the group allocation to their own group and the other group and treat the Ss as part of a whole group of boys. Now he would select the pair of points that, when added together, would give the highest joint amount of points. If all the boys had adopted this strategy and shared out the pennies earned from points at the end, they would have got the most money possible from the researchers.

- Maximum difference in favour of the in-group member – this choice ensured that his own group would get the highest possible points whilst making sure that his own group member would get higher than the other group member. This strategy would demonstrate discrimination in favour of the in-group, as in the first study.

Here is an example (again this shows an inter-group choice):

Rewards/penalties for member no. ... of your group	7	8	9	10	11	12	13	14	15	16	17	18	19
Rewards/penalties for member no. ... of the other group	1	3	5	7	9	11	13	15	17	19	21	23	25

These choices represented certain strategies:

Strategy:	Pair of points:
Maximum in-group profit	19 and 25 (this means giving more to the 'other' group)
Maximum joint profit	19 and 25
Maximising the difference in favour of the in-group	7 and 1
Fairness	13 and 13

Results

As in the first study, the results showed that maximising the difference between the two groups seemed to have the most effect: the boys again discriminated in favour of their in-group.

Maximum in-group profit was not the boys' priority in inter-group choices. In other words, they would rather give less than they could give to their own group in order to decrease still further the amount the other group received.

Maximum joint profit also had no impact on inter-group choices. However, it was seen as a strategy adopted by the boys for in-group choices. This suggests they were aware that this choice meant the most possible points for their group. When making out-group choices, however, they were less likely to select the pair of points representing maximum joint profit. Since this gave no disadvantage to the in-group, Tajfel describes this as 'gratuitous discrimination'.

Discussion

The study clearly shows that by simply grouping the subjects, even though they were unaware of who was part of their group, they demonstrated in-group preferences and out-group discrimination. The design ensured that subjects also had no existing hostility towards other subjects, and even if they had, they couldn't have put them into effect as all subjects were anonymous. Also, none of the boys gained anything for themselves by their choices, so the results must have been based purely on in-group/out-group discriminations. Tajfel concludes from this that 'out-group discrimination is extraordinarily easy to trigger off... it was enough for [Ss] to see themselves as clearly categorised into an ingroup, flimsy as the criteria for this division were' (Tajfel, 1970, p. 102).

Tajfel's explanation for the discrimination shown by the boys in his study is that 'to behave appropriately is... a powerful social motive'. Appropriate behaviour in this case meant following social norms. He sees two norms being used by the boys in the study, 'groupness' and 'fairness'.

Tajfel points out that further experiments had indicated that fairness seemed to be important in some of the choices made. He suggested that 'most of the choices must be understood as being a compromise between fairness and favoring one's own group.' Perhaps this is evidence that a culture for whom the values of 'fair play' are traditional instils this value, as well as the norm to discriminate in favour of one's own group, in its young people.

His final point is one for educators, the agents of socialisation. If discrimination is a side effect of the 'healthy competition' nurtured in our schools, perhaps they should rethink their emphasis on 'teams' and 'team spirit'.

Commentary

Is the study ecologically valid?

The artificial setting of the laboratory means that we cannot be sure that the behaviour being displayed is true to life. The groups themselves were meaningless, whereas in real life, group membership is based far more on something specific. Also, making judgements using pencil and paper tests may be easy to quantify, but lack the element of realism that would occur in a real-life situation. The study is therefore low in ecological validity.

Does the study raise any ethical concerns?

There is always a concern about consent when studying minors (children under 18). Who should give their consent? Are minors capable of deciding whether they want to be in a study or not for themselves?

The boys were deceived here, as the study could not have worked if they had been fully informed at the start that the allocation of points to their group was what the study was really about. The cover story was, therefore, necessary. Another concern relates to debriefing minors. Young children especially may be difficult to debrief as they may not have the maturity to understand. Do you think the 14–15 year old boys would understand what Tajfel was trying to demonstrate here? It is unlikely – we know of many psychology graduates and teachers who have yet to work out what Tajfel was up to here!

What are the strengths and weaknesses of using the experimental method in this study?

It would have been impossible for Tajfel to carry out his study objectively measuring discrimination if he hadn't used the controlled environment of the laboratory. Carrying out a laboratory experiment enabled him to isolate the IV, 'mere belonging to one group and knowledge of another group', in a way that no natural setting would permit, since you would have some hint of who was in your group and why, and this would confound the findings. This demonstrates clearly a major strengh of the experimental method in isolating the effects of a particular variable on another, known as experimental reductionism.

> **FOCUS ON THEMES:** reductionism and holism

Reductionism is a term once used by physicists to describe a method which would permit us to develop an understanding of the universe. It has its roots in Newton's mechanised version of the universe, wherein everything was interconnected and the smallest part of the universe, for example, an atom, was structured in the same pattern as the universe itself. Therefore, the theory was that by studying the smallest components of the universe, e.g. atoms, you would gain an understanding of the universe itself.

This came to dominate scientific investigation in many disciplines, and psychology was no exception. To gain scientific credibility, the behaviourists adopted a reductionist approach to the study of behaviour, assuming behaviours were interconnected and one led to the other (determinism). This led to their development of S–R (stimulus–response) psychology.

Reductionism has long been abandoned by physics, but the scientific approach it generated, of studying small components of, for example, behaviour, remains a useful tool for researchers trying to work out how certain variables interact with others.

However, some researchers see this approach as being too narrow, failing to see the whole picture. In particular, one school of psychologists, the Gestaltists, argued that human behaviour, especially perception, could not be described by breaking it down into its component parts as behaviour is an 'all at once' experience. For example, consider how we use cues to 'see' 3D in pictures

 CORE STUDY LINK – see Deregowski's study on perception).

The Gestalt approach is known as holism, and the famous quote which encompasses their anti-reductionist position is 'the whole is greater than

the sum of its parts'.

By this token we could argue that as well as being a strength in Tajfel's work, reductionism is also a weakness. Prejudice and discrimination are far more complex than the theory of in-group preference suggests. Scapegoating, economic and social inequality, historical relationships (e.g. imperialism), and many other factors impact on prejudice, and 'reducing' it to merely favouring one's own group over another is to fail to see the whole picture.

In terms of the weaknesses of studying behaviour in the laboratory, one problem is subject reactivity. As we know, human subjects are not passive and they try to work out what is going on. The subjects may have been simply conforming to demand characteristics. They may have worked out what the researchers were looking for; this would be supported by the fact that the matrices were fairly transparent – you could work out what they were trying to show by comparing the numbers in the upper and lower rows. They may have chosen to discriminate against the in-group to please the experimenter rather than due to the pressure to respond appropriately as dictated by social norms. Since they could have adapted their answers to meet what they saw as the requirements of the study, this means we have to question the validity of the findings.

What if the sample were different?

The subjects were hardly representative of people in general – many boys aged between 14 and 15 are far more sporty and competitive than the population as a whole. In fact, if the study had been conducted using females as subjects, it is possible that the idea of fairness would have been demonstrated to a greater extent than it was.

Is the study useful?

Given that we have suggested that the study lacks ecological validity and that internal validity can be questioned because of subject bias in the sample and the possibility of demand characteristics affecting the results, we have to concede that the usefulness of the findings may be limited.

However, Tajfel has tried to answer one of the big questions – why do we discriminate? His answer seems to suggest that at some level discrimination is learned. That is, we develop our discriminatory behaviour through the process of socialisation. In this respect he gives us useful food for thought: perhaps we should rethink how and what we are teaching our children if we hope ever to eliminate discriminatory behaviour.

Key questions

1. Explain what is meant by the following terms:
- In-group and out-group

- Maximum joint profit
- Maximum in-group profit
- Maximising the difference in favour of the in-group.

2. In the study, Tajfel says that the choices are best described as a compromise between maximising the difference in favour of the in-group and fairness. Look at the example matrix in study two above. Which pair of points do you think a boy would select if both fairness and maximising the difference were influencing his choices?

3. If the study was carried out on a sample of 60-year-old men, do you think the findings would be the same or different? Explain your answer.

4. Explain how reductionism can be both a positive issue and a negative issue in Tajfel's study.

Example Answers are on page 452.

Further reading

- Aronson, E. (1994), *The Social Animal*, New York: W.H. Freeman & Co., 7th edition.
- Brown, R. (1995), *Prejudice: Its Social psychology*, Oxford: Blackwell.

Cognitive psychology

Almost everything we do causes us to think. We think about what we are going to do and then think about what we have done. We plan, we discuss, we imagine, we remember, we try to make sense of the world around us and even when we can't, we try to work out why not. Sometimes working out why produces the wrong answer, but the processes involved are all interlinked. All these processes involve cognition.

Before the invention of computers, the understanding of how we processed information was limited. Prior to this time, much of the work in psychology involved simply looking at behaviour by observing the type of responses that were produced by different types of stimuli. There was little research on what happened between the stimulus and response, because not only were the techniques to investigate these processes limited but also the knowledge in this area was quite basic. However, the computer analogy opened up a whole new way of looking at the way the brain processes information. This information-processing approach works in the following way:

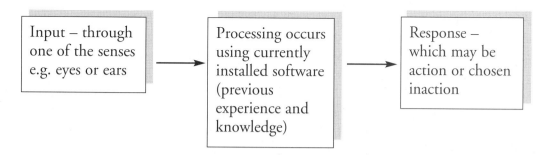

| Input – through one of the senses e.g. eyes or ears | → | Processing occurs using currently installed software (previous experience and knowledge) | → | Response – which may be action or chosen inaction |

Cognitive psychology is involved in understanding the middle process, that is, how the information is processed and what kind of choices will be made. Many of the choices we make may not always be rational. For example, we may know that chocolate is fattening and that we desperately want to lose weight, but still we buy a large bar of chocolate and eat it. Logic suggests that this would not happen if processing was based purely on logic, but we are often totally illogical. However, this information-processing model has opened up study in this area, allowing us to investigate these processes using laboratory-based methods and experiments.

This idea of information processing is somewhat removed from the perspective of reductionism which suggests that all our responses can be reduced to the most basic explanation. Take, for example, the chocolate-eating analogy. The reductionist explanation might go along the lines of 'chocolate-eating produces a feeling of happiness which the body desires. Therefore, the decision to eat chocolate can be reduced to the most basic explanation, that is, that we are simply responding to a biological need produced by our bodies', which sounds like a very good explanation if you want to excuse chocolate eating in the future! However, in order to satiate this feeling, we have to have knowledge of where to obtain chocolate, what is required to buy it, how to get to the shop and so on. Therefore, the reductionist approach might be considered to help aid our understanding of how cognitive processes work and how they interrelate.

Cognitive psychology therefore covers a number of areas: memory, perception, language, thinking and attention, and all these processes are interconnected because you will find it very difficult to do one without involving another. You cannot identify a seen object without thinking what it is called. In fact, you won't even try to identify it unless you happen to be looking in the right place at the right time (paying attention to it), and if you identify it as something frightening you will have to work out how to escape. There is also a huge debate about the fact that you cannot think without language, and this is mentioned later in the section on language at the end of this chapter.

One of the questions psychologists frequently ask is whether we are actually born with cognitive skills or whether we acquire them as we mature? Most psychologists believe that we are born with very basic skills, but the majority develop through a process of maturation and experience. This nature–nurture debate constantly appears in all areas of psychology but it is particularly evident in the area of cognition, and this is addressed by the study by Deregowski in this chapter.

The following sections of this chapter focus on four key areas of cognition. The topic of memory is addressed by looking at its structure and function and how accurate it really is. Perception is considered by investigating, among other things, whether our abilities are innate or learned and whether there are cross-cultural differences in how we interpret the same stimulus. Thinking is addressed by considering how children begin to work out that other people do not see the world in the same way as they do. The last section focuses on whether language is an innate ability in humans or is simply learned, and whether it is beyond the capability of other species to acquire language.

Memory

We will begin this section by looking at one of the most fundamental and complex of human cognitive abilities, the human memory. In fact, when considering cognition, it is hard to start anywhere else because what we have stored in our memory is the basis of what makes us who we are and dictates how we behave. It is for this reason that the section on memory is the longest in this book.

It is difficult to find a precise definition of 'memory', but it is often referred to as 'the ability to retain information and demonstrate retention through behaviour'. If we could not retain and use information that we have already discovered, it would mean that for every new experience, we would have to process huge amounts of information and this could be very costly in terms of the time it might take.

Brian was on holiday in Africa. He was sitting down by the lake, watching some beautiful creatures flying above the surface of the water. He was not sure what they were but they looked so beautiful, almost translucent, reflected in the sunlight. Then he noticed a ripple on the water and suddenly something long started to appear. It was green in colour and looked quite shiny. Whatever it was seemed to be getting longer as it approached him out of the water. Then he saw what looked like two little beady eyes on the top of what must have been its head and they were looking at him. Suddenly it came out of the water towards him, its long body propelled by four short thick legs and it flicked its long leathery tail. Its mouth opened and snap...

If Brian had been able to store information in his memory, he would have been aware that lakes in Africa may well be inhabited by crocodiles, therefore their shores are not the safest places to sit and contemplate the day. Because he had to process each piece of information as he received it, the time it would have taken to realise that the creature was not friendly was too long to enable him to save himself.

Memory is a fundamental part of us and our everyday lives. Our memories serve to tell us who we are, help us to make sense of the situations in which we find ourselves and enable us to make plans for the future. In fact, memory is so much a part of what and who we are, that it is almost impossible to imagine what it must be like to have no recollection of anything. Think of all the things you do automatically every day which rely on stored knowledge, such as getting dressed, finding your way around, talking, writing and reading, recognising people, remembering past events or information you have been told. Is there anything you can do without referring to something you have stored in your memory?

People who have lost their memory, for whatever reason, are called amnesics.

The classic portrayal of amnesics in the media tend to suggest that they forget everything, but this is not actually the case. If you think of the things we learn and therefore store in our memories, such as a knowledge of language or a knowledge of how to dress ourselves, you will realise that amnesics rarely lose these abilities. What they seem to lose is the memory of who they are, because they have no information relating to their past. These past memories are not stored as if they were recorded on a video recorder, although this is a commonly held belief by people who do not understand how memory works. In fact, television dramas tend to support this idea with dramatic scenes of hypnotherapists gaining access to previously lost information by hypnotising their clients. What actually happens is that we seem to unconsciously select information to store and overwrite similar experiences until they become merged into one memory. Memory is, in fact, a dynamic process which is constantly being updated or changed by the experiences we have.

Although psychologists who are interested in memory often consider what happens when memory becomes disrupted, they are also interested in how memory is structured and how it actually works. The structures are the various component parts, like short-term memory and long-term memory, and the processes are how information is taken in and how it is stored and then recalled. They have also discovered that there are a number of factors which influence whether information is stored or simply forgotten. You don't remember all the information you are told: you may remember the gist of it or a reasonable amount, but only for a limited amount of time, no matter how hard you tried to learn it (think of examination revision). However, it has been found that we do tend to store information on a more long-term basis if it is very different to other information, if it is rich in detail, if it is connected to other things we know or if it is personally important to us.

THE THREE PROCESSES OF MEMORY

The next section is going to look at how we take in information and store it and how we can then get at it when we need it. These processes are known as the three processes of memory.

In order to understand what these processes are, imagine looking up a telephone number in your local directory. Then you put the directory away and finally write down the number.

The first process involves *encoding* the information, that is, you took the relevant numbers into your memory system. Therefore, encoding is 'the acquisition of knowledge and creation of an internal representation to be stored'.

There are three types of encoding:
a) Acoustic/phonetic encoding or encoding for sound. This is when you hear in your head what someone has just said to you or you keep words in your head,

in this case, the telephone number. Psychologists have found that it is really easy to get muddled up when the sounds are similar, for example, if you try to remember a list of words that all sound the same such as bee, tree, three, he, me, see, wee, flee, tea, you will find it harder to remember the exact words than a list of words that sound dissimilar.

b) Visual encoding is used to produce an image of what something or someone looks like.

c) Semantic encoding or encoding for meaning is where you process information by thinking about what it actually means rather than what it looks or sounds like. This seems to produce the best storage. In fact, this method is so good that it is often used to remember lists of things. Take, for example, the colours of the spectrum. You probably know that they are red, orange, yellow, green, blue, indigo and violet. How can you remember what order they come in? The best way is to take the first letters of each word, R O Y G B I V, and then make a sentence which has meaning from those meaningless initials – Richard of York gave battle in vain. This method of semantic encoding is called using mnemonics or 'memory aids'.

Interestingly enough, many of the memory problems you may suffer from are due to failure of encoding – that is, you do not pay attention to them. Imagine someone has the phone number of Mr Bloggs the builder, and they read it out to you. You would probably think 'so what', and instantly forget it. However, supposing they said to you that they had the phone number of a stunningly attractive actor/actress, you would probably be more likely to remember it.

The second process is the *storage* of the information. This requires you to retain the information in an understandable form so that you can then go on to the third process. With our phone number, we will more than likely have to keep saying it to ourselves as a way of storing it. This is probably because the numbers have little meaning and are not really of any great importance to us.

Finally, you have to undertake the *retrieval* of the information, that is, you would have to get the information back from where you stored it. This is done either by recognition, which involves matching a stored item with something in your environment, or by recalling it, that is, bringing it back into your conscious awareness.

I was walking down the road the other day and this woman came up to me and said hello and started asking me how I was and if I was still at school. She said I looked really nice and asked if I had just had my hair done and if I was still going to the same hairdresser. I knew I recognised her but I hadn't got any idea who she was. She even knew my name. I just kind of stood there, answering her questions and being as nice as possible, while all the time I was trying to work out how I knew her. In the end, she said goodbye and that she would see me again soon, but I still have absolutely no idea who she was. It's really bugging me!

What was happening here was that the girl had no problems with recognition, but was unable to recall any information about the person she was talking to.

Returning to the idea of the telephone number that was read out to you, when you tried to remember it, you would have had to recall it as you would not be matching it against any other numbers. However, the chances of you remembering it for any length of time are fairly remote. On the other hand, you are unlikely to have problems remembering your own phone number, no matter how long ago you moved into your house. This tends to indicate that there is more than one type of memory: memory which doesn't last for very long (known as short-term memory – STM) and memory which lasts perhaps for ever (known as long-term memory – LTM).

The first psychologists to notice this fact also discovered that people who sustained brain damage sometimes lost either their STM or their LTM. This indicated that there must be different types of memory store, and they used this information to try to help them understand the component parts of memory and how they fit together.

SENSORY MEMORY

The first type of memory is known as sensory memory. This type of memory is necessary because if we don't retain an impression of what we have experienced, we will be unable to decide whether or not we actually want to begin to process it adequately in order to understand it, or even decide to disregard it. Let me explain this further. Look around the room you are in. There are lots of objects in the room which you are aware of, but not in any detail. If you were then asked to look for a pen you would need to be aware of the potential of all the objects that are there before you could decide whether or not they are pens or whether they are likely to contain a pen. If the impression is that a pen may be present then you would decide not to disregard the objects and therefore process them further.

It is called sensory memory because it refers to a 'fleeting' memory, which is registered by the sensory receptors of sight (iconic memory) and sound (echoic memory). This information is stored within these receptors and not at a central location, lasts for seconds and is then gone. For example, imagine you are watching TV or reading when someone speaks to you. Just as you are about to say 'What did you say?' you realise that you can 'play back' the words that are still echoing in your head, but only for a few seconds after the event and then that 'sensation' is gone.

SHORT-TERM MEMORY

Psychologists, including Atkinson and Shiffrin (1971), decided that information which stayed in consciousness after encoding entered short-term memory, whereas information that left conscious awareness but could later be recalled had been put into long-term memory.

Evidence to support this idea has come from studies of both brain-damaged people and those suffering from Korsakoff's syndrome (amnesia caused by alcohol abuse). These people can retain information in conscious awareness (STM) but have problems remembering information from the past (LTM).

It seems that some information from sensory memory is successfully passed on to the STM, which allows us to store it for long enough to enable us to use it – for example, retaining the phone number long enough to dial it, although it may be forgotten soon after. It is also a memory store that allows us to have a conversation with another person. You can't remember the whole content of a conversation, but if you can't remember what the person you are talking to has just said to you, how could you answer them? Therefore, you need to retain that information for a short period of time.

We know that the capacity of STM is limited. In fact, in 1956, George Miller gave the most famous account of the capacity of STM in his article, 'The magic number seven, plus or minus two'. Here he claims that we can retain between five and nine pieces of information in STM. He also explained that we can increase the capacity of STM by putting together pieces of information. If I asked you to remember the digits 0 2 0 7 9 4 6 1 4 3 2 individually, you would find that your STM memory was full, but if you put those letters together to form chunks, you would not have a problem remembering them – 020 7946 1432.

Another example of how we can increase this capacity is by putting together information that would otherwise have no meaning. If you were asked to remember the letters T W A I B M B A B B C, you might be able to, but if you were asked to remember TWA (Trans World Airlines) IBM (the computer company) BA (British Airways) and BBC (British Broadcasting Corporation), you would probably have no trouble at all. This organisation increases the storage capacity of STM by imposing units of meaning on otherwise unrelated numbers, each unit equalling one 'chunk'.

The duration of STM (how long the information is retained), according to Atkinson and Shiffrin (1971), is between 15 and 30 seconds. It can be easily disrupted; for example, someone asking you a question while you are trying to keep something in your mind by saying it to yourself.

Andrew was trying to work out why his bank statement said he was overdrawn. He was sure he'd put enough money in this month to cover all the things he had bought. Yes, OK, he had gone a bit mad when he went clothes shopping, but not that mad! He decided that the bank must have made a mistake. The trouble was that there were so many transactions that month, so he would have to add them all up. That way he could find out whether the bank had made a mistake or not.

Right, he said to himself, I have used two chequebooks this month, so if I add up all the items in one, and then add them to the other, I should work out how much I have spent. He started to add them up and had just got to the end of the first one when he realised he had got the wrong second chequebook. He kept saying the amount to himself in his head while he looked for the right book. Just then his mother called out, 'Andrew, that girl is on the phone again. Do you want to talk to her?'

Andrew completely forgot the amount he had totalled so far, because he was too busy thinking about the phone call. This should give you some idea how fragile STM really is.

LONG-TERM MEMORY

Some of the things we experience or learn as we grow up stay with us for very long periods, and others for the whole of our lives. This information has gone into long-term memory and seems to be fairly stable. No one has ever filled a long-term memory, although sometimes it feels as if you cannot store any more information. When we say we have forgotten something, this often means that we are unable to retrieve information from our long-term memory. We believe that one cause of forgetting happens as a result of the memory trace no longer being available (having decayed), and this could be through lack of activation of information or through interference from other memories. This interference could be in the form of overwriting the memory or confusing it with other similar memories. The other cause of forgetting may be a result of not actually being able to get at the stored information, i.e. lack of accessibility. This is when you know you know something but cannot actually remember what it is you know.

Using the information-processing idea, psychologists have constructed a number of models of memory to explain how memory works. Obviously, you can't test a model unless you have a model in the first place, so you should think of a model as being no more than a theory. Psychologists then use various experiments to try to support the model, but if the results show that the model is not quite right, they then have to modify their original design.

THE MULTI-STORE MODEL (ATKINSON AND SHIFFRIN, 1968)

Atkinson and Shiffrin proposed the first model of memory, which was very simple and involved information passing into sensory memory, then into short-term memory and, finally, into long-term memory.

According to this model, incoming information is received by the sensory register and is either selected for further processing or lost. If it is selected, it then goes into short-term memory. Here it can be retained for a limited period of time before it is lost, unless we choose to transfer it to long-term memory. The way this happens is that we have to say it over and over again to ourselves, which is called 'rehearsal'. In the diagram, rehearsal is shown by the 'loop' between STM and LTM. According to this model, unrehearsed items are forgotten.

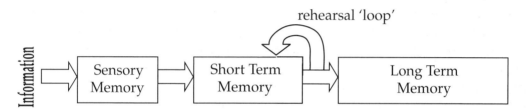

rehearsal 'loop'

There is quite a lot of evidence to support the multi-store model, and it is worth considering the evidence in order to decide whether the model is acceptable or just too simplistic.

The first kind of evidence comes from free recall experiments, which are experiments where people are asked to remember lists (of 20 words, for example), and then recall the words in any order they like. Evidence has shown that subjects usually recall more items from the end of the list, but they also recall quite a few from the beginning of the list.

It has been suggested that this is because the first words enter the STM, where there is probably no other material, and so they are likely to be rehearsed and thus transferred to LTM (called the primacy effect). As more words are presented, the STM capacity fills up and there is no chance to rehearse or transfer later words to LTM. Therefore, the items at the end of the list can only be retained in STM (the recency effect, Murdock, 1962). It is believed that the reason why the words in the middle are usually lost is because they cannot be rehearsed sufficiently to transfer them into LTM. You may have experienced something similar yourself when you are in a lesson or a lecture. Immediately after the lesson you may recall the beginning and end, but remember very little of the information you were given in the middle.

There is further evidence for the multi-store model from people who have sustained brain damage. Patients have been found who have lost one part of their memory but the other is intact, i.e. they have either lost their STM or their LTM.

One piece of evidence comes from a person, known by his initials, KF who was studied by Shallice and Warrington (1970). KF was in his twenties when he had a motorcycle accident, as a result of which he suffered damage to the left parieto-occipital region of his brain, which left him with a damaged STM. If he was given a list of numbers to learn he found he could sometimes recall two items, but often only one. His LTM was not damaged, however, and he could remember things that he had 'stored' before his accident. The strange thing about him was that he seemed to be able to learn new information even though his STM was impaired.

Although this evidence supports the multi-store model, it also leads to a question about the accuracy of the model as it challenges how the model works. The model states that the only way we can store information in LTM is by first taking it into the STM, then 'rehearsing' it, and finally passing it into LTM. If KF had a damaged STM, how then did the information get into LTM? This is the kind of evidence which led people to question how valid the model really was and to undertake further research into alternative explanations for the working of memory.

There are a number of further examples of amnesics who support the model. One was known as HM and the other was a man called Clive Wearing. HM suffered with severe epilepsy from the age of 16. In fact, his epilepsy was so bad that he had a number of seizures on a daily basis and this seriously impaired his quality of life. In 1953 he went into hospital for surgery to remove part of his temporal lobes as it was there that the seizures originated. The surgery was a success as the seizures stopped immediately, but within hours of the surgery the medical staff discovered that HM could not recognise the medical staff and could not find his bedroom in the hospital. It appeared that he was also unable to store any new information. Although the operation was a success, the cost to him was the loss of his ability to transfer any new information to his LTM, although his STM was seemingly intact. Interestingly though, he can remember his life up until a few years before the operation, but any new information is lost as soon as it is learned. Again, this gives us evidence that STM and LTM are separate systems, although perhaps they are not as simple as was first hypothesised.

Clive Wearing was very different. He was the chorus master of the London Sinfonietta, and although we cannot claim he gives much support for the multi-store model, as both his long- and short-term store are gone, he illustrates how important our memories are to us and how they make us the people we are today with our past experiences and our future aspirations.

Clive Wearing was a brilliant musician, with a wonderful career and a delightful young wife. One day he complained of a headache, which was the beginning of a cruel and vicious illness. The cold sore virus (herpes simplex) had attacked part of his brain and caused irreversible damage. This resulted in the loss of both his STM and LTM. According to his wife, 'He lives in a blinkered moment in time with no past to anchor it to and no future to look ahead to'. He recognises his wife when she visits but will forget having seen her the minute she goes out of the door. If she walks back into the room again he cannot remember the previous encounter, so he acts as if he has not seen her for years and greets her with the same enthusiasm as he did only five minutes before. His case is one of the most upsetting as he has lost all sense of who he is and where he is going. He has no recollection of his past and no idea of any future.

The multi-store model has a number of weaknesses. You may well have experienced instances where something fairly meaningless has happened to you and you probably don't think about it again. Then suddenly, out of the blue, whatever it was springs to mind. That incident has been transferred to long-term memory without you having repeated it over and over to yourself. According to the model, this cannot happen.

The other problem with the model is the description of STM. Remember that

STM is believed to have a limited capacity and is 'fragile' in that the information can be disrupted easily or lost. If it is simply a passive 'holding bay' for information which can be disrupted easily, this would indicate that the information is not processed in any way. But how do you decide what information to store long term and what information you can lose?

Imagine you are given a tube containing seven sweets. If you try to push another sweet into the end of the tube nearest you, a sweet falls out of the far end.

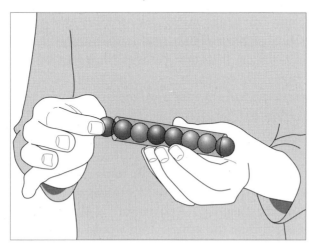

No matter what you do, you can't get more than 7 sweets in that tube. Now imagine every piece of information around you as sweets. There are so many sweets that could enter into the tube that there is never a shortage (these sweets could be spoken or read words or numbers, or they could be visual images such as faces or objects). But you can't 'see' the sweets unless they are in the tube.

How do you decide which ones to eat (i.e. store on a permanent basis). If they are rushing through the tube (STM) quickly and are simply filling vacant spots, then this implies that you are passive in the process. The problem is you cannot be passive, because if you were you wouldn't actually analyse the nature of the sweets enough to decide which sweets are worth eating and which ones to allow to fall out of the tube (i.e. you would not be able to decide which information to send into LTM). Therefore, you must analyse these sweets (information) to a certain extent.

This whole idea contradicts the multi-store model, which states that the STM is a passive store where no information processing takes place. But as we have seen, you must process the information in order to decide whether you want to store it or not.

Carole was on a diet, but she was given a large box of sweets for her birthday. When she was given them, she decided that she would eat them slowly, a couple every day, in order not to make her diet pointless. For the first couple of days, she looked at each one before deciding whether she wanted to eat it or not. She looked for the soft centres, and noticed the shape and whether it was milk or plain chocolate. She could describe in detail which sweets she had eaten and what they were like. On the third day she felt really miserable. When she got in from college, she grabbed the box of chocolates and sat down in front of the TV and proceeded to eat her way through the remainder of the box. She paid no attention to the type of chocolate and didn't even notice what each one tasted like. She was so fed up she just kept on eating until they were all gone, whereupon she felt sick!

If you asked Carole what the chocolates were like, do you think she could tell you about all the different types or would she only remember the ones she had deliberated over when she first got the box? Carole would probably only remember the ones she ate on the first day. The reason is that she 'processed' far more information about them than the others. This would indicate that the information she has stored is the information which has received more processing. The information which received little processing was forgotten. As we have seen, Atkinson and Shiffrin's model would claim that the only way the information would have been stored in LTM was if it was rehearsed, or said over and over again. Surely Carole did not say 'dark chocolate truffle' over and over again to herself?

It would make sense to conclude that perhaps rehearsal is not necessarily the process we use to transfer information from STM to LTM. It would seem likely that it is not simply repeating information to ourselves that decides whether it should be put into long-term storage or not. Perhaps it is something to do with the amount of processing we give to pieces of information. Craik and Lockhart (1972) supported this theory with their 'model' of memory. They argued that it is not rehearsal as such that is important, but more important is what is done with the material during that rehearsal (i.e. how well it is processed), and it is this alone which will determine the duration of the memory. The methods we use for this processing are the ones we have already talked about when we talked about encoding, that is, what it looks like, what it sounds like and what it means.

Craik and Lockhart claim that iconic processing (what something looks like) requires shallow processing; if you then consider what something sounds like, this requires more processing; and if you then take into account what this thing actually means, you will have to process the information more deeply still.

ACTIVITY

Here is an example of the way you can test this out. Compose a list of about 21 words, for example, house, egg, shoes. Divide the list into three so that you have seven words in each list. For the first seven words, you should have a question which asks about the structure of the word e.g. is the word in capital letters or lower case. For the second seven words, find some words that rhyme and some that don't rhyme. For the last seven words, ask something to do with the meaning of the word. Then put them in a random order on a sheet similar to the example given below:

Please answer the following questions and then complete the task at the bottom of the page:

Answer
1 Is the word in capital letters or lower case?   EGG
2 Does the word rhyme with spell?   Shoes
3 Do people live in it?   House
4 Do we wear them on our feet?   Gloves
5 Is the word in capital letters?   Book
6 Does the word rhyme with tree?   Knee
7
8
9

etc.

Please count backwards from 20 to 1.
Now turn over the page for the next instruction.

At the bottom of the page you should tell your subject to count backwards from 20 to one and then turn over, and on the back of the page you should ask them to recall as many of the words as they can. This process prevents them from continuing to rehearse the information, so the words they remember will only be the ones they have transferred into LTM.

The first question asked the person to look at the physical features of the object and nothing more, so this is an example of iconic or structural processing.

The second question asked the person what the sound of the word is like, so this is an example of phonetic (also known as acoustic) encoding. This requires more processing than iconic but less than semantic.

The third is an example of semantic encoding, where you are actually asking the person to process the meaning of the word. This method uses the deepest level of processing of them all.

Give the list to a number of people, and then ask them to recall the words. Then count up the number of words remembered and look at the way they were processed; the chances are that the highest number recalled will be those that were semantically encoded. This will give evidence to support the levels of processing model, but the problem is that the theory is really more descriptive than explanatory and does not really explain why deep processing is so effective.

There is another problem – the only way we can test what has been stored is to look at what we can remember. If the only way we can test depth is to look at how many words we can remember, and if how many words we can remember is taken as a measure of depth, then what we are really saying is the only things which will be retrievable will be things that have been stored and the only things that have been stored will be things that are retrievable. The problem is that this gives us no idea of how well we processed the information we have retrieved, so if we accept the levels of processing model, we have to conclude that the processing used to store information must have been semantic processing. However, further research has shown that it is the information and its relevance to the subject that will be more effective in deciding whether information is stored or not.

WORKING MEMORY

Before we move on, it is worth mentioning that there was another criticism of the multi-store model of memory. Baddeley and Hitch (1974) suggested that the idea of short-term memory being a kind of passive store (and a small one at that) was inadequate. They said that this idea of short-term memory should be replaced with a 'working memory' store, which is really like a kind of conscious memory. According to their model, working memory consists of three parts:

- The central executive, which is like our attention – the area focusing on the task in hand.
- The phonological loop, which is like an inner voice.
- The visuospatial sketch pad, which is like an inner eye.

The concept of working memory is not really of great concern to us here, but if you are interested in reading more about the workings of our memory, this model is the one which is now more widely accepted as an explanation of how we actively process information in conscious awareness and briefly store the information to be processed. It can help to explain tasks such as verbal reasoning or mental arithmetic, although there is still a lack of evidence to support all aspects of the model.

So far we have looked at how memory seems to be structured. We need to return now to the notion that information is not stored in our memory in the same way as a video recorder would record information, unchanged throughout the course of our lives. Our memory does not document everything we experience and recall it as necessary. In fact, many of the things we experience are not stored, and other things are stored, but not accurately.

It was a cold afternoon in late September and two women were standing talking outside their adjacent front gates. Both carried bags of shopping and one woman had a young girl standing by her side.

'I can't believe your Emily is going off to university. It only seems like yesterday when she was playing in the front garden with our Paul,' said the other woman to the girl's mother.

The young girl shuffled. God, she was bored and all she wanted to do was go inside and watch TV.

'Come on, mum, I'm cold, and I want to finish packing.'

'I remember the first day your mum and I took you to school,' said the other woman, totally ignoring her comment. 'You had a cream-coloured coat on, and just as you were going into the school you slipped over on the ice and made your coat all dirty, and you cried and cried. You refused to go in and you were clinging to your mum's hand and begging her to take you home. It only seems like yesterday.'

'No, Elsie, that wasn't her first day at school. That was when we took the children to see Father Christmas, and she had asked me if she could wear her new coat so she would look smart when she went in to tell him what she wanted for Christmas. Don't you remember, it was your Paul who pushed her over on the way into the shop?' said Emily's mother.

'No it wasn't,' said Emily. 'I remember that coat and falling over, but it was when I was on my way to Sophie's birthday party and I didn't want to go in because I had mud on my knees.'

How do we know which was the true story? Each version was true for the teller, but the truth may have been a different version altogether!

The next section is perhaps the most interesting, because it helps to explain how we use our memories in order to make sense of our environment rather than simply having a list of information that we draw on as and when necessary. Hopefully it will also help you to understand how our memories become distorted or positively inaccurate.

SCHEMA THEORY

We are going to consider schema theory and this will help to explain many pieces of research, especially the work of Loftus and Palmer, the core study described in this chapter, which focuses on memory.

Endel Tulving (1972) suggested that we have two different types of memory: episodic memory, which is a memory of episodes (or events in our lives) and semantic memory, which is a memory of facts (such as, trees lose their leaves in winter). Sometimes the experience of an episode leads us to learn new facts. Often (even when we don't have a damaged memory) we remember the facts rather than the actual episode. Why this happens can be explained in part by schema theory.

Each fact that we learn as a result of our experiences becomes part of a schema, which is a kind of packet of information about something. It may help you to think of our schema (the plural is schemata) as files in the drawer of a filing cabinet. You have schemas about school, work, holidays, clubs, picnics, parties, etc. You simply open the drawer of the filing cabinet in your head, take out the relevant file and look up the information, in a fraction of a second.

We have schemata for all different types of objects, events and situations, and they are put together from the experiences we have had and the information we have gathered. They seem to contain a kind of prototype which develops from this information, and the amount of detail they contain will vary accordingly. Think back to your fifth birthday. What do you think you did on that day? The majority of you would say you had a party and a cake and cards and presents – but you probably don't actually remember the event itself.

It is very unlikely that you really remember your fifth birthday, but you will have no problem thinking what it was probably like. Therefore you make inferences about the situation using information about what happens at birthday parties, stored from past experiences and acquired information. In other words, you are describing what your schemata lead you to believe it was like, rather than how it actually was. As you will see in the Loftus and Palmer study, the expectations caused by our schemata can lead to us to produce inaccurate and distorted versions of events. This is another example of the errors in human processing that make us question the machine analogy proposed by the information-processing model.

Schema theory is a theory that shows how we make use of our memory to enable us to quickly and efficiently repeat behaviours or experiences we regularly experience or to manage experiences similar to those we have experienced before. Our knowledge of a typical (or perhaps stereotypical) trip to the supermarket means we are able to do the weekly shop efficiently and without having to repeatedly learn how to do it. By putting schemata in order we are able to produce a script or template for what to expect and how to behave.

As we have seen, schema theory emphasises the fact that what we remember is influenced by what we already know. It also helps to explain how the ideas, beliefs and attitudes we hold have an effect on what we will remember of an event.

ACTIVITY	

Ask someone you know (a friend, family member or classmate) to describe a trip to the supermarket; it will probably go something like this:

'I drive to the supermarket and park my car in the car park. I collect a trolley at the entrance and go into the store. I make my way up and down the aisles, putting the items I want to buy in the trolley. I go to the checkout and wait in the long queue and when it is my turn I drag all my goods out of the trolley onto the conveyor belt. They are scanned in by the checkout girl and I put them in bags and back in the trolley. I pay the girl and take the trolley out to my car, put the stuff in the boot, return the trolley and drive back home.'

From this script, do you think the author finds supermarket shopping an uplifting experience? Well, no. The author's negative attitude can be seen in the expectation of a 'long queue' and having to 'drag' stuff out of the trolley. What's more, our prejudices are also apparent in our schemata. Would you expect the checkout assistant to be female, as the author did?

Other areas of research have demonstrated how our schemata influence our memories using studies similar to the activity above. If you were asked to imagine going to a restaurant and told to list 20 things that happened throughout the course of your time there, you would include many of the same things as other people. They would be things like being seated, reading the menu, ordering food, having drinks and paying the bill. This study, conducted by Bower, Black and Turner (1979), involved asking 32 people to list the 20 most important events associated with having a meal at a restaurant. What they found was that 73% included the following six events on their list: sitting down, looking at a menu, ordering, eating, paying the bill and leaving the restaurant.

All the subjects of this piece of research named the same events as they had obviously had experience of restaurants and knew exactly what went on. Now imagine that you are a small child and the only 'restaurant' you have been to is McDonald's. What sort of things would you describe if you were asked the same question? Then you visit a Harvester or Beefeater restaurant and your knowledge of restaurants would increase enormously, so you would realise that restaurants involve sitting down at a table and reading the menu and having the food brought to you rather than having to queue for it. Then you visit somewhere like the Savoy in London and things would be different again.

You can see how, with an increase in experience and knowledge, the packet of information contained in your brain which stores information about a certain event will increase in size as you get older. You will then be able to use this stored knowledge to answer questions and interpret conversations without having to have all the details presented to you at the beginning of the conversation. You would understand what was meant by, 'We went to the Harvester last night and the service was excellent,' without wondering what on earth the person was going on about.

How do schemata affect memories?

1. The schema guides the selection of what is encoded and stored in memory. You are unlikely to remember irrelevant details of events, e.g. what clothes you wore when you sat your GCSEs, assuming that it wasn't school uniform. The schema also provides a framework to store new information, like a file marked 'restaurant'.

2. You abstract information from events. This means that you take out and store only some of the information from different events if there are a number of them and they are all very similar. Remember your fifth birthday? All you can remember is general information about birthdays – presents, cakes, parties, etc. This also happens with conversations – you only remember the gist of them, not all the contents.

3. Because we have integrated lots of information into our schemata, they help us interpret different situations about which we have very limited knowledge. We may end up having to use inferences in the light of past knowledge and previous experience.

4. Memories can also be distorted to fit prior expectations and in order to make them consistent with your existing schema, they may actually be transformed. This is how eyewitness testimony gets blurred – you see what you expect to see.

5. Schemata may also aid retrieval. You can sometimes remember what happened by searching through the information you have already stored in your schema, to see if you recognise what was required.

The idea of schema theory was introduced by Frederick Bartlett in 1932 in order to explain why, when people remember stories, they regularly leave out some details and introduce what he called 'rationalisations' which they use to make the stories make sense. He investigated this using a story called 'The War of the Ghosts', asking people to recall a story which contained unfamiliar information. He found that they didn't remember the story as it was told, but made errors in their recall because they used their schemata to interpret the story and provide information they believed was in the story, rather than what was actually there.

ACTIVITY	
In order to demonstrate how this occurs, read the story used by Bartlett which is printed below, and five minutes later write down what you can remember.	

The War of the Ghosts (Bartlett, 1932)

One night, two young men from Egulac went down to the river to hunt seals, and while they were there it became foggy and calm. Then they heard war cries and they thought, 'Maybe this is a war-party'. They escaped to the shore and hid behind a log. Now canoes came up and they heard the noise of paddles and saw one canoe coming up to them. There were five men in the canoe and they said, 'What do you think? We wish to take you along. We are going up the river to make war on the people.'

One of the young men said, 'I have no arrows.' 'Arrows are in the canoe', they said. 'I will not go. I might be killed. My relatives do not know where I have gone. But you,' he said, turning to the other, 'may go with them.' So one of the young men went, but the other returned home. And the warriors went on up the river to a town on the other side of Kalama. The people came down to the water and they began to fight and many were killed. But presently the young man heard one of the warriors say, 'Quick, let us go home: that Indian has been hit.' Now he thought, 'Oh, they are ghosts.' He did not feel sick, but they said that he had been shot.

So the canoes went back to Egulac, and the young man went ashore to his house and made a fire. And he told everybody and said, 'Behold, I accompanied the ghosts, and we went to fight. Many of our fellows were killed. They said I was hit but I did not feel sick.'

He told it all and then became quiet. When the sun rose he fell down. Something black came out of his mouth. His face became contorted. The people jumped and cried. He was dead.

Bartlett asked people to recall this study at intervals over time and showed that distortions occurred. The story was made more westernised; for example, fishing was substituted for hunting seals. In addition, the amount recalled decreased over time, and further distortions occurred.

Bartlett believed that when people remember stories, there is a tendency for them to sacrifice detailed recall in favour of 'making sense' of the information given. Bartlett demonstrated that rather than being like computer memory where input information is retrieved unaltered, human memory is *reconstructive* in nature. When we process information we try to make it logical, sensible and coherent. As we've seen above, this means that we include what could or should have happened according to our expectations, illustrating that our memory is likely to be an imperfect record of events and can be a complete distortion governed by our biases and prejudices. You may be unaware of ever doing this, as it isn't a conscious process, but if you want to see a real-life version of it in action, just ask two squabbling siblings for their version of events and see how much they differ.

E.F. Loftus and J.J. Palmer (1974), 'Reconstruction of automobile destruction: An example of the interaction between language and memory', *Journal of Verbal Learning and Verbal Behaviour,* 13, 585–9

Background

Bartlett's ideas are still widely accepted as they explain how the information we take in is affected by already existing schemata representing previous knowledge. His work, however, has its critics. His findings were largely qualitative, as of course it is very difficult to establish objective measures of memory distortion. Later researchers, however, have undertaken laboratory studies to scientifically investigate the reconstructive nature of human memory and to consider some of the factors which lead to these distortions. An eminent researcher in this field is Elizabeth Loftus, who, along with colleagues, has carried out a series of studies, particularly concerning the reliability of eyewitness testimony.

It is interesting that eyewitness testimony was once considered one of the most important factors in court cases. Many suspects were found guilty as a result of their identification by witnesses and witness reports of events. But if human memory is reconstructive, should we rely on this in a court of law?

Loftus was concerned not only with the fragility of memory, but also with the effects of stress on the ability of victims to recall facts. Loftus and Burns (1982) showed their subjects a film of a hold-up and then tested their memory for details. The experimental group saw a violent version of the film where one of the members of a group of young boys is shot and collapses on the floor, clutching his bleeding face. The control group saw the same film, but this scene was omitted. Instead their film changed to a scene inside the bank where the manager is explaining to staff and customers exactly what has happened.

Loftus and Burns found that subjects who saw the violent version had significantly less memory for details of events before the shooting. Most subjects failed to mention that one of the boys had a large number '17' on his jersey, which was very obvious from the film. There were actually 16 items that subjects could have recalled, but those who had seen the violent version of the film recalled significantly less than the other group on 14 of those items.

The core study that we are concerned with here focuses on the effects of language on memory changes. Loftus suggested that there are two types of information that affect our memory of an event:
• information gained at the time of the event
• information gained after the event (subsequent information).

Loftus was interested in how you can actually change a witness's recollection of an incident by subtly introducing new and subsequent information during questioning, and therefore after the event. This depends on how language is used.

For example, one study showed how the changing of the structure of a question could lead people to reconstruct an event and 'remember' false facts. In the stud, film clips were shown and the independent variable was manipulated by asking one of two versions of the critical question. In one condition subjects were asked: 'Did you see a broken headlight?' – this question suggests there may or may not have been a broken headlight. In the second condition subjects were asked: 'Did you see the broken headlight?' – the use of the definite article here suggests there definitely was a broken headlight so the subject should have seen it. The results showed that more of those in the second condition reported seeing a broken headlight, even though there was no broken headlight in the film.

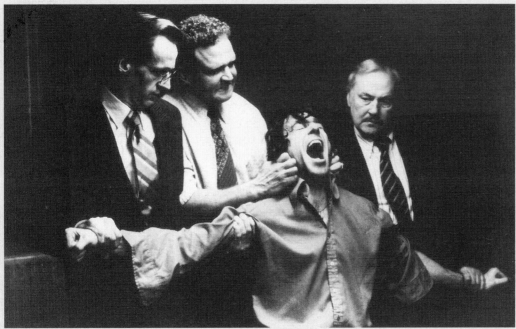

If we accept that stress affects memory, imagine how accurate any testimony would be if a witness were subjected to pressure. This scene from the film *In the Name of the Father,* starring Daniel Day Lewis, illustrates how someone could be 'encouraged' to remember something which may later become part of his actual memory.

Aim

Loftus and Palmer carried out two experiments to investigate the effects of language on memory. Their expectation was that information received after the event in the form of leading questions would be integrated into a person's memory. It would form part of the memory and cause the event to be recalled in a way consistent with the subsequent information they were given.

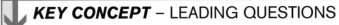

KEY CONCEPT – LEADING QUESTIONS

Loftus and Palmer point out that it was already known that 'some questions are... more suggestive than others', and that a legal concept of 'leading questions' existed, along with rules for the use of such questions in the courtroom.

Their definition is as follows: 'A leading question is simply one that, by its form or content, suggests to the witness what answer is desired or leads him to the desired answer'.

An example is the one about headlights given above: 'Did you see the broken headlight?' leads you to believe that there was one, and therefore you ought to have seen it, and so the expected answer is 'Yes'.

Examples from everyday life might include: 'You don't mind babysitting your little brother, do you?' or 'My bum doesn't look too big in these jeans, does it?'

CORE STUDY LINK – in the study of Little Hans by Freud, Hans' father uses leading questions in his analysis of the boy. e.g. 'When the horse fell over did you think of your daddy?'

Two experiments were carried out to see whether leading questions could change a person's memory for an event. The first experiment also tested the established theory that witnesses are not very good at estimating the speed of vehicles.

Experiment 1

Method

Design

This was a laboratory experiment, and the experimental design used was independent groups.

Subjects

Forty-five student subjects were tested. They were tested in groups of various sizes, but for test purposes it was designed that overall there would be five conditions with nine subjects providing data for each condition.

Apparatus

Equipment to screen seven film segments from the Evergreen Safety Council of the Seattle Police Department. Each segment lasted between five and 30 seconds. The films were safety promotion films, and four of the seven clips contained staged crashes. There would have been serious ethical concerns about showing real crashes and the advantage of the staged crashes was that the speed at which the vehicles had been travelling when they crashed was known: for two of the films, it was 40 mph, for one, 20 mph and for the other, 30 mph. This would mean the accuracy of estimating speeds could be measured.

There were also sets of questionnaires, corresponding to the film clips, one per subject, to be completed after each clip.

Procedure

All the subjects were shown the seven film clips and were given a questionnaire to complete after each clip. There were two parts to each questionnaire. First, they were asked to 'Give an account of the accident you have just seen', and second, to answer a set of questions relating to the accident. Of the questions being asked, the question the researchers were interested in was about the speed of the vehicles at the time of the accident.

In order to counteract order effects, the groups were presented with a different order of films. The entire experiment lasted about an hour and a half.

FOCUS ON RESEARCH METHODS – critical questions

In an experiment, the critical question (or questions) is what is used to measure the dependent variable. It is common for these to be masked in a questionnaire by the use of distractor questions, so that the Ss cannot respond to the demand characteristics present where just one question is asked. The fewer the questions asked, the more likely it is that Ss will work out the purpose of the study and behave so as to support the hypothesis or to scupper the study. This needs to be avoided as it affects the internal validity of the study.

The independent variable was manipulated by changing the wording of the critical question about the speed of vehicles at the time of the accident, using a different verb in the question. The authors theorised that the stronger the verb, the higher the speed estimate would be. The standard format of the critical question was, 'About how fast were the cars going when they _____ each other?'

There were five verb conditions: contacted, hit, bumped, collided and smashed.

Each subject received one of the five critical questions in their questionnaires. This means that the independent variable in this experiment was which verb condition the subject was tested in. The dependent variable was the mean speed estimate in miles per hour per condition, thus giving a quantitative measure.

Results

Let's look at these in two parts. First, how accurate are the witnesses' speed estimates?

The accuracy of subjects' speed estimates in miles per hour for the four staged crashes were:

Film no.	Actual speed	Mean estimated speed
1	20	37.7
2	30	36.2
3	40	39.7
4	40	36.1

These results support previous studies in that they indicate that people are not very good at judging how fast a vehicle is actually travelling.

Second, does changing the verb in the critical question affect speed estimates?

The mean speed estimates in miles per hour for each of the five verb conditions were:

Verb	Mean speed estimate in mph
Smashed	40.8
Collided	39.3
Bumped	38.1
Hit	34
Contacted	31.8

Inferential analysis of these results showed that they were significant at the $p < 0.05$ level. This shows that the form of the question affected the witnesses' answers.

Why does the wording affect the subject? Loftus and Palmer give two interpretations. First, it may be due to response bias. This is the tendency to give a response in a certain direction according to the situation. If a subject can't decide between 30 and 40, the word 'smashed' may cue the response of 40 as it suggests a higher speed. Second, it may be that the language used causes a change in the subject's memory representation of events. Loftus and Palmer say 'The verb "smashed" may change a subject's memory such that he "sees" that accident as being more severe than it was'.

Loftus and Palmer carried out a second experiment to try to establish which of these interpretations was true. They theorised that if the person's memory had been changed, then they could be expected to 'remember' other details that didn't occur, but would fit in with their belief that the accident took place at a higher speed.

Experiment two

Aim

To see if subjects asked the 'smashed' question would be more likely than 2 other groups to report seeing broken glass in the filmed accident, when tested one week later. They were compared to a group asked the 'hit' question and a control group asked to make no speed estimate. Broken glass would be expected in an accident occurring at high speed, but no broken glass was actually shown on the film. A positive report of broken glass would suggest that the memory of the event was being reconstructed as a result of information (in the form of leading questions) received after the event.

Method

Design
This was again a laboratory experiment, and again used an independent groups design.

Subjects
One hundred and fifty student subjects were divided into three groups, with 50 subjects in each condition.

Apparatus
Equipment to screen a film showing a multiple car crash. The clip lasted less than one minute, with the accident itself lasting less than four seconds.

Each subject completed two questionnaires. The questionnaires completed immediately after viewing the film clip asked subjects to describe the accident in their own words and to answer a series of questions (Questionnaire one). The critical question asked subjects to estimate the speed of the vehicles.

There were three conditions:
50 subjects were asked, 'About how fast were the cars going when they smashed into each other?'
50 subjects were asked, 'About how fast were the cars going when they hit each other?'
The remaining 50 subjects were not asked about the speed of vehicles, and thus acted as a control condition.

A second questionnaire (Questionnaire two) contained ten questions about the accident. The critical question was, 'Did you see any broken glass?' Subjects responded to this by ticking yes or no.

Procedure
This was a two-part procedure, with subjects seeing the film and filling in one of the three versions of Questionnaire one on one day, and returning a week later to complete Questionnaire two.

Results
Subjects in the 'smashed' condition gave a significantly higher speed estimate than those in the 'hit' condition, 10.46 mph and 8.0 mph respectively, supporting the

finding from experiment one that the wording of the question can have a considerable effect on the estimate of speed.

Subjects in the 'smashed' condition were also significantly more likely to answer 'yes' to the question, 'Did you see any broken glass?' than those in the 'hit' and control conditions. The differences between the control and the 'hit' condition were negligible.

Distribution of yes and no responses to the question, 'Did you see any broken glass?' was:

Response	Verb condition: SMASHED	Verb condition: HIT	CONTROL
YES	16	7	6
NO	34	43	44

Discussion

The conclusion of the second study was that the verb not only affected the estimate of speed, but also the likelihood of subjects thinking they had seen broken glass. Loftus and Palmer explain this by suggesting that subjects took in information from the original scene, and then merged this with information given after the event. This produced a memory of the event made up of some of the original information and subsequent information received when they were questioned about it. We are inclined to make our memory make sense, so those subjects who believed the accident had been at a higher speed and was, therefore, more severe (those in the 'smashed' condition) were more likely to think that broken glass was present.

Commentary

Is the study useful?

Loftus and Palmer's study is one in a series of studies that showed that it is possible to distort the memories of witnesses. This has considerable repercussions for the police. Such studies have led to a great deal of research being carried out into the best way for police officers to question witnesses. However, if the misleading information is blatantly incorrect, people are less likely to take it in and overwrite previous information. Look again at the responses of subjects in experiment two. Of 150 subjects questioned, 121 answered correctly, no, including over two-thirds of the subjects in the 'smashed' condition. So perhaps it is not so easy to change a memory for an important event after all, and we must be careful not to exaggerate the extent to which the recall of witnesses is affected by leading questions.

Is the study ecologically valid?

As the study is carried out in the controlled conditions of the laboratory, it is low in ecological validity. In the study, the subjects were asked to watch the film clips and were prepared to recall what they had seen. Accidents happen spontaneously in the real world, and our memories of such events will obviously be different without the luxury of prior warning. We also have to question whether watching film clips of staged accidents leads to memories being laid down or recalled in the same way as they might be under the stressful and distressing circumstances of being witness to a real car crash happening to real people.

FOCUS ON RESEARCH METHODS – students as subjects in psychological research

Since most psychologists undertake research whilst working at a university, the student body provides them with the perfect opportunity sample. The researcher just needs to put up an ad on the noticeboard with the offer of money (or, for psychology students, the possibility of marks towards their course) and stand back to avoid being killed in the rush. Maybe that's an exaggeration, but the fact is that students are plentiful on campus, and many researchers have benefited from using the time- and cost-effective sample that an undergraduate sample base can provide. The researcher gets to carry out the study from the comfort of their workplace and the students earn some money, so why are student samples a problem?

Well, a sample is supposed to be generalisable, and to be generalisable to people in general, you need a broader sample than that enticed out of the uni library or the student bar. Sears (1986) reviewed the use of student samples in psychology and considered both the problems presented in terms of biasing factors that reduce generalisability and the consequences of basing our view of human psychology on such a narrow sample base.

Biasing factors include the fact that students represent only a narrow age range and only the upper levels of family income and educational background. This obviously means that they present us with a biased sample as no other age groups are represented; moreover, students aren't even typical of their age group, as they are only students because they have displayed the cognitive skills required of them to gain entry to college, and in order to do this they tend to be more compliant to authority than their peers in general.

Sears goes on to say that laboratory studies, such as the study by Loftus and Palmer, compound the problems since the students will be more willing to comply with researchers' requests, especially if studies they participate in form part of their course. So we should always be cautious when making generalisations from studies using student samples.

For a well-written and concise review of Sears' work see Banyard and Grayson (2000), *Introducing Psychological Research*, Palgrave.

What does the study illustrate about the cognitive approach?

What this study shows us about memory as a cognitive process is that rather than the 'tape recorder' or 'computer memory' model that the information-processing approach might lead us to expect, human memory is a distortion of observed events. Moreover memory is a dynamic process, changing over time and affected by the person's subsequent experiences, driven by their need to make sense of their surroundings and experiences.

The study is an excellent example of how the scientific method is used in the cognitive approach. The reductionist approach is used here, homing in on one variable, the changing of the form of a question, and how it impacts on memory. This shows us the strength of such an approach in enabling researchers to identify the relationships between variables. Critics of the cognitive approach would see this narrow focus as a weakness, giving a restricted and limited perspective on behaviour.

Key questions

1. Explain what is meant by the term 'reconstructive memory'.

2. What is a leading question?

3. Why is watching a filmed accident different from being witness to an accident in real life?

4. Identify how the dependent variable was measured for both experiment one and experiment two. What advantages are there in gathering quantitative data in this study?

5. What if the sample were different? Suggest one other sample that could have been used for this study, and explain how you think this sample may affect the results.

Example Answers are on page 452.

Further reading:

Loftus and Palmer

- Loftus, Elizabeth F. (1996), *Eyewitness Testimony*, Cambridge, MA: Harvard University Press.
- http://faculty.washington.edu/eloftus/ – Elizabeth Loftus' site at Washington University.
- www.pbs.org/wgbh/pages/frontline/shows/dna/interviews/loftus.htm – an interview with Elizabeth Loftus.

Perception

When information from the outside world reaches us, either by touch, sight, smell, taste or hearing, we need to make sense of what that information is in order to identify it. The information may vary in form, for example, the 'things' we experience when we smell something are chemicals, and the 'sounds' that we hear are actually waves of different frequencies. Each of our senses has a specific organ which contains receptors for taking in information, for example, our eyes have receptor cells based at the back of the retina, which convert images into a type of electrochemical energy. This energy is transmitted via an internal 'wiring system', better known as neurons, to a specific part of the brain. (If you wonder where nerves feature here, nerves are simply a collection of neurons; so if you imagine a cable made up of lots of wires, this is what a nerve, made up of a collection of neurons, is like.) This energy is then 'decoded' by the brain into something we understand. The process we use to decode or understand what we have just experienced is called perception.

Look at the following picture and see if you can work out what it is.

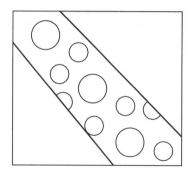

Could it possibly be a giraffe going past a window? It is certainly possible; however, what you actually see is a square with two lines which are almost parallel, and a number of circles. If you 'saw' a giraffe, what you have done is to use the information stored in your memory to help you identify what you have seen – you have perceived it as a giraffe.

If you had never seen a giraffe before, you would have trouble believing the giraffe suggestion. You would not have had the relevant information stored in order to help you decode the sensory input, and you would have identified it as what it is – lines and circles. Now imagine that you had never seen a circle before. Although you would have seen the shape, you would not be able to name it, but you would have been able to describe its properties, that is, that it was a line that was curved and had no end. Again, what you would be trying to do is to make sense of what you have seen.

Most psychologists believe that we can't make sense of any stimulus on its own, and that we need to use stored information to help us interpret it. Let's look at another example. We sense the presence of a stimulus, in this case, a noise. Our sense organs (ears) react to that external stimulus by detecting the sounds. What we actually perceive is music because we have interpreted that sensation as something we have heard before, which is called music.

Perhaps the best definition of perception is 'making sense of sensation'. In vision, sensation refers to the reaction of the retina to light or stimulus, and perception refers to our organisation, integration and recognition of these patterns, from an upside-down, blurred, double image which does not relate to the size of the object, into a clear, three-dimensional colourful image which is the right way up.

Research on the subject of perception has focused mainly on visual perception because it is estimated that 90% of the information we receive about the external world reaches us through our eyes. It would make sense, then, for vision to be the dominant sense and for the information we perceive visually to be so dominant that it can overrule the information taken in by other sense modalities.

This was demonstrated in an experiment carried out some time ago by James Gibson (1933). He asked his subjects to put on some glasses which made straight edges appear curved. He then asked them to run their hands along a straight edge. The subjects all agreed that the straight edge felt as if it were curved, even though it was not. The evidence of the subjects' eyes was contradicting what they knew to be true.

Although Gibson's experiment indicates that visual information is very powerful, most psychologists argue that we need to have had some experience of the things we see in order to make sense of them. We use visual cues to help us understand and make sense of the large amount of information in our world, and many of these cues are learned.

We are now going to look at the types of cues we use in order to identify how far away things are from us. Depth perception is one of our major achievements because it is astonishing how we can turn a two-dimensional retinal image into a three-dimensional world. We must remember that many of the depth cues that are available are given by our movement or the movement of objects around us. For example, if we have been driving along a road, we know how far away something behind us actually is, because we know how long ago we passed it. However, sometimes we are stationary and the objects we are observing are also stationary, and yet we can still work out, very accurately, how far away from us they are.

The cues we use can be divided into monocular and binocular cues. Monocular cues only require the use of one eye, although they can also be used easily when someone has two eyes open, and binocular cues are cues which need both eyes to be used together.

MONOCULAR CUES

Monocular cues are the cues that are used by artists to help give depth to a painting. They are also used if we only have one eye (but more of that later). Below are listed the monocular cues and examples of how they work.

Linear perspective

One of the most powerful monocular cues is linear perspective. This is where parallel lines pointing directly away from us seem to get closer together as they recede into the distance. An example of this is if you imagine railway tracks going off into the distance – they don't seem to be parallel.

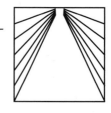

Linear perspective – parallel lines converge as they recede into the distance

117

Texture gradient

Most objects possess texture (e.g. carpets, pebbled beaches) and the texture of objects appears more dense the closer the object is to you.

Texture gradient – the texture or gradient becomes finer as it gets further away

Interposition

Interposition is where a near object hides an object a little further away. Many illusions are based on this depth cue, for example, Kanizsa's (1976) illusory square is an example of how strong this can be.

Shading

If you look at an object in a picture and there is no shadow, that object appears flat. This is because you know that flat surfaces don't cast shadows. The minute that a shadow is present, that object has depth.

Motion parallax

If you are on a train, the objects near to you seem to rush past whereas the objects on the horizon stay still for much longer. This is because the images of the nearer objects rush over the retina, whereas the images of the distant ones do not move across the retina as fast and the brain compares the speed of movement of the two objects and interprets this as distance.

Emily was looking out of the window of the car on the way home from holiday. 'Look, mummy, there's the moon,' she said, as she saw the moon in the sky. 'Is it the same moon that we saw on holiday?'

'Yes, darling,' said her mother.

Emily continued to watch the moon out of the car window, and when they pulled into the driveway, Emily leapt out of the car. 'Look, it's followed us all the way home.'

This happens because the moon is such a long way away that the retinal image does not appear to move, whereas objects very close to us move at great speed.

Height in the vertical plane

Objects that are a long way away from us are seen as being closer to the horizon. Therefore, if one object appears to be lower than another, we perceive that it is further away. The depth cue is so great that even without background we know where the objects are in relation to each other.

Height in the visual field – *the closer to the horizon that the object is, the further away it is*

Relative size

Objects which are some distance away produce a small retinal image, whereas objects which are

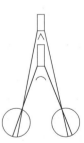

much closer produce a larger retinal image. The brain interprets this information in the light of what it knows about objects and uses this to work out how near or how far away objects that we are looking at really are.

BINOCULAR CUES

If you have one eye you will not be able to use binocular cues as they involve both eyes being used together.

Convergence

This cue refers to the way the eyes need to turn inwards to a greater extent to focus on closer objects compared with those further away. Note the difference of the angles when the eyes are looking at near and more distant images.

Accommodation

This refers to the way the lenses of the eyes change shape when we focus on objects at different distances. If we look at objects that are near to us, the lenses thicken, but they flatten for objects which are further away. The brain interprets this movement of the lenses to help give an idea of how near or far the objects are.

Stereopsis

Because your eyes are slightly apart, you actually see two very slightly different images at the same time, one from each eye. These two images are put together by the brain and this gives a very strong depth effect. To see how different the images are, first of all close one eye. Then hold something like a pen or pencil vertically in front of you and line it up with the side of a window or door so it is actually 'sitting over' the line of the chosen object. Keeping your hand still, now open the eye that was closed and close the one that was open. You will see how far the pen has 'jumped' away from its original position.

You may have experienced this by wearing special glasses which give you a three-dimensional effect at a cinema or a museum, or by looking at a stereoscope which contains two pictures which are almost identical, but when you look at them through a stereoscopic viewer the brain amalgamates the images into one three-dimensional one. (In fact, the 'magic eye' pictures work on this principle by overlaying one image made up of computer-generated sets of dots with another. The reason some people can't see them is because one eye is not working as efficiently as the other.)

VISUAL CONSTANCIES

Have you noticed that objects seem to retain their shape, even when you look at them from different angles? Even though the size and shape of the image which appears on the retina changes considerably as an object moves or as we move, the size and shape of the object seems to remain constant. There are a large number of these 'visual constancies', which will become clearer as you read on.

Shape constancy

Have you ever noticed that it doesn't seem to matter at what angle you look at a door, either open or shut, or half open, it always looks like a rectangle. Shape constancy refers to the fact that the shape of an object looks the same despite changes in orientation. This is a really good illustration of perception: you do not actually 'see' what the retinal image looks like, rather you 'see' the object as you know it to be.

Colour constancy

This refers to the fact that the colour of an object looks the same even when the colour changes. An example of this may occur when you are at a club which has red lighting. Although it may make your friends' faces look more red, you simply take into account the colour of the lighting and perceive their faces as the usual colour.

Size constancy

Size constancy involves objects looking the same size in spite of changes in the size of the retinal image. For example, cars at the end of a car park do not look like toy cars, even though the retinal image is very small. If you want to compare retinal images, first of all find an object like a tree or a car which you can see out of the window some distance away. Then hold your hand up and fit the image between your thumb and forefinger (as if you are holding it between them). Remember how far they are apart. Now do the same for a near object, and you will have a comparison in retinal sizes. Here is an amazingly effective example of how this works:

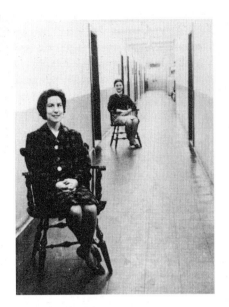

However, size constancy is not always found. Have you noticed if you look out of the window of a plane, or down from a very high building, that the scene below does not look real and objects like cars look more like toys? This is because it is an unfamiliar experience for us. This should give you some idea about how experience helps us to perceive accurately.

If we accept that the relationship between size and distance is very strong, it would seem quite reasonable for it to work in reverse, that is perceived distance is influenced by familiar size.

A cunning piece of research by Ittelson (1951) illustrates how well this works. He showed participants playing cards through a peephole into a long box that gave no indication of distance other than familiar size. There were actually three different sizes of playing cards (normal, half and double size). They were attached to some wire and put through the top of the box in exactly the same place, at a distance of two.three metres from the observer. When asked how far away the cards were from the observer, the half-size playing card was estimated to be on average 4.6 metres away, whereas the double size card was thought to be 1.3 metres away. Therefore, familiar size had a significant effect on distance judgements and, as the only way we know about familiar size is to have stored it in our memories, this must indicate that size constancy is learned.

Here is another example of size constancy which you may well have experienced.

You are away on holiday and you meet a whole crowd of really excellent people. You decide that you want to remember them, so you take a photo of them in front of a stunning view. When your holiday photos are developed you turn with excitement to the one of the group of people but, to your dismay, the people look so tiny that you can hardly make out their features. They look much smaller against the background than you remember them to be when you were taking the photo, and you think to yourself it would have been better to have had them closer.

When something moves away from us the size of the image cast on the retina diminishes rapidly, but we know that they aren't really shrinking. Our visual systems compensate for this decrease in size by making us see receding people and objects as larger than they really are, which makes them seem closer than they really are. Richard Gregory (1977) thinks this is why certain visual illusions work. He says that these illusions give up depth cues that line B is longer than line A in each case.

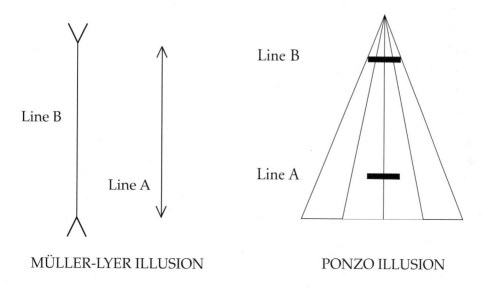

Müller-Lyer illusion and Ponzo illusion

The Müller-Lyer line B looks like the inside corner of a room. A looks like the outside corner of a building which emerges towards us. We compensate for line B because it looks further away than A.

The Ponzo illusion suggests parallel lines receding into the distance (like railway tracks), which leads us to think that line B is further away. So we compensate for the size of line B by making it look bigger to us.

However, as you will see later, other cultures are not always taken in by this because they live in a different environment, with round houses rather than rectangular ones – this kind of cue is not available to them, as it has not formed part of their experience. Gregory concluded that experience, therefore, affects the unconscious cues we use to interpret visual stimuli, and that Europeans and Zulus have what are known as different learning sets (or learning experiences).

There is one more example of how perceived distance can affect size judgements and this is an 'everyday' illusion which we have probably all experienced at some time. Have you ever noticed how the moon looks much larger when it is close to the horizon than when it is high in the sky? Part of the reason is that the moon looks further away from us when it is near the horizon because there are many depth cues present and we know that the horizon is a long way away. We therefore compensate for that distance by increasing the perceived size of the moon and so it looks quite large. When it is high up in the sky we have nothing to relate it to, and so although the retinal size of the moon is the same as it is at the horizon, we perceive it as much smaller.

This was demonstrated by Kaufman and Rock (1962) when they asked their participants to look at the moon on the horizon through a small hole in a card, thus depriving them of the distance cues provided by the horizon. They reported seeing the image as very small, in fact, much smaller than when they looked at it without the card. They also asked participants to look at the moon high in the sky through a sheet of clear plastic with an artificial horizon drawn on it. This resulted in them reporting an apparent increase in the size of the moon.

MOTION PERCEPTION

Motion perception is another example of how the brain intervenes in what we actually see. When we follow moving objects with our eyes, our eyes make small irregular jerky movements, but we perceive a smooth continuous motion. We can therefore conclude that we interpret what we see and make sense of it in light of what we know, rather than what we actually see, because we know, for example, that cars do not jerk along roads.

Have you ever been sitting on a train in a station, and the train next door to you starts to pull away, but you feel that it is you that is moving rather than the other train? Another example is going through a car wash – you feel that your car is moving backwards and forwards rather than the brushes either side of the car. There is also the example of the moon in the sky which has a thin layer of clouds across it which are moving along, but we think the clouds are stationary and the moon is what is moving.

All these relate to motion perception and stored information. We are much better at detecting motion when we see a moving object against a background which isn't moving. We also have the expectation that a car moves along the road, rather than the road moving and the car staying still. This is why, when we look at real moving things, we find that if the largest object which surrounds a smaller object is the one that is moving, it makes the small object appear to move. Now think of this in relation to the train: the carriage we are in seems small in relation to the rest of the world, therefore we think that we are moving and the rest of the world is stationary.

Our ability to perceive is amazing and depends a great deal on our past experiences and stored information. If you accept this you will realise how the whole area relates to our memory and past memory representations, and why we need to understand memory in order to be able to comprehend perception.

PERCEPTUAL SET

There are a number of cues which influence our perception, both external and internal: external are due to the nature of the object being seen, and internal are directly related to stored knowledge. So far we have focused on the most basic factors, but we are now going to consider a few of the factors which are largely unconscious. These factors are known as 'perceptual set' and are defined by Allport (1955) as 'a perceptual bias or predisposition or readiness to perceive particular features of a stimulus'. They are, of course, influenced by past experience and learning.

The first of these is **context**, that is, *where* you see something will influence your identification of that object. If you saw something that was a sort of golden orange colour and shiny, in the middle of a golf course, you would be very unlikely to identify it as a goldfish from a distance. Whereas, if you saw the same object in the middle of a tank of water in a hotel, you would have no problems identifying it from the far side of the lobby.

Your **motivation** will also affect your perception of an object. If you are trying to avoid someone in a blue Fiesta car, isn't it amazing how many blue Fiestas there are on the road? In fact, every third car seems to be a blue Fiesta! Gilchrist and Nesberg (1952) looked at the effects of deprivation on perception by using participants who were either very hungry or very thirsty, having gone without food or water for a number of hours. They were asked to rate the brightness of pictures of food or liquid, and it was found that the longer they had been deprived, the brighter the pictures were rated.

Another of these predispositions is what is called **expectancy bias**. This is where you are meeting the man/woman of your dreams off the train and you misrecognise all sorts of people because you are so desperate to see the person you are meeting. This was investigated by Bruner and Goodman (1947) when they asked rich and poor children to estimate the sizes of coins. The poor children overestimated the size of every coin in comparison to the rich children, which could be explained by the fact that the money had a much greater value to the poor children. We mustn't forget that it may also have been due to the fact that the poor children had not had much experience of handling money.

Another example is perhaps one of the most impressive ways of demonstrating expectancy – looking at the mask of a face. If we see it from the outside it is obviously convex. If we rotate it very slowly so we are looking at the inside of the mask, the concave inside will suddenly seem to 'spring out', so it looks convex again. This is because we know that faces are convex, not concave, and so we perceive the image as it should be seen and not how it actually is.

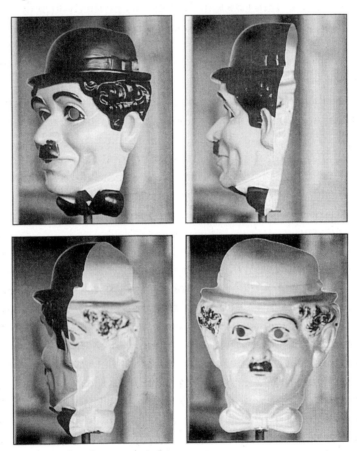

The rotating face mask

PSYCHOLOGY AND THE NATURE–NURTURE ARGUMENT

If we accept that perception requires the use of stored information, it would seem a reasonable argument to suggest that we have to learn how to perceive. But is this really the case? Perhaps we are born with the ability to perceive some things but not others. If this is so, what things are we able to perceive when we are born and how on earth could we find out (after all, you cannot question a newborn baby). Needless to say, some psychologists believe our abilities are innate and others believe they are learned, and therefore a huge amount of research has been generated in investigating this area.

The ideal method used to investigate this area is to study humans who have no perceptual experience. If we are born with the ability to perceive, then our ability to process visual information and make sense of it should be no different to that of an adult. If, on the other hand, it depends on learning, it should be totally inadequate. Where do we find these inexperienced humans who can both communicate and who have had no perceptual experience? As a response to this problem, a number of methods have been devised, some involving humans and others involving animals. It isn't necessary here to go into the studies in any detail, but the following will give you a general idea of the type of research and the findings.

One way of checking if babies can discriminate between different visual stimuli is to see if they have a preference for one picture over another. To investigate this, psychologists have looked at babies' eyes to see if they look more at one picture than another. The overall findings are that, even from a very early age, they prefer more complex pictures and pictures which resemble a human face (Ahrens, 1954, Fantz, 1961).

Bushnell and Sai (1987) conducted a study which looked at very young babies who had not had the chance to experience much in the way of visual stimuli to see if they could tell two faces apart. They showed newborn babies their mother's face and the face of a female stranger, both of whom had the same level of contrast and the same hair colour. The babies, who had an average age of two days and five hours, showed a clear preference for their mothers. This also indicates that it is likely that infants have a preference for faces, especially familiar ones. Why do you think this may be? Well, if nothing else, perhaps babies are born with the ability to perceive familiar and unfamiliar faces as this would be a useful survival mechanism. The problem, even with this piece of research, was that the babies were still not experiencing visual stimuli for the first time, and therefore it may have been a preference for learned things, which could have been associated with food and comfort.

The other area which has been investigated with regard to infant perception is depth perception, as it was reasoned that if babies are able to perceive depth at birth or very soon afterwards, the ability is likely to be innate. The most famous study was that done by Gibson and Walk (1966), using the visual cliff apparatus – a large step with a perspex cover over it.

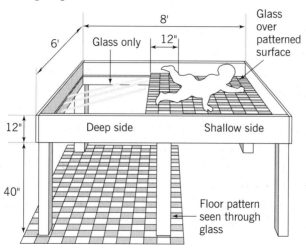

They tested babies between the ages of six and 14 months and found that they would not crawl onto the deep side. They claimed that this indicated that depth perception is innate. The problem was that babies can't crawl when they are born. In fact, they can't crawl until they are about four months of age. Does this indicate that depth perception may have been learned?

Although this study is somewhat inadequate, other research has shown that other species who are able to move almost from birth, for example day-old chicks, goat kids and lambs, would not go over to the deep side. If they were put on the deep side, they tended to freeze with fear. I have visions of researchers, sitting in fields, waiting for lambs to be born, and then running them into a laboratory and putting them on the deep side of the visual cliff. The 'freeze' may well have been the result of this trauma rather than the sight of the visual cliff!

Earlier we mentioned that studies into perceptual development have been done on animals, and these are the kind of studies which would be impossible on humans. They involve keeping animals in the dark and then investigating how much they are able to visually discriminate after a given period of time, compared to animals reared in the light. If there were different visual abilities between the two groups, this would indicate that visual perception must be learned rather than innate.

The problem with the original studies which kept animals in the dark was that the animals' visual 'machinery' did not develop properly. Post-mortem examination showed that the cells of the retina, and occasionally the optic nerve, had degenerated. Therefore other studies reared some animals in diffuse light, allowing the cells to develop, or kept them in a visually deprived or controlled environment where they had no experience of some stimuli, for example, horizontal lines. Needless to say, the visual abilities of the two groups of animals were very different. Studies such as the ones by Blakemore and Cooper (1966) showed that if kittens were visually deprived of, for example, the experience of horizontal lines, they were perceptually inferior to non-deprived kittens. An example of their behaviour was that they did not put their paws out to land when they were put onto a table, and they did not chase a horizontal stick when it moved up and down, but were able to play with a vertical one. Although some of their abilities improved with normal visual experience, they were not as effective as normally reared kittens.

None of these studies mentioned are really adequate as methods of investigating whether perception is innate or learned. It would be far better to have a person who had grown up without sight, and who had then been granted sight at an adult age, to ask them what sense they made of their environment. One such study was done by Gregory and Wallace (1963), who investigated the case of SB. He was 52 when he was given his sight after a corneal graft operation.

When bandages were first removed from his eyes, so that he was no longer blind, he heard the voice of the surgeon. He turned to the voice, and saw nothing but a blur. He realised that this must be a face, because of the voice, but he could not see it. He did not suddenly see the world of objects as we do when we open our eyes.

But within a few days he could use his eyes to good effect. He could walk along the hospital corridors without recourse to touch – he could even tell the time from a large wall clock, having all his life carried a pocket watch with no glass, so that he could feel the time from its hands. He would get up at dawn and watch from his window the cars and trucks pass by. He was delighted with his progress, which was extremely rapid.

When he left the hospital, we took him to London and showed him many things he never knew from touch, but he became curiously dispirited. At the zoo he was able to name most of the animals correctly, having stroked pet animals and enquired how other animals differed from the cats and dogs he knew by touch. He was also of course familiar with toys and models. He certainly used his previous knowledge from touch, and reports from sighted people to help him name objects by sight, which he did largely by seeking their characteristic features. But he found the world drab, and was upset by flaking paint and blemishes on things. He liked bright colours, but became depressed when the light faded. His depressions became marked, and general. He gradually gave up active living, and three years later he died.

From this case study, it is obvious that SB's perceptual abilities weren't as sophisticated as those of an adult with normal vision when he was first given his sight, and that he took some time to perceive objects with the same degree of accuracy as the majority of us. The problem is that he was not a naïve adult, as he had developed other perceptual skills, such as feeling objects, and he combined what he could see with what he felt in order to perceive and therefore identify objects in front of him.

CROSS-CULTURAL STUDIES

There is one final method that has been used to investigate the question of whether perceptual skills are innate or learned. This method has used what are known as cross-cultural studies. The idea here is to see whether people from different cultural groups perceive things in the same way. If they do, this would indicate that perception is a biological skill rather than something which is learned. It does make sense to look for comparisons when we think of the amount of cultural diversity there is on our planet, in terms of environment, lifestyle and beliefs. If perceptual skills are learned, then people from primitive tribes would not have the same learning experiences as white Europeans from developed cultures and the two groups would be unlikely to perceive things in the same way.

The other thing we need to consider before we look at cross-cultural studies is that many Westerners are guilty of considering themselves educationally superior, culturally more advanced and basically 'normal'. This is called ethnocentrism, the belief that we are the 'centre of the universe', the prototype of normality, and therefore that anyone else should be judged by our standards.

> **CORE STUDY LINK** – Tajfel showed that we make ethnocentric choices in favour of our 'own' group in order to create self-esteem from group membership.

Unfortunately, much psychological research is guilty of this ethnocentrism, as it was undertaken using white Western subjects, many of whom were middle-class, undergraduate, American, male students.

The method used to test members of different cultural groups is to use the same stimulus material in the form of pictures and to take the stimulus to the subjects.

One amusing piece of research, which actually took the subject to the stimulus, was done by Turnbull (1961). Bambuti pygmies live in the tropical rainforests of the Congo, where they are unable to see any distance in front of them due to the dense undergrowth. Consequently they have virtually no experience of looking at objects in the distance. Turnbull took one of the pygmies to an open plain and showed him a herd of buffalo a long way away. He identified the buffalo as insects and refused to believe that they were really buffalo. He became very distressed when he found that they appeared to increase in size in front of his eyes, as Turnbull took him closer to them. The only way the pygmy could deal with the situation was by telling himself that this was really due to witchcraft. (It's also worth bearing in mind ethical considerations here: perhaps this experience had long-term effects, perhaps even detrimental effects on the pygmy.)

One of the first studies where the stimulus was taken to the subjects was carried out by Rivers *et al.* (1901) on the Murray Islanders, who live on a group of islands between New Guinea and Australia. They were found to be less influenced by the Müller-Lyer illusion than English people. The reason for this was thought to be because they focused on the figure as a whole (including the arrowheads) rather than the shafts alone. Rivers believed this was due to something in their biological make-up which made them perceive things in a different way to the British.

Segall *et al.* (1963) undertook a study which took a number of years to investigate the cultural differences in perception. His subjects were taken from many different cultural groups, including Americans and Africans. He found, amongst other things, that Africans and Filipinos were less likely to fall for the Müller-Lyer Illusion than more Westernised cultural groups. Segall *et al.* concluded that there was a relationship between the physical environment inhabited by the subjects and their likelihood of being susceptible to visual illusions. As a result of this they came up with what is known as the 'carpentered world hypothesis'. According to Segall, we in the West live in a world full of right angles and straight lines, whereas other cultural groups live in environments where there are no straight lines or right angles. Instead, dwellings tend to be round huts with little or no symmetry. The conclusion was that we were, therefore, using our cultural experience to help us to try and interpret an ambiguous figure by changing the way that it is perceived.

There is, however, considerable research which has disputed these findings, claiming that other cultures who live in very different environments show no differences in their assessment of visual illusions. One such piece of research was undertaken by Gregor and McPherson (1965). They found that there was less difference in the responses of two groups of Australian aborigines when shown the Müller-Lyer illusion, despite one group living in a relatively carpentered environment and the other living in primitive conditions, outdoors.

These findings may be explained by the fact that some cultures are more familiar with elements of Western culture – namely, pictures. If you had never seen a picture or photograph before, you would probably find it fairly amazing and difficult to understand. We find that hard to believe, but to give you an idea of how hard it might be, if you have never seen a technical drawing before, you would find it really difficult to interpret, whereas someone who either designs or works with technical drawings every day would have no problem understanding them.

From the above findings, we realise that familiarity or lack of familiarity with an environment affects the way we interpret it. Returning to the idea of depth cues and constancies discussed about earlier, we use these all the time to make sense of what we see. If we are not familiar with them, we will misinterpret the stimulus and this will give supportive evidence that perceptual abilities are learned. This whole idea was addressed in the article by Deregowski (1972), where he considers whether people from different cultures see and interpret pictures in the same way.

Jan B. Deregowski (1972), 'Pictorial perception and culture'.
Scientific American, 227, 82–8.

The intention of the article is to present the findings from a series of cross-cultural studies, in order to answer the question: Do people from different cultures perceive pictures in the same way and if so, can we consider pictures to be a universal means of communication which go beyond language and culture?'

> **FOCUS ON THEMES** – cultural universals and the nature–nurture debate
>
> Cross-cultural studies are quasi-experiments where culture is observed as the independent variable and differences and similarities between cultures can be observed.
>
> If a behaviour is observed to be the same across cultures it is called a *cultural universal.* It can be assumed that, provided the cultures have not been 'contaminated' by exposure to each other, such behaviours are governed at least in part by biology. Similarly, if there are clear differences between cultures with regard to a behaviour or custom, then we can assume that this is as a result of environmental influence. Thus cross-cultural studies are seen as having an important contribution to make to the nature–nurture question.

Method

Deregowski's article is what is referred to as a research review. This means that he referred to previously conducted research in order to draw the findings together to establish whether or not the perception of drawings was innate or learned.

Deregowski used a number of different sources of information in order to gather evidence to answer his questions. He included the findings from experiments, together with anecdotal and empirical evidence, in his article.

> **FOCUS ON RESEARCH METHODS** – anecdotal and empirical evidence
>
> An anecdote is a short narrative or story of an incident. It is evidence based on a story either heard from someone else or recalled after an event. Anecdotes are subjective in nature, being told from one person's point of view. Anecdotal evidence is usually qualitative in nature, subjective and likely to be affected by the teller's attitudes and prejudices.
>
> Empirical evidence is evidence based on research carried out systematically, usually scientifically, providing quantitative data for analysis. The aim is to provide objective and scientific evidence to test hypotheses (although it is important to remember that even the most controlled experiments can still be affected by the biases of both experimenter and subject).

The conclusion that was drawn was that there were cultural differences in the perception of depth in the pictures. Africans did not read the depth cues in the pictures in the way that Westerners would. This suggests that we have to learn to perceive depth in pictures, so perception of pictures is not innate.

Anecdotal evidence

Deregowski describes a number of anecdotal reports from missionaries, explorers and anthropologists visiting remote cultures. An example of this comes from Mrs Donald Fraser (missionary teaching health care in Africa in the 1920s). She found that an African woman traced the outline of a profile of a head with her finger in order to understand it, but found it hard to understand why the head had only one eye. A further report attributed to Mrs Fraser described how, when a picture of an elephant was projected onto a sheet, the people present jumped up shouting and the ones nearest the picture ran out, as they all feared the elephant was alive. The chief was reported to have crept behind the sheet to find out if the animal had a body and let out a great roar when he discovered that it was only the thickness of the sheet.

> ### FOCUS ON THEMES – ethnocentrism
>
> As described earlier in this chapter, one of the problems with cross-cultural studies is ethnocentrism. This 'amusing' anecdote about how people ran away from the slide of an elephant is written in pretty condescending terms and could be interpreted as typical of the superior attitude of Western missionaries going abroad to 'educate the natives'. Should Deregowski have included this kind of anecdote in his work?

Empirical evidence

Deregowski describes a number of experiments carried out by William Hudson, a researcher based in Johannesburg in the 1960s. The first set of three studies considers whether there are differences between people in the way they perceive depth in drawings.

1. The pictures task

Hudson tested South African Bantu workers and other tribal and linguistic groups from different parts of Africa to see if they could identify the relative positions of objects, for example, a man, a tree, an elephant, an antelope, mountains, in a series of pictures, using three pictorial depth cues. A depth cue is a technique used to encourage a viewer to see depth in a flat, two-dimensional drawing.

These depth cues were:
• Familiar size – the same object will be drawn smaller if it is supposed to be further away. Also if you are aware of the relative size of objects, this acts

as a depth cue. If a drawing showed a cat and a house as being the same size, you would see the house as being in the background and the cat in the foreground.

- Overlap – a nearer object may obscure part of an object that is further away.
- Perspective – parallel lines appear to converge as they reach the horizon.

A three-dimensional perceiver would know the man is about to spear the antelope whereas a two-dimensional perceiver would say he was about to spear the elephant.

The subjects were asked what the man was doing, and which object on the picture was closer to the man. Depending on the accuracy of the answer and the ability of the subject to interpret the depth cues, the subject would have been classified as either a two-dimensional (2D) or three-dimensional (3D) perceiver. A 3D perceiver would be able to read the depth cues in the pictures.

The findings were that both children and adults from different educational and social levels found the depth cues in the pictures hard to interpret and were therefore classified as 2D perceivers (although Hudson's original data showed that schoolchildren showed much higher rates of three-dimensional perception than adults).

There were some problems with the pictures task, however, such as the omission of certain depth cues (for example, texture gradient), which could mean that the results were not valid and that the distinction between 2D and 3D perceivers was only a product of the task.

In order to ensure that the results were not simply due to the nature of the drawings, further studies were carried out.

2. The model-building test

Subjects were shown a drawing of two squares – one behind the other, connected by a single rod. They were then asked to make a model of what they saw using modelling clay and sticks. It was expected that the 2D perceivers would build flat models, and 3D perceivers would build cube-like models.

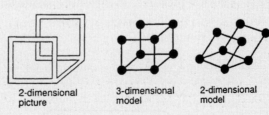

2-dimensional picture   3-dimensional model   2-dimensional model

Subjects who found it hard to see depth in pictures generally made a flat model, whereas most of the 3D perceivers made a cube-like model, as expected.

3. The tridents task

A group of Zambian schoolchildren had taken part in the the model-building test and had been categorised as either 2D or 3D perceivers. A further test was conducted to see whether they really were 2D and 3D perceivers, which would suggest that the distinction was a valid one.

The children were asked to copy two pictures: a simple trident figure and an ambiguous figure of a trident.

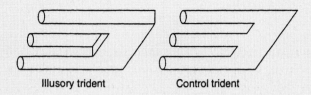

Illusory trident   Control trident

This figure is a type of optical illusion called an 'impossible figure'. This is because it appears to have two square prongs at one end, but the other end looks like three cylindrical prongs. It could not exist in three dimensions. Three-dimensional perceivers are more confused by the impossible figure and would find it harder to copy. In order to see the figure, the subjects had to lift a flap and then put it down again whilst they drew. It was expected that the 3D perceivers would have to hold up the flap for longer to try to make sense of the figure, so the time the flap was held up was timed by the researchers. The subjects also had to wait for ten seconds between lowering the flap and starting to draw.

The results, as expected, were that the 2D perceivers spent approximately the same amount of time looking at the two figures, whereas the 3D perceivers spent much longer looking at the ambiguous figure. These results support the idea that there were indeed those who read the picture as a 2D image and those who read it as a representation of a 3D figure, and that the distinction between the two was in fact a valid one.

The conclusion drawn from Hudson's work on 2D and 3D perceivers was that there were cultural differences in the perception of depth in the pictures. Africans did not read the depth cues in the pictures in the way that Westerners would. This suggests that we have to learn to perceive depth in pictures, so perception of pictures is not innate.

Having looked at depth perception, Deregowski went on to review findings relating to preferences for different styles of drawing. It was found that people who had difficulty interpreting pictures containing perspective had a tendency to prefer pictures that showed all the details of an object, known as a split-style drawing, even though the details would not really be able to be seen from the position of an observer.

Hudson showed African adults and children pictures of elephants. The first was an elephant seen from above (although this was not what you actually see if you are above an elephant, it was close to a real bird's-eye view) and the second was a split-style drawing. All but one said they preferred the split drawing, and the one who didn't said it was because the elephant was jumping around dangerously.

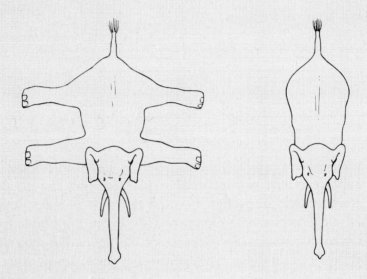

It is evident that certain cultures have a preference for this type of drawing, as demonstrated by the artistic styles of certain cultures, e.g. Indians of the north-western coast of North America and rock paintings in the caves of the Sahara. The split style is found in the drawings of children from all cultures.

Deregowski describes attempts by two anthropologists to explain where split-style drawings originated. Franz Boas sees them as a stage of ornamentation where 3D sculpture was adapted to fit on a bowl or bracelet, resulting in a split-style drawing. Deregowski suggests this is a complicated explanation and points out that it has no historical support. A second explanation comes from Claude Levi Strauss, who saw the split style as representing the split personality caused by the stress in mask cultures, where the pressure of taking on the role associated with the mask leads to split personalities and split-style art. (It seems surprising that Deregowski commented on how complicated Boas' theory was, but did not make the same criticism of that of Levi Strauss!)

Deregowski criticises both theories for their failure to acknowledge or explain the universality of the split style of drawing in children's art.

Is it just children who prefer split-style drawings?

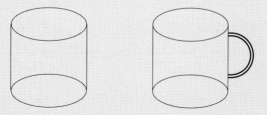

Which drawing of a coffee mug do you prefer? In the 'accurate' drawing, the handle is round the back. A split-style drawing (right) includes the handle. Look again at Hudson's two pictures of an elephant. Which one do you like best?

Deregowski suggests that although children in all societies have an aesthetic preference for split-style drawings, this preference is suppressed in most societies in favour of perspective drawings which convey information about the object more accurately. What Deregowski says is happening in the West is that perspective drawings are taught as, and therefore become, the preferred style as they are more efficient in communicating information than the more eye-pleasing split style of drawing.

Conclusion

Deregowski unequivocally states that to the question as to whether perception of drawings is a universal language, with pictures being perceived the same by all people and in all cultures, 'The answer is no'.

Commentary

Is the study valid? Are there differences in picture perception?

Although the article indicated that people from different cultures do not perceive and interpret pictures in the same way, some of the evidence is anecdotal and therefore possibly inaccurate. A number of evaluative points have been made about the empirical findings, which have looked at the nature of the materials and the way they are presented.

- The drawings used by Hudson were very simple and all but one lacked texture gradient. Unpublished research by Kingsley *et al.* found that by adding texture gradient to pictures the amount of three-dimensional answers increased from 54% to 64%.
- They also lacked binocular disparity and motion parallax, which we use for depth cues in real life (although no picture contains these two cues).

- They were also presented on paper, which was probably unfamiliar to some of the subjects and could have distracted them.
- Subjects were also spoken to via an interpreter and this means that misinterpretation on the part of both the subject and the researcher is a possibility. The language barriers between researcher and subject, as well as the possible misinterpretation of cultural differences in behaviour, can make cross-cultural studies problematic.

Key questions
1. What question was Deregowski trying to answer in his research review?
2. Describe what is wrong with using the descriptions given by the anthropologists and missionaries.
3. Explain how Hudson established the validity of his finding that some people see pictures in 2D and some see them in 3D.
4. What advantage does split-style drawing have over Western-style drawing?
5. Draw a split-style drawing of a hamster.

Example Answers are on page 453.

Further reading:
- Gregory, R. (1977), *Eye and Brain*, London: Weidenfeld and Nicolson.
- http://www.yorku.ca/eye/ is the joy of visual perception website, which you may find interesting.

Autism and the theory of mind

As children grow up in a social world it is important that they learn to understand the way social relationships, which are a feature of their lives from birth, operate. If they manage to master this aspect of growing up, they will be able to deal effectively with social interaction, no matter how complex, throughout their lives. The way they come to understand the world initially is through their social interaction with family members. It is here that most children learn what sort of behaviour is acceptable and what is not, although obviously this will vary from family to family. In fact, it is interesting to note that most children who have no developmental problems, seem to share an understanding of unwritten social rules.

Jean Piaget argued that children between the ages of two and seven years, who are in what he called the pre-operational stage, are very egocentric. To put it simply, they are centred on their own egos to the extent that they are unaware and unconcerned about others, because they do not understand that others are not the same as they are and may have different perspectives and different feelings. This is the difference between selfishness and self-centredness. Self-centredness is being centred on self, where all your thoughts and feelings focus on you, what you want, what you need, what you feel. Self-centredness is not the same as selfishness. Selfishness is where you know what effect you are having on others but choose to ignore it and simply gratify yourself, so in some respects selfishness is much worse than self-centredness.

An example of how egocentricity influences the behaviour of small children can often be seen in a supermarket. Have you ever noticed when you are waiting in the checkout queue, the little child hanging about in front of you. Mother is there, trying to unpack a huge pile of food from the supermarket trolley, with a tiny baby in a sling, crying! She is obviously fraught and wanting to escape and, the next thing you know, the toddler is whining, 'I want some sweeties.' This whining gets more and more insistent until he is having a full-blown tantrum, lying on the floor, screaming and wailing and gnashing his teeth. Although you may feel like physically ejecting him from your vicinity, remember Piaget would argue that he has absolutely no idea how his mother feels and that is why he is behaving in this way.

CORE STUDY LINK – the Samuel and Bryant study of conservation in pre-operational children, looks at another aspect of children's development (see p. 183).

Piaget claimed that this kind of egocentrism (or self-centredness) continues until the child is leaving the pre-operational stage, which he suggested was approximately seven years of age. However, later research has indicated that children as young as four have begun to see things from the point of view of others. The big problem with much of the early research on children's development was that the children were often tested in unfamiliar or unnatural situations.

FOCUS ON RESEARCH METHODS – naturalistic environmnets

Conducting research in an unfamiliar environment is likely to produce results which may be caused by the design, rather than being the result of the manipulation of the independent variable.

The best idea would be to look at the child in their normal environment, and, bearing in mind the family environment will have the most influence on a young child, it would make sense to carry out this kind of research in the child's own home. In fact, Hinde (1987) argued that unless we look at relationships in their social and cultural contexts, they will have little meaning as we will be unaware that some behaviours, which may appear unusual out of context, would actually have a great deal of meaning in the relevant environment.

Considerable research has questioned the lack of social awareness suggested by Piaget. If children really are totally egocentric, they are unlikely even to be aware of the moods of other people. However, researchers such as Stern (1977) have suggested that this awareness occurs much earlier. Stern noticed that children as young as one year can tune in to the moods of others. We have all seen instances where a baby will cry if the mother cries, and laugh if the mother laughs. Stern (1977) called this ability 'affective tuning' and claimed that it becomes more highly developed during the second and third years of the child's life. It seems that they are extremely interested in emotional states and ready and willing to learn about them, and, more to the point, that this is a normal developmental process which is generated by biologically hard-wired tendencies. This suggests that children have an innate predisposition to learn about the emotions of other people and to develop an awareness of what other people are thinking. When children have mastered this ability, they will have developed what is known as 'a theory of mind'.

The way that researchers have investigated the theory of mind is by looking at children's abilities to understand false beliefs. One of the original studies was that undertaken by Heinz Wimmer and Josef Perner (1983) and involved a small boy called Maxi and a bar of chocolate. The story required children of different ages to attribute a false belief to another person and was acted out with dolls. The story went something like this.

Maxi puts his chocolate in a red cupboard and then goes to play outside. Unknown to Maxi, his mother moves the chocolate to a blue cupboard. Maxi then comes back from playing and wants to get his chocolate. A child who has observed this will be asked, 'Where will Maxi look for the chocolate when he comes back?'

Obviously the correct answer is the red cupboard, because that is where Maxi put it and where he believes it still is. If the child has an understanding of false beliefs, he will realise that Maxi will have a false belief as to where his chocolate will be found. If, on the other hand, the child does not understand that people can see things differently from the way that he sees them, he will answer that Maxi will look for the chocolate in the blue cupboard because that is where it really is.

Wimmer and Perner found that all children any younger than four years of age typically said that Maxi would look in the blue cupboard. This indicated that they could not take into account the fact that Maxi did not know that the chocolate has been moved.

Having an idea of how children discover the mind, and how important this is to their social functioning, we can imagine how awful it must be for a child who has no concept of other people's minds. If they are unaware that other people have thoughts and beliefs which are totally different from their own, they will be unable to predict what other people feel and how they will react to different situations. Imagine being unable to assess how someone is responding to you when you meet them? How would you feel if you were not sure whether they liked you or not, or whether they were angry, upset or bored with your company? Under normal circumstances, having a theory of mind would help you in the following interaction.

> 'Do you like my new dress, Miriam?' squeaked Edna, as she wrestled with the buttons at the front of the vivid purple dress. 'I think it is soooo sexy, and I love the way the front shows off my cleavage.' Miriam grimaced. The buttons looked like they were on maximum tension, hanging on to both sides of the dress and trying to hold back the flow of excess flesh between them. One more inhalation of breath would result in the whole row just popping off and projecting across the other side of the room. As for the cleavage, it was more like two giant marshmallows trying to escape from the tight line of the bodice. If she bent over, they would escape, projecting out and smothering the top of the dress. And why that colour? It would make someone with even the strongest constitution feel nauseous.
>
> 'Yes, it looks lovely!'

Now imagine the same situation, but in this instance Miriam has no theory of mind. Her answer would have been something along the lines of, 'It looks absolutely awful. You are much too fat to wear it and the buttons look like they you are about to burst. And the colour makes me feel sick!'

What would Edna's response be like? She would either become extremely upset or incredibly angry; but Miriam would have no concept of what her response would be because she had simply told Edna the truth.

There is one group of children who rarely seem to develop any sort of theory of mind – autistic children – and this is the next topic we will consider.

WHAT IS AUTISM?

Autism is often referred to as a communication disorder. It is characterised by three main features, which are problems in social interaction, problems with communication and restricted imagination or inflexibility of thought (Scott, 2003). Having considered the necessity to be able to communicate and understand the thoughts and feelings of others, and having an understanding of how important it is to be flexible in our behaviours, you will probably realise how a problem with these core skills will produce significant difficulties for autistics.

Autism, however, is a relatively rare condition, affecting only one or two children in every thousand (Frith, 1993). Although we hear a great deal more about autism and the prevalence of autistic spectrum disorders, much of this is to do with the syndrome (collection of symptoms) being in the public eye, partially as a result of the MMR vaccine and partially to do with better diagnosis.

The ratio of boys to girls with autism is estimated at 3:1, but apart from this difference autism is a disorder that is found across all socio-economic classes and across all racial and ethnic groups. People who are diagnosed as being on the autistic spectrum will have a tremendous variation in the degree to which they are affected. This means that no two children with the disorder will be totally alike, as some have little or no speech whilst others may have fluent speech, some may shy away from social contact whilst others will tolerate considerable interaction. This makes the disorder difficult to identify because of the extremes that are seen.

However, a child on the more extreme end of the autistic spectrum is likely to suffer from severe disabilities which will continue into adulthood. Thus autism is not simply a childhood disorder, but rather one which may extend the dependence we associate with childhood across the adult lives of people with autism, leaving families and authorities to deal with those who need lifelong care.

Autism is often associated with mental retardation, and this intensifies the need for those with autism to be under the supervision of people who can look out for their welfare. This is not always the case, however, and many people diagnosed with autism have average, or even above-average, IQ in some skill areas.

> **CORE STUDY LINK** – for an explanation of IQ, see the Gould study (p. 323).

Oliver Sacks (1995) has written about Temple Grandin, an autistic adult who holds a PhD. in animal sciences, teaches at Colorado state university and runs her own business. Temple has developed ways of coping with the symptoms of her autism and is able to live a full and independent life, although it has to be pointed out that her social skills remain highly impaired – she chooses to live alone, and admits she has a better understanding of the feelings of cattle than she has of the feelings of her fellow humans. The way she deals with human interaction is to refer consciously to a kind of database in her memory which has stored factual information about how to behave and respond rather than having the kind of innate skills that most of us have.

DIAGNOSIS AND SYMPTOMS

Although autism was first recognised in 1943 by Kanner, it was not accepted as an official diagnosis until 1980. Until this point it had been considered a type of childhood schizophrenia – the 'aloneness' of the autistic child is very like the behaviour of people with schizophrenia, whose disordered thought cuts them off from others. However, it became clear that this was not the case, as autistic children do not develop schizophrenic symptoms as adults.

The criteria for diagnosis are based on the four major features of autism originally identified by Kanner:

i   inability to form relationships with other people
ii lack of spontaneous play, especially pretend-play
iii serious abnormalities in the development of language and communication
iv obsessive insistence on particular routines or interests.

Here are some examples of these:

The inability to form relationships with other people

The bond between parent/caregiver and child develops in normal children very early on. Babies make eye contact with their parents when being fed, they cry for attention or to be picked up, they smile from about four weeks of age, they are active in their communication with parents and quickly learn how a smile, giggle or happy scream can draw attention from others. From about seven months they develop stranger fear and separation anxiety, showing that they have developed emotional attachments.

 CORE STUDY LINK – for information on emotional attachments, see the Hodges and Tizard study (p. 219).

Autistic children do not develop in this way. Those on the extreme end of the spectrum do not seek attention as babies unless they are uncomfortable or wet. They do not make eye contact, even seeming to look through you rather than at you. They do not smile, and they appear to be unaware of others. Not until they are two or three do they form some sort of attachment to their caregivers/parents, and even then this may not be of the same quality as a normal child–parent bond.

The lack of spontaneous play, especially pretend-play

An autistic child will join in and play only if an adult insists. They usually play alone, and tend to focus on repetitive actions with an object, e.g. spinning a hoop repeatedly on their arm, passing keys repeatedly from one hand to the other. They do not engage in what is called socio-dramatic play, or pretend-play, such as playing house, pretending to be superman or dressing up, whereas normal children do this and also engage in joint games where they take on different roles and act out scenarios together, using their imaginations and social skills to move the plot forward.

Serious abnormalities in the development of language and communication

Lack of eye contact in children with autism is often the first indication of their poor communication skills. Their language development is very slow, and in fact 50% of people with autism never learn to speak. The language they do develop may differ from the normal use of language, for instance, they may repeat what others say. The child is not responding to the meaning of what is being said, simply repeating the words. This is known as echolalia. If all the child does is repeat back parrot-fashion what you have said, then the conversation is non-existent.

These difficulties with play and communication lead to severe social difficulties for the autistic child. At their most extreme, the child can be left in total isolation, in an apparently impenetrable world of their own.

An obsessive insistence on particular routines or interests

If you watch the film *Rainman* you will see Dustin Hoffman giving a very good portrayal of an autistic adult. The character is very upset by any change in his routine; any alteration, however small, can set off a person with autism in an inexplicable rage, where they will scream wildly, lash out and can be very difficult to calm down. Their resistance to any change, and their extremely negative responses to such changes in routine, can make living and dealing with autistic adults and children very challenging.

In the film 'Rainman', Dustin Hoffman accurately portrayed the fear and discomfort of an autistic subjected to a change in routine.

This need for sameness is an obsession for the autistic person. The world must seem like a very strange place to a person unable to fully engage in or understand the social world of others. It is believed that they use routines as a way keeping their environment under control. In fact many of the ritualistic and repetitive actions of autistics, such as twiddling objects or tapping, are simply a way to reduce their overarousal and consequent discomfort by focusing on one small and apparently meaningless action.

In addition to obsession with routine, children and adults develop obsessions with specific tasks or objects. As children in the playground, we were all familiar with the idea of crazes, such as collecting and swapping football stickers, playing marbles, etc. The obsessions of the autistic person are extreme versions of this type of behaviour. They become focused on one particular activity or interest, such as the weather, train timetables, even types of burglar alarm system, and the level of detailed and complex knowledge acquired about their interest can be mind-boggling.

It may be through such enthusiasms that one in ten people with autism seem to develop a particular skill or gift. Baron-Cohen calls these 'islets of ability'. The autistic person paradoxically develops skills which normal people cannot, such as playing a piece of music immediately after hearing it, being able to draw architecturally detailed drawings of buildings from memory, or specific and unusual mathematical skills, such as the card-counting skill that Raymond has in *Rainman*. A real-life example comes from Oliver Sacks (1985). He described the particular skills of John and Michael, 26-year-old twins with autism. They both had a remarkable memory for digits and could remember up to 300 digits with ease, even though they could not manage simple addition or subtraction. If you gave them a date in the past or future they could immediately tell you on what day of the week it would fall.

Whilst the existence of such skills is academically fascinating, and attracts a great deal of attention, it is not usually the case that they are of any benefit to the individual who possesses them.

The intriguing puzzle of autism has attracted a great deal of research. The particular study we are going to look at considers whether or not there is a core deficit of autism which is common to all people with autism and which could help explain why people with autism behave the way they do. Any discovery of a core deficit would also help in the diagnosis of autism in the future.

Simon Baron-Cohen, Alan. M. Leslie and Uta Frith (1985), *Does the autistic child have a theory of mind?*
Cognition, 21, 37–46

Background

Baron-Cohen *et al.* take a cognitive view, that there is a deficiency in the development of a way of thinking which means that autistic children are unable to comprehend and therefore fully engage in the social world. They describe this deficiency as lacking a theory of mind.

> ### *KEY CONCEPT* – theory of mind
>
> If you have a theory of mind this means you are able to recognise that mental states exist. That is, you recognise that both you and other people have ideas, beliefs and thoughts about the world, and that these thoughts, beliefs and ideas may differ from person to person. You understand that minds exist.
>
> If you lack a theory of mind this means you lack the ability to think about mental states. This is also known as 'mind-blindness', the inability to attribute belief states to oneself and others. The consequence of this is that you believe that everyone knows what you know.

Baron-Cohen and Bolton demonstrate how children's fiction confuses autistic children. They give the example of the story of Snow White. As you will remember, filled with jealousy now that she is no longer the fairest in the land, Snow White's evil stepmother tries to have Snow White killed so that once again she will be the most beautiful. Towards the end of the story it seems that she has succeeded. In her disguise as a nice old pedlar, she gets Snow White to bite the poisoned half of an apple, and Snow White collapses, apparently dead. Now, it only makes sense that Snow White eats the poisoned apple if you believe that she does not know that it's poisoned, that she thinks it is a delicious juicy apple offered to her by the nice old lady. In other words, Snow White eats the apple because she has a false belief. The readers know that this nice old lady is actually the wicked stepmother and that the apple is intended to get rid of Snow White. Autistic children do not understand that they and Snow White believe different things, and assume that since they know the apple is poisoned, Snow White must also know, so it makes no sense to them that she eats it.

The autistic child is fooled by fiction because they lack a theory of mind. The fact that they do not recognise another's thoughts as different from their own can be clearly seen in the Snow White example. Using this idea as a technique to test theory of mind in children, Wimmer and Perner originally explored the development of theory of mind using what they called the Maxi doll test. Baron-Cohen took the same idea and developed a shorter test with the intention of exploring the existence of a theory of mind in autistic children. Using this test, Baron-Cohen *et al.* were able to operationalise (measure) the variable, theory of mind.

Aim

In their study, Baron-Cohen *et al.* were aiming to show that the lack of theory of mind was a core deficit in all autistic children. So the title of this study gives us their research question: Does the autistic child have a theory of mind?

Method

Design

The study uses the experimental method. It is a quasi-experiment.

Independent variable: whether the child had autism, Down's syndrome or was 'normal'.

Dependent variable: whether or not the child had a theory of mind. This was operationalised by whether or not the child got the belief question in the Sally-Anne test right.

Subjects

Sixty-one children were tested: 20 children with autism, 14 children with Down's syndrome and 27 normal children.

Type of child	Mean chronological age	Mean verbal mental age	Mean non-verbal mental age
Autistic	11 years 11 months	5 years 5 months	9 years 3 months
Down's	10 years 11 months	2 years 11 months	5 years 11 months
Normal	4 years 5 months	4 years 5 months	4 years 5 months

The Down's syndrome and autistic children were tested prior to the study to establish their average verbal and non-verbal mental ages. It was assumed that the normal children's average mental ages would be equivalent to their age in years.

The children were selected according to their verbal mental ages. This was for two reasons:
- autistic children's language development is retarded and it would be unfair to compare them with children of the same chronological age. To complete the Sally-Anne test, a certain level of linguistic competence was necessary. With their communication problems, this might further disadvantage the autistic children.

- to ensure that linguistic skill did not confound the study, the autistic children were selected to have a higher level of linguistic ability. Thus if this was to be an advantage, it should favour the autistic children.

Conditions

The three groups of children give us the three conditions for this study. The autistic children are the experimental condition. The other two groups act as control (comparison) groups. The normal children were used to show any difference from the norm in the autistic children's performance, and the Down's syndrome group was used to prevent mental retardation from becoming a confounding variable. If there was a difference between the normal and autistic children, two variables could account for this, either autism or mental retardation.

In order to isolate autism as the independent variable it was necessary to introduce a group to cancel out the effects of mental retardation on the findings. This was why the Down's syndrome children were used, as this syndrome is associated with mental retardation. If the Down's syndrome children performed similarly to the autistic children (both differed in a similar way from the normal children), then this would suggest mental retardation and not autism was causing the results. If, on the other hand, the autistic children differed from the norm and the Down's syndrome children were more in line with the normal children's performance, this would point to the findings being a result of autism.

Apparatus

A table with a chair on one side for the subject and another chair on the other side for the researcher. On the table were placed two dolls, 'Sally' and 'Anne'. In front of the Sally doll was a basket, with a lid, and a marble. In front of the Anne doll was a box, also with a lid.

Procedure

Each child was tested alone, seated at the table opposite the researcher. They were then tested using the Sally-Anne test.

The researcher told the child that the first doll with the basket was called Sally, and the second doll was called Anne, who had a box. The child was then asked the first of four questions, the naming question: 'Which doll is Sally and which one is Anne?'

The researcher then went on to explain that Sally has a marble. Sally puts the marble in her basket and then 'goes out of the room'. While Sally is away, Anne takes the marble out of Sally's basket and puts it in her box. This is, of course, all acted out by the researcher. Sally returns. Now the child is asked: 'Where will Sally look for her marble?' This is the belief question. It is the critical question in this study (a critical question is one by which we will measure the dependent variable).

The right answer is 'in her basket', or to point to the basket. Sally should look there because that is where she believes she has left her marble. To get the question right, however, the child must realise that Sally has a different belief from theirs, and that Sally has a false belief about where her marble is. In other words, to get the right answer, the child must have a theory of mind. The wrong answer, of course, given by children who lack a theory of mind, is 'in the box', or to point to the box.

Two control questions were also asked: the reality question: 'Where is the marble really?' and the memory question: 'Where was the marble in the beginning?' These last two questions are intended to ensure that the child is actually aware of what is going on. If the child gets these questions wrong, we would have to assume that the test is beyond the capability of the child.

The child was then tested a second time, using the same questions, but this time hiding the marble in the researcher's pocket. Thus each child had the possibility of giving either two correct answers, one right and one wrong answer or two wrong answers.

Results

The results were presented quantitatively as percentages of each condition giving the correct response to the questions.

	Naming?	Reality?	Memory?	Belief?	Actual no. giving correct answer
Autistic	100%	100%	100%	20%	4/20
Down's	100%	100%	100%	86%	12/14
Normal	100%	100%	100%	85%	23/27

From the responses to the naming, reality and memory questions, it is clear that all the children tested had a clear understanding of the test. For the belief question, however, we can see that the children with autism performed very differently from the other two groups of children. Only 20% (4/20) of them answered this question correctly, compared to around 85% of all the other children. The other 80% (16/20) of autistic children had pointed to where the marble really was (box or pocket) each time.

Inferential statistics showed that the autistic children performed significantly differently on the belief question at a significance level of $p < 0.001$. This means that the probability of the results being due to chance are less than one in a thousand. It can therefore be argued that it is statistically more likely for the results to be due to the IV, autism, than to chance or random factors.

Discussion

All the children managed to answer the control questions correctly, which gives evidence that they were aware of what was going on in the study and understood that the marble had been moved. The belief question was the only one which caused problems, in particular for the autistic children. This suggests that the majority of the autistic children did not have a theory of mind.

The interesting factor in these results is that some of the autistic children could answer the belief question correctly, and some of the children in the other groups couldn't. This indicates that while the results lean towards the direction of supporting the hypothesis that the autistic child lacks a theory of mind, they are inconclusive since this is not true of some autistic children.

What we may conclude is that there is evidence that theory of mind is under-developed in autistic children, but not that a lack of theory of mind is a core deficit in autism.

Commentary

Is the study useful?

In terms of understanding the bemusing behaviours of people with autism, that they may lack a theory of mind is a useful concept.

If the autistic person can't 'read' the other person (i.e. can't imagine what they may be thinking), this makes it difficult for them to understand the behaviour of others. Lacking a theory of mind may explain why emotions such as embarrassment, which relies on social understanding in many cases, may never be understood by those with autism. You cannot worry what other people may think of you if you don't have a theory of mind.

The poor communication skills of autistic people may also be explained by a lack of theory of mind. We communicate in order to make our desires, intentions and needs known to others. If autistic people believe that we already share knowledge of these, what would be the need to communicate them?

Just as those with autism have difficulty with other's thoughts, children with autism cannot understand the meaning of deception, and this may leave them 'wide open to potential exploitation' (Baron-Cohen and Bolton). This has implications for those responsible for the welfare of these vulnerable children.

Is the study ecologically valid?

Given that the study tests children individually in the lab (see Focus on research methods regarding the testing of children), it is low in ecological validity. Critics of the study also pointed out that far from getting the answer wrong, it could be that the autistic children were just being accurate – dolls can't think. They suggest that the use of dolls lacks ecological validity and forced the autistic children to make errors in the test. However, this does not explain why the autistic children pointed to the box rather than not answering the question or even saying 'dolls don't think'. Indeed, further work by Leslie and Frith (1988) using actual people instead of dolls refuted this criticism, as autistic children made the same errors in the 'human Sally and Anne' trial.

Which psychological approach is illustrated in this study?

Of all the core studies, this one demonstrates that research can be used to illustrate a number of different perspectives. First, since it is about autism, this study is an example of abnormal psychology, and in the syllabus could just as easily be in the individual differences section. The study considers the development of theory of mind, and could also happily sit in the developmental psychology section. However, the specification places this study in the cognitive psychology section.

What this study shows us about cognitive processes is that theory of mind is a key factor in helping us make sense of our social world. Most normal children have developed a theory of mind by the age of four years and five months. We also learn that children with autism have an underdeveloped theory of mind and that this can account for their retarded language and communication skills and also for their poor understanding of emotions and social behaviour.

Is the study ethical?

FOCUS ON RESEARCH METHODS – this study illustrates both practical and ethical issues concerning the testing of children.

Practical issues
Children are often tested individually, under laboratory conditions, sometimes by an adult they are not familiar with. This set-up is designed to ensure that children do not contaminate one another's results, that they do not simple copy a friend's answers or respond to peer pressure. However, it is not usual for children to be out of their social environment and in the lab with a stranger. Therefore, we have to question the ecological validity of this method of testing children.

Ethical issues
Can informed consent be obtained from children? Can those with Down's syndrome/autism give their informed consent? Parental consent is usually sought. At what age do you think a child should be asked to give their consent? If a parent gives consent but a child does not, should the child be tested? Do you think the children have the right to withdraw? What about debriefing? Could the children in this study be debriefed?

● **Key questions**
1. Explain what is meant by a theory of mind.
2. Describe the Sally-Anne test.
3. In the Sally-Anne test, what could the autistic children not do?
4. Describe two features of autism that can be explained by the fact that autistic children have an underdeveloped theory of mind.
5. How do you think the findings of this study might help teachers or parents and autistic children?

Example Answers are on page 454.

● **Further reading:**
- Baron-Cohen, S., Cosmides, L. and Tooby, J. (1997), *Mindblindness: An Essay on Autism and Theory of Mind*, Cambridge, MA: MIT Press.
- Baron-Cohen, S. and Bolton, P. (1993), *Autism: The Facts*, Oxford: Oxford University Press.
- Frith, U. (2002), *Autism: Explaining the Enigma*, Oxford: Blackwell.
- Haddon, M. (2003) *The Curious Incident of the Dog in the Night-time*. London: Jonathan Cape. A brilliant novel written from the point of view of a young boy with Asberger Syndrome (which falls at the mild end of the Autistic Spectrum).
- Wilde Astington, J. (1994), *The Child's Discovery of the Mind*, London: Fontana Press.

Language

The last area of cognition that we are going to consider is language, and the core study in this topic area focuses on two interesting questions. The first question is whether the ability to learn language is unique to humans, and the second focuses on the nature–nurture debate and how far language is pre-programmed or hard-wired into the human brain, or whether it is dependent on the environment in which the child is raised.

We are born with certain abilities, but these abilities improve as we get older as a result of learning. However, some of these abilities not only involve learning experiences but also require physical maturity in order for them to reach the level of skill we have as an adult. For example, children cannot walk when they are first born, although they are born with a reflex which allows them, if supported, to move their legs as if they can walk. The problem is that they cannot fully support their own weight on their legs and their necks are not strong enough to support their heads. They are unlikely to be able to walk before ten months of age and often they may be over a year old before they launch themselves into action without needing to hold on to things. By this stage their physical body will have developed sufficiently to allow them to master this skill.

The development of language follows a very similar route because a baby is born with the ability to make a noise – it can cry! However, even if it was familiar with language, understood it and knew the words it wanted to say, it could not speak as soon as it was born because its mouth is not the right shape to do so.

When we are born our tongue is too big and our palate is too low. As we mature, the relative sizes of these parts will change and soon we are able to make the sounds which are the first steps in developing language.

A summary of the stages of language development in human infants between the ages of 0 and two

Age	Approx. two months
Stage	Cooing (pre-linguistic child)
Description	Baby makes 'ooh' and 'aah' sounds, which generally signal pleasure or excitement.
Nature or nurture?	Nature – cooing is a 'cultural universal', that is, it occurs in all babies in all cultures at approximately the same stage, and this implies that the behaviour is innate.
Age	Approx. six months
stage	Reduplicated babbling (pre-linguistic child)
Description	Babies babble in all sounds, even those not present in the language spoken around them. The sounds are repeated e.g. 'mamama' or 'dadada'.
Nature or nurture?	Nature – supported by the argument that even profoundly deaf babies babble at this time and in this way. This is also a cultural universal.
Age	Approx. 11 months
Stage	Jargon babbling (pre-linguistic child)
Descripton	Babbling changes to use only the sounds present in the language to which the child is exposed. This process of reducing the sounds used to babble in is known as 'phonemic contraction'. The child babbles in sentence patterns and rhythms (knows the tune but doesn't yet know the words).
Nature or nurture?	Nature – emergence of this type of babbling in children at the same age universally suggests some inborn potential is maturing in the child.
	Nurture – phonemic contraction and copying sentence rhythm and inflections are only possible if the child has been exposed in the environment to spoken language. The fact that deaf babies do not babble in this way, and,

in fact, stop babbling altogether at about nine months, shows the importance of environmental influence at this stage of development.

Age	Approx. 1 year
Stage	One-word stage
Description	Children produce single words, with names of objects usually being the first words to appear, tending to centre on things that are important to the baby, such as food, animals and toys. Using single words, the baby can convey more than the meaning of the word itself. This use of one word to represent a whole concept is called 'holophrastic speech'. Depending on the context, if a child says 'milk' this could mean, 'That is milk', 'I want some milk', 'The cat is drinking its milk', or even, as the child upturns its glass on the table, 'Oops, I appear to have accidentally spilled my milk, Daddy'.
Nature or nurture?	Nature – emergence of this stage in children at the same age universally suggests some inborn potential is maturing in the child. Nurture – the words acquired by the child are dependent on the language they are exposed to. For example, a child growing up in a German-speaking environment will not refer to milk as 'lait', as a similar French child would.
Age	Towards the end of the child's second year
Stage	Two-word stage
Description	Combining words to make two-word utterances enables the child to be clearer about the meaning of what is being said. Combining words to create novel utterances or extend the meaning of utterances is called creativity. These two-word utterances again convey more meaning than you think. For example, 'That car' may mean, 'That is a car', with 'is' and 'a' left out; this omission of the little words is typical at this stage. The structure of these two-word utterances led to early researchers describing them as 'telegraphic speech'.*

*Telegrams were communications sent by morse code, each letter tapped in laboriously by the operator. As a result, the sender paid by the word, so to save money telegrams developed their own language, in the same way that text messaging has a language of its own. For example, instead of sending, 'I'll see you on Sunday afternoon', you might send, 'See Sun afternoon'. The most famous example of this (and it may be a myth that it was ever used) is the message 'Stop Press!' sent by newspaper journalists who wanted the printing presses to be halted in order for their hot story to take preference.

Note: Children develop the type of two-word utterances in a universal sequence:
Agent + Action (Daddy run)
Action + Object (Eat biscuit)
Location (Mummy chair)
Possession (My ball)

Nature or nurture?

Nature – the sequence of the development from one- to two-word utterances in children at the same age universally suggests some inborn potential is maturing in the child. This is also supported by the fact that the development of the type of two-word utterance also occurs universally, again illustrating the importance of maturation in the development of language.

Nurture – the words acquired by the child are again dependent on the language they are exposed to.

From the age of three, children continue to learn new words, increasing their vocabulary further and allowing them to express themselves more effectively. They also continue to develop an understanding of grammatical rules.

One of the studies which actually gives an indication of just how much our vocabulary increases over the first years of our lives, and how much learning we undertake without realising, was carried out by Seashore and Eckerson (1940). They concluded that 19-year-old college students had a vocabulary in the region of 150,000 (other samples have estimated as many as 250,000). This means that between the ages of one and 19 we have to learn, on average, 21 words a day! This means that we are on our way to being equipped to produce complex sentences, providing that we master syntax.

Syntax refers to rules of grammar, such as using the pronoun 'he' for a male or adding an 's' to a noun to make it plural. Syntax also dictates the structure of utterances, commonly referred to as word order. Even in the two-word stage it is apparent that children have some understanding of word order, for example a child will say 'my mummy' rather than 'mummy my'. From the age of three, children's utterances increase in length and complexity, and up until the age of six or seven, children will be learning to master all the rules of grammar.

This involves applying the rules with increasing effectiveness. Interestingly, the rules are ones the child has deduced and inferred rather than rules that have been formally taught. We can see the rules the child is using in the kind of errors they make, which are particularly obvious because English is not a completely regular language and has exceptions to the general rules of grammar. These errors are called 'virtuous errors', because if English were regular, the child would be getting it right. For example, the child may have deduced that to talk about something that has already happened, they need to add 'ed' to the verb (obviously they don't analyse it exactly in these terms), so 'I look' would become 'I looked'. However, the verb 'to run' is irregular, and the child might say 'I runned', because he/she is over-generalising the rule.

Plural forming also produces some errors, as the rule 'add "s" to make a plural' doesn't always work. For instance, 'cat' becomes 'cats', but we don't refer to more than one sheep as 'sheeps'. One of the nicest examples of this was given by Hetherington and Parke (1986), when they described a child they knew who 'used the word "clothes" and insisted on calling one piece of clothing a "clo"'.

Parents are not unduly concerned about these errors, as the important thing is to get the meaning of the message across, and 'I runned' achieves this. It is only later that the child will get formal instruction on the irregularities of the language that they haven't managed to pick up for themselves along the way.

SO DO WE DEVELOP LANGUAGE AS A RESULT OF NATURE OR NURTURE?

The easy answer to this question is that language development relies on both nature and nurture. Certainly the universal sequence and timing of the stages of language development indicate the key role of nature in the process. Children with the most diverse levels of cognitive ability still manage to master the complex rules of grammar with little or no problem and no formal teaching. This should really reinforce the idea that there must be some sort of pre-programming to allow this level of learning to take place. Perhaps we have a kind of language 'processing box', which, once it starts to work, allows us to extract the rules of grammar of our native language without any conscious effort on our part. This suggests that the physical construction of our brains, which, through maturation seem to be hard-wired to assist language development, are important precursors for the development of human language.

But what about the role of nurture? Does the processing box work by simply being placed within earshot of a television or radio which emits the spoken word? It seems that this is not the case, as evidence has indicated that children only develop language provided they are given the opportunity to interact with other children or adults. We know this from studies of children who have been raised without language.

One study by Bard and Sachs (1977) looked at whether children simply pick up language from hearing it spoken around them. They studied a child called Jim whose parents were both deaf, although he had normal hearing. The parents used sign language to each other, but they did not use it with him. He listened to the radio and watched television, so he heard spoken language regularly, but he was unable to pick up the rules of grammar from passively experiencing language. His speech was seriously retarded and was not corrected until he started sessions with a speech therapist at the age of about 3½. Fortunately, his speech from then on improved dramatically. This study provides us with evidence that we need to talk with other people in order for normal linguistic skills to develop, and shows that nurture is important.

It seems that adults alter their use of language when talking to young children by simplifying it – using what is known as 'motherese'. It seems to be unconscious, although we all do it. Obviously, whatever the reason for doing it, it is easier for children to understand. It goes without saying that mothers and caretakers play a particularly important role in the child's language development, and the kind of conversations they have with babies seem to follow a pattern:

- they hold one-way conversations (before the child has started to speak).
- they take turns with the baby, first with sounds, then with words, so that they respond to the baby's noise by making one back, and then the baby will make the next noise (this seemingly simple activity is an important part of the socialisation process).

Adults interacting with very young children frequently interpret and often expand what the child says, for example, if the child says, 'My book', the mother might respond by saying, 'Yes, that's your red book over on the table.' They will describe objects surrounding the child and explain things in simple terms, and they also answer questions with simple language. These basic activities are the building blocks to language development, and it seems that without them children's linguistic skills fail to develop at the usual rate. In fact, children who have delayed language are often found to have parents who have not followed these seemingly natural patterns of response.

In 1967 Lenneberg suggested that there was what he called a critical period for language development and language learning. By this he meant that learning would take place with ease during a certain period of time but after the critical period learning language would become much harder. He pointed out that the stages of linguistic development were both uniform and universal, which could only mean that children are somehow biologically prepared for language. He justified this critical period by suggesting that it was controlled by physical changes in the brain and maintained that up to puberty it was possible to learn language easily, but after puberty it would cause problems. It seems that there is no convincing evidence for the physical changes in the brain and there are many instances of adults who move abroad, learning new languages fluently with little effort.

One study which gives some support to Lenneberg's ideas was the case of Genie, a child who was found in Los Angeles in 1970. She was discovered when she was 13, although she looked about eight. She had been kept in a small room from the age of 20 months and punished if she made any noise. She was confined to a small curtained room and strapped to a bed or a 'potty chair', so she could not walk around or interact with other people. In fact, she was beaten if she made any noise and so she grew up in an environment of extreme social and physical deprivation. Her case was reported by Curtiss (1977) as she was an ideal subject for an in-depth case study on late language development. According to Lenneberg, Genie had passed the critical period and therefore should have had tremendous problems learning language. However, she did learn a kind of primitive language, although her speech was never normal and she spoke in a kind of high-pitched, squeaky voice. She also lacked the ability to speak spontaneously and often had to deliberate about what she wanted to say. She managed to learn some elements of sign language too, but as a case subject Genie was not ideal. It seems that she had some kind of brain damage, but unfortunately it was impossible to work out whether this damage had occurred at birth or was a result of her early years of deprivation – so really, it was a flawed study from the start.

THE MAJOR THEORIES OF LANGUAGE ACQUISITION

We have now mentioned the two main theories of language acquisition – the nature theory (processing box) and the nurture theory, which involves the child having verbal interactions with adults and other children. It is important to understand a little more about the nature of these theories.

If you accept that children need to interact with other people in order to learn language and that the type of linguistic interaction varies according to the age of the child, you must accept that nurture is extremely important in the development of language. However, we have not considered how the child actually learns language. The first major theory of language acquisition suggests that language is simply learned in the same way as we learn other behaviours, that is, we learn by operant conditioning. This theory was proposed by Skinner in 1957. Skinner is a behaviourist, and 'hard' behaviourists believe that all behaviours and abilities are learned. Skinner therefore suggested that if adults praise the child, reinforcing whatever it is doing, this will make it more likely for that behaviour to be repeated (remember the idea of a child learning to say mama and dada – the excitement that mummy and daddy demonstrate would be enough of a reinforcement to make it more likely to happen again).

The idea behind this kind of learning is that we learn by making an association between what we are doing and a positive result. The result, as we have already said, may be that the parent praises or laughs at the child. This means that the child is more likely to repeat the sound it has made, and gradually it comes to shape the sounds into actual words. It may also be that the child gets something as a result of what it says or does; for example, if the child asks for a sweet and is given one, this will be the reinforcement for that kind of vocalisation. This would continue while the child learns the rules of grammar, because they will receive approval for grammatical correctness, even if this is not directly obvious.

Critics of this theory argue that it is difficult to explain how children learn the sheer number of words, especially words which do not relate to anything physical. How does a child learn abstract words such as 'thinking', 'wondering', 'explicit' or 'positive', by operant conditioning? This theory also implies that children go through a gradual and lengthy process of trial-and-error learning but as we know, children learn language extremely quickly and these rules would not be mastered in as short a time as six years. The other aspect of language acquisition that is not explained by the theory is how we come to make up our own unique sentences and change the words which have been spoken as a statement into a question. Surely we would only use language that we have heard before? Yet we produce totally novel sentences every day of our lives. Also, parents prefer their child to speak the truth rather than lie, and they have been observed reinforcing ungrammatical truths, rather than grammatical lies (Slobin, 1975). Why, then, do children not grow up speaking ungrammatically when this kind of language was the language which was reinforced?

The other contender for the explanation of language acquisition is Noam Chomsky, who put forward his opposing theory in 1965. Chomsky is a nativist and believes that we are biologically programmed to learn language. His argument suggests that parents do not pay close enough attention to children to provide the kind of systematic reinforcement that would be needed for this kind of learning. He agrees that language must be learned – because if you'd been born in Italy you would speak Italian not English – but he believes that we are in some way biologically programmed to learn language and that this biological programming explains how we manage to do it so successfully and so quickly.

Chomsky proposed that children have an innate processing box which he calls a 'language acquisition device' (LAD), and this enables them to collect the information about grammatical rules and vocabulary from the world around them. He believes that the child acquires a 'deep and abstract theory' which lays behind the words of the language, regardless of whether the language is French, English or Chinese. This explains why any child can be brought up in any country and can effortlessly pick up the general grammatical principles of that language (what he termed the deep structure), even though the surface structure or actual words change.

To back up his theory, he states that children pick up rules about language too rapidly for it to have come from the child's experience. An example of this is their ability to reverse pronouns in a sentence depending on who is speaking.

Mummy says to little Johnny, 'I am going shopping now. Would you like to come with me?'

Little Johnny replies, 'Yes, I would like to come with you.'

The child refers to itself as 'I' and the person he is talking to as 'you' very easily, yet the language the child hears from the other person has them the other way around.

He also argued that of all the noises children are subjected to, speech is the only one they pick up, and they master its complexities even though they are never formally taught grammar. They cannot acquire language simply by imitating parents either, because parents do not speak to their offspring in two-word sentences, but this is still a recognised stage in language development.

Having covered the development of language in children, and considering the two main theories as to how this happens, this brings us on to another point. Are humans the only species with the capacity for language?

One way that this has been investigated is the attempt to teach language to other species. What better species than those closest to us on the philogenetic scale – primates. If we are biologically programmed to learn language (as suggested by Chomsky) and no other species has that ability, then perhaps it is an innate ability. However, if other species can be taught to use language then it means that language is not only a human skill, but also suggests that perhaps we do learn language after all, which would support Skinner's theory.

Do animals communicate? Your initial response is probably one along the lines of 'of course they do', and you would be right. But what we need to be aware of here is exactly what we mean by communication. Most other animals communicate with each other by gesture, by smell and even by sound. The bee dances as a way of communicating to the other members of the hive where they can find pollen. If it dances in a sickle shape this would indicate a different direction to a figure of eight. Monkeys can indicate whether impending danger is in the sky or on the ground according to what kind of shriek they make. Dogs, foxes, cats, etc. communicate their territory by scent. Most animals and birds communicate threats to others of the same species by patterns of behaviour that are easily understood. The male stickleback, for example, uses the red underside of his belly as a way of demonstrating territorial aggression to other sticklebacks. However, most commentators are quick to distinguish between communication and language.

SO WHAT IS 'LANGUAGE'?

According to Banyard (1996) it is 'a small number of signals (sounds, letters, gestures) that by themselves are meaningless, but can be put together according to certain rules to make an infinite number of messages'. The key factors here are the rules that we use which are well defined. An example of one of the rules we use is the rule of syntax. As we mentioned earlier, syntax is the order of the words we use in a sentence, for example, subject – verb – object:

He hat the put on.
The lorry green out of the garage rolled.

It is interesting that although we may think we know very little about English grammar, the sentences above are obviously wrong. On the other hand, communication is the way in which one animal or person transmits information to another and influences them, e.g. screeching to warn of impending danger.

As we know, language is important because it is necessary to help us socialise with others and we are creatures who need to be social. Deaf and dumb people use sign language, which has the same grammatical structure as spoken language and is able to transmit the same information. It is vital for the transmission of ideas, to help us understand the world, to organise our thoughts and as a useful tool in learning about our personalities from how other people react to us.

In order to consider whether animals have the capacity for language, we really need to consider what we mean by language. A number of researchers have described lists of features which seem to be the essence of language, for example, Hockett (1959) listed 13 design features and Aitchison (1983) proposed that there were only ten which he considered were essential to make the difference between communication and language. We must remember too that language and speech are not the same. After all, a parrot can be taught to speak, but this does not mean it understands what it is saying.

It may be helpful to think of language in the following way, using some of Aitchison's criteria:
- The function of speech is purely as a means of communication, not a by-product of other behaviours, and it uses the vocal and auditory channels.
- It is also a process whereby we usually take turns to speak with other people.
- Words have meanings or semanticity, that is, they refer to things.
- Sentences are governed by grammatical rules (e.g. syntax), so the same few words can be organised in a different way to give different meanings to the sentence.
- Words do not resemble their meaning (they are arbitrary); the word 'cat', for example, does not sound like or even look like the animal we know to be a cat.
- Language can be passed on from one generation to the next.
- Language allows us to refer to things which are not actually present.
- Language can be used to generate novel utterances, that is, utterances which have never been spoken before.
- Language allows us to talk about things which did not happen or could never happen, in other words, to lie.

If you are happy with this outline of what we mean by language, it is obvious that many of these don't seem to appear in the communications of animals. There again, we need to consider whether this description of language is somewhat ethnocentric. It's a bit like the goalkeeper in a game of football, selecting a place to put the goalposts after the match has finished. Still, we have to accept that language needs to be defined and the above outline will serve us for the time being.

R. Allan Gardner and Beatrice T. Gardner (1969), 'Teaching Sign Language to a Chimpanzee',

Science, vol. 165 (3894), 664–72

Background

So our question is: 'Are humans the only species with the capacity for language?' Supposing we gave animals the tools to acquire language, would they then be able to develop the language skills of a human?

The first consideration was which animals should be used in language research. Since the 1930s, attempts have been made to raise chimps (and, more recently, gorillas) to communicate linguistically. As they are supposedly our closest relatives on the evolutionary scale, you can see that if they could learn language this would strengthen the nurture side of the nature–nurture debate – showing that innate predisposition is not necessary or exclusively human, i.e. anti-Chomsky.

The problem was that early attempts were unsuccessful, which is not surprising, as the vocal equipment of apes is not equipped to deal with the range of sounds used in human language. Although they make lots of different sounds, these sounds are more like shrieks and are very unrefined. Also they are usually made when the chimps are either excited or frightened, and seem to relate to the situation they are in. The rest of the time they are silent, so we could interpret the sounds they do make as being a very primitive, situation-specific noise rather than anything else. In fact, I find it quite hard to imagine why the researchers believed that chimps could speak in the first place. However, Kellogg and Kellogg (1933) attempted to raise a chimp with their own child, but she never managed to utter a word! Hayes and Hayes (1951) tried with Viki, who after six years only succeeded in saying the words 'up' and 'cup', 'mama' and 'papa', and these words were somewhat unclear. It seemed that the chimpanzee lacked the vocal equipment to enable it to make human vocalisations, even if it were so inclined.

Despite failing to teach Viki to speak, the Hayes' study did spark an idea for a method of teaching language to a chimpanzee that might be more likely to succeed. When she 'spoke' her words, Viki always accompanied the word with the same gesture, such as covering her nose as she said the word.

A further study by the Gardners noted that chimps beg and make similar gestures spontaneously, and therefore they might be able to learn a language if it were based on gesture rather than vocalisation. In other words, could a chimpanzee be taught sign language, the language used by deaf humans? The language selected was American Sign Language (ASL). In order to use this, the Gardners and those research assistants who would be Washoe the chimp's human companions had to learn to sign. They found that 'a good way to practice signing amongst ourselves was to render familiar songs and poetry into signs: as far as we can judge, there is no message that cannot be rendered into sign'.

Aim

The aim of the study was to investigate whether a chimp could be taught to use human sign language (ASL), which contains all the features of spoken language.

Method

Design

The case study method was used, employing a longitudinal design. The study started in June 1966 and continued for 22 months.

> **CORE STUDY LINK** – for a description of longitudinal studies, see the Hodges and Tizard study (p. 221), and for a description of case studies, see Freud (p. 241).

Subject

Washoe (named after Washoe county – the location of the University of Nevada) was a wild captured infant female chimp, at the age of eight to 14 months at the beginning of the study.

Studying chimpanzees

Thanks to films such as *King Kong* and *Congo* most of us would think twice about poking a gorilla with a big stick. However, *Tarzan* and his sidekick chimp, Cheetah, and those cute tea adverts on the TV have given the chimpanzee an altogether more cuddly image. The Gardners, who took on the task of raising Washoe in a human environment, were under no illusions. Specialists in rats and spiders, they were more used to animals that were bred for study and could be kept in a box on the laboratory counter. They were quick to point out that 'affectionate as chimps are, they are still wild animals'.

Adult chimps can weigh up to 120 pounds and be three to five times as strong as a man, pound for pound; therefore, one of the advantages of studying Washoe was that she was young enough to be kept under reasonable control. The Gardners realised that when she reached physical maturity, it would become prohibitively dangerous to keep her in a human-like environment, and possibly for this reason 'Project Washoe' was designed to run until just before Washoe was three. She was very young when she arrived and the first few months were spent getting her used to her environment and carers. From 0 to two years, chimps are completely dependent, and then semi-dependent until they are four. They reach the equivalent of adulthood somewhere between 12 and 16, so at the age of three Washoe was still an infant. In captivity, chimps can survive to be over 40 years old, and at the time of writing Washoe lives in the Chimpanzee and Human Communication Institute (CHCI) at Central Washington University in Ellensburg, Washington. You can make a virtual visit by going to www.cwu.edu/~cwuchci/chimpcams/main_cam.htm – there are 'chimp cams' and if you are lucky you may catch a glimpse of her!

Materials/Apparatus

Washoe was raised in a fully equipped house trailer. This was in the Gardners' own yard. She had the constant company of at least one human companion while she was awake. The environment was rich in stimulation, with toys and games which promoted interaction and gave her as much freedom as a young child. The Gardners created this human-like and stimulating environment in order to encourage Washoe to learn signs to obtain food (even cats learn to vocalise to their human owners for their food).

The Gardners explained that 'for the project to be a success, we felt that something more must be developed. We wanted Washoe not only to ask for objects but to answer questions about them and also to ask us questions... With this in mind, we attempted to provide Washoe with an environment that might be conducive to this sort of behaviour' (Gardner and Gardner, 1965, p. 665). After all, if she didn't have an interesting life, what would she have to talk about?

Life also revolved around routines such as bathing, feeding and dressing, which are activities involving rituals that have been identified as important in children's language development. During her period with the Gardners, Washoe's human companions never spoke in her presence, using only American Sign Language to communicate. However, they made other sounds, e.g. laughing and indicating joy or anger, and making noises with toys such as drums. The rule was that every sound that was made had to be possible for the chimp to imitate.

American Sign Language (ASL) has a grammatical structure so it can be compared with spoken language. Some of the signs have no relationship to the objects they represent, whereas others are iconic, that is, they look like the object or action they represent; for example, the sign for a toothbrush is the index finger used as if it is a brush to rub the front teeth. ASL users often use finger spelling to spell unusual words but it was not used by the researchers, and isn't used with very young children. By electing to teach ASL to a chimpanzee, the Gardners were able to take advantage of a naturally occurring control group, the deaf children of deaf adults raised in a signing environment.

Procedure

Two training methods were used.

1. Imitation

Capitalising on chimpanzee's natural propensity to copy, imitation of gestures and signs was encouraged. The Hayes' had trained Viki to produce her 'words' with the prompt 'Do this', and a similar game was developed in order to encourage Washoe to imitate signs. She would happily imitate actions, but not always when asked or in the appropriate situation. The trainers would tickle her as a reward (or reinforcement) for that behaviour. However, she was not always cooperative and even when she was she would sometimes became angry, sometimes aggressive, and would not take part any more. The Gardners remind us this is one of the drawbacks of working with a wild animal: 'Pressed too hard, Washoe can become completely diverted from her original object; she may ask for something entirely different, run away, go into a tantrum, or even bite her tutor' (p. 666).

2. Instrumental condition

Washoe was also trained by the use of operant conditioning techniques. If she made a sign that wasn't totally accurate, the trainers would aim to get her to produce a better sign by shaping her fingers. This 'shaping' of the sign was progressive and eventually she could be expected to produce a clear sign before it was accepted, acknowledged or rewarded. In this respect, Washoe's language learning was not like the acquisition of children's language. Children do not need to be instrumentally conditioned to acquire language; both vocabulary and syntax are acquired spontaneously in children.

To gather data, black and white silent film recordings were made of as much of Washoe's interactions and time awake as possible, and up to 16 months, a full record of her signing was kept, but after that they introduced a set of criteria that had to be fulfilled before a new sign could be added to Washoe's vocabulary of acquired signs. From this point, they only recorded a new sign after three different observers had recorded it being used in the correct context, the sign was made spontaneously (the only prompts allowed were questions such as 'What is it?' or 'What do you want'), and the sign was then said to be acquired only when it was used appropriately and spontaneously on 15 consecutive days. This was a very strict set of rules. Careful observation was also made of the way that Washoe combined signs, as this is part of the development of grammatical understanding.

Results

By setting the strict criteria at 16 months, it was possible for the Gardners to provide quantitative data for the signs acquired during the study. They identified 30 signs which had met the criteria. Washoe also signed a further four signs (dog, smell, me and clean) which were judged to be 'stable' signs. These four signs had not appeared for the prescribed 15 consecutive days, but had been recorded on at least half the days in a period of 30 days of recordings. So 22 months into the study, Washoe had 34 stable signs, although she used many more signs which did not meet the criteria at this stage.

Examples of these 34 signs and the context in which they were used can be seen in the following table.

Sign	Context
Come-gimme	Beckoning sign made to persons or animals. Often combined: 'come tickle', 'gimme sweet'.
Open	At door of house, room, car, refrigerator or cupboard; on containers such as jars, and on taps.
Sweet	For dessert; used spontaneously at end of meal. Also when asking for candy.
Out (also 'in')	Out was used for both in and out at first, but later 'in' appeared.
Toothbrush	When Washoe had finished her meal, or at other times when shown a toothbrush.
Sorry	After biting someone, or when someone has been hurt in another way (not necessarily by Washoe). When told to apologise for mischief.
Food-eat	During meals and preparation of meals.
Dog	For dogs and barking.
Shoes	For shoes and boots.
Clean	When washing/being washed. Also used for soap.

The Gardners recorded when the signs had appeared. Four signs appeared in the first seven months, nine during the next seven, and 21 during the remaining time. In the final month of the study, the variety of signs being used was also recorded. Of the 34 signs she had officially acquired at this point, the smallest number of signs used in a single day was 23, with 28 of the 34 signs being observed on 20 of the days in the month. The use of the signs as arbitrary symbols is an aspect of Aitchison's (1983) criteria, supposedly unique to humans.

In addition to this quantitative data, qualitative results were presented to consider how Washoe was using the signs and further parallels that could be drawn with human use of language.

- **Manual babbling**
  The Gardners identified her random gestures as a kind of 'manual babbling'. They used sign-like movements to assist the shaping of signs and suggest how a particular sign was acquired.

- **Combinations: creativity**
  Once she had about eight to ten signs in her vocabulary, she started to combine them, sometimes spontaneously rather than imitating researchers.

Washoe was not conditioned to produce combinations, although the Gardners concede, 'we may have responded more readily to strings of two or more signs than to single signs', possibly reinforcing the combining of signs with attention. Combining words to increase the meaning of utterances is known as creativity, and Aitchison (1983) considers this aspect of language to be unique to humans. However, the Gardners suggest that Washoe was producing novel utterances that she had not seen human carers sign and so could not be simply imitating. Two examples of this are 'open key' for a locked door to be opened and 'go sweet' to be carried to the raspberry bush.

- **Generalising signs and transfering signs from one context to another**
  She transferred signs from one context to another, e.g. 'open' from one specific door to a number of doors, and even 'open' for turning on a tap. Washoe also generalised the sign for one specific object to different objects, e.g. 'dog' from one specific dog to all dogs.

ACTIVITY

What stage of human language development does this combining of signs correspond to?

- **Differentiation**
  She also learned to differentiate new signs, e.g. she learned the sign for 'flower' and used it to indicate smell. With 'shaping' of her behaviour, she later became able to differentiate between the sign for 'flower' (all fingers and thumb put together as if tapered and then held to one then the other nostril) and 'smell' (palm held before nose and moved up to nose as if to smell, several times).

- **Discussion**

The Gardners' conclusions were that at the time of writing Washoe's utterances did indeed 'resemble a short sentence', and that their work showed that the 'writers who would predict just what it is that no chimpanzee will ever do... must proceed with caution'. Although they clearly state that they cannot answer the often asked question, 'Do you think that Washoe has language?' they explain that this is because there is no universally accepted distinction between language and communication. In fact, they suggest work with other species should be carried out extensively before 'theories of language that depend upon the identification of aspects that are exclusively human' are accepted. They also believed that with refinements to their training process, work with other chimpanzees would exceed what they had achieved with Washoe in this first attempt at teaching sign language to a chimpanzee.

Commentary

Did Washoe develop 'language'?

Interestingly, we are no nearer today to an operational definition of language. We have been using some of Aitchison's (1983) definition to help us try to answer this question, but the answer remains elusive.

Washoe developed a number of basic abilities which indicated that perhaps she was beginning to develop what has been defined as language; the way these were taught did not resemble the way that human infants acquire language. Washoe needed to be taught and her signing was dependent on external reinforcers, whereas children spontaneously acquire both grammar and vocabulary simultaneously.

She displayed semanticity (knowing that the signs had meaning, that they stood for something), and creativity (combining signs to produce novel utterances that increase the meaning of the utterance), but her ability to produce correct word order was limited. She was not reinforced for grammar and this may explain her poor skills. Washoe clearly did not have the skills human infants display in their effortless acquisition of syntax.

In another comparison with human infants the Gardners 'expected a great deal of manual babbling'. In fact, Washoe did not manually babble early in the project, which would have been the time that a baby would have babbled. The behaviour referred to as babbling may well have been a result of reinforcement and therefore not comparable with the babbling stage in human infants, which is clearly innate and requires no reinforcement. This illustrates how the findings in this study may have been subject to experimenter bias; for example, did the Gardners see Washoe's gesticulations as manual babbling because that is what they wanted, and expected, to see?

One of the biggest criticisms is that many of Washoe's 'utterances' were no more than imitations, and video footage of the original study did indicate that this may have been the case. Despite the fact that Washoe's vocabulary increased over the following two years, it had only increased to 132 signs after four years of training. The conclusion must therefore be that although the chimpanzee had been taught simple two-way communication, she seemed to lack the development shown by a human child. Children initiate conversations, they are highly skilled in turn-taking and the rules of grammar and word order and their utterances increase as they get older. Further attempts to teach different forms of language to primates, such as using tokens and symbols, have lacked any of these characteristics and the primates have simply retained the very basic elements of communication.

Is the study useful?

As the first study to successfully question whether or not language is a skill unique to humans, Project Washoe was groundbreaking.

In addition, the skills and behaviours that Washoe, and primates studied subsequently, did not display spontaneously, and which human infants do, have provided evidence for the role of nature in the acquisition of language in humans.

Is the study ecologically valid?

The study is low in ecological validity. As we stated earlier, Washoe's environment was designed to be comparable with the learning environment of a deaf child with signing deaf parents. However, Washoe had more carers than a child would have and much more testing of the chimpanzee was carried out than would be permitted with any child. Clearly, Washoe was a wild animal isolated from other members of its own species and in an environment very different from its natural habitat. In the wild, chimps are not trained to use a potty chair and you can be sure that they do not clean their teeth with a toothbrush.

Is the study ethical?

Ethical implications as to the rights of primates have not been considered by this study. Is it acceptable to bring them up in an environment which is so totally different from their natural lifestyle? What happens to them after the study is finished? Is it acceptable to then remove the primate from the humanised environment it has grown up in, and relegate it to a primate organisation or other holding area?

Key questions

1. Explain what is meant by the term experimenter bias. Why might it be a problem in this study?
2. If you were designing ethical guidelines for psychological researchers testing chimpanzees, what would you include?
3. What comparisons can be drawn between Washoe's language learning and children's language acquisition?
4. Do you think that Washoe uses language?

Example Answers are on page 454.

Further reading:

- http://www.uapress.arisona.edu/samples/sam1011.htm – a summary of the work of the Gardners.
- http://www.cwu.edu/~cwuchci – Roger and Deborah Fouts' website includes a biography of Washoe. You can see the ChimpCam, which gives live footage of the chimps. The trouble is there is a time difference between them and the UK, so it's best at night! http://www.cwu.edu/~cwuchci/washoebio.html – links to the Washoe section

You can get leaflets on the work of the Fouts here and they will answer queries from students – email them at chimplab@cwu.edu

Koko the Gorilla also has a website – http://www.koko.org/

• Harris, J. (1990), *Early Language Development*, London: Routledge, part two.

Children's development

Most adults go through life without questioning where our abilities and skills come from and whether they are due to the process of maturation or whether they are the result of learning. In fact, unless you study psychology, it is quite likely that this question would not be of any importance to you until you had children of your own. How many times have you heard your parents say things like, 'You are just like your father/mother/grandma', or 'Your father was always good with numbers/drawing'? This implies that many of the skills you have were passed down from your parents or grandparents, but when you were first born you were unable to sit, walk or hold a pencil, and you certainly couldn't count. Therefore these skills, *if* they were inherited, must have taken time to emerge, which suggests that maturation must have played a part.

From the previous chapter on cognition, you have already been introduced to the idea that many of the things we are able to do as we get older are as a result of the interaction between nature and nurture – you are born with some abilities, others develop as the result of maturation and many more are actually learned, either from adults or from experiences we have whilst interacting with the world. You have also learned about the development of one aspect of children's cognition (what we mean by cognition is the higher order thinking and reasoning capabilities, rather than simply the instinctive and innate processes in the study by Baron-Cohen *et al.* in chapter three).

In this chapter we are going to look at the subject of children's development, and the four core studies in this area can be considered to be an important part of the nature–nurture debate. Evidence has shown that much of what happens to us as children shapes what we become as adults, and therefore it is obvious how important childhood experiences really are. Each study takes a very different perspective on the development of children and will give you an excellent introduction as to how nature and nurture combine.

Cognitive development

If you were told that you would have to entertain a child for the afternoon, one of the things you would probably want to know is how old the child is. Without being an authority on children's development, you would still be aware that small children have very different abilities to older children, and this will influence what they enjoy doing. This is because children's cognitive abilities, especially their thinking and reasoning, differ from age to age, just as they differ from the thinking of an adult. Therefore, the things that would amuse a small child would be very different from the things which would amuse a 16-year-old. This way of thinking is very different from how adults used to think of children a few hundred years ago. In fact, in the seventeenth century it was believed that children's minds were a *tabula rasa* or blank slate, as they entered the world without any knowledge or skills. This implies that *everything* we know is learned (which is really the argument of the pure behaviourists – that is, that *all* behaviour is learned). At that time, most people also believed that children were simply miniature adults, with the same thinking and reasoning skills. This was why many children were punished for behaviours which to us would seem quite normal for a child, and why they were expected to accept the behaviour of the adults in their lives without question or explanation.

Nowadays we consider childhood to be a special time for learning, demonstrated by a strong focus on nursery schools and educational toys. We also no longer believe that children think in the same way as adults and much of this knowledge is thanks to a man called Jean Piaget (1896–1980). He developed not only one of the most comprehensive theories of children's development, but also one of the most influential theories of our time. Piaget's theory focuses on the idea that development is maturational (to do with the increasing maturity of the child), age-related and universal across cultures.

CORE STUDY LINK – as you may remember from the Deregowski study (p. 130), behaviours observed to be the same across cultures are called cultural universals. It can be assumed that, provided the cultures have not been contaminated by exposure to each other, such behaviours are governed, at least in part, by biology and therefore lend support to the nurture side of the nature–nurture debate.

PIAGET'S THEORY

Jean Piaget was not actually a psychologist, which is quite surprising when you consider how important he is in the world of developmental psychology. He was born in Switzerland and initially trained as a biologist and zoologist. He became interested in the relationship between biology and psychology in the early 1920s, especially in how animals adapt to their environment.

Piaget went to work in Paris for Alfred Binet, who was responsible for developing the first intelligence tests for the French Education Department as a way of testing children to identify those who had learning difficulties.

 CORE STUDY LINK – the study by Gould (p. 334) looks at the use of intelligence tests.

172

The idea behind the intelligence tests was to compare children on what was believed to be a fixed ability – their innate intelligence. We would expect that Piaget would have been interested in the number of correct answers children gave to questions, but what he started to notice was that they seemed to give the same wrong answers, and these wrong answers depended on their age. It was almost as if the children went through different stages of reasoning according to what age they were, with younger children producing similar errors in reasoning to each other. These errors would then differ from the errors of slightly older children.

This led him to formulate a theory that intelligence must be a kind of biological adaptation which allowed the child to develop more efficient interactions between them and the world in which they live. Small children do not need to interact in a very complex way because their needs are taken care of by parents of caregivers. Once they are able to interact (and operate) in the world by doing things and making things happen, they need to develop a greater understanding of how things work. This would require more complicated thought processes and so the child develops these as necessary.

Piaget realised that the development of mental abilities was not simply the result of the child maturing, but also required the child to be able to interact with its environment. He also believed that children are self-motivated to discover the world – almost to the point that if you put a child in a room with lots and lots of stimulating and interesting toys and games and objects, they would find out for themselves about the properties of those objects and universal rules that apply to them. Teachers would therefore be seen as facilitators rather than directors of a child's education. This means that they should provide the help the child asks for, and should make the environment as stimulating as possible by providing the facilities required to allow the child to learn for itself, rather than directing the child to learn. This stimulated a massive change in education where children no longer sat passively in rows of desks, but instead became active learners, working in small groups to seek out information.

Piaget also recognised that the development of a child's knowledge and under-standing seemed to involve a number of stages. They would start with a primitive understanding which was often slightly incorrect, and this would transform as they got older into an increasingly more sophisticated understanding of the nature of the world, as a direct result of interaction with their environment. He also noticed that this transformation often happened almost instantly, as if they suddenly gained insight into what they were doing wrong. Once they had gained this insight, they were unable to return to a previous stage of more basic understanding.

This following story will probably help to explain this kind of change in thinking, which we will refer back to later.

Little Johnny had his friend Nigel round to play, and mother offered them each a drink of cola. She got two glasses out of the cupboard and poured out the same amount of Cola into each glass so that they were both half full. Little Johnny started wailing (as small children do), 'I want it in my special glass.' Mother looked annoyed, anticipating what might happen next. The special glass that Little Johnny referred to was a tall thin glass, rather than the two identical, transparent, unbreakable beakers she had used originally.

She poured the cola into Little Johnny's special glass, which ended up being full to the brim. This produced a huge wail from Nigel who started bleating, 'It's not fair, he's got more than me now.'

Mother tried to remain calm. 'There is the same amount in both glasses.'

'No there isn't – he's got more.'

'I'll show you. Let me pour this back into the glass I got out in the first place.' She proceeded to pour the cola back into the unbreakable plastic beaker. 'Look, there is the same amount in both glasses now.'

Nigel was silent for a moment.

'I want my special glass, I want my special glass,' shrieked Little Johnny.

'It's not fair if you do,' said Nigel. 'It means you get more.'

At this point mother wanted to give up.

'Do it again,' said Little Johnny.

Both boys looked in wonderment as the liquid seemed to change volume before their very eyes. Suddenly Nigel let out a shriek: 'It's because the glass is thinner that it makes it all squashed up, isn't it, Mrs Brown? There's not really more in there. It's not really magic, is it?'

'That's right, dear.'

173

Piaget claimed that once a child reached a certain stage they could not return to a previous stage, but would have graduated up the developmental ladder. He claimed that each stage or step was like a building block and was dependent on having reached the previous stage first. These stages were age-related and cumulative.

In order to test out his ideas, Piaget undertook a longitudinal case study on his own three children, whereby he observed and questioned them as they grew up and noticed the differences in the quality of answers and explanations they gave to different problems.

> ## KEY CONCEPT – open-ended questions
>
> Piaget believed that unstructured and unstandardised questioning, which was dependent on the responses of the children, was a far better way of finding out what they were thinking. This would allow him to follow up ideas and beliefs that the children held which, in turn, would give him greater insight into their cognitive abilities. The disadvantage of open-ended questions is that they may be misinterpreted and the wrong conclusions drawn. Although this methodology could be considered somewhat unscientific, Piaget did test some of his hypotheses on other children, so at least his research was not so biased as we might think.
>
> Due to the nature of his research, Piaget was not really interested in gathering quantifiable data. However, other researchers using open-ended questioning may find it very hard to analyse and quantify the answers.

THE CENTRAL FEATURES OF PIAGET'S THEORY

Piaget said that all babies are born with similar biological equipment (he used the term 'structures'). These biological structures were the senses, the brain and reflexes (such as sucking and grasping). He proposed that the complex achievements of older children must have developed in some way from these basic reflexes.

He also used the term schemata to all the cognitive structures or interrelated and organised groups of memories, thoughts, actions and knowledge, which represented everything that the baby or child knew about objects or actions. He said that these schemata develop from the child's own interactions with the environment and any new experiences the child had would lead to new schemata being developed. The way the schemata develop and become more complex involves organising their past experiences and adapting them to any new information they come across.

Piaget claimed that adaptation has two components: *assimilation* and *accommodation*. He saw assimilation as the process of fitting new information and experiences into existing schemata, while accommodation is the process of changing the existing schemata when new information cannot be assimilated.

To return to the restaurant example used on page 103, if the only type of restaurant you had been to before was like McDonald's, where you don't have a waiter or a menu to order from while you sit at the table, the first time you went to a restaurant where the waiter took your order, you would be experiencing new information which could be fitted into your current 'restaurant' schema. If, on the other hand, you had no idea that you could buy food ready-cooked and eat it on someone else's property because you had only ever eaten at home, you could not assimilate the new experience in the light of anything you already knew about, so you would have to set up a new schema in order to accommodate the new information.

Piaget used these concepts to help explain the different kinds of thinking that occur during different stages in a child's development. One way to think of a stage is that it is a time of relative stability when a child will think in a similar way across a wide range of situations or problems. Remember Little Johnny and Nigel? What happened for them was that their thinking (and understanding) was challenged by a new experience which gave them new information they could not fit into their old schemata, so they had to reorganise them in order to make sense of the new information. This process of accommodation resulted in their ability to understand a process at a new advanced level or stage.

Piaget identified four major stages in the development of a child's thought and claimed that all children progress through these stages in this fixed order, although not everyone reaches the final stage. He also suggested ages for each stage, although he was aware that the ages were averages rather than actual ages, and he also said that children move through the stages at slightly different speeds, dependent on their experiences.

The stages are listed below and we will look at each one in some detail:
1. The sensorimotor stage (0 to two years)
2. The pre-operational stage (two to seven years)
3. The concrete operational stage (seven to 11 years)
4. The formal operational stage (11+ years)

As we have already mentioned, Piaget's belief was that children are internally driven to find out about their world, which implies that if a child is provided with a stimulating and well-equipped environment, they will explore the environment themselves and find out about the properties of the objects within that environment with little or no guidance.

The sensorimotor stage (birth to two years)

When a baby is very young, the only knowledge it has about the world is based on what it can experience and what it can do, both of which are somewhat limited. Babies are born with reflexes such as sucking and grasping and they can also move their limbs, for example, kicking and waving their arms. This restricted repertoire of movement limits what they can actually do, although each one of these actions results in some kind of sensual experience. They can also see, hear, taste, touch and smell the world around them and they begin to put together very primitive schemata about the world. This is why the stage is called the sensorimotor stage, because it is to do with the child's sensual experiences and their motor movements.

During this stage we see one of the biggest leaps in development because they go from being helpless, incontinent blobs, with limited reflex behaviours, to becoming able to turn their parents' world completely upside down by exerting their will, arguing and forming strong bonds. They will be able to speak; they may well be potty-trained; they will be able to throw things around; and they will understand that when people leave the room they haven't vanished off the face of the earth. They will also be able to solve simple problems, like finding the things you don't want them to find, and they will have developed their own little personalities.

What happens is that biological maturation has a huge part to play here. When they are born they are unable to sit up or make words, but the growth and development of the body makes each achievement possible. The child realises that it actually gains control over what was initially random movement, and this increases their understanding about their ability to interact with the world. These skills become internalised and they begin to think when they want to display various movements, rather than the movements simply occurring by chance.

Piaget noted one crucial development that takes place during this stage, and that is the child's sudden understanding of object permanence – realising that objects continue to exist even when they can't be seen, which he said occurred when the baby is about eight months of age. He tested this by looking at whether babies search for objects which are hidden from view. Prior to eight months, babies cease to look for an object which has been covered, but once they get to about eight months, they continue to look for that object in the place that they last saw it, but will not look for it in alternative places. Obviously this is quite a significant development in children's understanding as the phrase 'out of sight, out of mind' becomes more a case of 'out of sight – I'm going to scream and scream until it comes back again!'

The pre-operational stage (two to seven years)

During this stage, Piaget suggested that children become more able to represent the world using mental images and symbols. As we have already noted, words are really just sound symbols for objects, and it is at this stage that a child's linguistic skills really develop. We all use mental images or pictures in our mind's eye, and even speak to ourselves 'inside our heads', and this is the time when this kind of skill develops in a child. If we have access to very few symbols it would follow that our thoughts may also be limited, but the more they increase, the more sophisticated our thoughts become. Children of this age also demonstrate symbolism in their play, for example, using a banana as a telephone or a stick as a gun.

It is important not to imagine that the pre-operational child's thoughts are anywhere near as sophisticated as the thoughts of an adult. Their world is still very concrete – things are what they seem, so the child is more influenced by appearance than anything else. However, sometimes their thoughts may be intuitive, that is, based on what they feel or sense is true without being able to explain the underlying principles. This may be why sometimes a child may seem to be very bright when really it has made an intuitive guess without any logical reasoning to back it up.

Piaget's descriptions of children with pre-operational intelligence tended to focus on their limitations because he believed that they could not yet apply logical mental rules to actual objects in the world. He described these logical mental rules as 'operations', for example, addition and subtraction are reversible operations because adding three to a number can be reversed by taking three away again. Piaget suggested that a child would not be able to apply logical operations until they are about seven years old.

The main limitations of pre-operational thought

1. Egocentrism

According to Piaget, pre-operational children are egocentric. This means that they see the world from their point of view and are unaware that others see it differently. We talked about egocentrism in the section on autism, and how it explains the behaviour of small children having tantrums in supermarkets. Remember, too, that egocentrism is not the same as selfishness, because it is an *inability* to see something from someone else's point of view. Actually, Piaget thought this was the most serious deficiency in pre-operational children's thinking.

Piaget and Inhelder (1956) tested egocentrism with their famous study known as the 'three mountains task'. They asked children to look at a three-dimensional model of a mountain scene, which was based on a large mountain called La Saleve, across the lake from the city of Geneva. The mountains were placed so that one had snow on the top, one had a cross, and one had a small house. The child would have a good look at the model and then sit down at

The 'three mountains' task

one of the chairs placed around the table. The child would then have a doll placed opposite to where they were sitting and would have to choose a picture showing what the doll could see from their side of the table.

Piaget found that children under the age of five always seemed to pick out the view of what they could see from their own position and seemed to be unaware that the doll would see something different. He also found that between the ages of five and seven they knew there would be a difference but they weren't sure what it was. Then, when they reached seven years, they seemed to be able to cope with the 'in front' and 'behind' perspectives, but not the 'left' and 'right' perspectives. By the age of eight or nine, they would be able to choose the right pictures for all the positions around the table. According to Piaget, these findings clearly demonstrated that children are unable to see things from someone else's point of view until they are at least seven years old.

2. Conservation

Do you remember Johnny and Nigel? They did not understand initially that even though Johnny's mother had not put any more cola in the glass, it looked as if there were more because the glass was taller and thinner. This is a demonstration of lack of conservation. The pre-operational child is unable to 'conserve' because they don't understand that the basic properties of matter are not changed by superficial changes in their appearance. The serving of cola looked more in the tall glass, and this proved to be even more confusing when it was returned to the original glass.

This example deals with conservation of volume and is probably the best known example of a conservation experiment (although studies have also been carried out on conservation of number and weight). In fact, Piaget demonstrated this in exactly the same way with three beakers, two short beakers and one tall one. Both short beakers had the same amount of liquid in them and the tall one was empty. He then poured the liquid from one of the short beakers into the tall beaker and discovered that pre-operational children thought this changed the amount of water in the tall thin one.

When investigating number, Piaget used two rows of counters, equally spaced, and asked the child if there was the same number of counters in each row. The child would dutifully say 'Yes'. Piaget would then spread the second row of counters out and ask the child again if there was the same number of counters. At this point the child would say 'No'.

The conservation of weight would be tested using plasticine. Two balls of plasticine of equal size would be shown to the child and the child would be asked if there was the same amount in each. The child would say 'Yes'. Then one of the balls would be rolled into a sausage shape and the child would again be asked if there was the same amount of plasticine in each ball at which point the child would say 'No'.

○ ○ ○ ○ ○ ○ ○ ○ ○   Pre-transformation

● ● ● ● ● ● ● ● ●

○ ○ ○ ○ ○ ○ ○ ○   Post-transformation

● ● ● ● ● ● ● ● ●

The second row of counters are now spread out and a child without the ability to conserve will see the black array as one which contains more counters

3. Irreversibility

Piaget also demonstrated another limitation in pre-operational children's thought by these experiments. If we use the liquid experiment as an example, when the water from the tall thin beaker was then poured back into the short beaker, the child would be quite satisfied that there was again the same amount of water in both of them. The problem was that the child couldn't really understand why this was and was unable to work it out. Therefore they would be unable to 'reverse' the operation in their heads.

Reversibility is the ability to reverse the logic of a train of thought. According to Piaget, a three-year-old girl would be unable to do this. An example is the following conversation:

Adult: Do you have an older brother?
Child: Yes.
Adult: Does he have a younger sister?
Child: No.

4. Centration

This refers to the way a child will focus or centre attention on only one aspect of a task and ignore all the other aspects. This is when they rely on their intuition about what they can see rather than what they can reason. An example would be to put three sticks of equal length on the table in front of a child. The child would then be asked if the three sticks are the same length or if one is longer than the others. The centre stick would then be moved slightly so they are no longer in line. It is very likely that the child would then say that the sticks are no longer the same length (in fact, the centre stick will possibly be seen as either longer or shorter), because they will tend to focus on only one end of the stick, and not both ends.

179

Child

Child

5. Seriation

Piaget maintained that pre-operational children were unable to put things in order of sequence, for example, size or height.

These examples are the main limitations to pre-operational thought according to Piaget, although he identified other weaknesses in children's ability to reason. For example, children up to the age of four often develop what Piaget called pre-concepts, which are generalised rules. An example of this is when a child knows that as daddy owns a blue car, therefore all blue cars must be daddy's car.

Julie had a very interesting private life, having had numerous relationships in the past. She had finally settled down with Richard and they were looking forward to the birth of their first baby. The trouble was Richard was still somewhat insecure about her past. However, they were both delighted when Rosie was born and they seemed to become much closer.

One day, when Rosie was nearly three years old, they were all out shopping. Richard stopped to look in a shop window whilst Julie walked slowly ahead. Rosie was toddling along in front of her when suddenly one of Julie's past 'relationships' recognised her, broke into a smile, walked towards her and kissed her on the cheek. Rosie ran up to the man and said in a very loud voice, 'Daddy, Daddy.'

You can imagine the rest…

Here, what was happening was the small child held the pre-concept that daddy was a man, this was also a man, therefore, he must be a daddy too! You can see the logic in the reasoning, and also the limitations.

Piaget also said that children of this age show *animism*, which is giving lifelike qualities to inanimate things. Here is an example of a child attributing life to an inanimate object when talking about the sun:

Piaget: Does the sun move?
Child: Yes, when I walk, it follows. When I turn around, it turns around too. Doesn't it ever follow you too?
Piaget: Why does it move?
Child: Because when we walk, it goes too.
Piaget: Why does it go?
Child: To hear what we say.
Piaget: Is it alive?
Child: Of course, otherwise it wouldn't follow us, it couldn't shine.

Piaget, 1960, p. 215

The concrete operational stage (seven to 11 years)

In this stage children cease to be egocentric and acquire 'cognitive operations', which are much more complex mental schemata which enable the child to come to logical conclusions about the world. This means that they are now able to put items in order, such as height order, whereas they were unable to do this before. They would also be able to put a sequence of pictures in the right order because they could logically work out which one comes before the next. However, they still have problems with abstract concepts and principles and tend to see rules as black and white, so when playing any games with a concrete operational child, they will insist that the rules are followed and that you cannot change them in any way.

Formal operational stage (11+ years)

The final stage of development involves the ability not only to reason logically, but also to deal with abstract concepts. Piaget referred to these abilities as the 'logic of combinations', where the child may need to deal with the mental manipulation of several factors at the same time. This stage is where children can do mental arithmetic, which involves retaining and manipulating a number of pieces of information.

Children at this stage also understand that rules can be broken if everyone agrees, such as the rules of board games and so on.

CRITICISMS OF PIAGET'S THEORY

There has been a great deal of criticism of Piaget's theory, much of which is based on the idea that children are far more competent at certain ages than Piaget reckoned. It has been suggested that the language and methodology used by Piaget in his questioning was responsible for many of the supposed inabilities of the children. Further research suggests that there do seem to be developmental stages that children go through, and that these stages do seem to be cumulative and age-related, therefore, we must use the suggested ages as guidelines only. For example, a child of five may be able to conserve liquid quantity whereas a different child of eight may be unable to, but their progress through the stages will be similar. It also appears that when children are faced with a difficult or stressful situation, they can return to an earlier stage of reasoning (which Piaget said would not occur). This has been seen to happen with the birth of a new baby in a family, when the older child, who had been showing a good rate of cognitive progression, suddenly regresses to a more babyish level. However, we can never be sure whether this is simply attention-seeking behaviour or whether they do actually forget what they knew.

One criticism of Piagetian theory relates to his ideas about object permanence. Later research has indicated that it is not a lack of object permanence that stops a small child from looking for a hidden object in the sensorimotor stage – it is more likely to be a memory problem. If a child is shown an object and then it is hidden they may attempt to see where it has gone but forget where they last saw it and then give up looking. Bower (1971) demonstrated this idea of 'fragile memory' by looking at the searching behaviour of babies as young as 20 days when a ball was hidden. By assessing their facial expressions, he discovered that even the youngest babies showed surprise when a ball was hidden from view and no surprise on its return. If they realised that the ball hadn't vanished off the face of the earth, it would make sense that its return into view would not cause them any surprise, whereas if they thought it had really vanished they would be amazed by its magical reappearance. By refining the methodology used, Bower demonstrated that babies of all ages show object permanence when the period between hiding and reappearance is short.

Another criticism involves Piaget's claims about the extent of egocentricity in young children. One of the biggest critics of Piaget's methodology was Hughes (1975), who suggested that when given a task that was more familiar to them, children are far less egocentric than Piaget suggested. Hughes arranged an experiment designed to test whether children could see something from someone else's perspective using objects which were more familiar to the children. If you think about it, unless you lived in the Alps, you wouldn't be very familiar with mountain scenery and would therefore find it hard to imagine what these large models in front of you were actually supposed to represent. Hughes set up a scene using dolls and asked children to put one doll in a position where it could not be seen by the other. Using this familiar game of hide-and-seek, Hughes found that 90% of children between the ages of 3½ and five had no trouble accurately placing the doll.

Another study investigated children's ability to conserve numbers by presenting a different version of the original Piagetian study using counters. The results also indicated that young children can think quite logically in situations they understand. In an experiment carried out by McGarrigle and Donaldson (1974), the children were again shown the two rows of counters on a table and asked if there was the same amount in each row. Then, instead of the experimenter changing the layout, a 'naughty teddy' appeared and made the change while the experimenter looked in the other direction. This resulted in the children realising that although the counters looked different, there was still the same amount on the table and they had no difficulty explaining what had happened.

J. Samuel and P. Bryant (1984), 'Asking only one question in the conservation experiment',

Journal of Child Psychology and Psychiatry, 25, 315–18

● Background

Margaret Donaldson suggested that Piaget actually underestimated the cognitive abilities of young children because he did not appreciate that their cognitive and social understanding are very closely related. In other words, young children fail to demonstrate their cognitive capabilities in Piaget's tests because of their social understanding of the situation. For example, if someone asks you the same question twice, you might think it is because you got the answer wrong the first time.

'What are two and two?'
'Five.'
'What are two and two?'
'Sorry – four.'

This is exactly what happens in Piaget's standard conservation tasks. If you remember, the methodology he used involved asking the children after presenting them with the two rows of counters, 'Are there the same number of counters in each row?' He would then widen the spaces between the counters on one of the rows and ask the child again, 'Are there the same number of counters in each row?' What Piaget found was that children under seven would largely answer the second question incorrectly and from this he deduced that they failed to conserve. From his studies he set the changeover from the pre-operational stage to the concrete operational stage at age about seven.

Rose and Blank (1974), however, suggested that the child's error was actually as a result of them demonstrating a very sophisticated social strategy by interpreting that the reason the second question was being asked was because they may have given an incorrect answer to the first question. They devised a study to test this where they dropped the pre-transformation question (the question asked before the change in appearance had been made). Their study showed that if children were simply shown the two rows evenly spaced and then shown one row being changed and were then asked if there were the same amount of counters in each row, more six-year-olds would get the answer right.

Samuel and Bryant were interested in these findings, which seemed to suggest that the younger children made errors in Piaget's traditional two-question task not because they couldn't conserve (understanding that a change in shape or form does not necessarily mean a change in quantity), but because they were simply misinterpreting what the experimenter wanted to hear.

The current study by Samuel and Bryant was designed both to establish the reliability of Rose and Blank's findings and to extend the study. Rose and Blank had tested only six-year-olds, so Samuel and Bryant tested children aged 5–8½ to see if older and younger children were affected in the same way by the one-question only task. Whereas Rose and Blank had only tested the conservation of number (counters task), Samuel and Bryant extended the study to include the two other versions of Piaget's conservation tasks: mass (using Play-Doh cylinders) and volume (pouring liquid into taller, narrower glasses or into shorter wider ones).

Aim

The aim of the study was to test whether the methodology used in Piaget's conservation experiments was the reason why children under eight years made errors, rather than any true lack of understanding of conservation. The study was designed to use Rose and Blank's one-question method.

Method

Design

This was a laboratory experiment using an independent groups design.

Subjects

The sample was made up of 252 children from schools in and around Crediton, Devon, UK. Their ages ranged from five to 8½ years.

The children were divided first according to age. This gave four groups, each consisting of 63 children. The first group had a mean age of five years three months, the second, six years three months, the third, seven years three months and the final group, eight years three months. Each age group was then further subdivided into three more groups consisting of 21 children, to provide the three experimental conditions.

Mean age in years	Standard (2-question) condition	One-judgement condition	Fixed array
	No. of children	No. of children	No. of children
5¼	21	21	21
6¼	21	21	21
7¼	21	21	21
8¼	21	21	21

Within each age group, 21 children were tested using the traditional two-question method as used by Piaget, 21 were tested using Rose and Blank's one-question method, asking only the post-transformation question, and a further 21 were tested in a control condition called the fixed array condition. In the fixed array condition, children were only shown the materials as they looked after they had been changed and therefore they did not witness the transformation. This condition would show that the other children were using the information about how the materials looked in the first place to inform their answers to the post-transformation question.

Materials

The materials used were the same as those used in the Piagetian experiments: two cylinders of Play-Doh of equal size (used for conservation of mass), two rows of counters with a maximum of six in a row (used for conservation of number) and three beakers of liquid, two beakers being the same size and the third being taller and thinner (used for conservation of volume).

Variables

There were a number of independent variables being tested:

1. The age of the child – would the older children do better than the younger children?
2. The way the task was carried out – would children do better on the one-question task than the traditional two-question task and the fixed array condition?
3. The materials used – Piaget suggested that children find the numbers task easier than the mass and volume tasks; would that be shown in this study?

The dependent variable was always whether or not the child got the answer to the post-transformation question right.

Procedure

Children were tested individually under laboratory conditions.

- The *standard group* was tested using the standard Piagetian task, which involved asking a pre- and post-transformation question and witnessing the transformation process.
- The *one judgement group* was tested using only the post-transformation question, after the children had witnessed the transformation process.
- The *fixed array group* was tested by being shown the post-transformation array (therefore, not having seen the transformation take place).

An example of the procedure for the standard task to demonstrate conservation of number follows:

Counters were spread out in two identical rows and the child was asked the pre-transformation question: 'Is there the same number of counters in each row?' The counters in one of the rows were then spread out and the child was asked the post-transformation question: 'Is there the same number of counters in each row?'

The procedure was the same for the mass and liquid experiments, with the mass (Play-Doh) involving flattening (into a pancake) or rolling (into a sausage) one cylinder of Play-Doh, and the liquid condition involving tipping the liquid from one beaker into another of different height and width.

Each child was tested four times on number, mass and volume tasks.

Controls

To ensure that the children really understood, there were four trials in each situation. The order in which the children undertook the tasks was systematically varied to prevent order effects.

First child	number	mass	volume
Second child	mass	volume	number
Third child	volume	number	mass
Fourth child	number	mass	volume

Results

The children were each tested 12 times (four times on each task), so they had 12 opportunities to get the answer right or wrong. Samuel and Bryant presented their data as mean number of errors per age group and per condition.

This table shows that the number of errors in the one judgement condition were lower than the other two in every case. It also indicates that the number of errors made by the children as they got older decreased in every condition. The fixed-array condition made most errors, showing that children did indeed use their witnessing of the transformation to inform their answer to the post-transformation question.

Mean age	Standard (2-question) condition	One-judgement condition	Fixed-array condition
5¼	8.5	7.3	8.6
6¼	5.7	4.3	6.4
7¼	3.2	2.6	4.9
8¼	1.7	1.3	3.3

This table shows that the mean number of errors in the 'number' test were lower than the mean number of errors in the mass and volume tests in the one judgement and fixed-array conditions.

Type of task	Standard (2-question) condition	One-judgement condition	Fixed-array condition
Number	1.476	1.024	1.536
Mass	1.512	1.190	1.714
Volume	1.810	1.595	2.500

After being subjected to a number of statistical analyses, the summary of the results was as follows:

- Children were significantly more able to conserve in the one-judgement condition than the two other conditions, with the fixed-array condition making the most errors. These results establish the reliability of findings in the Rose and Blank study.
- The older children were significantly more able to conserve than the younger children, with each age group doing better than all the children younger than themselves.
- The number task produced significantly fewer errors than the mass and volume tasks.

Discussion

First, it seems that Piaget was right to suggest that changes in a child's understanding take place over time. As children get older the more they understand that simply changing the appearance of something doesn't mean the quantity changes. This was shown by the fact that the children who only saw the fixed array were less able to appreciate this because they could not carry over previous information into the new situation. In fact, adults may well have the same problem; if you were to show an adult two glasses of different sizes containing liquid and ask them if there is the same amount of liquid in each, it is very likely they would either say 'Possibly' or 'No', but they could not be certain. Second, Piaget suggested that the number task would be the easiest task, and Samuel and Bryant's study clearly shows he was right in this regard.

However, the findings from the earlier study by Rose and Blank, and the present study by Samuel and Bryant, both suggest that Piaget's method of asking the child the same question twice led children to give the wrong answer when in fact they *could* conserve. This was a result of the children believing that because they were being asked the same question twice, a different response was required from their answer to the first question. The fact that children were better able to conserve on the one-judgement task suggests that Piaget's methodology led him to underestimate the cognitive capabilities of younger children.

Conclusion

The study provides some evidence that supports Piaget's theory of cognitive development and also some findings suggesting that his theory needs to be refined, particularly in relation to the age at which children can conserve.

Commentary

Is the study ethical?

Where minors are being studied it is always difficult to get informed consent from the subjects themselves, and where tests are carried out by adults on children in a school setting, it is highly unlikely that the child felt they could refuse to participate or withdraw from the study. However, the test itself was not stressful or harmful and only took a few minutes. In such tests the child would not be told they were 'wrong', but just 'well done and thank you' at the end of the procedure.

Is the study useful?

Piaget's work has been very influential in education. His theory helped to describe the child for teachers and helped to establish a curriculum, especially in maths and science, which encouraged active participation in the early years (you can thank Piaget for your hours of fun at the sand tray and water tray with beakers when you were in infant school) and would allow a child to learn at its own pace, depending on the stage of cognitive development it had reached. Studies such as Samuel and Bryant's further our understanding of how children think and also show that their cognitive development and social understanding are very closely related. Often it is the social situation that influences whether or not a child will show what they know!

Is the study ecologically valid?

As we discussed in the Baron-Cohen study on autism, testing children individually and under laboratory conditions is low in ecological validity.

Are there any problems with the methodology that lead us to question the general validity of the findings?

The study itself was well designed and accounted for many of the extraneous variables that could have interfered with the results. The possibility that the answers were given by chance was addressed by the children having to have 4 attempts at each conservation test, and order effects were accounted for by varying the order of tasks given. One criticism of the number test was that the children may have simply counted the number of counters used and this may have accounted for the level of accuracy with the number task. All the children used as subjects would have been capable of counting to six and it would take a very short space of time to add up the numbers on the table.

Children often get nervous in laboratory settings and they also have a limited attention span, which may have resulted in their answers being instantaneous rather than considered. On the other hand, the number of trials should also have prevented these factors from influencing the results. However, as with all research, we can never be absolutely certain that subjects are not simply responding to even the most carefully designed experimental situation.

Key questions

1. Describe the key features of pre-operational thought.
2. Why was a control group used in the study?
3. The study aimed to test the reliability of Rose and Blank's study. What does this mean and why is it important for findings to be reliable?
4. Give one way in which the findings of the study support Piaget and one way in which they criticise his theory of cognitive development.
5. Can you think of an alternative way of investigating conservation which may have been more true to life?

Example Answers are on page 454.

189

Further reading

- Bee, H. (1995), *The Growing Child*, New York: Harper Collins.
- Bee, H. (1992), *The Developing Child*, New York: Harper Collins.
- Donaldson, M. (1978), *Children's Minds*, London: Fontana.
- Hetherington, E.M. and Parke, R.D. (1987), *Child Psychology: A Contemporary Viewpoint*, New York: McGraw-Hill.
- Smith, P. and Cowie, H. (1988), *Understanding Children's Development*, Oxford: Blackwell.

Is aggression learned?

As we have already mentioned, one of the central debates in psychology focuses on whether behaviour is innate or learned. This next section focuses primarily on the influence of learning on behaviour, although the core study itself looks at the way in which children learn aggressive behaviour by observation. The main purpose of choosing this as one of the core studies is that it allows us to focus on the topic of learning and to consider the different ways that children learn. The study also adds fuel to the nature–nurture debate in so far as most of us believe we have an innate capacity for aggression, but the way in which it is demonstrated is learned.

In order to be able to judge effectively whether children actually learn aggressive behaviour, it may be useful for us to consider briefly the theories of aggression which suggest that it is an innate capacity. In fact, one argument supporting the idea that aggression is innate comes from the fact that few parents actually teach their children to be aggressive, and yet both boys and girls demonstrate aggressive behaviour from an early age. Therefore, we will begin with theories of learning, and later in the chapter (after the core study) we will look briefly at the innate theories of aggression.

It would also be useful here to note that most textbooks include the Bandura core study into the area of social psychology and how the media influences aggressive behaviour. Although we will touch on the 'media effects on violence' argument, as we said earlier, this study is primarily intended to increase your understanding of how children learn.

THEORIES OF LEARNING

If you remember, we discussed Skinner's theory of how children learn in the section on language acquisition. Skinner, who was a behaviourist, claimed that all behaviours are learned. He explained that when an adult praises a child for a specific behaviour, this praise will act as a reinforcement and will make it more likely that the behaviour will be repeated. The child will have learned that their action has produced a positive result and will therefore repeat the action. The idea behind this kind of learning is that we learn by making an association between what we are doing and a positive result – we are conditioned to make that association.

FOCUS ON PERSPECTIVES – behaviourism

The behaviourist school was originally established by J.B. Watson in 1913. Watson argued that in order for psychology to be scientific, it must focus on the things which could be objectively assessed rather than inferred.

If you think about it, human beings respond to a specific stimulus. We talk if someone talks to us, we eat if we are hungry, we get angry if someone provokes us. Each behaviour has an antecedent (a stimulus or rather something that provokes that behaviour). Although we may think about our response to a stimulus, we may simply act on instinct. Therefore, anyone trying to analyse human behaviour would find it very difficult to work out the 'thought' part because it may vary for each person, or may not be present at all, and ultimately unless we developed telepathic powers we would have no way of knowing whether we are correct!

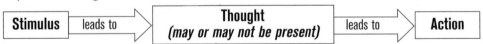

Behaviourism suggested that only the study of measurable behaviour could be considered scientific and therefore proposed that the 'thought' part of the equation should be ignored (this was the part that later interested cognitive psychologists). Watson also believed that all behaviour consisted of learned responses to different stimuli (which is really a reductionist approach where all behaviours are broken down to their basic components).

CLASSICAL AND OPERANT CONDITIONING

Although you have already been introduced to Skinner's ideas about how we learn in the section on language, there is much more to the theory than simply praising the sounds of a small child. Conditioning theory actually helps explain much of our behaviour, and is also extremely useful when trying to understand the behaviour of animals.

Imagine that you live in a huge house, with four floors. In fact, it is so big that in order for you to hear whether or not dinner is ready, the butler has to sound a huge gong which vibrates throughout the whole house. As you grow up, you always associate that sound with food, and it seems the minute you hear it you can feel your mouth watering in anticipation of the scrummy meal which awaits you.

When you leave home you move into a flat and become responsible for feeding yourself. One day you are walking down the road past some antique shops when you hear the sound of a gong being hit. It instantly makes you think of dinner and you can feel your mouth watering, so you have to go off to the nearest cake shop to get some food.

What you haven't realised is that you have become conditioned to associate the sound of a gong with food. Although you know that a gong does not indicate food when you are away from home, you cannot help the reflex response of your mouth watering when you hear the gong being hit.

This whole process is known as classical conditioning and was described by Pavlov in 1927, after he discovered that it was possible to teach dogs to salivate to the sound of a bell, rather than food. The reason was that the dogs did not consciously salivate to the sound of the bell in the first place, just as you did not consciously make your mouth water to the sound of the gong in the example above. The salivation was a reflex response to an unusual stimulus.

The way it happened with Pavlov was that he discovered that the dogs he was using for experiments started to drool before they were actually given any food. In fact, they drooled when the keeper approached the cage, or when they saw the bucket the food was carried in, or even the white coats of the keepers. Pavlov was actually interested in the digestion of dogs and was undertaking research which involved collecting dogs' saliva in a tube attached to the outside of its cheek. He decided to investigate this further, and wondered if he could teach the dog to salivate to the sound of a bell, which, as we have said, was a stimulus that under normal circumstances would not produce salivation.

For a while, Pavlov arranged for a bell to ring every time the dogs were fed. They learned to associate the sound of the bell with the fact that dinner was on its way, and soon they were slobbering the minute the bell was rung. He had taught them to make the association between a stimulus (the bell) which does not normally suggest food, and a reflex response (slobbering).

The process of classical conditioning is often referred to by a series of simple equations, but what you must remember is that classical conditioning involves training someone to produce a reflex response to something.

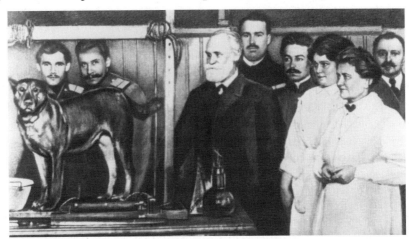

Ivan Pavlov is seen here with one of his dogs during a demonstration. His experiments in 1889 on the mechanism of digestion in dogs established the role of the ANS and won him a Nobel prize in 1904. He is best remembered for subsequent work on conditioned reflexes – conditioning a dog to salivate in anticipation of food by ringing a bell each meal time. Eventually the bell alone provoked salivation. These experiments founded behaviourist psychology.

Food (unconditioned stimulus) = Slobbering (unconditioned response)

BEFORE LEARNING

Food (unconditioned stimulus)
\+
Bell (conditioned stimulus) = Slobbering (conditioned response)

THE LEARNING PROCESS

Bell (conditioned stimulus) = Slobbering (conditioned response)

LEARNING HAVING TAKEN PLACE

The most important part of this concept is that it is possible to teach someone to respond with a reflex action to a certain stimulus. If we accept the idea that perhaps aggression is innate, and is a reflex response to certain stimuli, then we can see how some people can learn to be aggressive in specific situations. It also helps to explain how people develop phobias.

Probably the best-known example of how a phobia can develop is the case of Albert, reported by Watson and Rayner (1920). Poor little Albert was a 'stolid and unemotional' child who was healthy and happy. When he was nine months old, Watson and Rayner tested his response to a number of different things to find out if he was frightened of anything such as white rats, rabbits and masks (fear can be considered a reflex response). They discovered that the only thing that frightened him was a hammer hitting a steel bar, directly behind his head. Every time they showed him a white rat, they struck the steel bar, which was the conditioning process. After they had done this seven times over the next seven weeks, Albert showed fear and extreme distress every time a white rat was shown to him. In fact, this phobia had become so strong that he seemed to generalise the response to any furry creature, hair and even Santa Claus' beard! At this point his mother decided it was time to remove her son from the study.

Of course, there are only so many reflexes to retrain. It is possible to learn other things that have nothing to do with reflexes, such as teaching dogs to beg.

Mrs Evans had an old English sheepdog called Josephine. When Josephine was little, Mrs Evans decided to teach her to shake hands. She did this by saying 'Shake hands' to her, and holding her front paw and making her shake hands, and every time she did it, she gave Josephine a doggie chocolate as a reward. The dog soon learned that by 'shaking hands', she would be rewarded, but the trouble was when she had come in from the muddy garden, she would walk up to Mrs Evans and hit her with her front paw, leaving dirty marks all over whatever she was wearing.

What Mrs Evans had done was to use the process of conditioning to train Josephine to do something which was not a reflex response. She had learned that she would get something if she did something and this meant she was far more likely to do it. This process is called operant conditioning, and involves increasing the likelihood that a behaviour will happen again by rewarding that behaviour. Mrs Evans paired Josephine's behaviour of giving a paw with a treat (a reinforcement) until she could forget the reinforcement because the behaviour would happen anyway.

The difference between this and Pavlov's theory about how we learn is that Pavlov's learned responses would be automatically triggered by a stimulus without any sort of conscious awareness. B.F. Skinner pointed out that there was a difference between 'automatic responses' (where the response or action happens without conscious thought) and 'operants' where, initially, responses happen as a result of voluntary choice. Josephine could have chosen not to shake hands when the process of training started, although after a while the response became almost automatic.

Skinner (1938) described teaching rats how to press levers to gain food and explained how he would allow the release of a food pellet every time the rat approached the lever. Next time the rat would have to get just a little bit closer in order to get the food pellet. This would continue until the rat stepped on the lever, possibly by chance, and this released the food pellet. Finally, the rat would only get the pellet when pressing the lever. The rat learned by having its behaviour reinforced. Skinner shaped the rat's behaviour until the rat learned what was required. Sooner or later, the rat would not have to make the conscious decision 'Mmmm, now I'm hungry, I think I will go and press the lever.' It would simply do it without having to think through the process, having made an automatic association between the behaviour and the result.

As humans, we also make automatic associations, which we had to learn originally. In fact, you are doing exactly that now: you are reading without thinking about what each letter sounds like or what each word means. You actually learned to read by a process of operant conditioning, because each time you read a word either your parents or teachers would praise you, or you would feel so pleased with yourself that this would be sufficient reinforcement for you to continue. It is often the case that when you teach an animal something, and then take away the reinforcement or reward, they stop doing it. (Unfortunately, Josephine was reinforced sufficiently by pats and praise from others who had not experienced the muddy paw treatment for her to keep doing it.)

This theory can also be used to explain why some small children have screaming fits or behave very badly much of the time. Their parents are preoccupied with other things, and the child wants attention. The obvious way to get it, they have learned, is to start having a tantrum. That way, parents have to stop what they are doing and pay attention to the small child. In fact, many child guidance clinics specialise in dealing with children with behavioural problems. Frequently children who seem uncontrollable are referred and these clinics assess the parents' 'parenting skills'. The reason why the children are so badly behaved is often because they have learned that bad behaviour pays – they get the reward or reinforcement of their mum or dad's attention.

Now think about yourself. You have learned that certain types of behaviour get rewards – being nice to granny, working hard for exams, or even washing up! All of these have reinforcements which you have learned about, and which will make it more likely that you will do the same thing again. Being paid for working is a reinforcement – the harder you work, the more money you earn and the more likely your chances of promotion. You may even find that you self-reinforce by feeling good about what you are doing!

SOCIAL LEARNING THEORY

We learn the norms of our culture and acceptable patterns of social behaviour from the people in our environment. We are sometimes instructed or subtly cajoled by our parents, our teachers and our peers but more often we simply observe the way that others behave. We learn what is good and what is not acceptable within our culture by seeing who does well and who gets the rewards. Social learning theory suggests that we are more likely to learn these rules (which will vary between cultures) by the addition of rewards and reinforcements, by imitation and also by punishments such as social isolation or exclusion.

> Trevor decided to wear his sister's red dress to his fifth birthday party. After all, it was such a pretty dress and he liked the material and the beautiful lace around the neck. Everyone said his sister always looked nice when she wore it and he wanted to look nice too. Just before his guests arrived, he ran upstairs to get changed.
> When he came downstairs and walked into the sitting room to greet his school friends, they all stood and stared in horror at his appearance.

Trevor learned that at that point in time, it was not socially acceptable for him to wear a dress. In order to be accepted by his friends, he conformed to the norms of behaviour of his peer group. Let's now consider the kind of things you may have learned by observation.

You could probably list a dozen different ways of killing someone. Now imagine you have been told to disembowel them. In your mind, can you picture what you would have to do and what the person's innards look like? It is quite likely that you will be able to conjure up a totally gruesome picture, which is very messy and bloody and probably quite lifelike. But how do you know all these things? Most likely, you will have seen it on TV or at the cinema. You have learned by observing and have stored that information to be used if and when necessary. However, you have not been rewarded for learning these kinds of behaviours, which suggests that there is a difference between traditional theories of learning and social learning theory.

Bandura's early work indicated that children who have seen another person behaving aggressively will be increasingly likely to demonstrate aggressive behaviour. Later he suggested that aggression is actually something we learn to demonstrate because it seems to pay. An example of this is a child who has become a very aggressive bully at school because he has learned that he will get what he wants – sweets, money or status with the other children. But where has he learned to be aggressive? Bandura claims that children learn by seeing others behaving aggressively during their childhood or adolescence, through their own experience of being bullied, or through observation of the media. The likelihood of them imitating the behaviour will increase if they see the person being rewarded (reinforced) for their aggression, perhaps by getting what they want.

The implications that arise from our knowledge that we learn by observation must relate to the kinds of images we are exposed to on the television. In fact, a number of studies have been conducted to look at whether television and cinema violence really does result in violent behaviour. The problem with most of this research is that it is not ethical to expose groups of children to violent videos to see how they will act. Can you imagine the responses of parents if you asked them to allow their children to be tested in this way?

Research evidence has shown a link between television violence and later aggression. For example, an early study was carried out by Liebert and Baron (1972), where they showed one group of children a violent film and another control group an exciting but non-violent sporting event for the same length of time. Each of the children were then allowed to play with a group of children who had not seen the films and their behaviour was observed. The children who saw the violent film were far more aggressive than the control group. The problem is, we don't know if there was any measure of aggression in the children before the start of the study. It would have been a fluke, but it is possible that all the children who were aggressive before the start of the study may have been put in one group.

FOCUS ON RESEARCH METHODS – correlations

Research into the effects of watching violent films on subsequent behaviour involves using a correlational design. This means that the participant is measured on two variables, the first being the amount of time spent viewing (television/cinema) and the second being instances of aggressive behaviour. If there are high levels of one (lots of violent films having been watched) and high levels of the other (manifestations of violent behaviour), this would result in a positive correlation. However, correlations cannot show cause and effect, simply relationships between two variables, and therefore the cause of the behaviour may have been something different, such as a physiological defect in the brain (which links in with the study by Raine on p. 313).

Other studies have tried to measure aggression before the study starts in order to see how much more aggressive the children become. An example of this was the study by Williams (1986), who used observations of the children, together with teacher and peer reports, to get an idea of how aggressive they were at the beginning of the study. The idea was to compare the levels of aggression in children who lived in communities where television had only just become available with levels in children who already had access to television. They found that aggressive behaviour in the children aged six to 11 increased during the two years after television had been introduced, but was no different for the children who already had access to television. These results support the idea that being given access to images which will contain some aggressive acts will impact on the subsequent levels of aggressive behaviour of the child observers.

A. Bandura, D. Ross and S.A. Ross (1961) 'Transmission of aggression through imitation of aggressive models',

Journal of Abnormal & Social Psychology, 63, 575–82

Background

In order to demonstrate the power of social learning theory, Bandura designed a study which looked at whether children would imitate the actions of different role models when given the opportunity. If they did produce the same aggressive actions, this would show two things. First, learning can take place all at once, rather than by the step-by-step process which would involve reinforcement of all the component parts of a behaviour. This was the process advocated by Skinner, and Bandura criticised Skinner's approach as it would take too long for all behaviours to be acquired in this way. Second, direct reinforcement is not necessary for a behaviour to be learned. The original model need not be present. The behaviour can be stored up and demonstrated when the appropriate opportunity arises.

Aim

The aim of the study was to see whether children will imitate aggressive behaviour when given the opportunity, even if they saw these behaviours in a different environment and the original model they observed performing the aggressive act is no longer present.

Bandura's study aimed to test four hypotheses:

1. Ss exposed to an aggressive model would produce more imitative aggressive acts than Ss exposed to a non-aggressive model and Ss not exposed to a model at all (the control group).

2. Exposing Ss to a non-aggressive model would have an inhibiting effect on their aggressive behaviours and they would show significantly less aggression than the control group who saw no model.

3. It was assumed that pre-school children would have been reinforced for appropriate sex-role behaviour by their parents, that girls would have been positively reinforced for behaving in appropriate ways (*e.g.* cooking, being maternal), whereas boys would be negatively reinforced for these behaviours as they were not deemed appropriate for boys. Therefore, Bandura *et al.* predicted that the sex of the model would have an effect: children would be more likely to copy a same-sex model (girls would copy a woman more and boys would copy a man more).

4. Since aggression is stereotypically a male behaviour, boys would have been positively reinforced for this behaviour and girls negatively reinforced. Therefore, Bandura *et al.* expected boys to imitate more aggressive acts than girls, especially with a same-sex (male) model.

Method

Design

A laboratory experiment was carried out.

Variables

The independent variables were:
- whether there was an adult model present or not
- whether the model was male or female
- whether the model behaved aggressively or non-aggressively.

This meant different children were tested in the following conditions:
- observed an aggressive male model
- observed an aggressive female model
- observed a non-aggressive male model
- observed a non-aggressive female model
- no model (control condition).

This gives an independent groups design, where the overall performance of each group was compared with each of the other groups.

The dependent variable was the amount of aggression demonstrated by the child in a later situation (both imitative and non-imitative).

Subjects

In total, 72 children were tested: 36 boys and 36 girls from Stanford University Nursery School, aged between 37 and 69 months (mean age 52 months). The children were therefore between the ages of three and six.

The children were allocated to conditions as follows. The control group was made up of 24 children, 12 boys and 12 girls, who would see no role model. The two experimental groups were then subdivided into two groups of 24 subjects each: aggressive model observers (six female and six male Ss to see a female role model and six female and six male Ss to see a male role model), and non-aggressive model observers six female and six male Ss to see a female role model and six female and six male Ss to see a male role model.

Subjects	No role model (control group)	Aggressive model		Non-aggressive model	
		female	male	female	male
Boys	12	6	6	6	6
Girls	12	6	6	6	6

Controlling extraneous variables

Matching was carried out in order to prevent subject variables from influencing the results. Since some children are generally more aggressive than others anyway, the Ss were rated for aggression before being allocated into their groups. This was done by one of the female experimenters and the children's nursery school teacher, both of whom knew the children well prior to the study. The children were rated on a five-point scale for previous displays of physical and verbal aggression, aggression towards objects and their ability to control their behaviour when they were angry (aggressive inhibition).

The results of the two raters were considered to be reliable because they significantly correlated with each other. The groups of six children were then established to ensure the level of aggression shown previously by the children was matched across the groups so no one group was generally more aggressive than another at the outset.

FOCUS ON RESEARCH METHODS – establishing the reliability of findings and inter-observer reliability between observers/raters

If a test or measure is reliable this means that it gives significantly similar results on retesting. For a study or test to be established as reliable, it must be carried out using the same procedure on similar subjects under similar circumstances to give similar results. The way the results are tested to see if they are similar is to apply correlational statistics. If a significant positive correlation is established, this supports the reliability of the study's findings. This is important because if the findings are not reliable, they will not be valid.

In order to avoid observer bias, that is, an observer applying ratings or counting categories in a subjective rather than objective fashion, inter-observer reliability needs to be established. This means that two observers rate or observe the same behaviour and the two sets of ratings are correlated. If a significant positive correlation is seen, inter-observer reliability has been established and the objectivity of the results confirmed.

In the Bandura study this stops any conscious or unconscious bias occurring on the part of the teacher or experimenter in their assessment of the children's general aggression.

Materials

Role models: One male and one female role model, briefed to behave in a standardised way. The same male and female model were used throughout and therefore played both the aggressive and non-aggressive roles.

Location: The study took place at the Stanford University Nursery School.

There were three rooms used for the study, one in the children's nursery building and two set away from the children's main nursery building.

Room one: The experimental room had a table and chair in one corner with potato prints and picture stickers (selected because children like playing with them). In the other corner was another table and chair with a Tinkertoy set (which is a kind of construction set consisting of dowels and discs with holes in them to fit them together), a mallet and a five-foot high inflatable Bobo doll (which when you punch it, rocks back up again). This room was located in the main nursery school building and was therefore familiar to the children.

Room two: This room contained a number of very attractive toys, including a fire engine, a train, a plane and a doll with lots of clothes and a cot. The idea behind this room was to try to arouse aggression in all the children by letting them start to play with the toys and then taking them away, saying they were being saved for another group of children.

Room three: This room was next door to room two. These rooms were away from the main nursery building, so the setting was separate from where the observation of models took place. Many children thought they were no longer in the nursery school. Room three was also connected to an observation room with a one-way mirror through which observers could monitor the behaviour of the children. It contained a number of toys which were always placed in exactly the same position for each of the subjects. This standardisation of the setting of toys was done to ensure that one toy was not nearer to or more prominent for one child than for another, as this could have influenced their choice of which toys to play with.

The toys were either considered aggressive or non-aggressive. *Non-aggressive toys* were dolls, bears, construction toys, crayons, cars and plastic farm animals. *Aggressive toys* were a three-foot high Bobo doll, a mallet and peg board and dart guns.

Procedure

Each child was tested individually in a three-step procedure. The same female experimenter led each child through the three steps.

Step one (duration approximately ten minutes):
The children in the aggressive and non-aggressive conditions were tested in this step. The E took them into the first room, where they were seated at the child's table and encouraged to play with the potato prints and stickers. The model was then escorted into the opposite corner of the room and told that the Tinkertoy set, mallet and Bobo were for him/her to play with. Then the E left the room.

In the aggressive condition the model started by playing with the Tinkertoy set, but after a minute turned to the Bobo doll and started to act aggressively towards it. The aggressive acts were deliberately stylised so that imitation of them would be clear and not just examples of how children play with Bobo anyway. The physically aggressive acts were repeated about three times in the ten-minute period the child stayed in this room, and they were interpersed with the verbally aggressive responses and non aggressive phrases.

Physically aggressive acts	Laid Bobo on its side, sat on it and punched it on the nose. Raised Bobo up and hit it on the head with the mallet. Threw Bobo in the air and kicked it around the room.
Verbally aggressive responses	'Pow' 'Throw him in the air' 'Kick him' 'Sock him on the nose' 'Hit him down'
Non-aggressive phrases	'He keeps coming back for more' 'He sure is a tough fella'

In the non-aggressive condition, the procedure was the same except that once seated at the table the adult assembled the Tinkertoy set in a quiet, subdued way and ignored the Bobo doll for the ten minutes the child was in the room. After ten minutes, the experimenter came to collect the S saying they were going to another room now and said goodbye to the model.

Step two:
All the children, including the control group, were then taken into room two where they were subjected to mild aggression arousal. Having been allowed to play with the very attractive toys for two minutes, the experimenter stopped them and told them these were her very best toys and that she did not let just anyone play with them and she had decided to save them for the other boys and girls to play with. She then told each child that they could play with any of the toys in the next room and took them to room three.

The reason why this mild aggression arousal was induced for the aggression condition was that previous studies had shown that observing the aggression of others often inhibits (suppresses) a person's own aggressiveness, and this might mean the children in this condition were less inclined to be aggressive than the other two groups in room three, which would confound the study.

For the non-aggressive condition, the presence of the non-aggressive model was supposed to inhibit their aggressiveness, and this could be seen most clearly if the children were less aggressive in circumstances where they had good reason to be aggressive, and this is why their aggression was aroused in step two.

The control group was exposed to this stage to ensure fair comparisons could be made with the other two groups of children.

Step three (duration approximately 20 minutes):
The experimenter then took each child to room three and stayed with them, as some of the children refused to go into this room on their own or tried to leave before the end of the allotted time (this was because they had been upset by step two, presumably). To avoid affecting the children's behaviour, *the experimenter* worked discreetly at the other end of the room.

The child was able to play with the toys and their behaviour was observed for 20 minutes through the one-way mirror. Two observers scored the subjects' behaviour at five-second intervals, which gave 240 observations for each subject; the level of inter-observer reliability was highly significant.

The children were observed for the following categories of behaviour.

Three measures of direct imitation:
- imitation of aggressive acts
- imitation of aggressive phrases
- imitation of non-aggressive phrases.

Two measures of indirect imitation:
- the subject hit other things with the mallet (remember the subject only saw the model hit Bobo with the mallet)
- subject laid Bobo on its side and sat on it but was not aggressive towards it.

Four further types of aggressive behaviour which were not imitations of the adult role model (this would tell the researchers whether the general aggression of the children was inhibited or increased as a result of seeing one of the two models):
- striking, slapping or pushing the doll aggressively
- behaving aggressively to any other objects
- producing novel hostile remarks aimed at Bobo or other objects, e.g. 'Cut him', 'Shoot the Bobo', 'Knock over people', 'Horses fighting, biting'
- shooting darts or aiming the gun and pretending to shoot various objects in the room.

Results

The results have been broken down to make them easier to digest, but at the end of this section you will find the whole table for the mean aggression scores for all subjects.

What do the results tell us in relation to Bandura's four hypotheses?

Hypothesis	What the result showed
Hypothesis one: Subjects exposed to an aggressive model would produce more imitative aggressive acts than Ss not exposed to any model (the control group) and Ss exposed to a non-aggressive model.	The results show that this was true for all behaviours.
Hypothesis two: Ss exposed to a non-aggressive model would have an inhibiting effect on their aggressive behaviours and would show significantly less aggression than the control group who saw no model.	The researchers observed no significant general inhibiting effect, *but* when the results are looked at by sex of model, the male non-aggressive model had a significant inhibiting effect on the children.
Hypothesis three: The sex of the model would have an effect: children would be more likely to copy a same-sex model (girls would copy a woman more and boys copy a man more).	Boys showed more aggression if the model was male than if the model was female. Girls showed more PHYSICAL aggression if the model was male and more VERBAL aggression if the model was female. Subjects who saw the same-sex role model only imitated their behaviour in some categories.
Hypothesis four: Boys would imitate more aggressive acts than girls, especially with a same-sex (male) model.	Boys did display more PHYSICAL aggression than girls if the model was male, but girls displayed more VERBAL aggression than boys if the model was female.

	Female model	Male model
Imitative physical aggression		
Female subjects	5.5	7.2
Male subjects	12.4	25.8
Imitative verbal aggression		
Female subjects	13.7	4.3
Male subjects	2.0	12.7
Non-imitative aggression		
Female subjects	21.3	8.4
Male subjects	16.2	36.7
Aggressive gun play		
Female subjects	1.8	7.3
Male subjects	4.5	15.9

Table showing mean totals of aggressive behaviours and the gender of the role model

Response Category	Experimental groups				
	Aggressive		Non-aggressive		Control
	F model	M model	F model	M model	groups
Imitative physical aggression					
Female subjects	5.5	7.2	2.5	0.0	1.2
Male subjects	12.4	25.8	0.2	1.5	2.0
Imitative verbal aggression					
Female subjects	13.7	2.0	0.3	0.0	0.7
Male subjects	4.3	12.7	1.1	0.0	1.7
Mallet aggression					
Female subjects	17.2	18.7	0.5	0.5	13.1
Male subjects	15.5	28.8	18.7	6.7	13.5
Punches Bobo doll					
Female subjects	6.3	16.5	5.8	4.3	11.7
Male subjects	18.9	11.9	15.6	14.8	15.7
Non-imitative aggression					
Female subjects	21.3	8.4	7.2	1.4	6.1
Male subjects	16.2	36.7	26.1	22.3	24.6
Aggressive gun play					
Female subjects	1.8	4.5	2.6	2.5	3.7
Male subjects	7.3	15.9	8.9	16.7	14.3

Table showing mean totals of behaviour for all conditions

Discussion

It appears that although the children who saw the aggressive models were far more aggressive than the other two groups, the gender of the role model had a large impact on their behaviour.

The female role model seemed to cause confusion in the children, because she was not behaving in a way that they would expect for a female role model. They made comments like, 'Who is that lady? That's not the way for a lady to behave.' 'You should have seen what that girl did in there. She was just acting like a man. I never saw a girl act like that before. She was punching and fighting but not swearing' (p. 581).

The male role model's aggressive behaviour, on the other hand, was more likely to be seen as normal. The children made comments like, 'Al's a good socker, he beat up Bobo', 'I want to sock like Al', and so on. Bandura points out that this may be due in part to the children's expectations of behaviour: they already had ideas about what was sex-appropriate behaviour for men and women. For example, one girl said, 'That man is a strong fighter, he punched Bobo right down to the floor and if Bobo got up he said, "Punch your nose." He's a good fighter like Daddy'. The children's comments show us that they have clear ideas that fighting is acceptable, even desirable, for males and unacceptable for females.

Since girls are more likely to have been discouraged from behaving aggressively as this is male-typical behaviour, and boys will have been encouraged to behave this way, this explains Bandura *et al.*'s findings that the boys were more aggressive than girls, and that the male aggressive model elicited the most imitation. Learned appropriate behaviour also explains why the girls were more verbally aggressive and the boys were more physically aggressive in the male aggression condition.

Physical aggression is clearly a masculine-typed behaviour, therefore the boys' domain and not appropriate for the girls, whereas verbal aggression is not so clearly sex-typed and was therefore available as an aggressive outlet for the girls, who may have been suppressing their desire to behave in a physically aggressive way.

The inhibition of aggressive behaviour by the non-aggressive male model can be explained by the fact that male models have a greater effect due to male dominance in society, and also because by playing quietly with the Tinkertoy set, the male model was behaving in a non sex-typed manner.

Commentary

Do children learn by imitation?

This study certainly shows that children can learn as a result of imitation and without either the child or the model being reinforced. This suggests that modelling is a form of observational learning.

FOCUS ON THEMES – what does Bandura *et al.*'s study show us about reinforcement?

Bandura went on to investigate how modelling leads to learning in future studies, developing his social learning theory, which brings together the behaviourist concept of reinforcement and the Freudian concept of identification (which you will learn more about later in this chapter), since behaviour which is positively reinforced is more likely to be imitated, and the person is more likely to imitate a role model with whom they identify.

Bandura *et al.* showed that learning can occur without the learner receiving reinforcement, but suggested that reinforcement may play an important part in the learner's decision to perform the behaviour at an appropriate point. Therefore, reinforcement, whether direct, vicarious or self-reinforcement, is one factor which may influence the performance of a learned behaviour.

Remember, just because learning has occurred, it does not follow that the behaviour will be performed. We all know how to stick our heads in the oven, but we don't do it!

FOCUS ON THEMES – do Bandura *et al.*'s findings contribute to the nature–nurture debate?

Is aggression learned or innate? The study's results show us that there is a clear difference between the aggressive behaviour of boys and girls, but can this difference be attributed to biology or socialisation? Is it that boys have biological differences, such as higher levels of the male hormone testosterone that makes them more aggressive? Is it that both boys and girls are clearly taught their sex-appropriate behaviours by their parents, teachers and the media from an early age and this accounts for why boys are more aggressive than girls? Bandura *et al.*'s study fails to shed any light on this.

Is the study ecologically valid?

In terms of explaining the acquisition of aggressive behaviour, the study lacks ecological validity. Children are very rarely in a room with a strange adult on their own, and if they are then it would be unusual for the adult not to engage the child in conversation, or vice versa. Children tend to learn from adults and peers they know and who can offer their opinions and approval of what is going on, and they were isolated from this experience in this study.

The study could simply be said to be looking at how children learn to be aggressive to an inflatable doll. The fact that the object of aggression was not human may also limit the generalisability of the results. Also, a Bobo doll is supposed to be punched and hit. What if the adult had been aggressive towards a toy that would not usually elicit aggressive play? What if the adult tore the arms and legs off a cute teddy bear? Would the results have been the same, do you think?

Is the study ethical?

This study raises a number of ethical issues. First, there is no mention of informed consent being sought from parents. Certainly the young children would not have been in a position to give consent on their own behalf to taking part in the study. Perhaps consent was not sought because the researchers thought parents might not consent to their child being involved on a study on learning aggression! Remember, this study preceded Milgram's by two years, and researchers were not as concerned about strictly adhering to ethical guidelines prior to the debate on ethics in psychological research that followed Milgram's obedience experiments.

Second, the children were distressed during the study. The children were deliberately frustrated in step two when they were told the really good toys were to be reserved for the other children. We know this was significantly upsetting for some of the Ss because the E had to stay with the child in room three because some children were upset and refused to stay on their own or wanted to leave before the allotted time was up. The children were therefore encouraged (coerced?) into continuing with the study when they clearly did not want to. This implies they did not have the right to withdraw.

Finally, there is the problem of whether or not the children suffered any long-term consequences as a result of the study. It would have not been possible to debrief the children as they would not have understood what had been done, and it would be very difficult for the researchers to undo any harm that had been caused by the study.

Although it is unlikely that taking part in the study made the children significantly more aggressive in the future, we can never be certain. This is one of the major problems with any sort of study which involves looking at the origins of aggressive behaviour.

Is the study useful?

The study is useful to psychology in that it demonstrates observational learning in practice and shows how the different models affected the children.

In terms of applications to real-life settings, Bandura's work has been described as the first in a series of scientific studies into media violence. Later studies used video footage of Bobo-bashing as well as 'live' models. However, Bandura himself warned against interpreting his results as evidence of copycat TV violence, cautioning that learning does not necessarily lead to performance. We must therefore be careful not to assume that just because there are violent programmes on TV that the behaviours will be copied in the real world.

Key questions

1. Data was gathered by covert observation through a one-way mirror. Give one strength and one weakness of collecting data in this way.
2. What is interrater-reliability and how was it used in the study?
3. Explain the purpose for testing *all* the children in step two.
4. Why was the Bobo doll in room three only three feet high?
5. What are the ethical problems with this study?

Example Answers are on page 455.

Postscript – Innate theories of aggression

In order to complete the argument that perhaps we are just innately aggressive and that all this learning theory is just a way of reducing the 'blame', we will have a brief look at the three main theories suggesting that aggression is innate. You will probably find them relatively easy to accept, because at some point in your life you will have felt very angry, but on reflection may have realised that that anger was actually unreasonable. You will also probably be familiar with the fight/flight mechanism (which we will look at in more detail in chapter five), which suggests that when trapped, we either come out fighting or run away without really considering the consequences.

Lorenz (1950) proposed that aggression is innate in his hydraulic model of aggression. He suggested that aggression builds up within all species, both humans and animals, until something happens to trigger its release – and that this build-up is inevitable. The trigger is usually something specific to each species, for example, the baring of teeth in a dog or a cat arching its back and spitting. With humans the trigger could be as simple as a stare which is perceived as threatening. On the other hand, it could be as simple as someone driving into your parking space in a car park just as you are about to back into it.

Lorenz claimed that these aggressive energies continually build up inside us, just like a tank filling with liquid as a result of a constantly dripping tap. Obviously the tank will overflow unless the liquid is allowed to drain off from time to time. Therefore Lorenz believed that it was necessary for society to provide opportunities for this level of aggression to be released in a harmless way, such as playing football or doing national service.

Unfortunately, there is virtually no evidence to back up the idea that allowing a safe method of discharge actually reduces aggression. It may almost appear to work the other way, with people who engage in aggressive sports actually becoming more aggressive. You can probably imagine that if someone is trained to fight, as a boxer, for example, and they are better at it than the average person, then it will come easy to them to use it as a means of settling any sort of dispute – an automatic response.

Another explanation for aggressive behaviour focuses on biological factors (which may not be innate), such as hormone levels, chromosomes and abnormalities in the physiological structure of the brain (the physiological aspects of our behaviour will be discussed in more detail in chapter six). It has often been noted that high levels of the hormone testosterone result in aggressive behaviours (which helps to explain why men are more aggressive than women). To back up this argument, Maccoby and Jacklin (1974) concluded that boys are consistently more aggressive than girls after undertaking dozens of laboratory experiments and field studies amongst different social classes in various cultures. It is also the case that men are far more frequently charged with violent offences than women, whereas women are usually charged with offences against property. It has been found that testosterone levels are actually higher in both male and female prisoners who have been convicted of violent crimes compared with prisoners who have been convicted of non-violent offences (Dabbs *et al.*, 1995).

Gender as an explanation of crime provides a link to applied psychology. Statistics confirm that women are convicted of crimes to a far lesser extent than men and this pattern seems to hold true across the world. Studies from a variety of countries show that approximately 80% of crimes are committed by men. According to Home Office statistics (1992), one in three men and one in 13 women are likely to have a conviction for a serious offence by the age of 31. In England and Wales in 1993, women committed only 12% of all offences.

The general pattern is that although men and women commit similar crimes, they do so at very different rates; for example, women are far less likely to commit robbery, sexual offences or murder. The highest reported type of crime for women was fraud and forgery, but women still only committed around 20% of all those offences (Giddens, 1997).

Another explanation for aggression, which indicates that it takes more than a sign stimulus to produce an aggressive response, is Dollard *et al.*'s (1939) frustration–aggression hypothesis. Dollard suggests that if we feel frustrated in our efforts to achieve some kind of goal or to get what we want, we are more likely to become aggressive. Frustration can often lead to the expression of anger, much of which is not directly related to the situation itself.

There is a small problem with this argument, and that is that we don't always act in the same way if we are frustrated. Some people simply walk away from a situation if they can't get what they want and seem to be unharrassed by it. Seligman (1975) pointed out that continual frustration may lead to us becoming totally passive because we have learned that we are helpless. He calls this state a state of 'learned helplessness'.

Further reading

- Gunter B. and McAleer, J. (1990), *Children and Television*, London: Routledge.
- http://www.homeoffice.gov.uk/rds/pdfs2/hosb703chap123.pdf – Home Office Crime Survey.

http://www.psep.pl/a-eg/07cpgen.html
http://www.homeoffice.gov.uk/rds/pdfs2/hosb703chap123.pdf
(Home Office Crime Survey)

Maternal deprivation

When you listen to the news, have you noticed how reporters tend to focus on the background of the criminal who has been charged with an offence? They focus on things like coming from 'deprived backgrounds' or being part of a 'single-parent family' or having been 'abused as a child'. Although few of us have idyllic childhoods, and many of us come from single-parent families, we don't all turn into raving psychopaths – do we?

Carole: Do you know, if a child doesn't have a mother, it will turn into a weirdo and won't be able to form relationships with other people. It may even become a psychopath.

Alex: Where on earth did you get that rubbish from?

Carole: I read it in a book.

Alex: And how old is the book?

Carole: Dunno. It was an old book called 'Childcare and the Growth of Love' by a man called John Bowlby. I found it propping up the bottom of a bookshelf at my gran's.

Alex: Well, you should have left it there!

Carole found a book which was published in 1953 and had been commissioned by the World Health Organization as a way of looking into what was needed for the large number of children who, as a result of the Second World War, had become orphaned or separated from their parents and therefore had been taken into care. Bowlby had produced a report which not only drew on his own research, but also took into account the findings of other researchers, suggesting that if a child were deprived of its mother this would cause deep, long-lasting psychological problems for the child which would mean that they would be unable to form meaningful relationships with other people in later life.

Before we look at Bowlby and the evidence he used towards forming his theories, just think for a moment. You must realise that there are things that happen to us in our childhood which will have an effect on how we turn out as adults. Deprivation and neglect, experiencing family violence and learning from the behaviour of others are all likely to affect how we develop into adults. Whether we really believe that 'mother' is the key to our development, and lack of 'mother' is going to turn us into someone unable to function emotionally, is another matter.

It may also be useful to remember that Bowlby's *Childcare and the Growth of Love* was written in 1951 and its contents may well have been indirectly influenced by the war. Women had found a new kind of freedom during the war years – in effect, they had been running the country while their men were away fighting. This was the first time that women had demonstrated their abilities by showing a much greater equality with men, farming, working in factories, mending vehicles and so on. Pity the men on their return. Perhaps they felt superfluous to requirements and therefore unnecessary, and Bowlby's book was a move to put women back into their homes, in their rightful places!

The purpose behind Bowlby's study was to look at how the mental health of children may have been affected by being orphaned or separated from their families, resulting in them being placed in institutional care or foster homes. It was not intended to look at refugees, who would bring with them even more complex problems, such as cultural and language difficulties. The report focused on children who were in their native countries. Institutional care of the time focused on children's physical needs, but not on their emotional needs, and so the intention of the report was to try to identify the best kind of upbringing for these disadvantaged children.

Bowlby may not have been the ideal person to carry out such a study because he believed that mothers and babies had evolved a biological need for each other. He claimed that if they were separated from each other during the first five years of the child's life, this would result in emotional and social repercussions for the infant. Bowlby was strongly influenced by the teachings of Freud (who we will look at in the final section) and his work involved him in the psychoanalysis of people with emotional and social problems. He actually believed that children are genetically programmed to bond with a specific 'other' person during the first months of life and claimed that 'mother love in infancy and childhood is as important for mental health as are vitamins and proteins for physical health' (Bowlby, 1951). It therefore seems quite obvious that he would suggest having no mother would cause problems for a child's mental welfare. He does accept that sometimes the relationship between a mother and child is not always perfect, and that there are rejecting mothers (but this would be caused by the mother having suffered maternal deprivation in *her* childhood and, as a result, being unable to form a relationship with her baby).

To give you some idea how convinced Bowlby was about the importance of the mother, he states:

What is believed to be essential for mental health is that an infant and young child should experience a warm, intimate and continuous relationship with his mother (or permanent mother-substitute – one person who steadily 'mothers' him) in which both find satisfaction and enjoyment.

Bowlby, 1953, p. 1

In the book, he gives example after example of children who have been separated or have experienced what he calls 'grossly disturbed relationships with their mothers in their early years'. He gives a number of typical features which would be found, such as the following list (Bowlby, 1953, p. 37):
- superficial relationships
- no real feeling – no capacity to care for people or to make true friends
- an inaccessibility, exasperating to those trying to help
- no emotional response to situations where it is normal – a curious lack of concern
- deceit and evasion, often pointless; stealing; lack of concentration at school.

He also insisted that a baby can only form an attachment to its mother during the first two years of life as this was the 'critical period'. By this he was suggesting that if the child did not 'attach' during this time, it would lose the ability to do so, and this would result in serious long-term consequences for the child. (Although this sounds a bit extreme, Bowlby based many of his ideas on the work of ethologists who had looked at animal behaviours.) Therefore, the first two years of life were most important, although the risk of suffering damage due to lack of maternal care after that age was 'still serious, though much less so than earlier'.

The final conclusion to Bowlby's beliefs was that children who had been deprived of a mother over the first five years of life would have their social development affected and would be extremely likely to become juvenile delinquents. They may even develop what Bowlby described as 'affectionless psychopathy'.

Affectionless psychopaths have a disorder whereby they can't form personal relationships with others and are unaware of or (more likely) indifferent to other people's feelings, which would have come from lack of the primary relationship with their mothers. They are amoral, often very manipulative and frequently commit antisocial acts, such as using violence or demonstrating some kind of perverted behaviour. Most serial killers are psychopaths, as they experience no guilt about their behaviour, which allows them to go on killing.

What we need to consider is where all these ideas came from, because although Bowlby might have been somewhat extreme, he was not stupid, and he used documented evidence as a way of developing his ideas. As I mentioned earlier, studies of animal behaviour, especially work carried out by Lorenz, heavily influenced his thinking.

The influence of Lorenz

Lorenz was an ethologist. Ethologists study behaviours where they naturally occur because they believe that this is the only way the behaviour has meaning. Imagine a fox and a dog digging holes – the behaviour is the same for both, but the reasons are very different. The fox is digging a new home and the dog is burying something, but you wouldn't know this unless you watched them in their own natural environments.

Lorenz was interested in the way that young ducks and geese follow their parents around from very soon after they have hatched and seem to avoid any other creatures, even other ducks or geese. Lorenz found through laboratory experiments that young geese had an innate tendency to follow a large moving object if they encountered it soon after hatching. If the object was removed before they had been following it for ten minutes, they seemed to give up on it and then ignore it. But if they were allowed to follow it for more than ten minutes, they seemed to become extremely attached to it and they wouldn't follow anything else.

Lorenz called this process 'imprinting'. Imprinting is a rapid attachment which is formed as a result of a special kind of innate learning. This makes sense in evolutionary terms – in the natural environment the only large creature that is likely to stay around for ten minutes is the mother. Therefore, this time gap is perhaps a safety factor. Further research by Lorenz showed that if the birds did not see another large creature within 25 hours, they would lose the ability to imprint. This led to the conclusion that there was a 'critical period' during a young bird's development when it had to imprint. Bowlby transferred this idea of a critical period to humans and explains why he believed that young children had to form attachments within a certain time.

There are countless studies cited by Bowlby in his book, all of which point to the fact that maternal deprivation seems to be the key feature in children's lack of emotional development. It lists study after study which supports his idea that a child needs its mother, and if it suffers any separation is severely disadvantaged. Unfortunately, many of the studies are not actually named, but simply talked about in general terms, which means that you cannot check them or read any more about them. However, one study which is worth mentioning is one conducted by Bowlby himself, in 1946, when he was looking at juvenile delinquency. He had a child guidance clinic in London for disturbed teenagers and his subjects were selected from the people attending the clinic, which was hardly a representative sample of the population as a whole.

He compared a group of 44 emotionally disturbed teenagers, who had been reported as thieves, with a control group who were similar in number, age and gender and who were also emotionally disturbed, but who did not steal. Bowlby noticed that 14 of the thieves were 'affectionless characters', but none of the control group fitted this category. In fact, 17 of the thieves had been completely separated from their mothers or established foster mothers, for at least six months, if not more, during the first five years of their lives, whereas only two of the control group had experienced that type of separation. I suppose we could ask why, if 17 had been completely separated, only 14 developed 'affectionless characters'? What happened to the other three? Also, what made the two members of the control group 'normal'?

Unfortunately, Bowlby didn't answer these questions. He simply concluded:

'there can be no doubting that for the affectionless thief, nurture, not nature, is to blame… There is a very strong case indeed for believing that prolonged separation of a child from his mother (or mother substitute) during the first five years of life stands foremost among the causes of delinquent character development.'

Bowlby, 1953, p. 41

Perhaps we should simply put the results down to the methodology. As I said, he had a pre-selected sample. Bowlby chose delinquents as his subjects and used retrospective evidence, that is, evidence which is remembered. As we know, our memories are not always as accurate as we would like them to be and they can become distorted with time. Perhaps there were incomplete records of the children's childhoods and perhaps the children just felt really angry and upset about their experiences as little ones. They may well have had distorted memories about these events, and we have no idea what else had happened to them in the intervening years. Think of the other things which could have affected them – peer groups, institutions, poor fostering, physical deprivation, lower levels of intelligence and so on. Also, this study did not consider how many children were separated and *didn't* suffer from the same effects.

Before we go on to look at the research which disputes Bowlby, you may be interested in a study carried out after Bowlby's report by a man called Harry Harlow. Again, it was a study of animal behaviour, but in this instance it involved primates, rhesus monkeys to be precise. The idea behind the study was to look at why we form attachments. The obvious answer to this is that it must have something to do with survival. But why is it that we seem to form such a strong attachment to one person, usually the mother? Is there something biological there, or is it simply that we know when we are on to a good thing, and form attachments with the person who is most likely to do the best for us? We also know that sometimes mother is not the best caregiver around, and yet the attachment of the child to the mother is still very strong.

214

The primate study looked into what was called 'cupboard love theory'. This theory suggests that we attach to the person who feeds us. If this is the case, Bowlby's theory that the mother is the most important person factor in children's development would collapse in a heap because it would suggest that any old 'feeder' would do. Harlow and Zimmerman (1959) put a number of newborn rhesus monkeys in cages on their own with either a towelling 'mother' substitute or a wire 'mother'. The wire mother had a teat emerging from her 'chest' whilst the towelling mother had nothing. If food was the issue, the wire monkey would have become the surrogate mother for the tiny monkey. However, the towelling one became the mother substitute and the tiny monkey would run to cling to it whenever it was frightened.

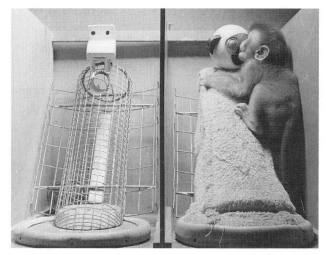

The tiny rhesus monkey clings to the towelling mother even though the wire mother is the one who provides the food

Three years later, Harlow reported on the monkeys who had now grown up. Although they had appeared physically normal and were fit and healthy, it seemed that they had not developed emotionally. They were much more timid than the other monkeys and didn't know how to act when put in a cage with other monkeys who had been raised normally. Because they had no idea how to behave in a social situation, the behaviours they did produce were quite unusual and they became prime targets for bullying.

The conclusion Harlow made as a result of this study was that their behaviour was due to maternal deprivation, and he claimed that if baby monkeys weren't allowed to form a relationship with their mother within the first six months, they would never form one. This, for them, was the critical period. When you think about it, they weren't just suffering from maternal deprivation, but also social deprivation. Further studies raised monkeys in isolation, but allowed them 20 minutes a day in a playroom with three other monkeys, and even this level of interaction was enough to teach them basic social skills. This suggests that perhaps the most important factor in predicting social inadequacy is *social* deprivation rather than simply maternal deprivation.

Henry clung to his mother's skirt and she tried to brush him off as if he were some irritating little fly hanging on for dear life. She caught sight of herself in the mirrors along the wall in the supermarket and adjusted her hair. 'Mmmm, not bad,' she thought as she turned as far as possible to see her profile. On her way to the checkout, she spied an attractive man in his early thirties, and gently manipulated her way in his general direction. Henry dragged behind. She tried to remove him with a well-aimed shove from her snakeskin high-heeled boots, but missed. She couldn't do it again without it becoming obvious and then she'd have one of the old dears in the supermarket wittering on about child cruelty.

Henry fell off. She launched forward, hoping to leave him behind for the few minutes it might take her to gently bump into her target. 'That should be long enough,' she thought, 'then I can go and find him again after I've been asked for a date.' She had already worked out that if they did go out together, she could leave Henry in his bedroom when she went. He should be all right there until the morning, even if she didn't come home. After all, she'd done it before. He even survived until the afternoon of the next day, although he was quite hungry and had wet himself. Still, that could be cleared up.

Suddenly there was an almighty crash from the other side of the shop and a huge scream, and then a child started to cry, large inconsolable sobs. 'Oh damn,' she said to herself as she guessed what had happened. Next minute, Henry was running towards her, covered in tomato ketchup, and made a huge lunge for her, crying, 'Mummy, mummy.' Her cover was blown. Tomato ketchup and white miniskirts don't go too well together. The man walked away.

Poor little Henry. His only caregiver was pretty hopeless, but she was all he had. What do you think he would be like when he grew up? Do you think he would be a secure, self-confident little boy, who valued his own worth, or would he be insecure, with low self-esteem? What about his role model for caring relationships? This should give you some idea how the nature of our early relationships give us a 'prototype' for our future. We learn patterns of behaviour, and he would be learning a very poor pattern. If Henry were to have a loving and caring father, or even grand-parents with whom he spent lots of time, they would teach him the other side of relationships. But if his mum was all he had, his prognosis would be pretty poor.

We are now going to consider evidence which supports the idea that it is the nature of the child's relationships which seems to be most important, no matter who that relationship is formed with. It has been shown on numerous occasions that children who are looked after by people who are sensitive and responsive to their needs form much more secure attachments with their caregivers. This leads to them being rated as more popular by their peers, showing leadership qualities, showing more initiative, being less aggressive and having higher self-esteem than children with insecure attachments.

The child with a rejecting carer, like Henry, will end up with a poor self-image believing that they are unacceptable and unworthy. This would come from the idea that if they had been better, nicer or more intelligent they would not have been rejected. Children with carers who are inconsistent will also have a negative self-image and will probably be attention-seeking in their behaviour as a way of getting some kind of recognition. This ties in with children with behaviour problems who are always naughty, as a way of gaining attention from their parents.

MICHAEL RUTTER

Michael Rutter is probably one of the most well-known critics of Bowlby, although he points out that Bowlby's writings are often misinterpreted. The idea that mother and mother alone should provide 24-hour care for her child, and any less than this would not be good enough, was never actually suggested by Bowlby, although many people believed this was what he was saying. In fact, Bowlby mellowed in later years and agreed that 'mother' may not be the most important person in some relationships after all, because children who formed a strong relationship with someone (be they father, nanny or whoever), often matured with no long-term problems. However, citing evidence from people such as Schaffer and Emmerson (1964) and Schaffer (1971), Rutter makes the point that it is the nature of the relationship which is the most important factor. He also goes on to say that a child does not necessarily need only one primary caregiver, although it seems that the attachments may be stronger if there are fewer rather than more. This would make sense, because if a child is with lots of different people who are all attentive, it is hard to like one of them more than the others.

Perhaps the most important argument that Rutter makes is that many children who have lost their mothers as a result of death do not suffer the long-term effects suggested by Bowlby. He says that it is more likely to be the type of arguments and bad feelings going on in families which will affect the child. If the child is part of a family where the parents are separating or divorcing, the arguments and atmospheres will frighten the children. They will probably not really understand what all the arguments are about, and may end up thinking that it is their fault that their parents have split up. It is very common for young children who do not have the situation explained to them, because they are too young, to try to make sense of it for themselves. Perhaps one parent has been unfaithful, and they are unlikely to go into such details in front of small children. The child may then attribute the break-up to the fact that they were naughty or didn't work hard enough at school.

Rutter (1970) studied boys between the ages of nine and 12 and looked into their backgrounds. Several had been separated from their mothers when they were little, but seemed to have adjusted well and appeared to have overcome the earlier problems. However, as they became older, some of them again seemed to be quite disturbed, and Rutter wondered what it was that had caused the differences in the two groups who supposedly had had the same early experiences.

The children who showed long-term effects seemed to have a different pattern of reasons for the earlier disruption. The reasons their families broke up seemed to be reasons the child found hard to understand, such as psychiatric illness or acrimonious divorces. The children who did not suffer later problems had reasons that were more concrete, such as physical illnesses or even death, problems with housing or even parental holidays. None of these involved a disturbance of the social relationships involved, so again, we return to the fact that it is the relationship that is important, rather than the mother herself.

Rutter (1981) also pointed out that we should be aware that there are different types of 'carer-deprivation' which the child may experience, and these types will also influence the way the child handles the situation.

- Deprivation is where you have had something which you later have taken away from you which is obviously going to cause pain, but may be overcome.
- Privation is when you never had it in the first place, so it is likely that you will suffer from a lack of any emotional experiences.
- Distortion is where there is stress caused by emotional upheavals, such as divorce or mental illness, and this is likely to result in more long-term effects.
- Disruption is where there may be separation caused by an event, but later the original situation will be reinstated (mother going into hospital but later coming home and family returning to normal). It may also mean that the original family situation may be superseded by another family situation (mother dies and father remarries). The most important factor is that even if the disruption seemed really horrific at the time, if the new situation is good, it will result in minimal, if any, long-term effects.

We also have to bear in mind that the age of the child when they first experienced the separation will be quite relevant. If you take a baby who is a month old, not only will it not realise what time of day it is, it will also likely have little preference for who actually looks after it, as long as it is taken care of. On the other hand, a two-year-old will know exactly what is going on. It would make sense to suggest that children who are old enough to know what is going on, and who have suffered long-term emotional deprivation, will probably develop some long-term consequences unless those deprivations are addressed.

However, if a child is put into a loving home, even if it is not the biological home, and made to feel of value and importance, it would seem likely that that child will develop into a well-balanced adult with high self-esteem. On the other hand, if they are not made to feel of value, they are likely to become attention-seeking and manipulative as a way of making themselves feel better. They will not have learned appropriate behaviours and may become too familiar with people in charge rather than associating with their peers, because they don't know how to form 'normal' relationships. This may also spin off into other aspects of their lives and they may spend so much time trying to deal with their emotional situation that they won't do very well at school. This will continue to reinforce the belief that they are useless – hence the low self-esteem.

218

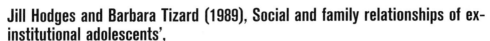

Jill Hodges and Barbara Tizard (1989), Social and family relationships of ex-institutional adolescents',

Journal of Child Psychology & Psychiatry, 30, 77–97

Background

The core study in this section is the conclusion to a study whose intention was to look at the long-term effects of being institutionalised as a young child. The first part of the study (Hodges and Tizard, 1978) had looked at a group of 65 children who were born to unmarried mothers and were placed in institutions before they were four months old. The children had all spent the first two years of their lives in institutions and were then either adopted, restored to their biological parents or remained in the institution.

The original 65 were studied when they were aged two, having been in the institution for over a year. The original study had focused on the type of care the children received in the institutions, which was good in terms of their physical needs. Yet they had very little chance to form strong attachments with the staff, as the institutions had a policy whereby they did not encourage such attachments. Consequently, most of the children experienced as many as 24 caregivers by the time they were two, and those that were still there at age four had experienced as many as 50.

What the children had experienced in their time in the institution was a period of privation, where they were unable to form close bonds with specific caregivers. They were assessed when aged four, then 51 of them were assessed when they were aged eight. The intention of the core study was to assess 31 of the 39 remaining children, now aged 16, who were still in contact with the researchers, to see if there were long-term effects which were still evident.

Findings from studies of the children aged two, four and eight

The children fell into three groups: a group that remained in the institutions, a group who were later adopted and a group who were returned to their natural mothers. Hodges and Tizard also included a control group, who were matched as far as possible for socio-economic status and came from intact families. The children's behaviours were compared between the restored group, the adopted group and those who remained in the institution, and all the children were also compared with the control group.

The adoptive parents were slightly older than the natural parents of the restored and control parents, and of slightly higher socio-economic status, which is not really surprising, as it probably took them a number of years to decide to adopt and then to be passed as suitable.

At age two, the children went to any known adult and were more frightened of strangers than the control group. By the age of four, the adopted group were indiscriminate and over-friendly towards strangers. The children who were still in the institution were attention-seeking and hung on to any available adults for attention. Any relationships they did form were very shallow and 70% of them were said to have no deep feelings for anyone (Tizard and Rees, 1974). They also had problems relating to other children as they were very argumentative and confrontational.

At age eight, the restored children weren't doing too well. They showed very weak attachments to their mothers and the mothers said they didn't feel very much for the children. In fact, two-thirds of the children who had been restored to their natural mothers had received professional help for behaviour problems, compared with less than a third of the children still in the institution and less than a third of the control group. This may be because the natural mothers were either one-parent families or part of another family, and this child was more of an outsider. On the other hand, the adopted children started to do better at this point, with less than one-tenth of them having behaviour problems. Of the adoptive parents, 90% said they played with their children every day, compared with half the restored children and 72% of the control group. How were they getting on when they reached the age of 16? What were their family relationships like as they approached adulthood?

Hodges and Tizard point out that, at 16, adolescents' relationships with peers increase as the child moves towards independence from the family. Earlier evidence from the ex-institutional children had shown difficulties in their peer relationships, and Hodges and Tizard were interested to see if this impeded their ability to make normal peer relationships in adolescence. Therefore the current study aimed to investigate their social relationships as well as their familial ones.

Aim

The aim of the study was to investigate whether children who had been placed in institutions before they were four months old, and who remained there until the age of two, would experience long-term problems in their social and family relationships, as suggested by Bowlby.

Following up investigations at two, four and eight years old, this final part of the study was intended to assess those children at age 16 who were still in contact with the researchers, to look for long-term effects of their early experiences on their social relationships, with adults outside the family and their peers, and on their family relationships.

Method

Design

The research method used was a quasi-experiment, where children who were already categorised by circumstances (adopted, restored to biological parents, still institutionalised) provided the independent variable. A longitudinal design was used.

FOCUS ON RESEARCH METHODS – longitudinal versus cross-sectional (snapshot) studies

In a cross-sectional design, different groups of people are tested at the same point in time and their performances compared. Examples from the core studies include the subway samaritan study by Piliavin *et al.*, the autism study by Baron-Cohen *et al.*, and Hraba and Grant's doll choice study.

The advantages that cross-sectional studies have over longitudinal studies is that they are relatively quick and inexpensive to carry out, can be easily replicated to test the reliability of findings and are relatively easy to modify. This final point means that if design faults become apparent, the study can be repeated with modifications to eliminate them. It also means that variations of the study can be easily carried out to investigate fully the variables that may affect behaviour. For example, a follow-up of the Baron-Cohen *et al.* study used a human Sally and a human Anne to answer critics who suggested that autistic children were simply being pedantically accurate in the first study since dolls can't think. This study supported the original findings that autistic children lack a theory of mind.

In a longitudinal study, one subject or one group of individuals is studied over a long period of time, for example, taking periodic samples of behaviour, as in the Hodges and Tizard study. This design allows us to track development and enables us to monitor changes over time. In the Hodges and Tizard study it enables us to establish a causal relationship between early negative experiences and relationships at age 16.

Other core studies which take a longitudinal approach include the Gardner and Gardner study of their attempt to teach sign language to a chimpanzee. Their longitudinal approach enabled them to make comparisons between Washoe's signing and the language acquisition of a deaf child born to deaf parents. Freud's study of Little Hans is also longitudinal, as is Thigpen and Cleckley's study of multiple personality disorder.

The major advantage of the longitudinal design is that it allows development over time to be studied and enables cause and effect to be established. It is also a repeated measures design, so subject variables are controlled. Where the same researcher oversees the study, trusting relation-ships can be built up with the subjects so that it is possible to gather valid data on sensitive issues, since subjects are more inclined to disclose information to someone they know and trust. Studying over time means a great deal of data can be gathered, which is usually qualitative in nature, and this also increases the validity of the findings.

There are, however, problems associated with this design. One of these is 'subject attrition', where the number of subjects available for study reduces as the study continues. This can be seen in the Hodges and Tizard study where, of the 65 children studied at age four, only 51 were studied at age eight, and only 39 were available for study at age 16. Losing subjects can be because, over time, the researchers lose contact with them, or because subjects decline the invitation to participate in the follow-up studies. With only those willing to be studied remaining at 16, the problem is that Hodges and Tizard's sample is affected by a volunteer bias, which means the sample studied at 16 may not be truly comparable with the original 65 studied at age four.

Subjects

NOTE: Although the following detailed information about the subjects and control groups does not appear in the actual core study, we have included it here as it is often used as a basis for examination questions. The authors of the study explain that the adolescents were described in a companion article in the *Journal of Child Psychology & Psychiatry*, 30, 53–75, 1989.

All the children in the groups were aged 16, and 39 of the original 65 were available for study. They fell into three categories: those that had been adopted, those that had been restored to their biological families and those living in institutions at age 16.

The numbers and gender breakdown of subjects was as follows:
• Adopted children: 23 (17 boys and six girls)
• Restored children: 11 (six boys and five girls)
(Note: 31 of these 34 children participated in this part of the study and are referred to as 'ex-institutionalised' children)
• Institutionalised children: five (three boys and two girls) who were interviewed but do not feature in the results.

There were two control groups used for comparison purposes:

Control group one: children who had been with their families continually, who were matched for sex, whether a one- or two-parent family, occupation of main breadwinner and position in family with the adopted and restored groups.

Control group two: in order to assess the information obtained from the schools, a second control group was established. The teacher compared the ex-institutionalised child to a same-sex classmate closest to them in age.

Variables

The independent variable was the environment in which the child had been brought up. The whole group of ex-institutionalised adolescents were compared with controls who had never been adopted and never been in care. Comparisons were made between the findings of the investigation which had taken place when the ex-institutionalised children had been eight years old. Also, comparisons were made within the ex-institutionalised adolescents at age 16, between those children who had been adopted and those who had been restored to their biological parents.

The dependent variable was the adolescent's family relationships, peer relationships and relationships with teachers and adults outside the family.

Procedure

The data was collected using a number of different methods:

1. Interview with subjects (recorded).
2. Interview with the subject's mother, sometimes with the father present, or care workers (recorded).
3. The parent or care worker completed the Rutter 'A' scale, a questionnaire about the adolescent's behaviour.
4. The subject completed a 46-point 'Questionnaire on Social Difficulty' (Lindsay and Lindsay, 1982), which asked them how well they got on in social relationships.
5. The teachers also completed two questionnaires, one about how the subject got on with their teachers and peers, and the same questionnaire about their same-sex classmate.
6. Teachers were asked to complete a postal questionnaire containing the Rutter 'B' scale, which is a psychometric test used to assess for any sort of psychiatric disorder.

Results

The results included data on a number of areas.

1. FAMILY RELATIONSHIPS

Attachment to parents:

Adopted adolescents were just as attached to their parents as the control group. Restored adolescents were less attached to their parents than the adopted group and control group.

Showing affection:

Control subjects were the most affectionate towards their parents, followed by the adopted group. The restored group were considerably less affectionate than the control group or the adopted group.

Relationships with siblings:

Ex-institutionalised adolescents, especially the restored group, had more problems with siblings than the control group.

Confiding and supporting:

No difference in both confiding in parents and support from parents between ex-institutionalised adolescents and controls was recorded, although restored mothers felt less certain that their children were willing to turn to them for advice.

Disagreements over control and discipline:
Fewer disagreements between the control group and their families were recorded than for all the ex-institutionalised adolescents. Of the ex-institutionalised adolescents, the restored group had the most disagreements. Disagreements about staying out, homework, helping round the house and pocket money were much less in evidence in adoptive families.

2. PEER RELATIONSHIPS (social relationships)

These were judged from the point of view of the adolescent, their mothers and their teacher.

- Ex-institutionalised adolescents had poorer peer relations than the controls, and were said to be less choosy about who they were friendly with.
- Compared to controls, ex-institutionalised adolescents said they were less likely to belong to a group or crowd of friends.
- Compared to controls, ex-institutionalised adolescents were less likely to confide in peers.
- Teachers said the ex-institutionalised adolescents were more often argumentative, less popular and more likely to bully others than the controls.
- According to mothers, ex-institutionalised adolescents were less likely to have a special friend than the control subjects.
- According to parents, ex-institutionalised adolescents were less likely to be selective when choosing their friends and would make friends with anyone.

3. RELATIONSHIPS TO TEACHERS (social relationships)

- Teachers believed the ex-institutionalised were more attention-seeking compared with classmates from the control groups, but no difference was shown in comparison with the matched control subjects.
- The restored group were seen by teachers as being more aggressive.

Summary of Hodges and Tizard's findings inrelation to the social and family relationships of 'adopted' and 'restored' adolescents compared with each other and with controls

	Type of relationship	
	Social relationships	Family relationships
Restored group	Adult/peer relationships were significantly WORSE than those of the two control groups	Family relationships were WORSE than those of the two control groups and WORSE than those of the adopted group.
Adopted group	Adult/peer relationships were significantly WORSE than those of the two control groups	Family relationships were NO DIFFERENT from those of the control groups so they were 'normal'

In summary, all the ex-institutionalised children showed differences in peer and adult relationships outside the home compared with the two control groups. However, the most relevant finding was that the restored group had worse family relationships than the other groups. They were less attached to their mother, showed less affection to both mother and father, identified less with their parents and had problems getting on with their siblings.

Discussion

The causes of the problems experienced by the ex-institutionalised children could be put down to the number of caregivers they had while they were in institutions, and the fact that they were unable to form any long-term bonds in what are considered the most critical years. However, this explanation is possibly too simplistic, as the results were not the same for all children.

All the ex-institutionalised children seemed to have problems with later relationships, but the results indicate that the restored group came off worse within their families, possibly due to a sense of betrayal and desertion – after all, they must have questioned why they were 'sent away' when they were tiny. The study doesn't explain the reasons why the adolescents were taken into institutions to start with and this may have had some kind of effect on the long-term consequences for the adolescents. We also don't know why some children were restored while others were adopted and whether this actually had anything to do with the nature of the child (Hodges and Tizard state that there was no evidence of differences in the children).

The study did indicate that there were a number of differences between the groups of children, but it also showed that maternal deprivation does not always lead to long-term irreversible effects, because many of the adopted children showed no effects of their early experiences in their family relationships. However, others did, and two of the adoptive placements failed.

In this study, the adoptive parents were very different from the restored parents because they really wanted the child, whereas the restored parents were often ambivalent about whether or not they wanted the child to return. Some had had further children in the time the restored child had been institutionalised, and this meant that the child was coming into a family where he/she couldn't understand why the new child had been kept at home while he/she had been in care. This resentment may account for the particular difficulties these children had getting along with these and subsequent siblings. Also it seems likely that the problems which had led to the child being in care in the first instance, e.g. financial problems, may not have been completely resolved, and so the child was not coming back into an environment where his/her increased need for attention and care could be effectively met.

Hodges and Tizard point out that the restored children's parents had expected a great deal of independence from them early on, and by the age of eight, one-third of them put themselves to bed or put their lights out compared to only one adopted child. Also, four of the restored group had demonstrated emotional or behavioural problems and spent time in residential units, although three of those had been returned to their families.

The adoptive parents were older, and had probably waited a long time before making the decision to adopt, whereas most couples can have a baby the natural way if biology permits, irrespective of their suitability. In fact, becoming an adoptive parent requires you to go through a rigorous assessment process, establishing your emotional and financial ability to be a parent. The adoptive parents were therefore prepared to make a lot of effort to make the relationship work. They had more resources, both emotional and financial, than the restored children's parents. They were accepting of a high level of dependency from the adopted child at the beginning of the relationship, in comparison to the restored parents, and were therefore primed to meet the needs of an emotionally demanding and attention-seeking child. This may well have been the explanation for many of the differences that appeared between the groups.

Finally, Hodges and Tizard conclude that since both the adopted and restored groups experienced problems that affected their social relationships with peers and adults outside the family, '[these problems] may have implications for the future adult relationships of these 16-year-olds. Whether these differences are now permanent, or further modifiable, we do not know.'

Conclusions

The early negative (privation) experiences of the ex-institutionalised adolescents can be observed at age 16 in terms of the problems they experienced in their social relationships. In the restored group there is also an observable negative effect on family relationships. The enrichment provided by adoption, however, appears to overcome the negative effects of the early privation experience as regards family relationships.

Commentary

Are there problems with the design that might affect the validity of the study?

As in many longitudinal studies, the findings from the Hodges and Tizard study are affected by subject attrition. The original study had 65 subjects and yet in this final part there were only 39. Some of the children from each group were unavailable or unwilling to take part in this follow-up study – why was this? Those available for study were the ones who continued to volunteer, and this brings in a bias which makes us question whether this final sample was actually representative of the original group.

As with any longitudinal study, it is not possible to establish for sure that the relationship problems observed at 16 were as a direct result of the early negative experience in an institution. The relationships could have been affected by other negative experiences in the meantime, or there could be subject variables such as personality differences which could account for the findings. These possible confounding variables make us question the validity of the findings.

What are the strengths and weaknesses of using self-report methods to gather data?

There were problems with the methodology because questionnaires are only as accurate as the answers given. Although they were given to both the children and their caregivers, there is no guarantee that they were really objective. One explanation for the reports made by teachers would be that they had little knowledge or understanding of the early experiences of the children, and therefore saw any sort of unusual behaviour as being unacceptable rather than understandable, and would thus judge it more harshly.

FOCUS ON RESEARCH METHODS – the strengths and weaknesses of self-report data

Self-report data is the data gathered from interviews, questionnaires and psychometric tests, as in this study by Hodges and Tizard, and the detailed case studies by Freud (Little Hans) and Thigpen and Cleckley (Three faces of Eve).

Self-report data can also mean simply asking Ss to answer questions, as in the Sally-Anne test by Baron-Cohen *et al.*, the conservation experiments carried out by Samuel and Bryant and the study on doll choice by Hraba and Grant.

The advantages of using self-report data are that we are able to measure cognitive variables such as memory, knowledge and attitudes, which cannot be either observed directly or tested for in any biological test. Without self-report, the study by Loftus and Palmer on memory and language would not be possible, for example.

However, the validity of self-report data can be questionned where Ss are able to deliberately falsify their answers. This can be because they are responding to demand characteristics present in the study or because of evaluation apprehension: they lie to give a socially desirable answer to avoid being judged negatively.

Is the study ecologically valid?

The data was collected using self-report methods and these methods are largely low in ecological validity. Where qualitative data is gathered (e.g. the recorded interviews with the subjects or their parents), the method can be more realistic. However, where subjects are asked to fill in questionnaires made up of restricted response answers to provide quantitative data for ease of analysis and comparison between subjects, the ecological validity of the study is reduced.

Is the study ethical?

The study was carried out ethically in terms of obtaining the informed consent of both the subjects and their parents. For example, in one case the subject agreed to take part and was interviewed, but the mother declined to be interviewed herself. Hodges and Tizard tell us that schools were approached only after subjects and their parents had given consent for the teacher to be involved in the study. The fact that the numbers of subjects available for study fell from 65 at age four to 39 by age 16 shows that parents and subjects felt free to refuse to continue; therefore their right to withdraw was clear.

Jill Hodges, who was familiar and trusted by the ex-institutionalised children and their parents, carried out all the interviewing. It is possible that some of those who were approached to take part but declined, and perhaps even some of those restored children and their families who agreed to take part, may have been upset at being reminded of past negative experiences which might open up old wounds, but there is evidence that the questionning was carried out sensitively and so this did not occur.

Is the study useful?

This study is one of many that has contributed to our understanding of the social and emotional needs of young children and the importance of secure attachments from an early age if emotional difficulties later on are to be avoided. It is the findings form such research that has affected current policy in the UK, whereby the aim is to provide foster homes for babies and infants who have to be taken into care rather than placing them in institutions.

Key questions

1. Describe the two control groups and explain the purpose of having the two control groups?
2. Why is subject attrition a problem in longitudinal studies? How might it have affected the findings in this study?
3. Give reasons why the restored group had more problems than the adopted group getting on with family members.
4. Why do you think the ex-institutionalised adolescents were more attention-seeking with adults?
5. Is this study useful? How?

Example Answers are on page 456.

Further Reading

- Bee, H. (1995), *The Growing Child*, New York: Harper Collins.
- Bee. H. (1992), *The Developing Child*, New York: Harper Collins.
- Bowlby, J. (1953), *Childcare and the Growth of Love*, London: Penguin.

The weird and wonderful world of Sigmund Freud

The core study in the last section relates to the development of a phobia in a five-year-old boy, whilst considering the unconscious drives which underlie much of human behaviour. Freud is often criticised as being a complete 'nutcase' and sex-mad, but despite some of his more extreme ideas, he must be commended for being the first person to actually make the point that things that we are not consciously aware of can have quite a strong influence on our behaviour.

Imagine you are a very small boy of three who is regularly beaten with a large cane. It doesn't matter what you do, you always seem to be in trouble, and every time you are in trouble, your dad beats you. He keeps the cane in a cupboard in the dining room and just before he actually beats you, he whips the air a couple of times with the cane just to make the point that it is going to hurt. One day, on his way home from work, your dad has an accident in the car and dies. Never again are you beaten, and over the course of the next couple of years the memory fades until you can hardly remember your dad, let alone the caning.

You are now 20, and you are round at a mate's house. You have somehow been roped into sorting out his shed. In the corner are some canes which have been used to support plants, but you haven't actually seen them. Your mate gets one of them and whips the air with it behind your back. Suddenly you feel this horrific feeling of coldness coming over you and all the hairs on the back of your neck stand on end. You aren't aware why the noise suddenly provoked such an extreme response because you have no recollection of being beaten when you were small. But the repressed memory has remained in your unconscious and is only triggered by the sound.

Many of the memories we have of painful or embarrassing incidents are pushed into our unconscious as our body's way of making it possible for us to cope with them. When we do repress memories, often the only way to get at them is through hypnosis, whereby the person is made to relax so deeply that the memories can be brought to the surface. This can also happen with frightening experiences, or when we are so ashamed of something we have done that in order to prevent ourselves from continual suffering, we push the memory into the deep recesses of our mind.

The other thing we must always remember was that Freud lived in a time of almost Victorian morality, where many aspects of our natural drives were considered base and crude. Consequently, people had far more reason to feel guilty than they would today. Perhaps some of his theories were a way of trying to explain these instincts as natural and normal. On the other hand, he was an unusual man and had many strange aspects to his personality, including the unerring belief that he was right in his ideas (a trait which often accompanies an innate lack of confidence – if you have confidence in yourself, you don't mind being wrong from time to time). He was also obsessive in his interests, very neat, tidy and controlled in his behaviour, and perhaps these traits gave him a sort of security.

FREUD'S BACKGROUND

Freud was born in Freiberg, Moravia in 1856, but lived for most of his life in Vienna. His father was a Jewish wool merchant who had been trading in Moravia, but on account of a failing business he moved his family first to Leipzig and then to Vienna. Life was not easy for the family as there was a great deal of anti-Jewish feeling, yet the family survived on a meagre income. When Freud was 17, he attended the University of Vienna where he studied medicine, although he did not graduate until March 1881.

Freud spent three years gaining experience as a clinical neurologist at both the Vienna General Hospital and the Salpêtrière Hospital in Paris. It was in Paris that he worked for the neurologist Jean Charcot, who had a keen interest in hysterical illnesses. In April 1886, Freud opened his own medical practice in Vienna and married Martha Bernays later that year, although they were extremely poor in the early years of marriage. The marriage lasted for 53 years, however, and Martha bore him six children, the youngest of whom was Anna Freud, born in 1895.

While treating his patients, Freud realised that some of them had what appeared to be real symptoms that had no physical basis (known as hysteria or hysterical illnesses). He became interested in what it was that caused these illnesses, which seemed to be more common in women. As part of his search to find an explanation, he was influenced by Charcot's ideas. Charcot taught that in order to understand hysteria he should look at psychology rather than physiology, and demonstrated the use of hypnosis as a way of gaining access to the underlying psychological causes for these symptoms. It seemed that many of the 'hysterical' patients had something troubling them which they had repressed, such as a painful memory. Once they had admitted their concerns, the symptoms seemed to disappear.

Freud also met and became friends with Josef Breuer, who used a different method of treating hysterical illness, which simply involved allowing the patient, in a totally safe and non-judgemental situation, to talk freely about his or her thoughts and feelings. Breuer believed that through this process, the problems would ultimately surface and, once expressed, would provide a kind of 'catharsis' or release, which would ultimately 'cure' the patient of his or her symptoms. Freud started to use Breuer's methods as he thought this was a way for his patients to gain access to the things they didn't want to talk about, the things they had buried in the deepest recesses of their mind.

Freud was totally committed to his work, practising during the day as a therapist and writing well into the night. Despite his theories being unpopular, his contributions to the world of psychoanalysis comprised 24 volumes. He was obviously an extremely intelligent man, although he was obsessive about his work and his private life and could be quite obstinate and very self-opinionated. He believed his ideas were right and he was very intolerant of others who disagreed with him, which resulted in him losing many of his friends. Freud finally fled Austria for London after the Nazi invasion in 1937 and, despite a long battle, finally died of cancer in 1939.

THE STRUCTURE OF THE MIND

Freud believed that the mind has three parts to it: the area which we are consciously aware of; another area, which he called the preconscious mind (not instantly accessible because it contains lots of things that we have temporarily forgotten, although a mere hint would bring them back into conscious awareness); and the unconscious mind, which contains all kinds of disturbing thoughts and memories which have been repressed. He believed that there was no point in trying to get direct access to the unconscious mind because people were not only unable to gain access to it, but probably not even aware that it was there. However, he did believe that when people weren't thinking they often gave away some information, like when they made slips of the tongue. This is what happens when you call your teacher 'mother', or call a recent boy/girlfriend by the name of the person you were dating previously.

Freud started using different techniques, such as dream analysis, as a way of gaining access to the unconscious with the patients who arrived with hysterical symptoms. Remember, many of them were young women. Freud unexpectedly discovered that some of them had suffered from sexual abuse as children. What you must remember was that when Freud was practising, 'sex' didn't exist. Of course it did, but it was not considered proper for women to enjoy sex. Sex was only for making babies. Men, on the other hand, had carnal desires and so if these were refused by their wife, they would have to either take cold showers or, if all else failed, seek some kind of solace elsewhere with ladies of the night.

Can you imagine the predicament Freud was put in? He couldn't blatantly admit that these eminent gentlemen, the fathers or brothers of his female patients, had abused them, and yet this was what he had discovered. He decided to present his findings in 1896, when he gave a lecture on the aetiology of hysteria. He explained that during therapy with patients who had previously unexplained hysteria, it had emerged that each child had been sexually abused in childhood, either by an adult or older sibling, and that until they had had therapy they had been unaware of this. The trouble was that the people Freud was speaking to were influential and well connected and their response to his finding was one of horror and disbelief (or even denial). Freud had to try to rectify the situation he now found himself in and return to a position of favour, so he replaced his theory the following year with what he called the 'Oedipus complex'. What happened, he claimed, was that the abuse was in the mind of the child – a fantasy rather than a reality, and if there was physical evidence of abuse, for example, a pregnancy, he explained this away by saying that the fantasy must have become so powerful that the children had initiated the sexual contact themselves.

If we return to Freud's ideas that much of our minds are actually unavailable to our conscious awareness, it links in with his theory of the adult personality which has three basic parts: the *id*, the *ego* and the *superego*. The ego is the only part that we are actually aware of, although the other two try their best to influence our conscious awareness.

Freud tried to explain the workings of the mind in a purely physiological way, although he realised that it was not that simple and that the workings of the mind change and evolve over time. He believed that when we are born, we are driven by what he called the 'pleasure principle', which means that we want to have lots of pleasure and avoid anything nasty. This pleasure principle or 'id' consists of primitive desires and primeval urges, which are often reflexes, so contain no logical or rational thought. Imagine the small child in the supermarket who we met in chapter three. He wants the sweeties and wants them now, no matter what state mother is in; he doesn't care because he is totally egocentric and driven by his own desires. We all retain these desires and urges and, ideally, would all like our desires met now, not next week or next year. Most of us, however, find ways of dealing with our id.

So how do we deal with our id? The next part of the personality to develop is what Freud called the ego. This operates according to what is known as the 'reality principle'. As we start to operate in the real world, we begin to realise that we can't always have what we want when we want it. We therefore work out ways of getting what we want by, for example, waiting for an appropriate moment, and this comes from our experiences and interactions with others. The ego has no moral basis; it doesn't consider the moral rights and wrongs of behaving in certain ways, although it does take into account what is and is not acceptable to other people. It realises that if we do follow our desires, we may be excluded by others and this would be pretty awful too (and might make matters worse in the long run). So it tries to satisfy the 'child' within us, in a realistic and acceptable way.

Have you considered where our morals come from? Perhaps Bandura would argue that we learn our moral code of behaviour by observing the behaviour of others, although Freud would disagree. He claimed that the little voice like a parent, which comes to most of us when we are about to do something wrong, is the part of personality called the superego. It develops as we start to internalise the rules and regulations of our parents and the society in which we live, so it becomes a kind of 'internal parent'. We will look at how this happens in the next section when we go into slightly more detail about the moral development of a child, but for the moment you should simply realise that in many ways the superego is as unrealistic as the id. If we always behaved according to a strict set of moral rules we would become rigid and inflexible.

Freud says the ego's job is to maintain a state of 'dynamic equilibrium' between these three parts. It has the position of trying to balance them out and satisfy the demands of both the id and the superego. One of the best descriptions of Freud's construct of the personality comes from Nicky Hayes (1994), when she claims that the relationship between the three parts is like, 'A battle between a sex-crazed monkey and a maiden aunt, being refereed by a rather nervous bank clerk!'

FREUD'S DEVELOPMENTAL THEORY

Freud's theory is called a psychodynamic theory because he claimed that there are psychological forces (psycho) that move or drive us forwards (dynamic) to do things – these forces are innate. As we have mentioned, the forces he is talking about are instincts and Freud identified two instinctive driving forces. The first is known as Eros, the life instinct, whose main active component is the sexual drive or libido. The second is Thanatos, the death instinct, and its main active component is aggression, both to ourselves and others. Freud initially ignored the aggressive instinct, but found it hard to explain the dreadful loss of life and carnage of the First World War, and so he later incorporated Thanatos as a representation of our innate destructiveness and aggression.

Freud believed that the development of a child's personality is based on these biological drives and the drives evolve through a number of biologically determined stages. He believed that the strongest drive was the libido or sexual instinct, and he maintained that babies and young children are capable of sexual pleasure. I think the word 'sexual' is too strong here, and that we should substitute 'sensual', because he was referring to physical pleasure from any area of the body rather than simply the genitals, which is what we as adults tend to think of as sexual pleasure.

Oral stage (0 to 15 months)

The first stage is the oral stage because the main areas of sensitivity and pleasure are the lips and mouth. The baby gets great pleasure in two ways from putting things in its mouth, even when it isn't feeding. One way is by sucking and swallowing and the other is from biting and chewing. According to Freud, if the child's desires are satisfied and they are not left to cry for hours on end without food, and they are weaned at the right time, they will be fine. If, however, they are weaned at the wrong time, they will become 'orally fixated', which means that as adults they will have an excessive interest in oral gratification. They will either become compulsive eaters, drinkers or smokers, or constantly chew things like gum, pens and fingernails. If they get excessive amounts of pleasure from sucking and swallowing, they will become too trusting and gullible and easily fooled, whereas if they enjoyed biting and chewing more they would become sarcastic and verbally aggressive. In fact, Freud believed that they even become incapable of personal love for other people, with a tendency to treat people as objects to be used to fulfil their needs.

The evidence to support this stage is somewhat sparse! Kline and Storey (1977) found evidence for two different types of oral characters. The first group showed a cluster of traits which could be called oral optimism: sociability, dependability and a relaxed nature. The other group showed a different cluster called oral pessimism: independence, verbal aggression, envy, hostility, ambition and impatience. What we have to remember here is that we can never be sure whether these were a result of their oral experiences or something completely different!

Anal stage (one to three years)

In this second stage, the sensitive area shifts from the mouth to the anus. Apparently the child now derives great pleasure from either expelling or retaining faeces. Although this seems somewhat weird, many children do have a fascination with their poos and often, when they first manage to go in a potty, will express interest and pleasure in what they have done.

During this stage the child is potty-trained, whereas before they could go where they liked, discreetly protected by the gentle comfort of clean nappies! Now the child learns that in order to get praise from its parents it has to behave in a certain way. No longer can it 'do as it pleases'. This may well be the first type of condition that will have been put on its behaviour and it learns that there is a huge significance to defecating. Therefore, if the parents are very strict and over-anxious about its bowel habits, the child will become almost too worried and frightened about going, and therefore will become an 'anal retentive'. Here the child will associate the normal functioning with messiness and dirt and may become preoccupied with orderliness and cleanliness as a reaction. Freud claims that this trait will continue as it gets older and it will become an adult who, instead of holding on to its faeces, will hold on to its possessions instead – in effect, a miser, hoarder or collector of some kind.

On the other hand, if the parents are extremely laid back and perhaps over-lenient about the child's ability to use the potty, the child will go anywhere! This child will become an 'anal expulsive', who will grow up to be over-generous, untidy and completely indifferent to material possessions. Again, these collections of traits are often found together and provide some support for his analysis, but the explanations he gives as to why they cluster together have received very little support.

Phallic stage (three to five years)

Freud claims that the area of sensuality shifts from the anus to the genitals when the child reaches the age of about three. This is the time when children play with their genitals and become inquisitive as to the differences between little boys and little girls. It is also quite normal to see small boys with their hands tucked down the front of their trousers at this age, which you could say lends support to Freud's ideas. The thing is, fascination and comfort (which is the main reason why most little boys hold on to their genitals) are not necessarily the same as sexual interest.

It is during this stage that Freud believes that the awareness of sex differences form the basis of what he calls the Oedipus complex. He claimed that girls feel inferior to or jealous of boys because they have a penis, and that boys believe that because girls don't have a penis, they must have been castrated. During this stage, children also have intense emotions, usually directed at the parent of the opposite sex. (How many males actually believe that girls are really castrated boys? Most will say that the thought has never entered their heads, although Freud would say that they were repressing their memories so of course they would not be able to recollect the idea.)

Before we talk about the Oedipus complex, it might be useful to explain who Oedipus was for those of you who are not into Greek mythology. Oedipus was the mythical son of the King of Thebes, but an oracle prophesised that Oedipus would kill his father and, in order to prevent this happening, his father ordered him to be put to death. He was rescued by a shepherd and brought up, unaware of his identity. One day, when he was on the road to Thebes, he quarrelled with a man and accidentally killed him, not realising that this man was his father. He was made King of Thebes as a result of an act of bravery against a mythical creature called the Sphinx, and subsequently married Jocasta, not realising that she was his mother. When he found out who she was, he gouged out his eyes.

As a result of this relationship between Oedipus and his mother, Freud coined the term Oedipus complex to describe the situation which occurs when boys develop an intense attachment to their mothers.

It often occurs that little boys become quite clingy to their mothers at this age, and often girls to their fathers, but we will stick with small boys for the moment. Freud believed that this attachment becomes increasingly intense and causes the boys to regard their fathers as rivals, especially as father sleeps with mother and has the closeness and familiarity with her that the boy would like. However, the boy also sees his father as a powerful and threatening figure who has the ultimate power to deal with this rivalry – namely to castrate him. The small boy is caught at this point between desire for his mother and fear of his father's power.

What we must remember here is that the boy does not have real sexual feelings that we know about as adults. Most of his feelings are unconscious and therefore cause a kind of internal conflict or anxiety which the small boy has to deal with. Anxiety is an unpleasant state, and we strive for much of our lives to find ways to reduce our feelings of anxiety, no matter how they are caused. Therefore, Freud claims that the boy deals with it by using a defensive process called sex-role identification. The boy will start to identify with his father and repress any further feelings he has for his mother into his unconscious. He will begin to spend more time with his father, wanting to be like daddy, and this in turn will reduce any further chance of being castrated, as his father will no longer see him as a rival. Through this process he will internalise his father's moral standards and this is the core of the child's superego.

> **KEY CONCEPT** – what does Freud's study show us about identification?
>
> The Freudian concept of identification suggests that we may identify with people whom we perceive as threatening as a way of reducing the threat. This comes from the idea that boys who suffer from castration anxiety realise that it will be impossible to beat their powerful father so it would make more sense to 'join' him. This process is known as identification with the aggressor.
>
> This helps to explain why schoolchildren often side with bullies, even though they don't agree with their behaviour, for fear of being bullied themselves.

So what about girls? The 'Electra complex' is the supposed female equivalent occurring in girls between the ages of three and six and is manifested by the excessive attachment of little girls to their fathers and corresponding hostility to their mothers. The term Electra complex also comes from Greek mythology. Electra, the daughter of the Greek leader Agamemnon, was famous for her devotion and loyalty to her father until he was murdered by her mother and her mother's lover. In order to avenge the death of her beloved father, Electra, with her younger brother's help, murdered the mother she detested and also the lover.

The problem was that Freud hadn't clearly worked out the female side of this developmental process, probably because he found women puzzling throughout his life. The course of the Electra complex goes something like this: the girl will be very close to her mother when she is little until she discovers that she doesn't have a penis. This makes her feel inferior and she will blame her mother for allowing her to be castrated. She does realise that one way she can feel equal to men is by producing a baby (and this is all at three+ years of age!), and so she sees her father as a potential impregnator to allow her to have a child of her own as a substitute for the missing penis. She will therefore transfer her affections from the mother to the father.

Why this happens is the main problem with the Electra complex. Boys renounce their feelings for their mother because of the fear of castration by their father, but this can't be the case with girls, who have already been 'castrated' by their mothers. Freud suggested that males do feel that their penis is the thing that they value most in the world, but the thing that girls value is loss of love. If the girl continues with her desire to have a relationship with her father she is likely to lose the love of her mother, so she will renounce her feelings for her father and do her best to make her mother love her by being a good girl. The problem is, the fear on the girl's part would be far less (according to Freud) than the boys' fear and this led him to suggest that girls will have a much less developed superego.

Latency stage (around five years to puberty)

The sexual drives seem to be removed from consciousness during the latency stage, although they are still there. According to Freud, the child has repressed its memories of the earlier sexual impulses by a phenomenon called 'infantile amnesia'. The child redirects the drives into intellectual development and social activities as it learns about the world beyond the family. The friendships it makes tend to be with children of the same sex, which helps the child deal with any possible sexual thoughts. The problem with this idea is that children from other cultures, where sexual activity is seen as acceptable, show interest in sexual matters throughout the whole of their childhood.

Genital stage (puberty onwards)

With puberty, there is a re-emergence of the earlier drives and the centre of attention is again the genitals, although this time an adult expression of sexuality is shown through relationships with members of the opposite sex.

Freud's developmental theory has been challenged and criticised by many researchers who claim that the theory is untestable. There is evidence from cross-cultural studies that children who are brought up with extended families show no problems with morals or sex-role development. If Freud was right, having a father (if you are a boy) is a prerequisite to developing morals, superego, appropriate sex-role behaviour etc. What happens to orphans and boys from single-parent families? He also claimed that the first five years of life are the most critical, but this implies that the next 80 are irrelevant.

Now we have been through the stages, you may wonder why these stages are so relevant. Freud believed that if an adult suffers from any kind of neurosis, it can be traced back to their progression through the stages of development. The poor old adult will either have unresolved problems due to lack of gratification or, on the other hand, will have achieved excessive gratification – both being a result of the parental treatment they received. What then happens is that the child will become fixated at one of these stages, either because they have enjoyed it too much, or because they have been deprived of what they really wanted. If they enjoyed it too much, they won't want to leave the stage they are in. If they have been deprived, they want to stay in the stage for a bit longer in order to achieve the level of gratification or satisfaction that they desire. Obviously this put a tremendous amount of pressure on mothers who were frightened of over- or under-feeding, or who over- or under-stressed the importance of potty training. The problem was, Freud gave no guidelines as to what the 'right' amount actually was!

The other possibility could be that something has happened to them during their lives that they have found distressing. For example, they may have had an experience they found unacceptable or very hurtful (such as rejection by a parent, or even sexual abuse), or they have done something very wicked or unpleasant (hurt or abused or murdered someone else). It may not be that enormous, because even having unpleasant or unacceptable thoughts can be tremendously upsetting to some people because they feel disgusted that they could even contemplate such horrendous ideas. Whatever the cause, their ego will have stepped in and dealt with the situation either by projecting the feelings onto something else more acceptable (such as developing a phobia about a related object), or by repressing the memory into the unconscious in order to protect the person. This may then result in the person developing an anxiety or panic attack when they experience a situation which reminds them of the thing they are trying to forget. The situation may also affect their behaviour, for example, they may become obsessive about certain things but not understand why. Only if that feeling is brought into conscious awareness can the person deal with the situation.

The following true story about Maurice explains how this works. Maurice had been referred to a psychiatrist as he was suffering from obsessive compulsive behaviour. Obsessive compulsive behaviour means that you have intrusive thoughts which are the obsessions, and a compulsion to keep doing certain things. Most people have small compulsions like going and checking if you have shut the door or turned off the gas, but Maurice's compulsion was getting the better of him.

Maurice explained to the psychiatrist that he was unable to get out of the house in the morning because he had to keep going back into the bathroom to check that the towel was hung straight on the hook behind the door. He told the psychiatrist that he had to make sure that when hung, both sides had to be of equal length and then he would close the door very carefully before he could leave. The trouble occurred when he got halfway down the stairs because he suddenly imagined that it had moved and slipped off the hook and so he would have to go back and check and would end up going through the ritual all over again.

After several hours of therapy the psychiatrist finally uncovered the cause of this obsessive compulsive behaviour. Maurice was about 45 and lived with his ageing mother, who was a bossy old woman and wouldn't let him do anything. He felt totally trapped living with her and secretly wished she would simply drop dead. One night, while he lay in his bed with his hot-water bottle, teddy bear and cocoa, he started to daydream. Apparently he had imagined that she had gone to the bathroom and tried to push the door open, but the towel had fallen off the back of the door and was stopping the door from opening. She pushed and shoved and pushed harder until the door flew open unexpectedly and she fell through the door head first, bashing her head on the loo (which was opposite the door), cracked her skull and died. Of course, this was too awful to contemplate and he felt absolutely mortified that he could think of such a dreadful event, so rather than live with the guilt, his ego had pushed the memory out of his conscious awareness and he therefore had no idea why he had begun this bizarre behaviour. Once he had admitted it to the therapist, the obsession and compulsive behaviour seemed to subside.

This example gives an illustration of how the unconscious can affect our behaviour. Often we repress memories or unpleasant thoughts in order to reduce our discomfort, and you may now have some idea of how this might affect our subsequent behaviour.

239

S. Freud (1909), 'Analysis of a phobia in a five-year-old boy',

In *The Pelican Freud Library* (1977), vol. 8, Case Histories 1, pp. 169–306

Background

In the introduction which formed the background to the study, Freud talked about Little Hans and the origins of this particular case study. He acknowledged that Hans was not a normal child and had a predisposition to neurosis, so he realised that it might not necessarily be valid to generalise from him to all children. He also said that the argument that children are untrustworthy was unfair. Adults are untrustworthy because they are prejudiced and this might influence what they say. Children, on the other hand, may lie but they lie for a reason and this reason may well be one of the most important things to consider.

Hans was described as being a cheerful and straightforward child, but when he became 'ill' (by this Freud meant that he developed his phobia), it was obvious that there was a difference in what he said and what he actually thought. Freud suggested that this was because of things that were going on in his unconscious of which he was unaware. In order to put this right, Freud decided that Hans' behaviour had to be interpreted and he had to be told why he was thinking and acting as he was. Freud was emphatic that this was not putting suggestions into the boy's mind but was only a way of helping him understand what already existed. This is the process of psychoanalysis, a form of talking cure used by Freud. The idea was for the client to talk freely and the analyst would then be able to interpret the client's unconscious desires and anxieties, which would reveal themselves to the analyst in symbolic form, for example, in the client's fantasies and dreams.

Aim

The aim of this case study is to document the case of Little Hans who developed a phobia of horses. It was also used by Freud to support his ideas about the origins of phobias and his belief that they are often influenced by unconscious forces. He also used it to support his ideas on psychosexual development and the Oedipus complex, and the effectiveness of psychoanalytic therapy.

The study therefore reports the analysis of the boy's phobia, a process which was intended to cure him of this 'illness'. It also shows how Freud explained Little Han's behaviour in terms of an unconscious Oedipal conflict.

Method

Design

A case study was carried out, longitudinally, over a period of months.

FOCUS ON RESEARCH METHODS – case study method

A case study is an in-depth study of one subject or a small group of subjects, often carried out over an extended period of time (longitudinally). Within the case study method a number of different data-gathering techniques can be used. For example, recorded interviews, case notes (of therapeutic interviews, for example), observation, as in the Washoe study, and psychometric tests.

The strengths of the case study include its usefulness in describing atypical, abnormal or rare behaviour. In abnormal psychology the case study is seen as a useful way of exploring a S's past experiences to help them deal with current difficulties. Freud's work derives predominantly from the case studies of his patients.

Another strength is that the data gathered is usually qualitative and rich in detail, so data from case studies can be highly valid.

The bond of trust that can be built up between the researcher and subject also means that the data is more likely to be valid than if the researcher were a stranger having only one interview with the subject.

The weaknesses of this method include the fact that replication is not usually possible, particularly where a therapeutic approach has been taken. This makes it hard to establish the reliability of findings from a case study.

The close bond that develops between the researcher and subject can be a weakness of the method too, as the researcher may lose their objectivity because of their personal relationship with the subject. Their interpretations of data may also be affected by biases formed as a result of their long-term investment in the project.

Generalising from the findings of case studies can also be difficult as the cases selected for study are often unusual or even unique.

Case studies can be costly in terms of both time and money.

Procedure

This case study and the analysis was actually conducted by Little Hans' father, a friend and supporter of Freud. Freud only met the boy twice, on one occasion for a therapeutic session and on another when he paid a social visit to deliver the boy a birthday present.

The father reported on the boy's behaviour via correspondence (including his own interpretations) and Freud gave directions as to how to deal with the situation based on his interpretations of the father's written reports and conversations.

Freud believed that the reason the analysis could progress using this kind of method was because the father and son had a very special and close relationship with each other.

It is important to note that Hans' father had been making notes on the boy's behaviour for a number of years and sending these to Freud. Freud had asked all his friends with young children to observe and record their behaviour in order to confirm his theory of psychosexual development.

Also, it is pertinent to point out that Hans' mother had been a patient of Freud's and had met Hans' father through him.

Hans' father's early notes on the boy and Freud's interpretations of these notes

The first information that Freud thought was interesting was Hans' interest in his 'widdler' (penis) when he was three years old. Hans thought everyone had a widdler, males and females alike, and the only things that didn't have widdlers were inanimate objects. He even thought his baby sister, Hanna, who arrived 'by stork' when he was 3½, hadn't grown hers yet. (Small children around this time were told that storks brought babies rather than explaining where they really came from.) In fact, Hans liked playing with his widdler, which is quite normal for small boys. However, as this behaviour is frowned upon, parents often tried to discourage their children from masturbating and Hans' mother was no different:

When he was 3½, his mother found him with his hand on his penis. She threatened him with these words: 'If you do that, I shall send for Dr A to cut off your widdler. And then what'll you widdle with?' Hans' reply, 'With my bottom', suggests he was none too perturbed by his mother's threat!

His interest in widdlers was quite extensive and he tried to see other people's widdlers and liked showing his off. He even said to his parents that he wanted to see theirs and Freud explained that this was probably because he wanted to see how theirs compared to his. Hans thought his mother must have a widdler 'like a horse' and presumably thought that as he got bigger his would grow too. In fact, much of the focus of his dreams and fantasies during this time concerned widdlers and what they do.

Hans wanted his father 'out of the way' so he could have his mother to himself and sleep with her. This idea had come from spending lots of time with her when his father was away one summer. He had become apprehensive and nervous about things and had been comforted by his mother who cuddled him in bed. He enjoyed her attention and probably resented having to 'share her' on his father's return. In fact, Freud believed that he attempted to seduce his mother when he was 4½ by asking her why she wouldn't put her finger on his penis when she was putting talcum powder on him after a bath. She answered that it was not proper, but according to Freud he had 'found an incidental channel of discharge' for his sexual feelings towards her and this resulted in his 'masturbating every evening, and in that way obtaining gratification'.

Freud claimed that Hans feared that another baby might come (more competition?), but suppressed his anxiety which surfaced in another form – a fear of the bath. Hans had said he was worried about drowning in the big bath having previously been bathed in a baby bath. Freud suggested this fear came from being frightened that if he was naughty his mother wouldn't love him anymore and therefore might let him drown. Hans also expressed jealousy towards his sister and was asked the following question: 'When you were watching Mummy giving Hanna her bath, perhaps you wished she would let go of her so that Hanna should fall in?' Hans answered yes to this question, which confirmed Freud's idea that this was evidence of his death wish towards Hanna.

Case history – the identification of Hans' phobia and the report on his psycho-analysis

Hans' father wrote to Freud describing the fact that Hans had developed an irrational fear that a horse would bite him in the street, and that the fear was in some way connected with his having been frightened by a large penis. His father believed that this was the onset of the illness, and that there was a motive for being ill – he wanted to stay with his mother and never be separated from her, which was the result of a dream where his mother had gone away.

This irrational fear probably developed from two events, overhearing a father say to his child, 'Don't put your finger to the white horse or it will bite you,' and seeing a horse pulling a carriage fall down and flay about in the road. It affected Hans sufficiently to make him fear that a horse would come into the room. Freud suggested that there was a connection between putting a finger towards the horse that may actually be bitten and the event when his mother wouldn't touch his penis with her finger after giving him a bath. This connection had something to do with Hans' knowledge that his parents thought masturbation was not a very good behaviour to indulge in. In fact, Hans' father said to him, 'If you don't put your hand to your widdler anymore, this nonsense of yours will soon get better'.

Freud also suggested that Hans' desire to see his mother's widdler was increasing. At this point, his father told him that women didn't have widdlers. Hans may have made the association between his mother's threat to castrate him if he didn't stop playing with himself and her lack of widdler. Perhaps she was in fact a castrated man who had played with hers too much in the past and had suffered the consequences!

Freud began to make the connection between Hans' father and Hans' fear of horses, and started to think that the fear was simply a symbolic representation of his fear of his father. His fear of his father punishing him as a result of his longing for his mother had been projected on to horses. This connection was made after Freud was informed about a daydream the boy had had, the fantasy of the giraffes.

243

The fantasy of the two giraffes:

Hans: In the night there was a big giraffe in the room and a crumpled one, and the big one called out because I took the crumpled one away from it. Then it stopped calling out, and then I sat down on top of the crumpled one…

Hans demonstrated what he meant by crumpled by crumpling up a piece of paper. Hans also explained that he had not dreamed about the giraffe.

Hans: No, I didn't dream. I thought it. I thought it all. I'd woken up earlier.

He then went on to explain that he knew you can't really squash a giraffe with your hands, but explained that he had picked up the crumpled giraffe and held it in his hands until the big one had stopped calling out. Once that had happened, he again explained that he sat down on the small crumpled giraffe.

Father: Why did the big one call out?

Hans: Because I'd taken the little one away from it.

This fantasy was recognised by the father as a re-enactment of what happened in the morning when Hans climbed into bed with his parents. Often his father objected and Freud believed that he was represented by the big giraffe who was calling because Hans had taken the little giraffe (mother) away. There was also some discussion about whether the long neck of the giraffe represented a penis, but this was denied by Hans.

Freud's interview with Hans and Freud's explanation for Hans' phobia

It was at this point that Freud himself chose to see Hans and asked him about his fear of horses. Freud suggested to the boy that the horse must represent Hans' father. Hans must be frightened of his father because he was jealous of him and felt hostile towards him (as outlined in Freud's Oedipus complex). The reason why Freud made this analogy between the horse and Hans' father was because Hans mentioned the black on horses' mouths and the things in front of their eyes (blinkers). Hans' father had a black moustache and wore glasses.

Hans explained that he was also afraid of horses biting him, as well as being afraid of loaded carts and buses, which was interpreted as having some kind of analogy with pregnancy, a 'loaded' body which would deliver a competitor for his mother's affections. He then told Freud about seeing the horse fall down and kick about with its feet, which terrified him because he thought the horse was dead and this led him to think that all horses would fall down. Hans' father suggested that when Hans saw the horse fall down he must have wished that his father would fall down and die in the same way. According to Freud, Hans' behaviour towards his father after this 'confession' became much less fearful and he was much more boisterous and overbearing. He did, however, still retain his fear of horses.

Hans then developed a preoccupation with his bowels and 'lumf' (German for faeces). He had been in the habit of accompanying his mother or the maid to the toilet until he was forbidden to do so. Father again recognised another analogy between a heavily loaded cart and a body loaded with faeces. Then Hans started to talk about Hanna and father concluded that the reason for the train of thought was because he thought his sister was lumf and was born in the same way as we produce lumf. This led on to the analogy between loaded carts and pregnancy, horses falling over and giving birth, '...the falling horse was not only his dying father but also his mother in childbirth.' He then described an imaginary friend called Lodi who was called after 'saffalodi', a German sausage. This time father pointed out that the sausage looked like 'lumf'.

The final fantasies Hans produced at the end of his conflicts focused around plumbers and being a parent himself.

The fantasy of the plumber:
The first fantasy involved a plumber who 'took away my behind with a pair of pincers and then gave me another, and then the same with my widdler.' Hans' father immediately interpreted this as the fact that they were replaced with bigger ones like his, which meant that Hans wanted to be like him.

The fantasy of being a parent to his mother's children:
The second fantasy was that he was the father of his own children (his mother was now his wife) and his father was their grandfather, in other words, no longer a threat to the boy as a result of his affection for his mother.

This was then the final piece of evidence that showed that the Oedipus conflict was the cause of Hans' problems, and that once he had acknowledged his desires towards his mother (which he did symbolically in his fantasies), his problems would be resolved.

FREUD'S DISCUSSION

The discussion focuses on the fact that this study offers support for Freud's theory of sexuality.

Support for the Oedipus complex:
- Hans was sexually aroused by his mother.
- He was jealous of his father's relationship with his mother and frightened of him (castration fear), symbolised by a fear of fingers being bitten by horses.
- He fantasised about taking mother from father (giraffe fantasy).
- He tried to seduce his mother by asking her to touch his widdler.
- He finally admitted he wanted to marry his mother.
- Resolution came with wanting to be like his father (the plumber removing his widdler and behind and giving him a bigger one).

Commentary

Is the study useful?

Little Hans was the only child studied by Freud and Freud had already formulated his Oedipus complex before he met him, supporting the idea that the report was extremely biased. Hans was probably quite normal, but became 'phobic' about horses because of a traumatic event which may well have frightened any small boy. It is quite likely that his fear of horses was absolutely nothing to do with his father but that this idea was introduced and stuck in Hans' memory.

Freud believed that phobias are a result of hidden conflicts found in the unconscious mind and, as such, interpreted everything on that basis. His questioning of Hans can therefore be understood as a way of getting at the unconscious mind and trying to resolve what he saw as a potential cause of trouble for the boy as he got older. Hans' agreement with many of the interpretations offered to him indicated to his father and Freud that they were correct in their beliefs about the origin of his phobia and the Oedipus complex. Hans' final fantasies about wanting to marry and have children with his mother was the final confirmation they needed.

Another way we could interpret the findings is that the boy was suffering from what Bowlby called 'separation anxiety'. Hans' mother frequently made alarming threats to Hans to make him behave, such as beating him with a carpet beater. His fear of castration was founded on firm ground – after all, his mother had threatened him when he wouldn't stop fiddling. She also threatened to leave the family, which would have made him quite insecure, and consequently he may have become very possessive and clingy. Hans was actually kept away from his mother when Hanna was born, and this must have made the situation worse: because he was frightened that his mother might leave him, he would have felt very angry and unhappy that she was the cause, so it would make sense that these feelings were directed towards her. However, it is not right to be fearful or angry with your mother, so he may have projected those feelings onto something else – horses. This idea is illustrated in the following conversation when Hans talked about a fantasy he had that he had taken a horse out of the stable:

Father: You took it out of the stables?

Hans: I took it out because I wanted to whip it.

Father: Which would you really like to beat – Mummy, Hanna or me?

Hans: Mummy.

Father: Why?

Hans: I should just like to beat her.

Father: When did you ever see someone beating their Mummy?

Hans: I've never seen anyone do it, never in all my life.

Father: And yet you'd just like to do it?

Hans: With a carpet beater.

As there are other explanations for the cause of Hans' phobia, we have to question the validity of Freud's interpretation, and this affects its usefulness. In fact, Freud's theory of psychosexual development is considered to be 'a nice story', but not an accurate description of personality development.

Are there any real-life applications of the study?

We must remember that this case study was intended to support the Oedipus complex which replaced Freud's earlier 'seduction theory'. The change from believing that the parent was responsible for child sexual abuse to suggesting that it was a fantasy in the mind of a child was, however, responsible for the resistance of society to acknowledge how widespread such abuse really was. Even if there were some overt physical evidence of abuse, such as a pregnancy, the child would be blamed. In this respect, it would have been better if Freud had stuck to his original ideas, and this suggests that Freud's work may have done more harm than good.

Are there any problems with the methods used?

- On the one hand, Freud suggested that children's memories were in fact quite accurate, but the next minute he was making some fairly stunning leaps by reinterpreting what Hans said to give it a different meaning! Perhaps Hans' memory was originally quite accurate but the likelihood of his father (and Freud) introducing new interpretations may have affected his subsequent memory of events or clouded their interpretation. In fact, the whole study brings new meaning to the idea of leading questions.

KEY CONCEPT – leading questions

We came across leading questions in the Loftus and Palmer study on eyewitness testimony. Their definition is as follows: 'A leading question is simply one that, by its form or content, suggests to the witness what answer is desired or leads him to the desired answer'

In the study of Little Hans by Freud, Hans' father uses leading questions in his analysis of the boy, e.g. 'When the horse fell over, did you think of your daddy?'. Hans replies, 'Perhaps. Yes. It is possible.'

This is a problem as it means that the child in being influenced by his father's expectations, which in this instance are very much in tune with Freud's theory of child development, and this means the findings are not objective.

- One of the biggest weaknesses of case studies is that contact with the subject over time may well lead to extreme subjectivity. This case study was even more subjective because the child was being 'treated' by his father (emotional

247

involvement) who was a strong Freud supporter (biased) and his mother had been treated by Freud before her marriage (it would be interesting to know why she was treated).

- Perhaps some of the interpretations were because the father was preoccupied with matters sexual or physical. After all, father was the one who suggested that a German sausage looked like a lumf. In fact, when he was aged between six and 19, Hans' mother and father divorced and both remarried; he went to stay with father while his sister went with mother. Perhaps the relationship between father and mother was somewhat strained during the time when Hans became phobic and in fact father was projecting his own preoccupations onto Hans.

- Psychoanalysts claim that they cannot be judged by anyone except a psychoanalyst because no one else would understand the procedures and would therefore be biased in some way. In effect, they are making their beliefs and profession unquestionable, so perhaps we should simply accept that the case history of Little Hans is true, because until we are psychoanalysts ourselves, we can't judge it!

Whether you think this case study was good or bad, Hans actually came out of it seemingly unscathed, although we cannot be sure that he wouldn't have been fine anyway. When he was 19, Hans met Freud and told him that he was well and that he had no troubles or inhibitions. He also claimed he had no memory of the discussions with his father or Freud which took place during his childhood and that he got on well with both parents despite their break-up, but actually missed his younger sister. However, we can never be sure whether this was because he was repressing the memory or not.

Despite the fact that Freud's theory of child development is without supporters today, very few people question the major contribution Freud made to our understanding of behaviour by describing the influence of unconscious motivation on behaviour and interpreting the purpose and meaning of dreams.

Key questions

1. Can you describe the strengths of a case study over a snapshot study?
2. Why was it a problem for the case study to be conducted by the boy's father?
3. Give one piece of evidence from the study which was used by Freud to show that Hans really was experiencing the Oedipus complex.
4. Is there any evidence in the study that Hans demonstrated castration fear?
5. Can you think of an alternative explanation for Hans' phobia to Freud's interpretation?

Example Answers are on page 457.

Further reading

- Jones, E. (1953–7), *Sigmund Freud: Life and Work*, New York: Basic Books, three vols.
- http://www.freud.org.uk/ – Freud's museum, London.
- http://users.rcn.com/brill/freudarc.html – a collection of links to different Freud-related sites.

CHAPTER
5

Physiological psychology

In many ways it is very easy to forget the physical basis of all human behaviour – our bodies. Our bodies are the most amazing organisms, which are so complicated that it is likely we will never understand absolutely everything there is to know about them. They have also been the basis of many heated debates that focus on whether our bodies are all there is to us, or whether we also have a spirit (or soul). If our bodies are all there is, when we die, we must cease to exist. If, on the other hand, we also have a spirit, when we die, does our spirit die too or does it go on existing? This is known as the mind–body problem and really questions the basis of consciousness and existence itself. Logic says that we are simply what goes on in our bodies and so when our body dies, our spirit must die too. There seems to be no easy answer to this conundrum.

If you are a biologist, you will have already some insight into how our bodies work and you will be familiar with the information in the next section (which is very basic). However, for those of you who have spent your time trying to ignore biology, hopefully this simplistic overview of the physiology of the nervous system will not put you off. You need to have some understanding of the structure of the nervous system because psychology also involves an understanding of physiology. Once we have done this, we can begin to look at the interaction between what goes on physically and our subsequent behaviour, as the topics in this section look at that interaction.

The physiology of the nervous system

The way the nervous system is structured is absolutely fascinating because it is so complex and each component is so tiny, and yet it seems our abilities are limitless. With all the technological knowledge in the world, we have not yet been able to mimic much more than the most basic of human abilities. Humans can make assumptions that are correct on the basis of very little information; computers are far more likely to make errors. They cannot use information that is not clear, whereas we process the past, the present and what we know about the future, at the same time. That is not to say that we don't make errors, we just make far fewer than computers.

We discussed in the chapter on cognition, the information-processing approach which makes the analogy between humans and computers. This analogy is not only relevant because of the way we both process information; it is also the case that we both use electricity. Obviously, we don't have to plug ourselves in to the mains, but we do actually work by a system of electrochemical changes and these are caused by external stimuli and also by changes in our bodies.

THE STRUCTURE OF THE NERVOUS SYSTEM

The nervous system includes the central nervous system (CNS), which is the brain and spinal cord. This is the central control for all the activities of the body, where information received is processed and there is coordination of actions and reactions, both conscious and unconscious. The other part is the peripheral nervous system (PNS), which consists of a network of neurons which are located around the whole body and are responsible for carrying information from the world to the CNS and from the CNS back to the different parts of the body.

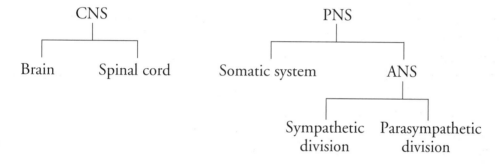

The PNS can also be subdivided into the somatic nervous system and the autonomic nervous system (ANS).

The somatic part is the part that is generally conscious of the responses it is making, for example, the sensory nerves of the somatic system carry information about external stimulation from the different receptors to the CNS. The information is 'decoded', and then messages are carried back from the CNS to the muscles of the body where action is then taken in response. Therefore, the somatic part of the nervous system is responsible for all the muscles we use in making voluntary movements, as well as involuntary adjustments in posture and balance.

The nerves of the ANS run to and from the internal organs and are affected generally by information from inside the body (although occasionally they may respond to external information) the messages transmitted by the ANS regulate the function of these internal organs, for example heart rate, speed of respiration and digestion. It is called the autonomic nervous system because many of the activities it controls are automatic and self-regulating and these continue whether a person is asleep or unconscious.

The ANS can be further subdivided:

- The sympathetic division is the mechanism that speeds bodily systems up and prepares the organism for activity so it has an excitatory function. It is the fight/flight mechanism which prepares the body for a response, for example, by speeding up the heart, dilating the arteries of the essential organs and constricting the arteries of the less essential organs, such as the skin and digestive organs. We need more blood to the vital organs in order for us to survive, whereas we don't need to digest things if we are running away (that can be done later).
- The parasympathetic division is responsible for returning the body to normal by slowing it down again and allowing bodily functions to return to their original state – so it is inhibitory.

In order for this to happen, neuronal fibres from both the sympathetic and parasympathetic divisions supply most organs, and the normal state of the body is maintained by a balance between these two systems.

What are neurons?

Neurons are the cells of the nervous system and are the things responsible for carrying messages from one part of the body to another. In our bodies we have three types of neuron: sensory neurons, motor neurons and inter-neurons. There are between ten and 12 billion neurons in the nervous system, which will give you an idea of how tiny they are. A nerve is actually a bundle of neurons (like a telephone cable) which are held together by glial cells. Glial cells are smaller cells than neurons and provide the neurons with nutrients and structural support.

The three different types of neurons all have different functions:

- Sensory neurons transmit impulses received by receptors to the central nervous system.

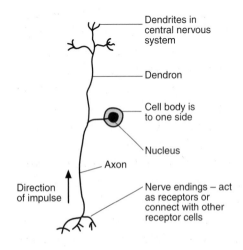

Dendrites in central nervous system

Dendron

Cell body is to one side

Nucleus

Axon

Direction of impulse

Nerve endings – act as receptors or connect with other receptor cells

Unbranched sensory neurone e.g. skin

A simple diagram of a motor neurone

- Inter-neurons receive the signals from the sensory neurons and send impulses to other inter-neurons or to motor neurons. They are found only in the brain or the spinal cord.
- Motor neurons carry outgoing signals from the brain or spinal cord to the effector organs such as the muscles or the heart and lungs.

All these neurons form connections with each other in order to carry information around the body by way of impulses or 'electric messages'. Some of these impulses are messages to do something, and in other cases they are messages to remain inactive.

The messages or impulses that travel along our neurons can be thought of as bursts of electrical energy. We talk about these bursts of electricity as bursts of 'fire'. A single neuron 'fires' when the stimulation reaching it from other neurons exceeds a certain threshold level. A way to imagine this is if you think of a number of drips coming from various branches of a tree into a large bath underneath – when the bath is full, a final drip will make it overflow. The firing of a neuron is just like this – a certain level has no effect, but a sum of lots of stimulations makes it reach a certain level, when it will fire.

What sets these cells apart from other cells is their shape. From the central body of the neuron come lots of small, thin fibres called dendrites. Some are very short and others extend for long distances, with lots of branches to them. Consequently the shape of a neuron can vary enormously, and it is their shape which dictates both the number of excitatory or inhibitory connections they make with other neurons and how each one will contribute to the overall functioning of the organism, although they all work in the same way. This should begin to give you an idea of the flexibility of the nervous system in terms of the number of connections that can be made between the many different components of the body. In fact, each neuron can make up to 10,000 connections with its neighbours.

If you imagine a set of roads converging with roundabouts and junctions and flyovers, which give you an unlimited choice as to where you can go, this should give you an idea of the choices of connections that can be made with the increasing numbers of junctions between neurons. No one neuron creates thoughts or behaviours, but it is the different patterns of activity that arise from the firings of millions of different neurons which result in our different activities. In fact, even when we think we are at rest (and neurons should be relatively quiet), if we scan the activity of our brains they still seem to be alive with constantly changing inter-connections. If you think how these patterns must increase and interconnect when we are engaged in any sort of task, from complex mental thought to physical activities, it will give you some idea how active our brains must be. Every time we experience a sensation this will result in new neuronal connections being made, and this pattern will fade away unless the information relating to this experience is stored in our brains for whatever reason.

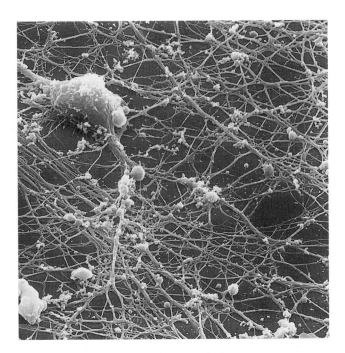

A photograph taken by an electron microscope to show the intricate network of neurones and their complex connections

THE BRAIN

The area of the body where most of our neurons are located is the brain. In fact, the brain consists of nothing but millions and millions of neurons. It is the most amazing wiring network and different areas seem to be responsible for different things. It looks like a walnut with lots of furrows or crevices that are known as sulci. Just like a walnut, it is divided into two halves which are known as hemispheres. The left hemisphere controls most of the right-hand side of the body, and the right hemisphere controls the left-hand side.

Each of these hemispheres has the equivalent of three layers: the hindbrain at the core, the midbrain and the forebrain (which contains the cerebral cortex). Although the cerebral cortex is the area most relevant to us, it may be useful to see how the other structures of the brain actually assist in our day-to-day activities.

The hindbrain

The hindbrain consists of the cerebellum, the pons and the medulla. The cerebellum plays an important part in movement. It is where memories for automatic sequences of actions are stored and any damage to it will cause problems in movement, such as walking or the coordination of fine movements. The pons is a kind of bridge or connection between the two halves of the cerebellum, whereas the medulla oblongata is the crossover point between the fibres from the brain and the spinal cord. The medulla also contains lots of vital reflex centres that control and regulate many of the basic bodily functions, such as the cardiovascular system and respiration.

The midbrain

The midbrain is smaller in humans and other mammals than in birds and reptiles. It is really the top of the brain stem and connects the cerebral cortex (or forebrain) to the spinal cord and hindbrain. At its core is the reticular activating system (RAS), which brings sensory information from the spinal cord to the cerebral cortex and takes back motor information. It plays a very important part in maintaining or controlling our levels of arousal and may even have an influence on our personalities. According to Eysenck (1970), people who fit the category of introverts have a high level of arousal in their RAS and therefore seek to reduce it, whereas extroverts have a low level of arousal and constantly seek to raise it by choosing external situations which are 'busier' than their introvert counterparts. It is the RAS which has an influence on our ability to pay attention selectively to different stimuli, and influences the way we become used to stimuli which are continuous and therefore not necessarily important. It also has a role in our sleeping and waking because when the level of activity in the RAS falls below a certain level, the person falls asleep.

How personality influences behaviour provides a link to applied psychology. Research into personality types suggest that extroverts prefer team sports, whilst introverts prefer solitary sports such as golf. It has been suggested that the reason for this is that extroverts seek the stimulation of playing with others whilst introverts perform better when they are less aroused by other people.

Personality has also been linked to other applied areas:
- It has been suggested that extroverts may be more likely to become involved in criminal activities (especially if they also score highly on tests of neuroticism).
- Extroverts prefer working with other people within organisations rather than alone. Introverts have been shown to be better at vigilance tasks such as air traffic control monitoring.
- Within health psychology, a link has been established between personality type and illness.

The brain stem, made up of the midbrain, pons and medulla, is really the most primitive part of the brain and probably evolved more than 500 million years ago. It is often referred to as the reptilian brain because it is like the brain of a reptile, controlling the basic elements of life but with no higher-order thought processes. You can't form a close and loving relationship with a reptile because it is incapable of thinking and feeling in the same way as even the lower-order mammals such as rats and mice. It simply functions from day-to-day, has a heart that beats, lungs that inflate and deflate, a maintained blood pressure level, can move, fight, mate and produce other stereotypical behaviours which give it the ability to survive. Beyond that, there are none of the characteristics we associate with intelligent life, simply instinctive behaviours.

The forebrain

The forebrain is the largest and most obvious part of a mammal's brain. The outer layer is called the cerebral cortex and consists of the cerebral hemispheres. Under the cortex are a number of other structures including the thalamus, the hypothalamus, the pituitary gland, the basal ganglia, hippocampus and amygdala, some of which form what is known as the limbic system (involved in emotional behaviour, motivation and learning). The limbic system is a kind of centre where the more primitive parts of the brain join with the 'newer' cortex and integrate information from the outside world and the internal functioning of the body.

Although these individual structures do not concern us directly, they all have an influence on our behaviour and, for that reason, they are briefly described below.

- The thalamus works as a kind of relay station by linking sensory signals between the cerebral cortex and the sense organs.
- The hypothalamus helps to control the body's internal environment such as temperature regulation, appetite and thirst. It also influences other motivated behaviours such as sexual behaviour and emotional arousal levels. Eating disorders can be triggered by a disorder of the hypothalamus, and if it is damaged the person's internal temperature regulation may well be affected, making them overheat or always feel extremely cold. The hypothalamus is also involved in the regulation of levels of hormones in the body and controls pituitary gland activity.
- The pituitary gland is actually an endocrine gland (produces hormones). It is attached to the base of the hypothalamus and responds to information from the hypothalamus to release hormones into the bloodstream. The secretions of the pituitary gland control the timing and amount of secretion by other endocrine glands.
- The basal ganglia plays a part in voluntary movements.
- The amygdala is important for feeding, drinking, sexual behaviour and

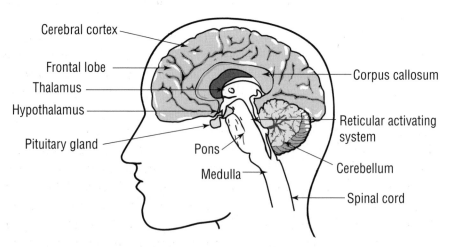

The main structures of the brain

aggression. If it is electrically stimulated in non-human animals, such as cats, they will either attack another individual or actually become very placid. Rabies, which causes animals to become violent, often involves the amygdala. What seems to happen is that it changes how animals interpret information and therefore affects their responses.

- The hippocampus plays an important role in the laying down of new memories and so any damage seems to result in a lack of ability to store new information. According to Colin Blakemore (1988), it is the 'printing press' for our stored memories.

The *cerebral cortex* itself consists, as we know, of two hemispheres, each receiving information from the opposite side of the body. The two sides, which are almost mirror images of each other, communicate via a tract of fibres called the corpus callosum. Each hemisphere is divided into four lobes which are defined by major sulci.

The *occipital lobes*, located at the back of the head, are the areas which receive the main input from the visual pathways. The rear of the lobe contains the primary visual cortex and if this is destroyed the person loses their sight.

The *parietal lobes* are located between the occipital lobe and the central sulcus (the central sulcus divides the parietal lobe from the frontal lobe). They are specialised to deal with information from the body such as touch and temperature, and also to help interpret body position. They also play a part in vision, because it has been found that damage in this area doesn't result in a failure of vision or touch, but it does produce disturbances in the integration and analysis of sensory information. This is explained well by the example of a man who had a tumour in his parietal lobe, recognised a clock as a clock but could not tell the time from the position of the hands.

The area directly to the rear of the central sulcus is known as the *sensory cortex* and is responsible for receiving any sensory information such as touch, pressure, pain, smell and temperature.

The *temporal lobes*, located on either side of the head near the ears, receive information from the ears about sounds and balance. They also contribute towards the more complex aspects of vision such as face recognition. They play a part in emotion and motivation and if they are damaged this may lead to extremes of emotional response. Wernicke's area is located in the temporal lobe on the left-hand side, and plays a critical role in language comprehension.

Finally, the *frontal lobes* seem to be responsible for all the higher-order and more complicated functions such as thinking, planning and forming ideas. They also play a part in memory formation and retention. Frontal lobes are said to contain our personalities, and have an input to our emotional responses and control our social inhibitions. This area is the last part of the brain to stop growing and it continues to change even after birth, because the numbers of neuronal connections that are located here seem to continue forming after birth. Broca's area is found in the left-frontal lobe in humans and is critical for the production of language. People who have left-sided strokes (burst blood vessels in the left-hand side of the brain) often lose their ability to speak and this would indicate that Broca's area has been affected.

The area at the back of the frontal cortex, directly in front of the central sulcus, is the *primary motor cortex* and this area is responsible for movement, especially fine movement.

Much of the evidence we have about what is known as 'localisation of function' (which bit does what!) comes from the investigation of people with areas of their brain which have been damaged at one time. If a certain area is damaged and this results in them not being able to do something, this would indicate that the damaged area is responsible for the non-function.

Having been through a brief guide to the physiology of the nervous system, we can now start to focus on the core studies. The first study we are going to look at involves the interpretation of many of the body's physical responses to a situation. The study questions whether each set of responses is different depending on whether we are frightened, excited or angry, or whether all the responses are the same and it is really down to how we interpret the responses, which will depend on the situation in which we find ourselves.

Emotions – are they real?

Have you ever wondered what emotions really are? Before we look at this topic, consider the following two situations.

> One dark damp night you are walking home from town alone and you have to go along a fairly narrow alleyway, which is dimly lit by street lamps from either end. You are late and you decide that although you would rather not walk along the alleyway, it will save you quite a lot of time. As you start to walk along, you think you hear footsteps behind you. You turn to look and you see a dark silhouette of a man against the street lamp. You start to walk faster and faster. Your heart is beating so fast now that you can almost hear it. You are breathing faster too and you can feel your mouth is dry and you are beginning to sweat. In fact you feel…

What is the emotion that you are feeling?

Imagine another situation (assuming you escaped from the first one in one piece).

You are at a nightclub and the music is excellent, the atmosphere is charged, and you feel you look really good tonight. Across the other side of the dance floor you see someone who seems to be looking at you, and at first glance you realise that this person is absolutely gorgeous. You can't believe that they are looking back at you and you look away. When you look back again, they are still looking and smiling and you realise that this is real. You smile back, they come over and you can feel the electricity between you. All you want is to touch this person but you go to the bar together and buy a drink. As the evening progresses, you become more and more infatuated and as the person stands in front of you can feel your heart beating so fast now that you can almost hear it. You are breathing faster too and you can feel your mouth is dry and you are beginning to sweat. In fact you feel…

The interesting thing about both of these situations is that the physical responses you have are the same, but the emotion you actually 'feel' is very different.

We need to stop and consider three possible alternatives to the question, 'What is an emotion?'

1. Do we simply interpret our body's physical response to a situation as an emotion?
2. Does what we think about a situation (our cognitions) constitute an emotion, irrespective of our body's physical response?
3. Are emotions actually a mixture of the two?

Just to recap, we know from the section on physiology, that we have a sympathetic division of the autonomic nervous system which is the part which prepares us for emergency action – the fight/flight response. This is the part that increases our heart rate and raises our blood pressure, makes us breathe faster, dilates our pupils and makes us sweat, while things like saliva secretion decrease. All the vital organs necessary for emergency action are supplied with blood, and other areas, which are not required in the immediate response, are put on hold. We also know that when the emergency subsides, the parasympathetic system, the energy-conserving system, takes over and returns the organism to its normal state. These activities are triggered by activity in certain critical regions of the brain, including the hypothalamus and parts of the limbic system.

The kind of heightened physiological arousal just described is characteristic of some emotional states, such as anger or fear, when we must prepare ourselves for some sort of action. The interesting part is that they are also present when we are extremely elated, excited or sexually aroused. It is only when we feel very sad that our bodily processes seem to be depressed or slowed.

So what is the relationship between heightened physiological arousal (the 'physical' bit) and our subjective experiences (the 'felt' bit) of an emotion? If we didn't have the physical bit, would we feel less? What we need to consider is whether or not our perception of our own arousal makes up part of the experience of the emotion?

One way to study this is to look at people who have spinal cord injuries. When the spinal cord is severed (or lesioned), the impulses sent by the sensory neurons which enter the spinal cord below the point of injury can't reach the brain, because the neurons in the spinal cord have been damaged and so the messages can't get through. Once they are damaged, the neurons in the spinal cord can't repair themselves, and so the person suffers a permanent lack of sensation. The actor Christopher Reeve suffered just such damage when he fell from a horse and severed his spinal cord at the level of his neck. He has no feeling in any areas of his body below the break, although his body still functions.

Some of the sensations from our body come from the somatic system, for example, we know if the temperature is hot or cold. Others come from the sympathetic nervous system – we know if our heart is pounding and whether or not we have a dry throat. Therefore, if people have suffered a spinal cord lesion they will no longer have an awareness of any bodily response to a situation and will suffer a reduction in any sort of contribution autonomic arousal may make to felt emotion. To put it more simply, if we don't get any sort of feedback from our bodies, and if this feedback is essential for the experience of an emotion, then people with spinal cord lesions will not feel any emotion.

Hohmann (1966) studied army veterans who had spinal cord injuries. He divided them into five groups, according to where the lesion was on their spine. In one group the lesions were near the neck, so there was very little feedback from the sympathetic system. In another group the lesion was near the base of the spine, so they had far more feedback from the sympathetic nerves. The other three groups fell between these two extremes.

The subjects were interviewed to find out what their feelings were in situations of fear, anger, grief and sexual excitement. They were asked to remember an emotion-arousing event that took place before they were injured, then to think of a comparable event which occurred after they were damaged, and try to compare their emotional experiences in each case to see if they were greater before the injury was sustained. It seemed that the higher the lesion (giving less feedback from the autonomic nervous system), the more they reported a decrease in emotionality, no matter what the original emotional feeling actually was. This tends to indicate that the less autonomic arousal we have available to us, the less intense the emotions are that we experience.

Patients who had the highest spinal cord lesions suggested that they could react emotionally to arousing situations, but that they did not really feel emotional:

'It's a sort of cold anger. Sometimes I act angry when I see some injustice. I yell and cuss and raise hell, because if you don't do it sometimes, I've learned people will take advantage of you; but it doesn't have the heat to it that it used to. It's a mental kind of anger…'

So we now have a useful but not entirely objective study, because the emotional situations would have varied from person to person and subjects rated their own experiences. What may be an intensely emotional experience for you may have been no more than a laugh for me.

Further studies, however, have shown that very similar findings have been made so the conclusions are that the less feedback we get from the autonomic system to the brain, the less intense is the feeling of emotion. It seems that autonomic arousal does contribute to the intensity of emotional experience, but does it actually differentiate the emotions? Is it really the case that there is one pattern of physiological activity for joy, another for anger and another for fear?

THE JAMES-LANGE THEORY

William James (1884) suggested that an 'emotion' is simply our interpretation of the physical responses our body might have to different stimuli. At about the same time, the Danish psychologist, Carl Lange, came to the same conclusion. This approach to emotions became known as the James-Lange theory and the theory suggested that there are different patterns of arousal according to the stimulus. These patterns form the experience of an emotion, but because the different emotions feel different, there must be a distinct pattern of autonomic activity for each one. A simplistic example of this would be that our hearts might beat faster if we are frightened than if we are excited, and we would interpret that speed of beating as the emotion of fear.

Here are two examples that may make it a little easier to understand. The first is: 'I am afraid because I run.' What is being suggested is that I have seen a situation and worked out that I really need to remove myself from whatever the situation is without necessarily feeling any kind of emotion. But, once I start to run, this physical act will involve a number of changes in my body's physiological system, including an increase in arousal in the autonomic nervous system. The brain detects these changes and interprets them as the emotion of fear. The second example is: 'I am happy because I laugh.' Here again, I have decided that an appropriate action for the situation I am in is to laugh, and as I laugh the physiological changes involved are interpreted as the emotion of happiness.

Here is another example.

> Katie was waiting by the kerb to cross the road. She was desperate to catch up with her friends, but she looked right and left as her mum had told her to do whenever she crossed the road. She was sure the road was clear and started to run across. Just as she got out into the road, a car flew round the corner and had to hoot at her and slam on the brakes in order to avoid hitting her. The sound of the horn stopped her in her tracks as she jumped back onto the pavement. The car drove off, leaving her standing on the pavement. She started to shake and a dreadful sick feeling had come from nowhere into her stomach as she realised how lucky she had been.

Have you ever been in that situation when you do the right thing at the time, but afterwards the emotions you feel are dreadful?

One study which offers support for the James-Lange theory was carried out by Valins (1966). He wired up his male subjects to a heart monitor in order to give them feedback about their heart rate. He then showed them arousing photographs of scantily clad ladies who had appeared in *Playboy* magazine. The heart rate feedback was rigged and appeared higher for about half the slides. Interestingly enough, subjects rated the slides that appeared when heart rate feedback was higher as being more attractive than when feedback was normal.

However, despite some supporting evidence, the theory has been criticised, especially by Walter Cannon (1929), who listed a number of specific faults with the theory.

1. Cannon claimed that the internal organs are really quite insensitive structures and internal changes happen quite slowly, whereas emotional feelings seem to happen more or less immediately.

2. He also said that the pattern of autonomic arousal does not seem to differ much from one emotional state to another; for example, while anger makes our heart beat faster, so does the sight of a loved one.

3. Although you can artificially induce the bodily changes associated with an emotion, for example injecting a drug such as adrenalin (the fight/flight hormone), this still does not produce the experience of a true emotion.

This was demonstrated by a study carried out by Maranon (1924), when he injected his subjects with adrenalin. About 71% of the 210 participants experienced physical symptoms such as a dry mouth or a pounding heart, but none of them felt real emotions, with 29% reporting that they felt *as if* they were afraid or angry. He discovered that a few of his subjects did actually seem to experience a genuine emotion rather than an 'as if' feeling. When they were asked about what they were feeling, they reported that they were remembering an emotional event from their past or imagining a highly emotional situation. This implies that they were using their cognitions (thoughts) as a way of interpreting the physiological responses they were having and labelling the response with the appropriate emotion for the situation they were in. To put it in simpler terms, it seems that the physiological arousal alone is not enough to give the feelings of an emotion unless the person is given (or produces) a suitable cognition such as an upsetting memory.

What we have to remember is that 71% of Maranons's subjects did not report an emotion. However, they knew they were receiving an injection and may well have known what it was and what the effects would be. Consequently they had a completely appropriate explanation as to why they were experiencing such physiological responses. Maybe this was why so few of the subjects reported any emotional experience.

4. Perhaps the physiological changes we associate with various emotions are not even necessary and it is quite possible to feel an emotion without autonomic feedback to the central nervous system.

There is some evidence to support this idea, although the evidence is really quite weak. Cannon (1927) removed the sympathetic nervous system of cats but they still showed a supposedly normal set of emotional responses – the question is, what are the normal emotional responses of a cat?

THE CANNON-BARD THEORY

As an alternative to the James-Lange theory, Cannon proposed what is known as the Cannon-Bard theory. This suggests that emotions can be felt without any change in the responses of the nervous system.

Cannon pointed out that incoming stimuli are processed through the thalamus in the brain. Messages then pass from the thalamus upwards to the cortex, where conscious emotional experience occurs. At the same time, messages are sent downwards to the hypothalamus and then on to the body, which would result in physiological arousal and muscle activity. If the spinal cord has been damaged, obviously the messages can't get back down to the body from the brain, so physiological arousal won't occur. However, the messages that are travelling from the thalamus to the cortex won't have been affected and so emotional feelings will still be preserved.

You will probably agree that neither of these theories really explains emotions adequately because, despite what Cannon believed, is it unlikely that an emotion could be complete without both the thoughts and the physical responses. Can you imagine feeling fear or anger without the stomach going into a knot and the heart pounding? Maybe the James-Lange theory is correct and there are subtly different responses for each emotion, but imagine how fast the interpretation of all these physical responses must be in order for you to work out what you feel almost instantaneously when something happens. If you were to see something ambiguous like a light in the sky, which may or may not be a flying saucer, you would need to have feedback from every part of your body in order to pick out all the slightly different rates of activity before you can decide if you feel frightened or excited about the object. By this time you may well have been massacred by whatever the object was. Do you think this is realistic?

SCHACHTER'S TWO-FACTOR THEORY OF EMOTION

Schachter (1964) suggested that there is a relationship between physiological arousal and emotion. He believed that most of the theories about emotions and the role of arousal had ignored the importance of cognition and how we use our cognitions to make sense of the situation. In effect, we label the situation according to the cognitions that are available to us. The two factors he referred to were the state of arousal and the cognitions that make sense of the situation.

He argued that when we feel emotions they are always about something – either an external stimulus or possibly a memory or thought. How often have you sat alone and thought about things and become very sad or very happy? You are not feeling these things out of the blue – they are related to past experiences. Emotions seem to be directly related to memories, and just thinking about past events can result in your heart beginning to beat faster or getting a really sick feeling in your stomach. Maybe thinking about the event produces the physical response and then you relate that response to the situation which makes you feel the original emotion, such as anger or embarrassment.

If this is the case, Schachter's explanation gives some support to the James-Lange theory that we do need to have some kind of physiological response first in order to feel emotions. But Schachter makes the point that it is how we interpret the physical response that really makes an emotion, and we do this according to the situation we find ourselves in. What he meant was that when we have a physical response we attribute it to something, and this attribution will suggest whether the emotion is labelled as fear or anger or whatever.

At this point, perhaps you can accept his theory that an emotion comes from a combination of a state of arousal and a cognition that makes the best sense of the situation the person is in. Let's look at a couple of examples.

It is a sunny summer afternoon and you have borrowed a car from a friend, with the intention of impressing your girlfriend by taking her out for the day. You decide to drive to a really romantic spot at the top of a steep hill, where there is a wonderful view over the sea. You pull the car up and look out over the landscape and then gaze into your girlfriend's eyes. What is this strange sensation you feel? A horrific awareness of what is going on suddenly occurs to you – the car has started to roll down a steep slope and you have no control over it. Not just the handbrake, but all the brakes have failed. You experience the emotion of absolute terror...

Now imagine the situation where the car is part of a roller coaster. The feeling you have will also be one of fear and excitement, but not the blind terror of the first situation. Here, our cognitive appraisal of the situation determines the intensity of the emotional experience.

One final piece of evidence which supported Schachter's theory of emotion comes from Dutton and Aron (1974). They manipulated the arousal of their subjects by choosing men who were crossing Capilano Canyon in Canada on either an unstable suspension bridge or a solid wooden bridge as part of their sight-seeing tour. The men, who were aged between 18 and 35, were approached by an attractive female and asked to take part in a survey on scenic attractions as they crossed one or the other bridges. She also asked the men to write a short story about an ambiguous picture of a woman which was assessed for sexual content (assumed to be a measure of sexual attraction to the female interviewer). The men on the unstable bridge wrote stories containing more sexual imagery than their 'wooden' counterparts and it was suggested that this significant difference could be explained by the wobbly bridge! (Do you think the participants might have wondered why – in a survey of tourist attractions – they were being asked to write a story?)

Schacter developed his two-factor theory (which is also known as 'cognitive labelling theory') in part as a result of past research. Schachter and Singer (1962) had joined forces to conduct some research to look into the notion of cognitive labelling. Their research was intended to test three propositions which would support the idea of the two-factor theory of emotion.

S. Schachter and J.E. Singer (1962), 'Cognitive, social and physiological determinants of emotional state',
Psychological Review, 89 (5), 379–99

Background

In their introduction, Schachter and Singer reviewed the James-Lange theory and Cannon's criticisms of it by showing that emotion is not simply cued by a physiological response. They also described the work of Maranon (see above) to show how someone could only be induced to experience an 'emotion' once they had been physiologically aroused only if an appropriate cognition was introduced. Maranon had done this by suggesting a 'memory with strong affective force... of their sick children or dead parents' to subjects. Schachter and Singer took this to show that both physiological arousal and cognition contributed to the experience of emotion. In this study, Schachter and Singer intended to test three propositions which would support the idea of the two-factor theory of emotion.

The study involved manipulating not only the arousal levels of the subjects, but also the situations they found themselves in, and the expectations of what the side effects should be. Their explanations of their feelings formed the interesting and relevant part for the researchers.

The question was whether emotion is made up of both a state of physiological arousal (biology) and a cognition (belief about the reasons for the arousal).

Aim

The aim of the study was to investigate the interaction between physiological responses and cognitive factors when experiencing an emotion (the two-factor theory).

In order to do this, three propositions were tested:

1. If a person experiences a state of physiological arousal that they can't explain, they will describe the state in terms of the cognitions available to them at the time. This means that the same state of arousal can be labelled as joy, fury, fear or lust, depending on the situation the person is in.

2. In order to test this, Ss would have to be put in a state of physiological arousal for which they had no explanation and then be put in a situation to try to manipulate their beliefs (cognitions) about their 'emotional state'.

3. If a person experiences a state of physiological arousal that they can explain, they are unlikely to try to re-explain the arousal as a result of the situation they are in. Here subjects would need to be put in a state of physiological arousal and given an explanation for it, and then tested to see if the situation they were put in really had no effect on their interpretation of their emotional state.

A state of physiological arousal needs to be present before an emotion is experienced. In order to test this, it was important that the Ss were not induced to a state of physiological arousal *before* they entered the study. This would therefore mean that their experience of an emotion would not be influenced by other factors such as the situation in which they were placed.

Method

Design

A laboratory experiment was conducted, using an independent groups design. Subjects were tested in one of seven ways.

Subjects

The Ss of the study were 184 male college students studying introductory psychology, who received extra points towards their exams. Their health records were checked to make sure that epinephrine (adrenalin) would not harm them.

Variables

There were two independent variables being manipulated.

The first IV was manipulated according to which experimental group the subject was tested in. There were four conditions, and they were injected and instructed as follows:

- **Epinephrine ignorant (Epi Ign)**
  Subjects were given an injection that they believed was Suproxin and were told by the doctor that the injection was mild and harmless and there would be no side effects.
- **Placebo condition (control group)**
  Subjects were given an injection that they believed was Suproxin but was in fact only saline solution, and were told by the doctor that there would be no side effects.
- **Epinephrine informed (Epi Inf)**
  Subjects were given an injection that they believed was Suproxin, and were told by the doctor of its real side effects, which were shaky hands, pounding heart, etc.
- **Epinephrine misinformed (Epi Mis)**
  Subjects were given an injection that they believed was Suproxin and were told by the experimenter (confirmed by doctor) of possible side effects, but these effects, were inaccurate (itching, numb feet and headaches).

All subjects believed they were being given Suproxin and that the purpose of the study was to test the effects of this on their vision.

Epi Ign	Epi Inf
These Ss were given adrenalin, told the injection was mild and harmless and there would be no side effects. This group would test the first proposition, as they were given no explanation for the physio-logical arousal they were to experience.	These Ss were given adrenalin and warned of the true side effects. This group would test the second proposition.
Placebo	**Epi Mis**
These Ss were given saline solution and were told the injection was mild and harmless and there would be no side effects. This group acted as a comparison group for the Epi Ign group. This group would also test the third proposition, and would show that arousal is necessary for a subject to experience 'emotion'.	These Ss were given adrenalin and told of wrong side effects (misinformed). The purpose for including this group was to control 'expectation of side effects' as a possible confounding variable in the results obtained from the Epi Inf group.

The second IV was whether an emotion inducing cognition could be established. This was tested by placing subjects in one of two conditions: the euphoria condition or the anger condition (described in the procedure below).

This would show whether Ss with no explanation for their arousal could be led to experience happiness or anger by being put in the context where they observed the behaviour of someone 'in the same chemical boat'. Would their emotion be cued by the what the context led them to believe they should be feeling?

	Epi Inf	Epi Ign	Epi Mis	Placebo
Anger	23	23		23
Euphoria	27	26	26	26

The DV was the subject's mood state at the end of the test, as measured by observation, and on a scale by self-report questionnaire.

Procedure

Subjects were told a cover story by the researchers, that the study was to look at the effects on vision of vitamin supplements called Suproxin. In fact it was to investigate the effects of physiological arousal and cognition on emotions. The Suproxin, which was administered by a doctor, was really epinephrine (adrenalin), which produces arousal similar to that when we are in the fight/flight situation – heart beating, increased respiration, pupils dilating, etc.

Subjects were tested individually. They were told that the aim of the study was to look at the effects of a vitamin injection called Suproxin, on visual skills. They were given an injection of either epinephrine (adrenalin) or a placebo (saline) and tested individually. The effects of epinephrine began after a period of three minutes and lasted up to an hour, although the average length of time was 15 to 20 minutes.

In the next stage of the experiment each subject was tested in one of two contexts, euphoria or anger.

Euphoria-inducing condition:
Subjects in the euphoria condition were put in a room with a stooge for 20 minutes to 'let the Suproxin be absorbed by the bloodstream' before they undertook their vision test. The room was slightly untidy and as soon as the experimenter left, the stooge made a number of friendly comments to the subject and began playing with items left in the room (paper, rubber bands, pencils, folders and hula hoops). He encouraged the subject to join in while he played basketball with crumpled paper, made paper airplanes, fired pieces of paper with rubber bands, made a tower of folders and played with one of the hula hoops. The routine was standardised but would be adjusted according to the behaviour of the subject and whether or not he joined in.

Anger-inducing condition:
Subjects in this condition were put in a room with a stooge and asked to spend the time waiting for the injection to take effect by filling in a questionnaire. The stooge began trying to wind up the subject by moaning about having injections. The questionnaire was also intended to annoy the subject by asking increasingly personal questions such as, 'Do you bathe and wash regularly?', 'What is your father's average annual income?', 'How many times a week do you have sexual intercourse?' and other very personal questions. The stooge would make comments to some of the more extraordinary questions, such as question nine, which asked, 'Do you ever hear bells? How often?' The stooge's remarks to this question were, 'Look at question nine. How ridiculous can you get? I hear bells every time I change classes.'

The stooge continued to make comments and then got very angry (again, in a standardised routine), ripped up his questionnaire, saying that he was not wasting any more time, picked up his books and left.

(In order to prevent any experimenter effects, the stooge had no idea which condition the subject was in.)

Measurement of the DV

During his time with the stooge, the subject was observed through a one-way mirror to take observational measurements of his emotional state.

For the next stage, the experimenter returned and took the subject's pulse. He told the subject that it was necessary to assess any side effects of Suproxin which may affect performance on the vision tests and this would involve filling out a questionnaire. This gave a second measure of the DV, a self-report measure from the questionnaire.

The questionnaire consisted of a number of irrelevant questions about the Ss' current mental and physical state. Some required answers on a four-point scale: others were open-ended questions. The critical questions used to measure mood and emotional state were on a five-point scale.

How irritated, angry or annoyed would you say you feel at present?	
I don't feel at all irritated or angry	(0)
I feel a little irritated and angry	(1)
I feel quite irritated and angry	(2)
I feel very irritated and angry	(3)
I feel extremely irritated and angry	(4)
How good or happy would you say you feel at present?	
I don't feel at all happy or good	(0)
I feel a little happy and good	(1)
I feel quite happy and good	(2)
I feel very happy and good	(3)
I feel extremely happy and good	(4)

Each subject was given an individual score by subtracting his anger score from his happiness score, so each subject could be placed on a scale between four and –four.

Finally the subjects were told about the nature of the experiment and debriefed. Eleven subjects expressed extreme suspicion about a crucial part of the experiment and their data was discarded.

Results

Results from self-report of mood

The subjects' scores for anger were subtracted from their scores for happiness. Therefore, if they had a positive value, it meant they were feeling more happy than angry.

In the euphoria condition, we can see that the misinformed group were feeling more happy than all the others. The second most happy group was the ignorant group and so on. These results were as predicted because subjects were more susceptible to the mood of the stooge when they had no explanation of why their body felt as it did, as was the case for both the Epi Mis and Epi Ign groups.

This also indicates that the informed (Epi Inf) group felt the least happiness because they understood why they were experiencing arousal and did not need to use the context they were in to give them a reason for it.

Results for the euphoria condition (the lower the score the higher the happiness)

Condition	Average score	
Misinformed	1.90	h a p p i n e s s
Ignorant	1.78	
Placebo	1.61	
Informed	0.98	

In the anger condition, we can see that the ignorant group were feeling the most angry (or rather, the least happy). The second most angry group was the placebo group, and the group who were informed felt the least upset by the questionnaire, as predicted. Again, this was because subjects were more susceptible to the mood of the stooge and the nature of the questionnaire when they had no explanation of why their body felt as it did.

Results for the anger condition (the lower the score the higher the 'anger')

Condition	Average score	
Ignorant	1.39	a n g e r
Placebo	1.63	
Informed	1.91	

N.B. the Epi Mis group was not tested in this condition.

Results from observations of behaviour

The behaviour of subjects in both conditions matched their self-reports. The euphoric condition produced the most manic behaviour from the misinformed group, followed by the ignorant group, and in the anger situation the ignorant group produced the most anger. This was probably because there was no misinformed group in the anger condition.

Discussion

The results of the study followed the expectations of the researchers and support Schacter's (1964) idea of cognitive labelling theory, which suggests that the physiological arousal in different emotions is the same – we just label it according to our cognitions.

Proposition one:

The findings from the Epi Inf and Epi Mis conditions support proposition one. It seems that if a person experiences a state of physiological arousal that they can't explain, they describe this arousal in terms of the situation they are in. They give a 'cognitive' reason for the arousal they feel rather than just feeling it and not understanding it.

Proposition two:

The results from the Epi Inf condition support proposition two. It seems that when a person experiences a state of physiological arousal that they can explain by way of an injection they have received, they are unlikely to try to explain it in any other way.

Proposition three:

For proposition three, it seems that the control group (who were not supposed to be feeling arousal) did not score the least happy or least angry, as might have been expected. However, this can be explained by the fact that the injection itself may have aroused them somewhat and this may be why the researchers suggest their support of this proposition is 'tentative', but claim their evidence supports it nonetheless.

However, the findings were not as impressive as expected. The subjects in the anger conditions were actually not angry (if they were angry, the numbers would have been minus numbers and they were all plus numbers). It seems that the researchers either didn't actually manage to make their subjects angry, or that subjects were reluctant to reveal their anger ('at the experimenter') on the self-report questionnaire. Remember the subjects had agreed to take part because they were to receive points towards their course, and therefore they may not have wished to displease the experimenter and risk losing these!

The researchers conclude that 'the pattern of data… falls in line with expectations', but we must note here that it was only after they had omitted a number of findings to account for 'experimental artefacts', such as subjects giving their own explanation for their arousal, subjects being suspicious of the procedure, etc.

Commentary

Is the study valid?

Epinephrine does not have the same effect on everyone, and five subjects who said they had no physiological symptoms had their data removed from the study.

Therefore we can't be sure that they were all experiencing the same level of arousal as a result of the injection.

It is also likely that subjects who did not have the epinephrine would still have felt aroused, simply because they were taking part in a study. In fact, the subject's arousal was not assessed before the study and this might have affected their subsequent behaviour. The researchers also failed to establish a baseline for the subject's mood, and therefore we cannot be sure whether they were more or less happy as a result of the study or whether the study had any effect at all on their mood prior to taking part.

These problems mean we have to question the validity of the findings. The use of an all-male student sample from the USA also means there are difficulties in genereralising the findings to a broader population and again, this means the validity of the study is low.

A problem with the design of the study was that Schachter and Singer failed to test the Epi Mis group in the anger condition. The reasons they gave for this omission was that this condition was intended to test for whether expectation of side effects was a possible confounding variable, and they thought they only needed to test this in the euphoria condition to see if this was the case or not. However, since this group gave the highest 'happiness score', it might be predicted that they would also give the most anger (or least happiness) in the anger condition. This might have affected the interpretation of the results, so the incomplete nature of the findings also leads us to question their validity.

Is the study ethical?

Ethically, the study involved considerable deception, although it was necessary in order to produce the conditions. The fact that the researchers intended to irritate the subjects in the anger condition is ethically questionable, but since they failed to do this we have to conclude that, apart from the use of the cover story, the study was carried out ethically. Health checks were carried out to ensure the subject would not be harmed by the adrenalin injection and the participants were fully debriefed at the end of the study.

Is the study ecologically valid?

Since this study was carried out in the laboratory, the behaviour observed may not have been a sample of the subject's true behaviour. Can the 'emotions' induced in a laboratory setting really be compared to those experienced in real life? The reliance on self-report to give a quantitative measure of emotional state also means that the study is low in ecological validity.

Key questions

1. Why does it matter that no baseline measure of either arousal or mood state was taken at the start of the study?

2. Why is it useful to study emotions?
3. Explain why we should be cautious in generalising the findings from this study to people in general.
4. Suggest a different sample that could have been used for this study and explain how you think this might affect the results.
5. Give one strength and one weakness of the use of the experimental method in this study.

Example Answers are on page 457.

Further reading

- If you are having trouble getting to grips with the theories of emotion in this study, go to http://changingminds.org/explanations/theories/twofactor_emotion.htm for some helpful explanations of the two-factor theory of emotion and a link to the James-Lange theory.

Circadian rhythms and sleep

Despite what you may think, sleep is actually a behaviour, although it is more often defined as a state of consciousness.

Because we all sleep, it is a topic that often crops up in conversation. Here is a list of phrases you will probably recognise:

How are you sleeping?
I'm so tired.
I'm not tired mum!
I stayed out until four o'clock in the morning and I'm dead today.
I must get some sleep.
I can't sleep, I just toss and turn all night.
I seem to wake up far too early.
Did the baby sleep all night?
I wish she'd go to sleep.
If I don't get eight hours of sleep I can't function.
I only need four hours of sleep a night.
She's overtired, that's why she's in such a bad mood.

It's not surprising that sleep is so relevant, after all we spend one-third of our lives asleep. We all know that we can't do without it, and yet it seems such a waste of time. Have you also noticed that during the week when you have to get up, you can't seem to wake up, and at the weekend when you can lie in bed, you wake up really early when you don't have to? That should give you the idea that perhaps our feelings of needing sleep seem also to relate to our state of mind. If we are enjoying ourselves at a party, we find it easy to stay awake, whereas if we are at home, bored, we feel very sleepy. People suffering from depression feel very tired all the time and sleep more than they would normally.

There are other aspects to sleep: the fact that while we are asleep we have periods of relative quiet and periods when we know we dream. We also vary in the amount of sleep we need throughout the course of our lives. When we are babies, we sleep and wake many times during the course of a day. As we get older, many of us only sleep once, at night, although people from very hot countries may well have a siesta during the day when the sun is at its highest in the sky. We also seem to need less sleep when we are in our teens and twenties, and yet, with the passing of the years we seem to need more sleep. When we are really old, our need for sleep often decreases again. The reasons for this are complex and are not only to do with our bodily requirements but are also related to the stresses and strains of everyday life. In many ways, the most stressful times seem to require the most sleep and yet they seem to be the times when we get the least.

One of the most exciting things about sleep can be the dreams we have. You can be anything in dreams, and yet they are not always about pleasant things. They are sometimes weird, sometimes very enjoyable or erotic, and sometimes they seem to perform the function of giving an insight into the solution of problems. The analysis of dreams was one of Freud's interests, and in some of the daily newspapers you will occasionally see articles on how to analyse your dreams. As to whether this dream analysis actually bears any relationship to reality is another matter!

In order to understand the nature of sleep it would help to have a brief introduction to the rhythms which govern our lives, whether they are 24-hour rhythms or annual rhythms. These cycles of sleeping and waking and the different levels of sleep seem to form regular patterns which are known as circadian rhythms, and these form part of the annual rhythms or cycles of life.

CIRCADIAN AND CIRCANNUAL RHYTHMS

Rhythms in behaviour and physiological processes are found throughout the plant and animal world. These cycles are generally called circadian rhythms ('circa' means about, and 'dies' means day, which explains why circadian rhythms are based on a 24-hour cycle), but they may be circannual (about a year). One of the reasons for these cycles seems to be related to the changing patterns of sunlight and temperature that vary from day to day across the seasons.

Plants and animals respond to these changing patterns by pursuing different behaviours according to the time of year or time of day. Some animals hibernate when the length of day shortens and the temperature falls. Even when the temperature remains mild, they become more sleepy, responding to the change in daylight. Other animals collect stores of food, a process triggered by their internal clocks rather than any conscious decision. Birds migrate south and plants begin to lose their leaves. There are similar positive patterns of behaviour in the spring, when animals, triggered by the increasing length of day and warmer temperature, come out of hibernation and begin to find mates and build nests. Humans, too, follow patterns of behaviour that seem to be stimulated by the length of day and amount of light.

Reseach has tried to identify what it is that makes us follow these rhythms and the conclusions are that although light plays a part, it is not that simple. Evidence from rats and birds, which were kept in a constant environment for prolonged periods of time, still demonstrated variations in behaviour on a regular basis, which indicates that we must produce endogenous rhythms (rhythms generated from within) which are unrelated to light, although they seem to follow a similar pattern to external cues. Research has also demonstrated that light seems to moderate the rhythms and prevents them from going too fast or too slow. Evidence to show the power of light as a 'zeitgeber' (timegiver) has been collected from animal studies, where animals which are kept in constant darkness will reset their internal clock, advancing or retarding it when shown no more than a brief flash of light (Aschoff, 1979). If however, there is no light available, other environmental stimuli, such as temperature, can serve as a zeitgeber, which is why hibernating animals know when to wake up, even if they are hibernating underground.

It seems that humans have a circadian rhythm which follows, approximately, a 25-hour sleep-waking cycle. This natural 25-hour clock can explain why, when we are on holiday, we often stay up later than we could do normally, and wake up later too – our biological clock is gaining one hour in 24, so in effect, if we had a 24-day holiday and we got up and went to bed when we wanted to, by the end of the holiday we would be back where we started again.

In humans, another cycle which seems to influence our behaviour is our temperature. Under normal circumstances, temperature in the body core (not skin temperature) will rise during the middle of the day and dip slightly by mid-afternoon. It will fall again at night, reaching its lowest point in the early hours of the morning whether or not our sleep follows that pattern (this is why we often wake up in the night and feel really cold). It therefore seems that temperature must have something to do with how well we sleep. Shift workers, for example, have dreadful problems trying to sleep when their body temperature tells them that they should be up and about.

THE FUNCTION OF SLEEP

Horne (1988) has conducted considerable amounts of research into sleep and has reviewed much of the literature on sleep. He points out that everything that is alive has some period of rest during a day – even plants, who seem to go into a period of quiescence or inactivity, at the same time every day. There are three theories which suggest why we need to sleep: for our bodies, for our minds, and as a result of evolution.

Physiological restoration – for our bodies

This theory suggests that the main reason we sleep is to allow our bodies to restore themselves after a hard day. Our bodies do seem to undertake certain processes which relate to restoration when we are asleep, such as digestion, the removal of waste products and protein synthesis, but these processes also happen when we are awake, so that can't be the only reason. The speed at which cell division takes place is also not affected by sleep – they divide at the normal rate for time of day, irrespective of whether the person is awake or asleep.

Psychological restoration – for our minds

Sleep may not be essential for our bodies, but it does seem to be essential for our brains. If we don't sleep we may become dizzy and irritable and find it much harder to concentrate or do complex tasks. Our memories seem less efficient and we may have problems finding the words to explain what we want to say.

We will consider sleep deprivation studies later in this section. The main finding with all of them is that they illustrate how lack of sleep causes problems with higher-order thinking and this seems directly related to the amount of REM (rapid eye movement) sleep we get (more about types of sleep later). There is evidence that people show higher levels of REM sleep following some kind of stressful life event or trauma. Therefore we can assume that perhaps the restorative function of sleep is not that accurate for the body, but certainly plays a part in restoring our psychological functioning to maximum efficiency.

Evolutionary theory

Because the length of time we sleep seems to have little or no relationship to what we did the day before, it has been suggested that perhaps the function of sleep is similar to hibernation. We may sleep to conserve energy when the environment is hostile, such as having limited food, or when we would be inefficient, such as in the dark. It is true that our bodies mimic a kind of mini-hibernation because we have a lower metabolic rate, lower temperature and lower blood pressure when we are asleep.

If we accept this theory, it would make sense to suggest that animals should vary how much sleep they need depending on different aspects of their lifestyles. For example, if it takes them long periods of time to search for food, they should sleep less. If their food is low in nutrients, such as for cattle and horses, they need to eat a great deal in order to survive so they should sleep less. How safe they are from predators should also enter the equation, with animals such as sheep sleeping less than foxes. Research evidence supporting this idea comes from the average amount of time various animals spend sleeping.

Humans sleep for an average of eight hours per day because the food consumed is much higher in nutritional value and can be eaten at more regularly spaced intervals. Most predators, such as foxes and cats, live in relative safety and will only eat one meal a day and that meal will contain all their nutritional requirements. Consequently they can sleep for much longer periods of time in relation to their body size, as foxes sleep for an average of 9.8 hours per day and cats for 14.5 hours per day.

The one problem with this theory, according to Hauri (1979), is that sheep and goats are extremely vulnerable to predators, and if sleep was purely an evolutionary activity, why would they sleep at all, bearing in mind that the minute they go to sleep they become even more vulnerable than usual?

HOW IS SLEEP INVESTIGATED?

Most of the work undertaken on sleep has been carried out in 'sleep laboratories'. These consist of one or several small bedrooms next to an observation room where the experimenter spends the night and monitors the sleeper's behaviour, both by observation and also by wiring the sleeper up to a series of recording instruments. The sleeper may also be videoed to record his/her behaviour. Can you imagine how difficult it would be not only to sleep in a strange bed, but also to know you were being watched?

In chapter one we mentioned that it is possible to monitor and measure the activity of the nervous system by taking physiological measurements. You can read more about the different types of machines in the next section, but in sleep laboratories subjects would be wired to three types of machines, which all work in the same way:

- An EEG measures brain activity (electroencephalogram) – here the electrodes are placed over the head to record the electrical activity of the underlying neurons.
- An EMG measures muscle activity (electromyogram) – here the facial and jaw muscle activity is monitored by electrodes being placed on the jaw area.
- An EOG measures eye movements (electrooculogram) – here the movement of the eyes is recorded by electrodes being placed around the eye socket.

The subjects who take part in such studies may have been deprived of sleep or allowed to sleep for limited periods. They may even have the type of sleep monitored to see what happens if, for example, they are not allowed to enter REM sleep. The types of measurements taken will give a good indication of what is going on. They may also be woken at regular intervals or specific times and questioned about dreams or feelings they may be having.

It seems that if we are deprived of sleep or sleep is limited for one night, it has no serious effects, but what happens is that we will simply fall asleep much more quickly and sleep longer the following night. If the amount of time we are allowed to sleep is gradually reduced, then we seem to suffer few effects, but if sleep is suddenly reduced, as in the case of hospital doctors who are on call, our ability to perform certain tasks is reduced. If the task is simple, no performance decrement

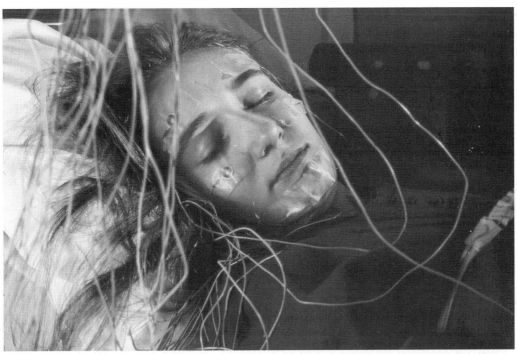

A subject who has been 'wired up' before sleeping. Would this affect your quality of sleep?

(decrease in performance) is shown, but if it is a complicated task which needs planning and thought, then performance declines. This goes along with the idea that the frontal cortex seems to be the area of the brain that requires sleep, as this is the area which is involved in things like higher-order thinking, planning and problem solving.

In order to test these effects out, subjects have been given a number of different tasks, such as problem-solving tasks, reaction-time tasks (to see how quickly they respond to a given stimulus) and also vigilance tasks (where they have to watch screens and report a change in the display, for example). Subjects showed a number of symptoms of sleep deprivation, such as no originality in their responses, staring into space, memory deficits for recent events or information, a decline in their spatial orientation, word fluency and spelling and, finally, speaking in a monotone.

FOCUS ON APPLIED PSYCHOLOGY – environmental disasters and catastrophes

If prolonged lack of sleep can be so debilitating, and sleeping in the day is so difficult, it doesn't say much for the people who work at night, does it? Think of hospital doctors, nurses, airport staff and so on. Without wishing to concern you unduly, it is interesting to note that two of the most frightening environmental disasters happened in the early hours of the morning.

In March 1979 there was an accident in unit two at the Three Mile Island nuclear power station. As a result of both equipment failure and human error, the core of the reactor was exposed. This generated extremely high temperatures which resulted in damage to the fuel and equipment inside the reactor. It took time to bring it back under control, but by then approximately 400,000 gallons of radioactive water had collected on the floor of the reactor building. Radioactive gases had also been released and remained trapped in the concrete container surrounding the reactor.

The incident at Chernobyl in Russia happened in 1986 as a result of a well-meaning safety check. It was considered the largest and most hazardous nuclear accident in history and involved an enormous amount of radiation being released into the atmosphere. There was even concern for the contamination of pasture and sheep kept in the Lake District during that time. It involved a huge number of people and the after-effects are still being dealt with today.

If these two events were the result of sleep deprivation in key personnel, surely it means that we shouldn't take the effects of sleep deprivation lightly.

Jim Horne of Loughborough University has reported that five to eight days of sleep deprivation has little effect on the body. However, motivation might be impaired and there are sometimes small effects on the immune system, but this is caused by the stress of not sleeping rather than the lack of sleep. If, however, we are deprived of sleep, it seems that there is what is called a 'rebound effect'.

In order to understand the rebound effect (which is described in more detail in the postscript), we need to briefly focus on the stages or levels of sleep which can be identified by changes in electrical activity in the brain.

Stage one sleep is the first 'drifting' stage that we go through on our way to deep sleep. It can occur when the natural light fades, as this information is transferred through the eyes to the pineal gland in the brain, which starts to produce a hormone called melatonin. Melatonin indirectly makes us feel sleepy and therefore, when it gets dark, we may begin to feel drowsy. If we are in bed, no problem, and so we start to drift off into stage one sleep. Have you ever noticed that just as you are drifting you jerk violently and it sometimes wakes you up? This is where the neurons are randomly discharging before you enter the second stage.

Stage two is deeper than stage one, but we can still be woken easily. The heart rate, breathing and brain activity is slower than at stage one.

Stage three is deeper still with more long, slow delta waves. The person is difficult to wake at this point and their heart rate, blood pressure and temperature are dropping.

Stage four is known as delta or quiet sleep. This is the stage where it is hardest to wake the person unless the stimulus is very relevant such as the alarm clock or a baby. This sleep lasts for approximately 30-minute bursts. During this stage we are able to toss and turn or move our limbs as necessary.

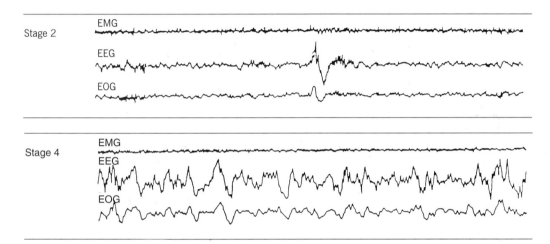

A whole sleep cycle lasts for about 90 minutes and involves us moving 'down' through all four stages and returning 'up' again during that time. This 90-minute cycle is present in infants, who are fed on demand, and has also been noticed in adult activities. We can be engaged in something for about 90 minutes, but suddenly have the urge to go and get a cup of coffee or have a break.

When we return to where stage one would be, we enter a different kind of sleep known as rapid eye movement sleep (REM sleep), where our eyes dart back and forth beneath closed eyelids. It is different because it is an active sleep – active in terms of our brainwaves and eye movements, but strangely enough, our bodies are actively inhibited from movement. That means that we are in effect 'paralysed', so we don't move during this period of sleep. Because the blood pressure rises, this is the time when men get erections in their sleep although the rest of their body is immobile. Our pulse, respiration rate and blood pressure increase and our brainwave patterns look like they would when we are awake. The trouble is, it is even harder to wake someone from this sleep than stage four. It is sometimes known as 'paradoxical sleep', a term coined by Michel Jouvet in the late 1950s. Jouvet was carrying out research into insomnia when he noticed how high brain activity occurred that resembled wakefulness, but at the same time the body was in extreme relaxation and was very hard to rouse. The term paradoxical literally means apparently self-contradictory, as the activity of the brain and body are in total contrast to each other.

Most of the research on sleep has either looked at types of sleep, sleep deprivation or dreaming, although early studies were beset with numerous difficulties in effectively determining and quantifying levels of sleep. The core study in this area is one that was undertaken by Dement and Kleitman and looked at the relationship between sleep patterns and dreaming using specialised equipment.

W. Dement and N. Kleitman (1957), 'The relation of eye movements during sleep to dream activity: an objective method for the study of dreaming',
Journal of Experimental Psychology, 53, 339–46

Background

One of the problems researchers in the field of sleep and dreaming were facing in the 1950s was the problem of measurement. How could you measure objectively if someone was dreaming or not? Prior to this study, researchers had had to rely on the self-report of subjects.

Dement and Kleitman theorised that it might be possible to find an objective way to tell whether someone was dreaming or not by investigating whether physiological phenomena correlate significantly with dreaming. You could then simply measure these physiological reactions and assume the person was dreaming. This would reduce the problems of forgetting, falsification and responses to demand characteristics that occur with the self-report method of measurement. A study by Aserinsky and Kleitman (1955) had shown that Ss in REM (rapid eye movement) sleep recorded dream activity more than when in NREM (non-rapid eye movement) sleep. Moreover, it was possible to measure REM sleep objectively using an EEG machine. REM sleep is characterised by a low-voltage, relatively fast pattern in the EEG. From this, Dement and Kleitman theorised that it might be possible to find an objective way of measuring whether someone was dreaming or not by investigating whether REM sleep correlated significantly with dreaming.

Aim

The aim of the study, then, was to see if the physiological aspects of REM sleep related to subjects' experience of dreaming.

The study aimed to investigate a number of factors. First, it was intended to observe and record the length, frequency and patterns of the subjects' of REM sleep. Second, three hypotheses were to be tested:

1. There is a significant association between REM and reported dreaming. This would establish that measuring REM sleep would be a valid and objective measure of dream activity for future researchers to employ.
2. There is a significant positive correlation between the estimate of time spent dreaming and the measurement of REM sleep.
3. There is a relationship between the pattern of eye movement and reported content of the dream.

283

● Method

Design

A laboratory experiment was carried out.

* For hypothesis one, the purpose was to compare dream recall in REM and NREM sleep.
* Dement and Kleitman measured whether the S was in REM or NREM sleep, as identified by the EEG pattern being recorded, and whether the subjects reported they had been dreaming or not on being awoken. These were then analysed to see if there were differences between REM and NREM sleep as regards dream recall.
* For hypothesis two, quantitative data was collected for correlational analysis, to establish whether there was a positive correlation between REM time and estimated time of dreaming.
* For hypothesis three, qualitative data was gathered regarding the content of subjects' dreams and this was compared with observations of the way the subjects' eyes were moving (REM movements can be observed with the naked eye).

Subjects

Seven adult males and two adult females were studied, with five studied intensively while the other four were used to confirm the findings.

Materials

Subjects were tested in a sleep laboratory using an EEG machine to measure sleep objectively. Electrodes were attached to subjects' eyes to measure eye movement, and to the subjects' scalps to measure brain activity. A doorbell was used to wake subjects and a tape recorder was used to record subjects' recollections of what they had been dreaming.

Procedure

Subjects were tested individually. They were instructed to report to the laboratory a little before their usual bedtime. Subjects were also told to avoid alcohol and caffeine, but to eat normally on the day of the experiment. This was done as a control to prevent the effects of caffeine or alcohol from affecting the findings.

Electrodes were applied to the subjects' heads and faces. To avoid entanglement and to allow the subjects free movement, all wires were gathered at the top of their heads and then led in a single cord to the lead box. Subjects slept on their own in a quiet, dark laboratory. Their brainwave patterns were recorded constantly throughout their period of sleep.

Testing hypothesis one:

At various times during the night, some of which were during REM and some during NREM, subjects were wakened by a doorbell. They had been instructed to record into a tape recorder immediately whether they had been dreaming or not. Return to sleep usually occurred in less than five minutes. To further control extraneous variables, there was no contact with the experimenter before dream reports in order to avoid experimenter bias.

Subjects were not told whether they had been in REM or NREM sleep and the pattern of awakenings for each subject was varied, again to avoid bias:

- Two subjects (initials PM and KC) were woken according to a random numbers table to remove any likely pattern.
- One subject (IR) was woken at the whim of the experimenter.
- One subject (DN) was woken during three REM periods and three NREM periods.
- One subject (WD) was told he would only be awakened in REM sleep, but was actually awoken in NREM sleep periods too.

Testing hypothesis two:
Subjects were woken either five or 15 mins after REM sleep began and were asked to estimate the length of their dream by choosing one or other length. These findings were then correlated with the length of time in REM sleep.

Subjects were also asked to relate the content of their dream, and the length of the narrative was correlated with the duration of REM sleep before they were woken.

Testing hypothesis three:
Subjects were woken one minute after one of four patterns of eye movement had occurred. The patterns were:

(a) mainly vertical (eyes moving up and down)
(b) mainly horizontal (eyes moving from side to side)
(c) both vertical and horizontal
(d) little/no eye movement.

They were asked what they had just been dreaming about, and the data was analysed to see if the pattern related to the content of the dream.

The total number of awakenings (for all nine subjects) was 351 times over 61 nights, which averaged out at 5.7 awakenings per subject per night. Awakenings were spread out over the night as follows: 21% in the first two hours; 29% in hours three and four; 28% in hours five and six; 22% in hours seven and eight.

Results
Dement and Kleitman observed the following about REM sleep:

- All subjects showed periods of REM every night that they slept in the laboratory and this was shown by low-voltage, fast EEG patterns.
- The average occurrence of REM was one period every 92 minutes for the whole group, with variations between 70 and 104 minutes.

- The length of REM was between three minutes and 50 minutes, and they tended to increase in length as the night progressed.

Hypothesis one: eye movement periods and dream recall

(Note that for all hypotheses, dreaming was deemed to have occurred if the subject could give a relatively coherent and detailed description of the dream).

- As shown in the following table, more dreams were reported in REM than NREM sleep.

Subject	REM SLEEP		NREM SLEEP	
	Dream recall	No recall	Dream recall	No recall
DN	17	9	3	21
IR	26	8	2	29
KC	36	4	3	31
WD	37	5	1	34
PM	24	6	2	23
KK	4	1	0	5
SM	2	2	0	2
DM	2	1	0	1
MG	4	3	0	3
Totals	152	39	11	149

Table showing instances of dream recall after awakenings during periods of rapid eye movements or periods of non-rapid eye movements (p. 341)

- Where no dream recall was recorded this tended to be in the earlier period of the night (19 of the 39 no-recalls in REM sleep were in hours one and two).
- Subjects were woken 132 times when they had ceased REM by more than eight minutes and, of these, only six subjects recalled dreams. However, when woken within eight minutes of ceasing REM, five out of 17 reported dreaming. This indicates that the closer subjects were to REM, the more likely they were to be able to recall their dreams. Where subjects were awoken from deep sleep (stage four sleep – a period of NREM sleep characterised by high-voltage, slow waves in the EEG), they were often bewildered and often reported that they must have been dreaming, although could not recall the dream content, or they said they had not been asleep at all. They sometimes described experiencing feelings such as pleasantness and anxiety but could not relate these to dream content.

Hypothesis two: length of rapid eye movement periods and subjective dream duration estimates

- As shown in the following table, there was a significant relationship between subjects' estimate of dream length and amount of time spent in REM for both the five- and 15-minute period. The table also shows that there were significantly more correct estimates of length of REM than incorrect estimates. It also shows that there were more wrong estimates after 15 minutes, so the longer the subject had been in REM sleep, the less accurate they were in estimating dream length.

Subject	Right	Wrong	Right	Wrong
DN	8	2	5	5
IR	11	1	7	3
KC	7	0	12	1
WD	13	1	15	1
PM	6	2	8	3
TOTAL	**45**	**6**	**47**	**13**

Results of dream duration estimates after five or 15 minutes of rapid eye movements (p. 343)

- There was also a significant relationship between length of narrative and REM period.

Hypothesis three: specific eye movement patterns and visual imagery of the dream

The study suggests that the eye movements of subjects related to dream content, indicating that the eyes are moving as if seeing what the subject was dreaming about:

- There was a strong association between the pattern of REMs and the content of the dream, with horizontal and vertical movements relating to dream reports of looking up and down or left and right. The kinds of situations reported by subjects were such events as looking up cliff faces or throwing tomatoes at each other.
- Periods where movements were mixed were associated with looking at close objects, and the periods where there was little or no movement were associated with dreams of looking at stationary or distant objects.

Discussion

The results obtained by waking subjects strongly support the connection between REM sleep and dreaming. Dement and Kleitman point out that, on the basis of their findings, 'it cannot be stated with complete certaintly that some sort of dream activity did not occur at other times' (p. 345), that is, in NREM periods but they considered this unlikely since their results had shown low recall of dreams in NREM sleep and because REM sleep occurs in the lightest level of sleep.

Dement and Kleitman had recorded that when woken within eight minutes of ceasing REM, five out of 17 subjects in NREM sleep reported dreaming. This may account for some of the recordings of dream recall in NREM, as it may be that those awoken within eight minutes were still recalling dreams they had been having whilst in REM sleep.

They suggested that their findings on the correlation between dream recall and length of time in REM sleep indicate that dreams are not instantaneous or happen very rapidly, but rather 'seemed to progress at a rate comparable to a real experience of the same sort' (p. 346). In other words, dreams occur in real time.

Dement and Kleitman considered their findings in relation to other studies of REM sleep and studies of dreaming and considered that any inconsistencies between findings were due to methodological issues. For example, whilst Dement and Kleitman recorded periods of REM sleep in their subjects for every night they had been tested, earlier work had not shown this. They put this down to earlier studies recording only samples of behaviour and therefore missing REM periods, or not amplifying the EEG high enough to make accurate recordings of when REM was occurring.

Conclusion

Dement and Kleitman concluded that the measurement of REM during sleep can be used as an objective measure of dreaming. They say that this then enables further studies to objectively study the effect of other factors such as envionmental change, drugs and stress on dreaming.

Commentary

Is the study useful?

This study was the first to try to study dream activity scientifically. It was highly generative, that is, it led to a great deal of further research in the area of sleep and dreaming. This means it was very useful to psychologists working in this field. On the other hand, issues such as low validity and low generalisability may mean that the findings are not very useful in describing real sleeping behaviour.

Is the study ethical?

Given the complicated instructions for data recording and the fact that the subject had to agree to sleep wired to an EEG machine in the laboratory and to be awoken in the night, we should assume that their informed consent was obtained for taking part in the study. Neither harm nor significant stress was caused to the subjects in the study, and so we can conclude that it was carried out ethically.

Is the study ecologically valid?

The situation may have affected the type of sleep shown by subjects; after all, sleeping wired up in a laboratory is not conducive to getting an excellent night's sleep. Therefore, we could criticise the study for a lack of ecological validity. Of course, this in turn limits its generalisability to real sleeping behaviour and this means we have to question the usefulness of the findings.

Are there any methodological problems?

Sample biases are present. The disproportionate number of males to females may have influenced the study. We cannot be sure that the results of this study were not simply biased towards the dream patterns of men rather than women.

The sample size was also extremely small, and this makes it difficult to generalise to people in general. Also, since this study used subjects who were able to report to the university laboratory just before bedtime and were people for whom periods of disturbed sleep were not going to cause problems, it may well be that the people who were studied were students, although this is not specified in the study.

The study was carried out in one university in America and therefore has an ethnocentric bias which means we have to be careful in any attempt to generalise these findings to a broader population.

The use of self-report measures for dream recall and dream content also presents a problem. As well as the general concerns about falsification of data by subjects and responses to demand characteristics, a number of factors suggest that the data collected by self-report from subjects in this study may not be accurate:

- Even though there were far more reports of dreaming during REM and no dreaming during NREM, the reason for the lack of reports of dreaming during NREM may have been something to do with the depth of sleep and the lack of ability of subjects to remember the dream as they awoke from such a deep level of sleep.
- The length of dream narrative was probably influenced by the talkativeness of the subjects, with subjects who were naturally more talkative giving a much longer description of their dreams. This in turn might have influenced how quickly they went back to sleep.
- The nature of the method of waking subjects (by doorbell) may have affected their ability to recall the dream.

There are also problems with correlational evidence. We must remember that this study was looking for a relationship between REM and dreaming. Even though a significant relationship was found, we still cannot confirm that one causes the other. Correlation does not mean causation. It may be that their co-occurrence has been caused by another variable.

Do the findings hold true in further studies? (Are they reliable and valid?)

The relationship between patterns of eye movements and dream content has not been supported by later studies. For example, babies in the womb and people blind from birth have periods of REM, and yet they must be unable to recall images of objects and events as they have had no experience of such objects.

Later studies have also indicated that not everyone follows the pattern of REM sleep being associated with dream recall. For example, some subjects who claim they rarely dream report a low level of dreaming during REM sleep. It seems likely therefore that there are individual differences between subjects.

Key questions

1. Why do you think that it was seen as important for an 'objective' measure of dreaming to be established?
2. Why were the subjects woken by a doorbell and asked to report the content of their dreams into tape recorders?
3. Using the study as an example, explain why sample bias is a problem in psychological research.
4. Identify and explain one weakness of using correlational analysis in this study.
5. Can you think of a way to carry out this study that would be higher in ecological validity?

Example Answers are on page 458.

Postscript

It was believed that we only dream during this REM sleep, however, it has now been shown that we do dream during stage four sleep, though the dreams are not stories like the ones we are used to. If people are awakened from stage four sleep, they are more likely to report a situation or some kind of feeling or awareness, although some of the most terrifying nightmares occur during stage four sleep.

We still don't know the function of dreaming. Some researchers suggest that it is simply a way of putting the events of the day in some kind of order. Others, like Freud, believed that it is our unconscious finally having free rein, and our id running away with itself. Others say it is simply random neuronal firings which trigger some distant memory or thought that we try to make sense of and therefore turn into part of a story. Whatever the reason, it seems that REM sleep is far more important to us than NREM sleep.

To return to the rebound effect, if we deprive someone of sleep for a night, they will spend more of the next night in REM sleep than normal, but will not necessarily increase the amount of NREM sleep they have missed. This is called the REM rebound, where we seem to compensate for the amount of REM sleep lost. This explains why people aren't too bad at having their sleeping hours slowly reduced. What they do is to pack their REM sleep into a shorter period and reduce the amount of NREM sleep. There have been a number of reports as to what happens to humans if they are deprived of REM sleep. Although the findings are contradictory, it seems that people may develop a kind of paranoia where they are very suspicious of other people's motives. They may also have what are often called hallucinations but are really visual illusions or distortions, that is, they are based on some external stimulus, but it is actually interpreted wrongly (Dement, 1960).

Further reading
- Kleitman, N. (1987) *Sleep and Wakefulness*. Chicago: University of Chicago Press.
- www.lboro.ac.uk/departments/hu/groups/sleep/ – Loughborough University's site, which has lots of interesting work on sleep.
- http://www.sro.org/
- http://www.sleepquest.com/ – website on sleep and sleep disorders, with a section by Dr Dement.

Hemisphere deconnection (or split brains)

As we have already discussed, the brain is divided into two relatively symmetrical halves. We also know that the left-hand side of the brain controls the right-hand side of the body and vice versa, but it is not known why that crossover occurs. The two hemispheres are joined by what are known as commissural fibres and the corpus callosum is by far the largest commissure (cross-hemisphere connection), responsible for carrying the majority of information between the two hemispheres.

It is often misconstrued that the two hemispheres have entirely different functions. It is true, they do differ in some ways, but they are nowhere near as different as we are led to believe by the large number of books which seem to suggest that the left-hand side of the brain is the clever side, and the right-hand side is the spiritual, artistic part.

In most people there is some 'lateralisation of function', which means that one side has a different role to the other. In the majority of people the language centres are on the left-hand side – Broca's area is responsible for speech production and Wernicke's area is responsible for speech comprehension. This is so for the majority of right-handed people, although people who are left-handed may well have their language centres on the right-hand side of their brain. However, it is virtually impossible to give exact percentages, so it is best to accept the fact that the majority of people, left- and right-handed, have their speech centres located in the left hemisphere. This would mean that any damage you may get to the left side of your head would probably leave you unable to speak or understand.

Why this is the case is another matter. One suggestion is that having speech centres in both hemispheres is likely to cause stuttering. It would seem quite likely that both centres would be sending impulses to the muscles responsible for speech, and these impulses may well arrive at slightly different times, so that speech will not be synchronised. Jones (1966) performed a number of operations on patients who had blood clots or tumours near their left hemisphere speech centres and who also stuttered. He knew in advance that they were quite unusual because he had discovered, by anaesthetising one hemisphere at a time with sodium amytal, that they could still carry on a conversation. This showed that they had speech centres in both hemispheres. He also discovered that after the operations their speech was quite normal and that they had stopped stuttering!

Much of the evidence which has been gathered about hemisphere function has come from people who have suffered strokes, or 'cerebrovascular accidents', as they are correctly called. This is the most common source of brain damage in old age and is caused by either a blood clot or other obstruction closing off an artery, or an artery rupturing. This will result in the area around the site being deprived of oxygen or nutrients and the relevant neurons dying. Because the left-hand side of the brain controls the right-hand side of the body, a left-sided stroke will result in right-sided lack of function. This can be quite mild, for example, a non-mobile side of the face, or more severe, as with hemiplegia, where the whole of the right side of the body ceases to function. What makes it worse is the fact that the person often loses the ability to either comprehend or produce words, and so not only are they non-mobile, but they are also isolated in their own little world.

Having made the point that one side of the brain controls the other side of the body, we should note that there are a couple of exceptions to this rule.

VISION

In vision, the input from the left half of each eye goes to the right hemisphere and the input from the right half of each eye goes to the left hemisphere, as seen below.

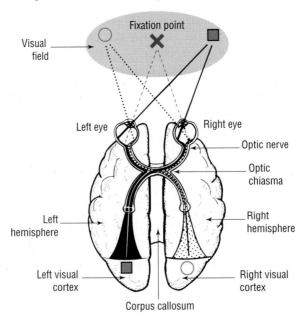

To explain this more simply:
- Light from the world stimulates the receptors at the back of the eye.
- The light from the left half of the world stimulates the receptors on the right half of both eyes (shown by the dotted line), and the light from the right half of the world stimulates the receptors on the left half of both eyes (shown by the black line).
- The right half of each retina connects to the right hemisphere and, thus, the right hemisphere sees the left visual field.

Although this seems complicated, it is actually accurate. The result is simply that things that appear to the right of your nose are 'seen' by your left hemisphere and things that appear to the left of your nose are 'seen' by your right hemisphere.

TOUCH

Information from the sensory receptors of the hands also crosses over so the information from the right hand goes to the left hemisphere and vice versa.

HEARING

Each ear receives sound from just one side, but sends 90% of its input to the other side of the brain, and retains 10% on the side it entered. The reason for this is so we can pinpoint where a noise is coming from by comparing the input from both ears – we couldn't do this if the information only went to one side.

SMELL

Information from each nostril remains on the same side as it enters, so odours that are experienced by the left-hand side of the brain are processed on the left.

ACTIVITY

If you want to look at the differences in hemispheres, there are some fun tasks you can do (although they only work for people with intact brains).

Kimura (1973) found that right-handed people move their right hand more often than their left when speaking. However, left-handed people show no hand preference. Watch your teachers or friends as they talk and notice whether hand movement and 'handedness' are related.

Kinsborne (1972) discovered that if one hemisphere becomes more active, the eyes tend to turn towards the visual field of that hemisphere. So if someone is trying to work out the answer to a verbal problem, they will gaze to the right significantly more often than they will gaze to the left. Similarly, if someone is trying to work out the answer to a spatial question, such as where something is located on a cognitive map (map inside your head), the eyes will turn significantly more to the left. However, this is only true for right-handed people, and left-handed people are inconsistent in their results. Try this by getting your friends to study puzzle books or puzzles printed in newspapers and watch their gaze direction.

Hicks (1975) suggested finding a stick that would be quite difficult to balance on your right index finger. Then start talking and see if the task gets harder. In fact, you can time how long you can balance it for when you are talking and not talking. However, if you are left-handed, again, the results may be quite variable.

If we return to the differences in the hemispheres, you will recall that the main differences between the two hemispheres relate to language. Ornstein (1986) suggested that the right-hand side of the brain is involved in pulling different things together to form a whole picture or concept, whereas the left-hand side is better for breaking down information into different units for analysis. This is why the right-hand side of the brain is better at spatial tasks and artistic activities and the left-hand side is better for analytical thought. There is some evidence to support the idea that the left-hand side of the brain is more analytical and logical and the right side is more holistic and sensory (Rasmussen and Milner, 1977). The right brain seems to be related to depression and pessimism. It has also been noted that people who get left brain strokes are often extremely depressed, irrespective of the amount of damage done to the brain, presumably because the right brain is the only normally functioning part now, and its whole outlook on life is more pessimistic than optimistic. On the other hand, right brain damage often leaves the person with an optimistic outlook, even though their prognosis is poor.

Rita Carter (1998) reports the tale of a senior American judge who suffered from a right brain stroke.

…he insisted on continuing at the bench despite having lost his ability to weigh evidence in anything like a sensible way. He maintained an exceptionally jolly courtroom, happily allowing serious criminals to go free while occasionally dispatching minor offenders to lifelong prison sentences. He resisted his colleagues' attempts to persuade him to retire and was finally sacked. Thanks to his right brain damage he seemed perfectly content – if puzzled – by this turn of events, and subsequently enjoyed a long and happy retirement.

Carter, 1998, p. 36

We have now considered that the two symmetrical hemispheres are only slightly different in the tasks they carry out. In order for us to function adequately, these two parts need to communicate with each other and we have mentioned that they do this by means of the corpus callosum. This gives the side of the brain without speech centres access to words and descriptions which it would be without if there was no bridge between the two. It does not take a huge amount of imagination to think what would happen if that bridge was not there. Such a thought gives new meaning to the phrase, 'the left hand does not know what the right hand is doing!'

There are rare instances of people having the connections between their two hemispheres severed, either as a result of accidents or, more likely, as one of the surgical treatments for epilepsy. Epileptic seizures are a result of abnormal electrical discharges of groups of brain neurons, described by Carlson (1986) as the 'wild sustained firing of cerebral neurons'. The source of the hyperactivity is usually in the temporal lobe and results in the person briefly losing contact with reality and even experiencing hallucinations. Sometimes the seizures can be more sustained, and these are known as 'grand mal' seizures. During one of these, the person becomes unconscious for a few minutes and experiences muscle spasms which may result in them breaking their bones or damaging themselves, and they may also lose bowel and bladder control. When the seizure is over the muscles relax and the person will wake up, but is often extremely disoriented and embarrassed. A seizure like this would obviously be quite debilitating and would put the person in some danger, so any way of trying to reduce the severity or frequency would obviously be of huge benefit.

One way of reducing the problem, developed by the late Wilder Penfield, is to remove the 'focal point' or original source of the seizures from the temporal lobe; operations of this type have been carried out on conscious patients. They need to be conscious in order to make sure that the surgeon doesn't take away too much brain tissue. The patient would be given a local anaesthetic, and the surgeon would remove the skull and layers of dura mata until the brain was exposed. The focus would have been identified by EEG recordings before surgery and checked by more recordings during surgery. The subject would also have areas surrounding the identified focal point stimulated with the tip of a metal electrode in order see what sort of response was made. If the area stimulated was part of the speech centre, then obviously that area would be avoided. The benefit of this method is that it prevents excess tissue or essential tissue from being removed. The by-product of these operations was to give us an excellent map of brain function.

An alternative way of preventing the spread of the wildly excited neuronal firings is to sever the corpus callosum, preventing the other side of the brain from becoming involved and thus reducing the severity of the effects. This method was very successful and it was found that it not only stopped the discharges from spreading, but it also reduced the epileptic seizures to negligible proportions. You would think that an operation of this severity would result in lots of side effects, but the extraordinary aspect is that most of the people who underwent surgery actually had very few side effects which were noticeable in their everyday lives. In effect, they were living with two brains in a single head, each one functioning adequately and seemingly suffering no real side effects from the surgery. However, there *were* side effects and it is these effects that form the focus of the core study undertaken by Roger Sperry in 1968.

R. W. Sperry (1968), 'Hemisphere deconnection and unity in conscious awareness',
American Psychologist, 23, 723–33

● Background

Before we look at the study itself, you need to know a little about Sperry and his work. It would be useful to explain how the studies were carried out and the expected results. Sperry is a neuropsychologist who has conducted a number of studies on split-brain patients whilst working at the California Institute of Technology. In the early 1950s he undertook research which involved 'splitting' the brains of cats and monkeys. He discovered, by training the animals, that you could teach one hemisphere a task, but the other hemisphere would remain unaware of the information learned. This supported his idea that the brain consisted of two separate modules rather than one unified whole. In fact, he shared the Nobel Prize for physiology and medicine with David Hubel and Torsten Wiesel in 1981. (Hubel and Wiesel pioneered a method of studying the physiology of vision by inserting very thin wire electrodes into the columns of neurons in the optic cortex and recording their response to different stimuli.)

Many of the effects of splitting brains were investigated in the laboratory with relatively simplistic tasks. They involved presenting information to one or other eye so that the information went to the opposite side of the brain.

The way this would work is as follows. If the information was presented to the far right visual field, it would go to the left-hand side of the brain which contains the speech centres. Therefore the person would be able to say what they had just seen. If the information was presented to the far left visual field, it would go to the right-hand side of the brain which has no speech production centre. Therefore the person would know what it was, but would not be able to say what they had just seen. However, if this person was then asked to draw the object with their left hand (and their eyes closed), they could draw the object.

From the diagram shown earlier, you may remember that each eye has information that goes to the opposite side of the brain, crossing over at a point called the optic chiasma. (If this crossover point were severed too, this would mean that information from one eye went to one side of the brain only, and in a few cases this has happened.) In order to sort out the situation with the rest of the subjects, they were asked to fixate (fix their eyes) on a spot in the centre of the screen. The image was projected for one-tenth of a second, which was insufficient time for them to move their eyes enough to send information to the opposite side of the brain. Therefore, for any of the split-brain studies which involve projecting objects for someone to look at, just accept the fact that the information projected on one side of the fixation point (that is, in the far left or far right visual field) was only seen by the corresponding eye and only went to the opposite side of the brain.

These studies aren't really ecologically valid because in the real world the situation would not occur, unless they only had one eye. However, a later set of studies on split-brain patients was conducted by Gazzaniga *et al.* (1977), and again, although they lack ecological validity, they also showed how important it is for the two hemispheres to connect.

Gazzaniga *et al.* developed a contact lens which allowed the presentation of sophisticated images to one side of the retina only and therefore to only one side of the cortex. In one study they presented a female subject, V.P., with a short film showing one person throwing another into a fire. The image was presented to the right hemisphere (with no language), and although the woman was fully alert throughout the course of the film she was only aware of having seen some kind of light. She reported that she felt scared and jumpy but was not sure why, and so she explained her feelings by saying that she felt scared of Gazzaniga, although she knew she liked him.

It seems she labelled her state of arousal by the situation she was in, namely having contact with her surgeon. She transferred the fear the film had created into a fear of Dr Gazzaniga. Does this remind you of the study by Schachter and Singer?

Beneath the corpus callosum is another tract of fibres that connect the more primitive part of the brain – the 'limbic system'. If you remember, the limbic system is found under the cortex, and forms the junction between the older, more primitive parts of the brain, with their unsophisticated emotional responses, and the more logical, reasoning cortex. Here there is another tract of fibres which connects the two hemispheres – the anterior commissure. Very basic information about emotional responses such as anger or fear are passed from this area to both sides of the cortex, but the more sophisticated responses of the cortex are missing.

The article by Sperry describes the results of a series of experiments undertaken on people who had already had their corpus callosum severed as a treatment for severe epilepsy. The aim was to investigate the effects of this deconnection and show that each hemisphere has different functions, in other words, to map lateralisation of brain function and show that information in one side of the brain is not accessible to the other side.

Method

Design

The design was a quasi-experiment which compared split-brain subjects with 'normal' subjects in laboratory tests, and case studies of all the individual patients.

Subjects

The split-brain subjects were 11 patients who had already experienced a commissurotomy prior to the study. The sample type is therefore an opportunity sample.

All subjects had a history of severe epilepsy which had not responded to drug therapy. Two of the patients had been successfully operated on to sever their corpus callosum some time before the experiments. The remaining nine had only recently undergone surgery.

Materials

The equipment used allowed for various types of sensory information to be presented to one or other hemisphere, in different combinations. Visual information was presented by projecting images on a screen in front of the subject. Tactile information would be presented to either the left or the right hand, or both hands, without the patients being able to see what the object was. A representation of the apparatus is given below.

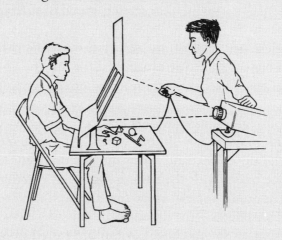

Procedure

Subjects had to remain in silence during the studies unless they were asked questions by the experimenter. This was to prevent them passing information from the left side of the brain to the right side (as sound can be taken in by both ears simultaneously; an example of this would have been if the subject identified an object and then said what it was, this information would then be available to both hemispheres).

Visual investigations:
Visual investigations involved showing one stimulus at a time to one visual field or showing two stimuli simultaneously to the two different visual fields.

One visual field (targeting only one side of the brain at once):
These tests required the subject to cover one eye. They were told to look at a fixation point in the centre of the screen. The image was projected for $1/10$th of a second on either the left or the right of the fixation point, which would send the image to either the far right or far left visual field. It was projected for that short space of time to prevent the information going to the wrong half of the visual field

if the subject moved their eye, therefore sending the information to both sides of the brain. This is because there is an overlap in the centre of the visual field (at the fixation point), which means that the right and left brain both get information about objects viewed at that point.

For example, this screen would be sending the image of a key to the right side of the brain, as it is projected in the far left visual field, picked up only by the left eye.

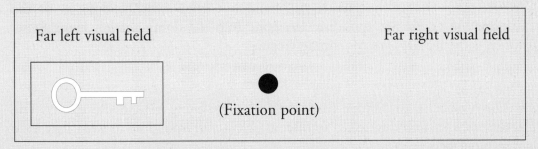

This screen would be sending the image of the key to the left side of the brain as it is projected in the far right visual field, picked up only by the right eye.

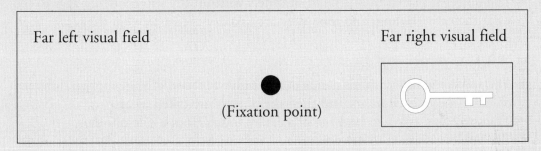

Both visual fields:
The subject would look at the fixation point on the screen while two images were flashed simultaneously either side of the fixation point.

This screen would be sending the image of a key to the left side of the brain (because it would be seen by the right eye in the far right visual field) and the image of an apple to the right side of the brain (because it would be seen by the left eye in the far left visual field).

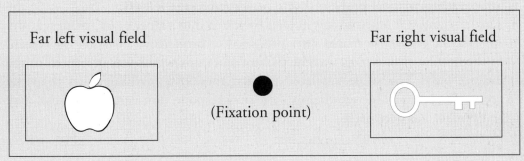

The subject would then be asked to say what he had seen. Typically he would say 'key', although he would not have a conscious awareness that he had seen anything else.

He would then be given a pen with his left hand and be asked to draw what he had just seen (although he would have to do this with his eyes closed or with his hand out of sight, because if he could see what he was doing, the dominant hemisphere would interfere with his recall). Typically he would draw an apple. If he was then shown the picture he would not know why he drew it, as the information about the apple had *not* gone into the dominant left hemisphere, which is the hemisphere containing language.

Tactile investigations:
One hand:
- The S's hands are hidden from their view by being behind the screen. The subject would then be asked to find an object corresponding to what they have seen on the screen.
- The object is placed in one hand or other, without the subject being able to see what they are holding, and then they are asked to say what they have been given.
- The object is placed in one hand or other, without the subject being able to see what they are holding, and then they are asked to point to what they have been given.

Both hands at the same time:
- The subject works with his hands out of sight. He would be given two different objects, one in each hand, and then the objects are taken away.
- The subject is asked to find the objects by touch from a pile of items.
- The subject is asked to say what they have just held.

Tests of the right hemisphere
Because the right hemisphere does not contain language, in order to test if it has any ability to make mental associations, work logically or experience separate emotions from the left hemisphere, the following tests were undertaken:
- The left eye (therefore right hemisphere) is presented with an object on the screen. The person would then be asked to pick out similar objects by touch from an array of objects.
- Simple mathematical problems were presented to the left eye.
- The left hand was asked to sort objects by touch into shapes or by size or texture.
- An array of geometric shapes were projected to both visual fields on the screen. In the middle of this array was the picture of a nude which was presented to the left eye only. The subject is later asked if they saw anything other than the geometric shapes. The right hemisphere may respond non-verbally and this may reveal what has been seen.

Results

Visual stimuli presented to one visual field

- When subjects were shown an image in one visual field, they would only recognise the image as one they had already seen if it was shown again to the same visual field. The reason for this is because that information would have gone only to one side of the brain and not the other.
- If it was shown in the right visual field (left hemisphere) the person was able to say what they had seen, could identify what it was from an array of pictures shown to the right eye by pointing to it, or could find it from an array of objects with their right hand.
- If it was shown to the left eye (right hemisphere) the person was unable to name it, but could draw it (with eyes closed) with the left hand, could identify what it was from an array of pictures shown to the left eye by pointing to it, or could find it from an array of objects with their left hand.

Visual stimuli presented to both visual fields

The subject would be able to say what he had seen presented in his right visual field, but would be unaware that he had seen anything else. If he was given a pen with this left hand and asked to draw with his eyes closed, he would again be able to draw what he had seen with his left eye, although he would seemingly have no conscious knowledge of having seen anything else and would be very surprised when he discovered what he had drawn. He would then be able to name the object, once he had seen his drawing with his right eye.

Tactile investigations

The results of the tactile investigations were the same irrespective of whether one hand held the object at a time or both hands held the objects simultaneously.

- The subject would have no problems identifying an object by name if it was put in the right hand, but if it was put in the left hand they would have no conscious awareness of it. However, they would be able to find it by touch if they put their left hand in a bag full of objects.
- When the objects were placed in one hand or other, subjects could point to what the object was with the same hand that held the object.

Tests of the right hemisphere

- Subjects were able to pick out semantically similar objects, for example, if they saw on the screen a picture of a wall clock with their left eye (therefore right hemisphere) and the only related item in a tactile array is a toy wristwatch, this would be the object chosen.
- Right hemispheres can carry out simple mathematical problems.
- Left hands were able to sort objects by shape, size and texture.
- When subjects saw the array of geometric shapes, they would giggle or look

embarrassed when the picture of the nude appeared, even though they could not say what they were responding to. This non-verbal response suggests the right hemisphere has a second conscious entity.

Discussion

The study gave considerable support to the idea that the brain consists of two seemingly independent hemispheres, each with its own consciousness, and that there is no transfer of information from one side to the other. For the subjects studied, the dominant hemisphere was the left-hand side, which contains the speech centres, and this explained why, when information was presented to the right hemisphere (via the left eye), they were unable to say what they had experienced. The final tests of the right hemisphere give further support to the idea that the two hemispheres have their own consciousness whereby one responds in a typically human way, by giggling at the nude, while the other one doesn't have a clue what is going on.

Commentary

Is the study ecologically valid?

The findings of the study would be unlikely to be found in a real-life situation, because a person with severed corpus callosum who had both eyes open would be able to compensate. This would be either because the information was received by both sides of the brain at the same time or because the information would be carried to the minor hemisphere by speech (and this indicates that the minor hemisphere – the right hemisphere in right-handed people – must have some speech abilities, or it would not understand); therefore, the study lacks ecological validity.

Is the study useful?

Certainly Sperry's work was ground-breaking in starting to understand the physiognomy of the brain, that is, how the brain works. It revealed the importance of the corpus callosum as a pathway for internal communication between the two sides of the brain. However, there are a number of problems with the findings that make us question their validity, and this limits the usefulness of the study.

First, the sample was extremely small as the condition is quite rare. Also we have to question whether studies of the 'abnormal' brain can really be generalised to the 'normal' brain. It may be that the experiences of the subjects prior to the surgery made their brains very different from normal brains anyway. These differences could have been caused by the epilepsy, the life-threatening nature of their disorder and the drug treatments used to try to treat it. Add to this the fact that the subjects have undergone major brain surgery and you can see that there are problems with the generalisability of the findings from these subjects.

Second, Sperry emphasises in his conclusion to the study that even within this small sample of 11 subjects there were 'with respect to the deconnection symptoms mentioned, striking modifications and even outright exceptions' found amongst the split-brain patients. If there are individual differences in brain lateralisation in a sample so small, imagine the extent of individual differences we might find in the human brain in the general population.

Is the study ethical?

The study is ethical as the Ss consented to be studied, no deception was used and they were neither harmed nor unduly stressed by the experimental tests.

Key questions

1. Why do 'normal' people have no problems with the tasks in Sperry's experiment?
2. Why must the researcher make sure that the stimulus is presented for such a short amount of time?
3. Why were the subjects not allowed to see their hands?

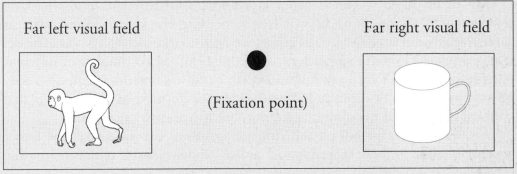

4. If the following screen was shown to a split-brain subject for one-tenth of a second:
   - what would the subject say if asked 'what did you see?' and why?
   - what would the subject draw with his left hand and why?
   - what will he say if you show him what he has drawn and why?
   - if the same monkey picture is then shown in the far right visual field, will the subject report having seen it before and why?
5. Outline two findings from the study that suggest that the two sides of the brain have different functions and that the one side does not know what the other is doing when tested under these conditions.

Example Answers are on page 458.

Further readng

- www.nobel.se/medicine/educational/split-brain/background.html – an excellent website, which allows you to conduct your own split-brain experiments.

- http://www.indiana.edu/~pietsch/split-brain.html – a website which describes the findings from split-brain patients.
- http://www.dushkin.com/connectext/psy/ch02/sperrybio.mhtml gives a short biography of Sperry.

The criminal brain

In the earlier section on learning and aggression, we looked at theories of aggression and considered whether aggression was an innate predisposition or was simply learned behaviour. In order to look at the next section, it may be helpful to clarify briefly what we mean by aggression, because at this point I want to talk about people who are considered criminals. Depending on your concept of aggression, you may feel that crime and aggression are not always one and the same thing.

Most of us, when we think about aggression, tend to relate it to whacking someone with a large lump of wood or something else quite violent, whereas aggressive acts can be very subtle. Perhaps we need to think of aggression as an act that is intended to harm someone or something but uses a number of different techniques. We can't even say it is antisocial, because sometimes aggression may be used as a means of defence. However, what we do need to remember is that criminal behaviour is not always aggressive, but it is always antisocial.

This next section focuses on the ultimate aggressor, one who takes the life of another person. Is their aggression an innate tendency or is it due to the life experiences they have had, and what they have learned?

The innate theories we have looked at so far have simply considered two possible explanations for antisocial behaviour. Lorenz believed that aggression was a biological drive which may be discharged in either antisocial or competitive ways; Dollard said it was only displayed as a result of frustration. Other theories suggest that it is the result of their genetic inheritance: some people are born with a predisposition or susceptibility to develop criminal tendencies in later life. It has been suggested that they have a cluster of symptoms which makes it impossible to develop the kind of moral control that normal people develop through their childhoods as a direct result of cortical under-arousal. In order to combat this under-arousal, they are hyperactive and inappropriate in their behaviour and often are diagnosed as having 'attention deficit hyperactivity disorder' (ADHD). It has also been suggested that this disorder can lead to criminal behaviour where the motive seems irrelevant or non-existent. However, we must not instantly assume that children diagnosed with ADHD automatically become criminals.

More recent research has suggested that there may be other kinds of biological malfunction, either an excess of hormones or some kind of physiological damage, which may have been present at birth or may have been caused by some kind of accident. It is this aspect of antisocial behaviour that we will be looking at in greater detail.

It is not our place here to consider the social explanations of crime, after all, we have touched on some of the explanations in earlier parts of this book. Here we are going to consider the idea that perhaps serious criminal actions may be brought about by an abnormality in the functioning of a person's brain. In fact, there are a number of studies which have shown that violent offenders have poorer brain functioning than normal controls (Eichelman, 1993, Eysenck and Gudjoinsson, 1989, Elliott, 1987, Lewis *et al.*, 1988, Moffitt, 1988, Raine, 1993). Until recently, however, trying to identify the particular part of the brain that is not functioning properly has been impossible.

Biological explanations of criminal behaviour provide a link to applied psychology There are a number of theories which claim that criminal behaviour has a biological basis. One theory claims that criminal behaviour is due to chromosomal abnormalities. Jacobs *et al.* (1965) found a higher percentage of people from a prison population with an XYY pattern of chromosomes than a similar sample of the general population. The problem was that even though it was higher than the population as a whole, it was still only 1.5%. This theory has really very little evidence to support it, especially after Witkin *et al.* (1976) tested over 4,500 men and found no evidence that the XYY individuals in the sample were any more aggressive than the rest.

BRAIN-IMAGING TECHNIQUES

Nowadays, it is possible to use a number of brain-imaging techniques in order to assess the functioning of our brains.

EEG machines

We looked at the EEG machine in the section on sleep, where brain activity is measured by tracing the electrical impulses under the surface of the skull by 'sticking' electrodes to the scalp. The electrical impulses from each of the electrodes are amplified and traced or drawn onto a roll of paper. This is what gives us the information about different types of sleep, for example. They are also used to pick up activity from different areas of the brain, and can be used to detect epilepsy in individuals.

CT scans

CT scans or CAT scans (computerised axial tomography) are used for the diagnosis of pathological conditions such as tumours or degenerative diseases. The patient's head is put in a large doughnut-shaped ring which contains an x-ray tube on one side and opposite an x-ray detector. The head is scanned from front to back and then the 'doughnut' is moved around a few degrees and another scan is taken.

306

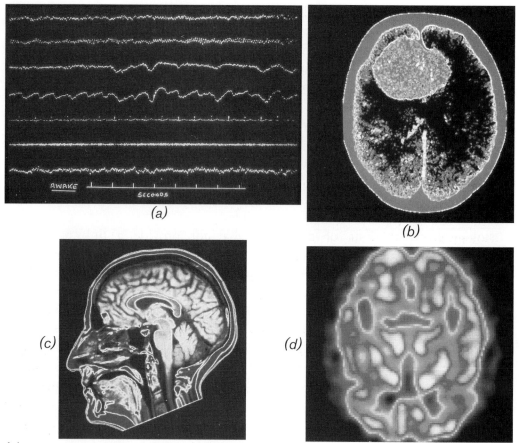

(a) Traces from EEG, EOG and ECG machines (b) A cross section of the skull from a CT scan (c) An MRI image (d) Activity in the brain from a PET scan which shows areas of differing activity.

These images are fed into a computer and this produces a cross-sectional image of the brain. The 'doughnut' can take images of the head from top to bottom so that a whole selection of cross-sectional images can be produced to show the size or site of any abnormalities.

MRI scans

MRI (magnetic resonance imaging) is more precise than the CT scanner as it shows far more detail in soft tissue. It works using strong magnetic field and radio pulses. Patients lay in a round tunnel surrounded by a large magnet which generates a powerful magnetic field. The required part of the anatomy is 'magnetised' and exposed to radio pulses which cause the tissues to give off radio signals that can be measured. Hundreds and hundreds of measurements are made which are converted by computer into a two-dimensional picture of the area.

PET scans

PET scans (positron emission tomography) work in a very different way to the other techniques. PET scans actually look at the different levels of metabolic activity in the brain. Every cell in the body needs energy in the form of glucose, and in the brain neurons use glucose from the bloodstream in order to function. Therefore, by injecting a person with glucose which has been mixed with a small amount of a radioactive tracer compound, it is possible to see how much glucose each area of the brain is using. The PET scan measures the amount of radioactivity and sends the information to a computer which will draw cross-sections of the brain, showing the areas using different amounts of glucose as different colours. If an area is working really hard, it is going to require more glucose and this technique makes it easy to see.

By comparing PET scans of normal people with those of people who have some kind of disorder, it is possible to identify the areas that differ. It is also used to identify which areas work hardest when we are doing specific tasks, such as listening to music or solving mathematical problems.

> **CORE STUDY LINK** – diagnosing insanity
> You may have heard of Peter Sutcliffe, the 'Yorkshire Ripper'. His defence was to plead insanity as the reason for murdering 13 women – this plea was discounted. One of the biggest problems is that we are unable to differentiate between the sane and the insane. You will see in the next chapter the core study by Rosenhan (p. 369), which shows how people who are totally normal can be judged as insane and admitted to psychiatric hospitals.

Wouldn't it be good if we could just test people with some equipment and scan their brains and then label them accordingly?

'Okay Mr Smith, come in. It's time for your annual scan to find out if you are normal or not.'

Mr Smith edged his way towards the door and kind of hung about, debating whether or not to run. Every year he had to go through this nightmare of being scanned to find out if he could go on living a normal life. His best friend was found abnormal just last month and had been disposed of in the Human Waste Disposal Institute attached to the council offices. He couldn't understand why. His friend wasn't abnormal. The only thing he had ever done wrong was to park on a double yellow line for a few minutes while picking up his daughter but the letter came the next week, saying that his scan was abnormal and he had to attend for termination.

'Come in, man, we haven't got all day,' said the official. 'Take off your shirt and lie down on the bed and whatever happens, don't move. You

307

know the procedure, after all, it is compulsory for everyone from the age of twelve.'

Mr Smith didn't run. What was the point? If he got out of the building, he would only be caught and taken back by the authorities, so he might as well do it now.

He lay down on the bed and put his arms down by his sides. The bed slid inside a giant tube and he closed his eyes. As he lay there, he felt the most horrific feeling. He wanted to sneeze. He mustn't move. Whatever happen he must stay still or the reading would show an abnormality. He could feel it coming and he tried to swallow and hold his breath, but suddenly, explosively, he sneezed. The machine whirred.

You will probably not need to be told about the ethical implications such a policy might have, but perhaps it might be worth considering what the results of an incorrect diagnosis might be.

We mustn't forget that brain scanning is useful for neurologists and neuropsychologists who look at normal functioning of the structures that make up our brains in order to understand why people behave as they do. You could also conclude that if brain scanning provided positive evidence that people who committed certain crimes (and who later pleaded not guilty because they were insane) really did have some kind of brain abnormality, it would make you much less worried about accepting their plea and treating them accordingly.

If you remember, the hypothalamus helps control our internal environment such as temperature regulation, appetite and thirst. It also influences other motivated behaviours such as sexual behaviour and emotional arousal levels. Therefore, if we could find the right part of the hypothalamus and stimulate it, we might be able to produce bizarre aggressive behaviours which are out of character for the situation. This would then indicate that if the hypothalamus were damaged in any way it may influence our behaviour, either making us much more aggressive or very passive.

Animal studies have backed up this idea. It has been shown that by giving certain animals mild electrical stimulation to a region of the hypothalamus, aggressive behaviour will result. For example, a cat will hiss, its hair will stand on end and it will attack an object placed in its cage when its hypothalamus is stimulated by electrodes. Another demonstration of the effects of hypothalamic stimulation is when a gentle, non-aggressive rat, who has lived peacefully in the same cage with a mouse, attacks and kills that mouse if its hypothalamus is stimulated. It is believed that the stimulation triggers an innate killing response.

But what has this got to do with humans? Obviously it wouldn't be acceptable to stick electrodes in people's heads and stimulate their hypothalamus in order to get a response; what researchers have done instead is to look at primates. The instinctive patterns of aggression in primates are moderated by the cortex and therefore they are influenced by experience rather than crude arousal. If you have a monkey that is at the top of the dominance hierarchy, he will only attack subordinate males if necessary and will not attack the females. Monkeys at the bottom of the dominance hierarchy are very submissive and won't attack anyone. Research shows that if two such monkeys have their hypothalamus electrically stimulated, the top monkey will attack subordinate males but still will not attack females. The bottom monkey will just cower and behave in a more submissive way than normal. This indicates that learned patterns of behaviour and experience have a very strong moderating force on even the electrical stimulation of part of the brain.

The functioning of the tracts of fibres between the two hemispheres, the corpus callosum, could also be assessed. As we saw in the section on split brains, the patients with split brains couldn't interpret the external environment in the same way as people with intact brains. Some studies have shown that the two hemispheres seem to work either at different speeds or one works harder than the other. The suggestion is that lack of coherence between the two hemispheres may be something to do with the corpus callosum not transferring information between the two hemispheres effectively, although this suggestion has not actually been tested.

We could also consider whether another part of the brain which usually moderates the hypothalamic drives is functioning. Supposing you feel really aggressive, under normal circumstances you wouldn't go out and whack someone with a large piece of wood. Something inside should say to you that this behaviour is not really appropriate and therefore you wouldn't do it. The moderator we do have – our cerebral cortex, especially the frontal lobes – seems to act to restrain our behaviours. It is in these frontal lobes that we store all the learned social behaviours and ways of acting that are accepted in our society, and store them as memories to be used when the need arises.

The story of Phineas Gage, a railway worker who lived in the nineteenth century, is perhaps the best illustration of the effects of damage to the frontal lobes. He suffered the most horrific injury when a steel rod was blown through his head, entering the cheek just below the socket of his left eye and leaving through the top of his skull. Obviously the damage done to his frontal cortex was immense and yet he survived. As the frontal cortex is the area which is involved in the regulation of behaviour, any damage to that area will result in the person behaving in a less acceptable manner. Phineas changed from being a restrained, polite, industrious worker to a drunken waster. He became obstinate and rude, urinated at will and seemed to have no controls on his behaviour. He made plans but never followed them through as he was lacking in any sort of direction. His intellect suffered too, and he became more like a child although he still had the physical strength and drives of a mature man which were no longer modified by acceptable social behaviour.

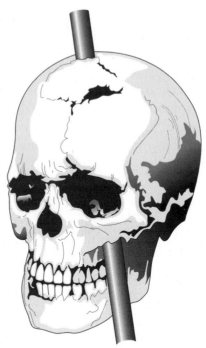

An impression of the skull of Phineas Gage showing the entry and exit points of the steel rod

Damage to our frontal lobes means we can't judge our own performance and compare it to others, and we no longer learn from our mistakes. It can damage our memories and make us absent-minded, although our long-term memory may remain intact. Another problem is that this kind of damage may leave us in a rut in terms of our thought processes; this is known as 'perseveration' and means that we always use the same strategy to try and deal with problems rather than using flexible problem-solving strategies. Perhaps the easiest way to describe this is the Wisconsin card sorting task. Here people are asked to sort playing cards into piles. The cards can be sorted according to shape – the four suits – or into colours – red and black. In fact they are more complex than our usual packs of cards but this is a good analogy. Whichever way subjects choose to sort them, the experimenter will tell them after a while that this is actually wrong. In response most people will try another tack and sort according to a different method, so if they started off with suits they will change to colours and so on. People with frontal lobe injuries will not be able to change their method but will continue sorting according to their original ideas. This kind of perseveration will cause them problems if it is carried into their everyday lives, because they will not be able to adjust their behaviour according to the situation but will continue to operate according to one set of rules.

In earlier sections we discussed the fact that both Piaget and Freud believed that young children find it hard to resist their impulses. Piaget said it was because they had not matured sufficiently in their cognitive development, whereas Freud blamed it on the primeval urges of the id, which have not yet been controlled by the ego. Physiologically, this is really because the frontal lobes are slow to mature and are really not fully matured until a person is in their twenties.

There is research evidence to back up the idea that dysfunction of the prefrontal cortex is likely to disrupt the regulation of aggression. Studies by Damasio *et al.* (1990) have shown this to be the case. Animal studies have indicated that there may be other structures involved in moderating aggression, such as the amygdala and hippocampus, although these are animal studies and are far removed from human beings.

311

Charles Whitman, who was responsible for the deaths of 48 innocent people when he went on a shooting spree at the University of Texas in 1966, provided a small amount of evidence that brain malfunction may have something to do with murder. As a small boy, his behaviour had been quite normal, but his behaviour seemed to changed after his mother left home as a result of his father's physical abuse. He often complained of headaches and occasionally fell into a rage for no obvious reason.

When Whitman was 25, he spent much of his time making detailed plans to carry out a massacre at the University of Texas on his chosen date of 1st August, 1966. He knew his mother would be upset at his plans, so he visited her on 31st July and, as she opened the door, he attacked her with a knife, stabbing her and then shooting her in the head. He put the body to bed and tidied up the apartment before returning home to his wife. This gave him time to make his final preparations for the following day before he went upstairs and, using a hunting knife, stabbed her three times in the heart.

The next day he left for the university wearing grey nylon overalls and strolled into the reception area of the observation tower. Here he struck a receptionist over the head with a rifle and ran up the stairs of the tower with an assortment of weapons, before barricading himself in. Two young brothers and their mother and aunt went to go up the stairs, unaware of what was happening, and he shot and killed two of them and seriously injured the other two. He then went back down and shot the receptionist.

Returning to the observation deck, from where he had an excellent view over the campus, he laid out his weapons. The first person he shot from the tower was a paperboy, cycling across the campus. He then shot and killed another three students before anyone realised what was going on. He then shot a traffic policeman who had come to investigate what was happening.

Over the next 96 minutes the police tried to do everything they could to deal with him including using a low-flying aeroplane. When all else failed they charged Whitman's barricade and finally shot and killed him. However, he had hit 48 people, many of whom died either instantly or later in hospital.

The curious thing about Whitman was that before he committed these murders he typed out a note saying, 'I am prepared to die. After my death I wish an autopsy on me to be performed to see if there is any mental disorder.' When this was done, he was found to be suffering from a tumour in the region of his hypothalamus. Although it seems likely that this tumour was what influenced him to carry out this massacre, no one could ever be totally sure. What this example should do is to give you some idea of how important any sort of brain damage or malfunction might be in explaining the behaviour of criminals and why the plea of 'not guilty by reason of insanity' should be considered acceptable. After all, was he responsible for his actions, or was the tumour making it impossible for him to reason about what he actually did? The trouble is we will never know.

You must always remember that the kind of social environment criminals come from, their early experiences within the family and their experience of the education system can have considerable effects on their later behaviour. Perhaps people who have behavioural problems end up in certain social situations, which then make the problems worse. Imagine a person with low intelligence who can't get work and therefore ends up with an inadequate diet. He may well be married with children, who will also be poorly nourished. This may contribute to their lack of physical development and, at the same time, they will be living in a poor area where perhaps others are engaged in criminal activities as a way of meeting the bills. There may also be an availability of drugs, or drugs and alcohol may be used as a way of making life more tolerable, and these may contribute to a lack of brain function by destroying neurons. There are so many factors which could result from a deprived childhood that it is impossible to say which came first, the abnormal brain or the abnormal behaviour. It is obvious that this nature–nurture debate is likely never to be completely solved.

However, each one of these explanations may have a place in our understanding of the causes of antisocial acts, although, as yet, no one theory has been accepted as the gospel truth. Perhaps that is the way it should be, after all the hardened killer is hardly the same as the single mother who hasn't enough money to survive and tries to supplement her meagre income with a bit of petty shoplifting – but they are both considered criminals and they have both carried out antisocial acts.

The core study: A. Raine, M. Buchsbaum and L. LaCasse (1997) 'Brain Abnormalities in Murderers Indicated by Positron Emission Tomography',
Biological Psychiatry, 1997, 42, 495–508

Background

Earlier work by Raine and others had demonstrated the relationship between low levels of activity in the prefrontal cortex and violent behaviour (Raine *et al.*, 1994). The prefrontal cortex is the area of the brain behind the forehead. Raine has described the function of this part of the brain as being a bit like 'the emergency brake on behaviour' which prevents us from acting on violent and aggressive impulses. He argues that this is gone in the violent offender and that this brain difference explains, in part, why some people are more violent than others. It is thought that the prefrontal cortex sends messages to the limbic system to tell us to fear the consequences of acting on our impulses, and this is how the 'emergency brake' mechanism works. The limbic system is a part of the 'old brain' which governs our emotional and aggressive impulses. The hippocampus and amygdala are key structures in the limbic system. (Don't let the complicated terms faze you – these names are simply Latin for what the part of the brain *looks* like: amygdala means 'almond' in Latin, and hippocampus means 'seahorse'!)

Raine suggests that violent offenders have shown abnormalities in these areas in the function of the different hemispheres. He suggests that this may be linked to dysfunction in the corpus callosum (see the Sperry study). Raine *et al.* point out that it is the advent of brain-imaging techniques which have allowed research to be carried out into the possible brain dysfunction in violent offenders.

Raine *et al.* had identified a particular group of violent offenders for study.

These were offenders who had committed murder and were pleading not guilty by reason of insanity (NGRI). Raine *et al.* (1994) had carried out a pilot study comparing 22 subjects pleading NGRI with controls and found that there was some evidence of prefrontal dysfunction. The present study expanded on this research increasing the sample size and increasing the number of areas of the brain for investigation.

Aim

The aim of the study was to look at direct measures of both cortical and subcortical brain functioning, using PET scans, in a group of murderers who had pleaded not guilty by reason of insanity (NGRI). (Raine *et al.* refer to this group as 'murderers' in their study for ease of reference, and we shall do the same here.)

The expectation was that the murderers would show evidence of brain dysfunction in their prefrontal cortex, as well as in other areas that have been linked to violent behaviour in the past, such as the limbic system and corpus callosum. It was also predicted that they would not show dysfunction in areas of the brain implicated in some psychiatric conditions but not related to violent behaviour.

Method

Design

The study was a laboratory experiment using an independent groups design.

Subjects

The experimental group (the 'murderers') consisted of 41 subjects (39 men and two women) with a mean age of 34.3 years. They had been charged with either murder or manslaughter, and were pleading NGRI.

They had been sent to the University of California imaging centre for one of the following reasons:
1. To obtain evidence as to whether they were NGRI.
2. To find out if they were competent to understand the judicial process.
3. To see if there was any evidence of diminished mental capacity, which may affect the nature of the sentencing they received.

They were referred for the following reasons:
- six had schizophrenia
- 23 had head injuries or organic brain damage
- three had a history of psychoactive substance abuse
- two had affective disorders
- two had epilepsy
- three had a history of hyperactivity and learning disability
- two had passive-aggressive or paranoid personality disorders

The control group of 41 people were matched by age and sex and had a mean age of 31.7 years which was considered not significantly different from that of the experimental group. The six schizophrenics in the experimental group were matched with six schizophrenic controls. The rest of the control group were thoroughly screened and showed no history of psychiatric illness. None of the controls had committed murder.

The consent forms and procedures for the participation of subjects in the study were approved by the Human Subjects Committee of the University of California.

Experimental controls

- All offenders were in custody and were kept medication-free for two weeks before the brain scanning. Urine tests at the time of scanning confirmed this. The control group were also medication-free.
- Tests were undertaken to make sure that being left-handed or right-handed had no effect on behaviour.
- Fourteen of the murderers were non-white, but when they were compared to

white murderers on PET measures there was no significant difference between them.

- Twenty-three murderers had a history of head injury, but again, they showed no difference between non-head injured murderers, except in the functioning of their corpus callosum, and the authors accepted that this may have contributed towards a reduction in the murderers' brain activity.

Materials

- Thermoplastic head-holder, individually modelled, to hold the subject's head still while being scanned.
- PET machine to image brain functioning. A colour 'map' of brain activity is generated by the machine.
- Fluorodeoxyglucose (FDG) – a tracer injected to trace brain metabolism. What this does is 'attaches' itself to the glucose being used by the brain. The tracer is radioactive so it, and therefore the glucose, can be picked up and 'mapped' by the scanner.
- Continuous performance task (CPT) which has been shown to make the frontal lobes work especially hard, together with the right temporal and parietal lobes. The task consisted of spotting targets on a screen and pressing a button to indicate the target had been recognised. The CPT lasted for 32 minutes.

Procedure

Ten minutes before the injection they were given practice trials at a CPT so they knew what to expect. Then, 30 seconds before they had their injection, they made a start at the actual task. This 30-second gap was to ensure that the novelty of the task didn't show up on the scan and thus confound the results. Once they had been injected they were monitored for 32 minutes and then they were scanned in the PET scanner, having their heads held still in the individually moulded plastic head-holders. Their brains were scanned ten times at ten-mm intervals to pick up differences in glucose metabolism in both the cerebral cortex and the subcortical layers. Glucose metabolism means the brain is using up glucose; the brain 'runs' on glucose like a car engine runs on petrol, and the PET scan shows where the glucose is being used. High levels of glucose means high levels of activity, and different levels of glucose metabolism show up as different colours on the PET scan, with the highest areas of activity showing up as red.

Results

Although there was no significant difference in the task performance between the two groups, there was evidence of a significant difference in brain metabolism of glucose in a number of areas.

The authors suggest that this gives preliminary but not complete evidence that muderers pleading NGRI have different brain functions compared to normal controls. The study also indicates which brain processes may mean a person is predisposed to violent behaviour.

Group means for murderers and controls for cortical and subcortical glucose metabolism

	Left Hemisphere		Right Hemisphere	
	Control	Murderer	Control	Murderer
Cortical				
Lateral Prefrontal Lobes	1.12	**1.09**	1.14	**1.11**
Medial Prefrontal Lobes	1.25	**1.20**	1.22	**1.17**
Parietal Lobes:	1.15	**1.10**	1.17	**1.13**
Temporal Lobes:	90	*.90*	.93	*.94*
Occipital Lobes:	1.09	**1.12**	1.11	**1.15**
Subcortical				
Corpus Callosum	68	**.56**	.67	**.56**
Amygdala	.97	**.94**	.83	**.88**
Medial temporal lobe incl.				
hippocampus	.95	*.91*	.93	*.96*
Thalamus	1.09	*1.09*	1.09	**1.15**

Numbers in **bold** means that the difference is significant.
Numbers in *italics* means that the difference is not significant.

CEREBRAL CORTEX

Frontal lobes:
The murderers had lower glucose metabolism relative to controls in both the lateral (left and right sides) and medial (middle) prefrontal cortical areas.

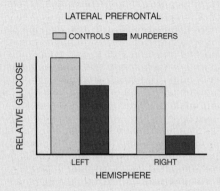

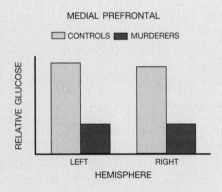

Parietal lobes:
Murderers had lower parietal glucose metabolism than controls.

Temporal lobes:
Temporal lobe glucose metabolism was identical between the two groups.

Occipital lobes:
The murderers had higher occipital lobe glucose metabolism than controls.

SUBCORTICAL REGIONS (areas beneath the cerebral cortex)

Corpus callosum:
Bilaterally lower glucose metabolism than controls.

Amygdala:
Reduced left and greater right amygdala activity than controls.

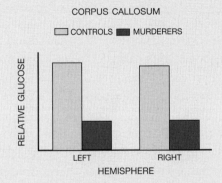

Medial temporal lobe including the hippocampus:
There was evidence of reduced left and greater right activity in the murderers, although the results were not significantly different to controls.

Thalamus:
Murderers had more right thalamic activity compared to controls.

Summary table of results for the prefrontal cortex, limbic system and corpus callosum: areas previously associated with violent and aggressive behaviours

Area of brain	Findings
Prefrontal cortex	Lower glucose metabolism (lower brain activity)
Limbic system	Abnormal asymmetries of brain activity observed in the amygdala and hippocampus
Corpus callosum	Lower glucose metabolism (lower brain activity)

Discussion

The results indicate that murderers pleading NGRI have significant differences in the metabolism of glucose in a number of different areas compared to controls. Lower glucose metabolism indicates a lack of activity in certain areas, and the findings that there was reduced activity in the prefrontal areas may explain impulsive behaviour, a loss of self-control, evidence of immaturity, altered emotionality and the inability to modify behaviour. All of these may make it easier to carry out different kinds of aggressive acts because the normal constraints on behaviour may be reduced (Damasio, 1985).

Lee *et al.* (1988) found that the amygdala plays a role in our ability to recognise socially significant stimuli, and the destruction of the amygdala in animals leads to a lack of fear. In man, the destruction of the amygdala has been shown to lead to a reduction of autonomic arousal, which could be relevant to a 'fearlessness theory' of violence. This means that a situation that most of us would find very frightening would have a minimal effect on violent offenders – this idea has been backed up by findings of reduced autonomic arousal in offenders.

To support this idea still further, Raine (1993) has found that abnormalities in the functioning of the hippocampus, amygdala and thalamus are important to learning, memory and attention. Therefore, any abnormalities may result in problems in learning relevant emotional responses, as well as the inability to learn from experience, which is often shown by criminal and violent offenders.

The study suggests that the neural processes which underlie violent behaviour can't simply be reduced to a single brain mechanism that causes violence. It seems that there are several processes involved, and if there are deficits in a number of these processes the likelihood of violent behaviour occurring is much greater.

The authors consider that although there are problems with their research, including the limitations placed on measurement of brain activity by present-day PET scan technology, the study provides a starting point for investigation in the field of forensic psychiatry of muderers pleading NGRI. They are also careful to suggest that the study requires independent replication before conclusions of any description could be drawn about the findings, which they again emphasise are preliminary.

The authors are at pains to point out what this study does not indicate. They say the findings cannot be taken as evidence:

1. that violence is determined by biology alone
2. that muderers pleading NGRI are not responsible for their actions
3. that PET scans cannot be used to 'diagnose' potential murderers
4. that the findings of these abnormalities in brain function can be generalised to other types of violent offenders
5. that the findings can be generalised to 'crime' in general as the study did not contain a non-violent criminal control group.

They conclude that what the study does show is that murderers pleading NGRI have significant differences in glucose metabolism in certain areas of the brain compared to controls. The findings also suggest, but do not conclusively demonstrate, that reduced brain activity in certain areas may be one of the many predispositions towards violence in this particular group of offenders.

Commentary

Is the study ethical?

The study is carried out ethically, with consent and procedures being overseen by the Human Subjects Committee of the University of California.

Is the study ecologically valid?

The laboratory is unlikely to produce behaviour in any circumstances that could be said to be highly ecologically valid. This study requires the subjects to carry out a target recognition task for 32 minutes. This is to get a comparable task that involves the prefrontal cortex that can be compared between subjects. This is clearly a task low in ecological validity as we would not do this in the course of our daily lives.

The task is also a non-violent task, and therefore we could argue that it is not one which will reveal the level of brain activity and dysfunction present when the subject is engaged in violent or aggressive activity, so again the ecological validity of the task is low. (Of course, there would be all sorts of ethical problems involved in inciting and studying violent behaviour in murderers!)

Evaluation of the measurement techniques

The main evaluation of the study is that it shows that a correlation exists between brain abnormalities and violent behaviour. The relationship, therefore, cannot be assumed to be causal. Although all the evidence indicates that brain dysfunction may contribute to the subjects committing murder, there are other factors which also need to be considered e.g. 'social, psychological, cultural and situational factors' (Raine *et al.*, 1997, p. 505).

Brain imaging techniques are a relatively new form of technology and may not produce a wholly accurate picture of brain activity. Also, we can see the brain is active, but we don't know what it is actively doing!

Is the study useful?

The study contributes to our understanding of how biology may influence violent behaviour, and this is useful. It also helps us to understand the physiognomy of the brain.

What we must be careful to avoid with studies such as this is the misuse of findings. If it were to be taken as evidence that low prefrontal activity meant that the person would inevitably become a violent criminal then it could lead to all kinds of abuse in testing and 'diagnosing' criminality. At particular risk would be children with ADHD, which has shown to be characterised by low prefrontal activity, who could be wrongly labelled as 'criminal types'.

Raine *et al.* are aware of the possibilities of such abuse of findings such as theirs and clearly caution us against over-generalisation and misinterpretation of the findings.

Key questions

1. Explain why it was important to have a matched control group.
2. Why were both groups of subjects kept medication-free for two weeks before the study took place?
3. What is meant by the following acronyms from the study?
- PET
- FDG
- CPT
- NGRI
4. Is the study ecologically valid?
5. Complete the following table:

Area of brain	Findings	How can the findings explain violent behaviour in the murderers?
Prefrontal cortex	Lower glucose metabolism (lower brain activity)	
Limbic system	Abnormal asymmetries of brain activity observed in the amygdala and hippocampus	
Corpus callosum	Lower glucose metabolism (lower brain activity)	

Example Answers are on page 459.

Further reading
- Blakemore, C. (1988) *The Mind Machine*. London: BBC Books.
- Carter, R. (1998), *Mapping the Mind*. London: Weidenfeld & Nicolson.
- www-rcf.usc.edu/~raine/ – Adrian Raine's website.
- more.abcnews.go.com/sections/living/inyourhead/allinyourhead_ 69.html
- www.deakin.edu.au/hbs/GAGEPAGE/index – website about Phineas Gage.

The psychology of individual differences

The last section in this book will look at individual differences, a term often used in psychology. What are individual differences? To put it simply, they are the differences between individuals which make it very difficult to group people together as one bunch or 'type'. Of course, we can find things that people have in common, such as their cultural backgrounds or their gender or age. We may even be able to identify things about their personality or how clever they are, which puts them in a group with others who share similar characteristics. What we must always remember is that although we may share characteristics or abilities with others, this is only part of the story. Each of us has also had a unique set of life experiences, which has contributed towards making us what we are, and this individuality must be acknowledged, irrespective of our opinions about the differences between us.

We are now living in a multicultural society and the world is more accessible to us than ever before. We now have a greater knowledge and understanding of the variation in cultures that exists; and the ease with which we can travel around the globe and experience different cultures makes this variation easier to understand. The climate, the terrain and the religion of people from other lands all impact on the way they see the world. Earlier we talked about ethnocentric bias and, hopefully, by now you have a greater understanding of how easy it is to 'measure people by our own yardstick'. This saying really explains the whole issue – that we are often too quick to measure people by our own values and measurements, and this 'yardstick' may be wholly inappropriate.

There are many examples in the literature of the social sciences describing the norms of different cultures that still appear to be quite bizarre by our standards. Gross (1992) cites a number of studies, by people like Margaret Mead and Malinowski, who describe patterns of behaviour totally different to ours. Malinowski studied the Trobriand islanders, from the South Pacific, in which culture both males and females had a reputation for being virile. As a way of keeping that reputation intact, groups of women from one tribe would go and seize a man from a different tribe and gang-rape him. There was nothing gentle and 'feminine' in the way that this was done, and what made it more extraordinary was that the women would boast of their conquests after the event. Can you imagine how a situation like this would be viewed in our society? It would be greeted with shock and horror, and we would consider it to be quite abnormal, whereas to the tribe concerned it was perfectly acceptable. However, who is to say that what we believe to be 'femininity' is how women really should be. Perhaps our idea of femininity is purely a social construct rather than what women are actually like.

Therefore, the area of individual differences involves not only differences between individuals, but also differences in cultures and lifestyles, and it is the way all these things interact that impacts on the way we are. These individual differences are one of a number of factors that make it quite difficult to carry out truly objective psychological research. In chapter one we talked about matching subjects and mentioned the fact that you can only match people on certain things. The problem comes when you try to compare them, because perhaps each one of those subjects will have an individual part of them which is totally unlike anyone else – not only life experiences, but also cultural and cross-cultural differences.

The studies in this section will be looking at a number of topics which consider the differences between individuals. The first section looks at intelligence and tries to provide some kind of definition as to what intelligence might be. However, if we aren't sure what it is, how can we accurately measure it? Man-made tests can only test what a man thinks something is, and if he's wrong, the test is worthless. The second study looks at the changing pattern of racial identity and preference, and how black people are more easily able to express their cultural identity nowadays, rather than years past when they were generally seen as inferior to white people. The third study looks at how we define abnormality – or indeed *if* we can. The implication here is that if we cannot tell the sane from the insane, does insanity actually exist? The final study looks at multiple personality, one of the most fascinating conditions in the field of psychopathology (the part of psychology that looks at the abnormal workings of the mind).

How clever are you?

Would you like to know what your IQ is? You would probably love to know, especially if it were high, but you would also be worried, just in case… But have you every really considered what we mean by IQ? Do you know what 'an IQ' is?

'So, what is an IQ?' I ask you.

'Everyone knows what an IQ is, it's how intelligent you are,' you answer.

Your clever friend, sitting next to you, suddenly adds, 'Actually, it's your Intelligence Quotient.'

'Well, excuse me,' you say.

'Yes, but what is an intelligence quotient and how do you measure it?' I ask again.

By this time you would start to look a little perplexed. 'Well, it's kind of how clever you are,' you would answer, 'and you measure it with an IQ test.'

'How clever you are at what?' I would reply.

'Well, er, everything, sums and things like that.'

'What do you mean – academic skills?' I say.

'Yes, that's what I mean'.

'Now think of the amazingly clever, academic professor who can recite theories of quantum physics in his sleep; but put him in a kitchen and ask him to boil an egg or mend a fuse, and he may have no idea at all how to do these things, which are really very simple. In fact, he may well have no common sense at all. Do you think he has a high IQ?'

'Well, yes of course he has,' you answer.

'But he can't even boil an egg. He wouldn't survive for long if he was dropped in the middle of a jungle, would he? Okay, now think of the bricklayer who has designed and built an ecologically friendly house with solar heating panels, from recycled building materials. He has no formal training in anything and left school when he was sixteen. He actually can't read very well either. Would you say he was intelligent?'

'Yes.'

'But he has no academic skills – they are purely practical.'

'Yes, I know, but he knew things from experience.'

'Ah-ha. So does that mean that intelligence comes from experience? What about someone who has done the same job for years and years? He or she is experienced, but is he or she intelligent?'

And so the conversation would go on. In fact, everything you may suggest could probably be contradicted in some way.

> ### ACTIVITY
>
> Spend five minutes jotting down on a piece of paper what you think intelligence is. At the end of this section, have another go at doing the same thing. Compare your answers and look for similarities and differences in what you have said.

We are going to begin by considering what we mean by intelligence and how we measure it. When you get to the end of the section, don't worry if you feel even more confused than ever – you can rest assured that you are in the majority. The other point is that if psychologists, as a profession, find it hard to agree what really is the essence of intelligence, then we must consider whether the techniques used to measure it have any validity. Also, if we do manage to get it wrong, what are the likely repercussions of labelling someone as either 'intelligent' or 'unintelligent' in terms of self-fulfilling prophecies.

FOCUS ON CONCEPTS – the self-fulfilling prophecy

The self-fulfilling prophecy comes from the work of Rosenthal and his colleagues and looks at how expectations about a person or group can influence the way they ultimately behave, therefore confirming the original expectation.

Rosenthal and Jacobson (1966) demonstrated this in a study which looked at teacher's expectancy of pupils' performance and how this translated into actual achievement. Teachers were told that 19 children from a total of 114 children had been identified by means of a non-verbal intelligence test to be 'bloomers' (children who were beginning to show signs of higher intellectual ability), although in fact the children were randomly allocated to each condition with no differences existing between them. The children were tested eight months later, and those identified as bloomers showed a significantly greater level of achievement than the other children over that time. The results suggest that it was the teacher's expectations of the children's performance, which translated into these increases in achievement, rather than any differences in the children's innate ability.

The way this would work is as follows: if you are told someone is unintelligent, you will probably not bother to explain things to them because you will assume that they would not understand. Because they have not had the information to help them understand, they will not develop in their knowledge and understanding of the world, which will make them seem intelligent.

The Rosenhan study on p. 369 also considers the impact of labelling on behaviour.

Interestingly enough, few concepts in psychology have received more devoted attention than that of 'intelligence', and few have proved so difficult to define. Despite many efforts over the years to come up with an adequate definition, it seems that all the attempts made have remained linked to the techniques developed for its measurement.

Let me explain this further: if you think that intelligence is your ability to use language and do mathematical calculations, the intelligence test you devise will contain these two topics. If you think it is to do with problem solving and spatial awareness, the test will have to cover these topics. It seems to be the case that we can only define intelligence in terms of measurable skills. What is the point of saying that intelligence is something intangible? If we believe it is intangible, it would be impossible to measure, which rather defeats the object.

THE HISTORY OF 'INTELLIGENCE'

Herbert Spencer (1820–1903) and Sir Frances Galton (1822–1911) were the first people to use the term intelligence in the way we use it today. They both believed in the existence of a 'general ability', which affects how well we perform at any sort of intellectual task. They acknowledged that some people might be good at one type of task, such as arithmetic calculations, or possibly two things, but maintained that unless they were good at all types of tasks they must lack the 'general ability' which they suggested was 'intelligence' and which was inherited.

Galton began the psychological investigation of intelligence in the 1860s. He believed that genius runs in families and supported this by the fact that the most eminent Victorian gentlemen had eminent fathers. He seemed to forget that these same gentlemen had the financial status to educate their children at public schools, and could give them far more opportunities to develop a career than the average person, by way of contacts and financial backing. He also thought the rulers of the British Empire must be the most intelligent people in the world (we can safely say he was ethnocentric). It was understandable, therefore, that he should believe that people who held lower positions in society (the working class, women and black people) must be of inferior intelligence.

As a result of his beliefs, Galton formed a movement known as the eugenics movement, which proposed that people of inferior abilities should be prevented from having families, because in some way this would result in a feebler society. He claimed that people who lived in poverty or squalor did so because of a 'natural depravity', which was inborn in them. He also suggested that different races, which were of inferior origin, should not be permitted to interbreed for fear of genetically contaminating the so-called superior races. Jewish people, Gypsies and Poles were some of the races considered inferior: this will give you some idea how ridiculous this actually was. The eugenics movement became very popular earlier in the twentieth century in many countries, especially Nazi Germany and South Africa, leading to the genocide of the Jews in Germany and the acceptance of apartheid in South Africa, where different races were segregated by law and brought up separately. Despite these beliefs, Galton failed to come up with any successful intelligence tests that could confirm his theories.

INTELLIGENCE – NATURE OR NURTURE?

Perhaps it would be useful to look at the arguments about whether intelligence is inherited or whether it is due to our environment. These ideas may help us to decide what intelligence actually is and whether it is a single factor or a number of abilities, and then we may be able to determine how we can assess how high or low it is.

Nature: is IQ inherited?

One of the people most influenced by Galton was Cyril Burt, who was mentioned in chapter one. If you remember, he was firmly committed to the idea that intelligence was inherited and that it was pointless to educate people beyond the limits of their capacity. Burt produced a large number of research papers, which seemed to provide unquestionable proof that intelligence was inherited. This led to the universal testing of children when they reached the age of eleven, to see whether they would receive an academic education or more practical training for later life. It was believed that the children who did not pass the eleven-plus were less academically able and therefore would not benefit in any way from a more formal, academic education. However, in 1974, Kamin re-analysed Burt's data and concluded that most of the data was extremely suspect and may well have been fiction. It seems that Burt believed so strongly that intelligence was inherited, he simply adjusted the evidence to support his ideas.

Hans Eysenck also believed that intelligence is purely inherited. He was a firm supporter of Jensen's (1969) idea that there was a difference in the abilities of racial groups. The findings were that, on average, black people's test results were about one standard deviation (15 IQ points) below the average of the white population. This fact was not disputed, but what was disputed was the explanation – that it was due to genetic factors. True, they had achieved a lower average score to the white population, but it was nothing to do with innate ability. The findings were due to the nature of the tests and that they were culturally biased towards the white population (more about this later).

There are two ways to investigate whether IQ is inherited or not. One way is to look at identical twins, reared in different homes and see if their IQs are the same. Because they are genetically identical, but have different life experiences, this method would test whether their IQ is caused by genetic factors rather than early experiences. An other way is to look at children who have been adopted and see if their IQ is closer to that of their adoptive parents or that of their natural parents.

Before we go on here, you should think about the likelihood of people, even if they do have the same genetic features, achieving exactly the same scores on tests if they have been brought up in different surroundings. Surely their early experiences must count for something? If one child experienced an enriched and advantaged life, whilst another had lived in an impoverished home with little in the way of food, material possessions or life experiences, would this not have a huge influence on their development? Even something as simple as parental influence will affect a child's development? If parents encourage their children at school and support and help them, they are far more likely to do well than those children whose parents have no interest in education or academic achievement.

Studies which have compared the IQs of twins reared together with twins who were reared apart have looked at the 'correlation coefficient', which is a statistical measure showing a relationship between two sets of data. If there is a relationship, we would expect the IQ scores to go up or down together, which would suggest that there is a genetic component to IQ. On the other hand, if the IQ scores of the pairs of twins show no relationship, we would conclude that their differences were due to environment alone.

Shields (1962) investigated 37 pairs of twins who had been reared apart and compared them with twins who had been brought up together. The criterion for inclusion in the study was that they should have been reared in different homes for at least five years, although the study didn't mention how old they should be at the age of separation. In fact, some of the separations did not occur until the twins were seven, eight or even nine years of age. By that time, they would have spent much of their 'formative' years together and this may have affected the results. The other problem was that the 'separated' were often living with other members of the same family, such as one being raised by the mother and the other by an aunt. Often the twins knew each other and were attending the same school, so in terms of totally different upbringings the findings were really not that valid.

When Shields took these factors into consideration, it only left 13 pairs of twins, and the correlation in IQ scores between these remaining pairs of twins was quite weak, giving very little support to the idea that IQ was inherited. Further research suffered from similar sampling problems to the Shields study, although Horn (1983) reported on a group of 300 children whose mothers had given them up within a week of birth, thus getting round some of the earlier methodological problems. He found that the identical twins (who shared the same genetic material) had very similar IQs, whereas the fraternal twins (non-identical twins, who only shared some of the same genetic material) had less similar IQs. He concluded that about 80% of the concordance of IQ in twins is due to genetics rather than environmental factors.

Studies investigating the relationship in the IQs of fostered or adopted children with their natural and adoptive parents found a closer correlation between adopted children's IQs and those of their biological mothers rather than their adoptive mothers (Skodak and Skeels, 1945). This now dated study seemed to show that there was a stronger genetic influence on intelligence than simply environmental factors. However, this study also had problems. The groups were supposed to be matched for age, sex, parental occupation, educational levels and type of neighbourhood, but the adoptive parents were older, more committed and turned out be a more successful group as parents (perhaps because they wanted the children). So overall, the adopted children's IQs were much higher than those of their biological mothers, and seemed to be closer to those of their adoptive parents, suggesting that intelligence wasn't inherited.

Nurture: so what about environment?

Alfred Binet did not believe that intelligence was a fixed capacity we inherit through birth. He believed that anyone is capable of learning, but that some learn faster than others. This suggests that the environment will have a large impact on achievement. We have already mentioned the impact of parenting and lifestyle on achievement, but there are other issues which have also been shown to impact on intelligence.

- The IQ of 300 children, who were born prematurely, was measured when they reached eight years of age. During the initial weeks of life, the diet of these premature infants was carefully monitored. The type of nutrients consumed had the effect of as much as ten IQ points difference.
- Malnourished children were found to have lower IQs than their well-nourished counterparts (Meyer and Harris, 1975).
- Studies suggest that between 0.25 and six IQ points can be lost per year of missed school.
- Toxins in the environment (e.g. lead in the air from car exhausts) in high doses are certainly toxic and can have severe effects on the central nervous system. Needleman *et al.* (1990) found that high levels of lead in early childhood are associated in adolescence with low vocabulary and grammatical reasoning scores, slow reaction times, poor hand-eye coordination and low reading scores.
- Dozens of animal studies have shown that a stimulating environment affects the structure of the brain. Rats that learn complicated tasks or have lots of toys develop thicker and heavier cortexes, and have a richer network of synaptic connections in certain brain areas than rats in unchallenging environments (Rosenzweig, 1984).
- The average IQ in a family tends to decline as the number of children rises (perhaps due to less parental time).
- Siblings growing up in the same environment often have different IQs. Dunn and Plomin (1990) have reasoned that this is due to individual experiences, like different teachers.
- Children who score well on IQ tests have parents who actively encourage their development.

Evidence to support the idea of early intervention came from the USA in the mid-1960s, when President Johnson started the Head Start Programme as part of a 'war on poverty'. Project Head Start was a comprehensive early child development programme, which was designed to provide learning experiences for two- to five-year-olds from poor homes. It provided different activities for both parents and children and was seen as a way of giving the children the pre-school educational experiences they would have missed otherwise. From its inception, Head Start recognised the need to address children's educational, physical and social-service needs holistically and also to extend help to their families and communities. Evaluations of Head Start programmes over the years (McCall, 1993) have found that they produces improvements in IQ scores and in academic readiness and achievement, greater self-esteem, and better social behaviour and health.

BUT WHAT IS INTELLIGENCE?

There is no universally agreed description of intelligence. Binet viewed it as 'a general capacity for comprehension and reasoning', while others, like Terman (1916), believe it is 'the ability to carry out abstract thinking'. Wechsler (1958) suggested it is 'the aggregate or global capacity of the individual to act purpose-fully, to think rationally and to deal effectively with his environment', while Heim (1970) argued that 'intelligent activity consists in grasping the essentials in a situation and responding appropriately to them'.

Charles Spearman (1904) questioned whether there is such a thing as 'general intelligence', which is what these other definitions suggest. He said that everyone has 'a general intelligence factor' (which he called 'g') in varying amounts. This 'g' will affect our achievements in various specific areas (which he called 's'). Linguistic skills and numeracy are examples of 's', so if we had a high 'g' we would be good at languages and maths. However, if we follow this idea through, it doesn't follow that we have to be good at everything, which would make it easier to accept that the professor who can't boil an egg is intelligent after all!

Eysenck (1986) believed that intelligence is linked to our physiology. He argued that approaches to intelligence can be categorised into biological approaches, psychometric approaches (which means they can be measured) and social approaches (which is how we behave in social situations). In short, he said that there are actually three ways of looking at intelligence, but he believed that the biological approach was by far the most acceptable and objective. He suggested that we should try and find out if there are any physical characteristics or mechanisms which are responsible for intelligent behaviour. If we can look at intelligence in terms of biological functioning, then it would stand to reason that any measurement would be objective rather than subjective. He said that by using physiological measurements, such as reaction times, and 'evoked potentials' (where you measure the speed of transmission of an electrical impulse in the nervous system), and looking to see if these bear any relationship to IQ test scores, it is possible to see that speed of information processing seems to be a fundamental property of biological intelligence. There is some evidence to show that there is a relationship between reaction times and intelligence, but as the evidence is correlational, we cannot be sure that one causes the other.

There is a little more evidence to back up the fact that there might be a biological component to intelligence. Investigations into the neuroanatomy of Albert Einstein's brain (which was preserved in case anyone wanted to look at in it detail) resulted in the discovery that in one area there were more glial cells per neuron than in control brains from 11 non-geniuses (these cells supply nutrients to neurons). But what does this show? Was he clever because he had a lot of glial cells, or did his glial cells multiply because he used his brain more than other people? Most neuropsychologists doubt that differences in intelligence are due to the anatomy of the brain. It is more likely that the wiring of neural circuits, the amount or efficiency of neurotransmitters, or the metabolic rates of cells are what matter.

If you are now less sure than before about the nature of intelligence, and wish that perhaps you had not been given this information, this links nicely with the next section. If we are still not absolutely sure what intelligence is, how on earth can we measure it?

INTELLIGENCE TESTING

Psychometric testing is what we do when we test or measure mental characteristics such as intelligence or even personality. It is a way of quantifying what we are, and it is believed by many theorists to be possible. These theorists are called 'nomothetic', theorists and they say that we are all made up of the same skills, abilities, characteristics and traits, but just have them in lesser or greater amounts, so we should be able to measure them. This also means that we should be able to work out what makes an 'average person', and then we can see how far away we are from the average or norm. Of course, others say it is impossible or pointless to measure and compare people because we are all individuals and, by trying to categorise people, we lose the essence of that individuality. These theorists are called idiographic theorists.

Galton was believed to be the first to try measuring intelligence, which he did by measuring people's sensory sensitivity (by their ability to distinguish subtly different colours, for example). He believed these measures would serve as indicators of intelligence because he assumed that more intelligent people would have better discriminating powers when looking at colours or feeling pinpricks. Needless to say, he was not very successful.

He might not have been too good at measuring intelligence, but he wasn't completely unsuccessful. In fact, in 1885, Galton was the first person to identify the 'normal distribution curve'. He set up an anthropometric centre as a tourist attraction in London, and people paid to come and have their physical characteristics measured – like height, weight, width of upper arm, lung capacity and strength of grip. He collected reams and reams of data about different physical characteristics from thousands of people. Then he plotted their scores from each characteristic on a graph and found he had a normal distribution curve. He therefore assumed that as mental characteristics were presumably dependent on physical ones, the mental ones would also show a normal distribution curve.

The normal distribution curve (also known as the Gaussian distribution) is a bell-shaped curve that has special mathematical properties. The mean or average score falls in the middle because it is the most frequently occurring score – but note this is only the case in a normal distribution. Using another calculation, which comes directly from the mean (called the standard deviation), allows us to find out the percentage of people who fall either side of the mean. This can be used mathematically to predict how similar or dissimilar someone is to the population as a whole. If we finally manage to measure IQ and then look for an average amongst a large number of people in the population, it would make it possible to see how normal or abnormal an individual is, in terms of measured IQ score.

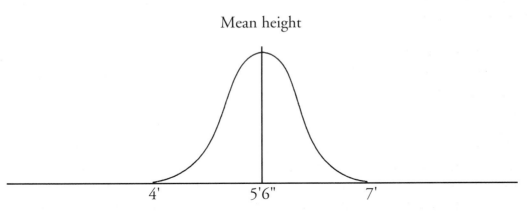

This normal distribution curve illustrates adult height. The curve indicates that most people are 5'6" tall, whereas there are very few who are 4' and very few who are 7'

The first intelligence tests

In 1881, the French government passed a law making school attendance compulsory for all children. Then, in 1904, the administrators of the Paris school system asked Alfred Binet and Theophile Simon to devise a method of identifying children who found learning in normal classroom settings very difficult. The school system was extremely overcrowded and the idea was that these children should be given the opportunity for special education, which might help them keep up and take some of the pressure off the rest of the classes.

The few tests that had been given to children in the past were very simple tests, which just looked at things like spelling and addition. Binet decided to put together a new kind of test, which involved reasoning and problem solving, areas which are probably more suited to measuring this illusive thing called intelligence. Binet's test was published in 1905 and the format of the test has provided the basis for most intelligence tests ever since. Binet believed that a 'slow' or 'dull' child was no different to a 'normal' child, but that it took longer for their mental abilities to develop, which meant that they would simply perform like a younger child. Binet was therefore measuring what he called 'mental age', which would then be compared with the child's 'chronological age' (how old they really were).

In 1916, Terman developed a version of Binet's intelligence test, which was suitable for North American populations. This became known as the Stanford-Binet test. This test is still the most well-known test for children today. IQ is calculated by comparing a child's mental age, as measured on a test, with their real or chronological age:

The formula used is: $$IQ = \frac{\text{mental age (MA)} \times 100}{\text{chronological age (CA)}}$$

The 100 is used so that the IQ will have a value of 100 when the child's mental age equals their chronological age. If their mental age is lower than their chronological age, their IQ will be less than 100. If it is the other way round the IQ will be more than 100.

The Stanford-Binet test has used a number of different items to test intelligence, and until 1986, all the items tested had an equal weighting towards the final IQ score. Since then, verbal reasoning, abstract/visual reasoning, quantitative reasoning and short-term memory have become the areas that are used as an acceptable measure of intelligence.

Today the Wechsler Scales are probably the most widely used individual intelligence tests and have been standardised for different populations in different cultures. They consist of 11 sub-tests, six of which are designed to measure 'verbal intelligence'. The verbal intelligence sub-tests are tests of vocabulary, general comprehension, general knowledge, mental arithmetic, identifying similarities between pairs and digit memory span. This is fine for people who are literate and numerate, but what about someone who has problems with language? The remaining tests involve things like spatial relationships, using tests involving picture completion, object assembly and copying a block design.

The one disadvantage of these tests is the amount of time they take to administer. Each sub-test requires the administrator to give standardised instructions in order to provide each person with the same experience and prevent any sort of confounding variables interfering with their score. In fact, the tests themselves can take up to half a day to administer if every sub-test is used. Therefore, tests of this nature are not suitable for testing large groups of people. If the situation arose where it was necessary to test a larger group, the test would need to be carefully redesigned in order to allow the candidate to understand what they are expected to do.

The key study looks at the development of these 'mass' tests and how they were used inappropriately. The first test was called the 'Army Alpha Test', which consisted of a number of different types of questions, including questions which asked people to unscramble mixed sentences and say whether they were true or false. They were also asked for the next number in a sequence, to identify words with the same or opposite meanings, and so on, all of which were obviously language-based questions. Because it was likely that people were not always suitably literate, or perhaps didn't speak English, the 'Army Beta Test' was developed, which involved tasks like tracing the outcome of a maze, picture completion, counting the number of cubes in a stack and combining several shapes to make others. The tests took about one hour, and could be given to lots of people at the same time.

Earlier in this section we mentioned that, on average, black people's test results on IQ tests were about 15 points below the average of the white population. The results of the tests were not actually wrong, but the reasons for the results were not due to the black population being less intelligent, but because tests were culturally biased in favour of the white population. In the early part of this century, American intelligence testers applied tests which had been standardised on white English-speaking Americans to people from other ethnic and cultural groups. Not surprisingly, they found East European immigrants, Mexicans, American Indians and blacks to be of much 'lower' intelligence. These American testers believed they had shown that white English-speaking people were of superior intelligence, but their critics pointed out that they were misusing their tests – tests standardised on one population cannot be used to measure the IQ of people from different populations.

In theory, it should be possible to develop tests which look at many different types of skills and establish norms that are taken from the groups of people likely to be tested. You may therefore have a high standardised score for people who have the same culture as the testers, and a lower score for immigrants from certain countries, but at least there would be norms established for each cultural group. Then a group of people who have completed the test could be compared to the relevant cultural group rather than a group which may suggest that they are less able.

At the end of the day, can we really measure this elusive ability? What we have to accept is that we do all vary and some of us find things easier than others. The concept of intelligence is very useful in life in order to make comparisons and estimations about people, but what we must always remember is that it may simply be a concept rather than a reality. So we should never use intelligence as the only criteria for judging others, but should look at that person as a whole and value them for what they are.

Stephen Jay Gould (1982) 'A Nation of Morons,'

New Scientist (6 May 1982), 349–52

● **Background**

To help you get an understanding of Gould's work, have a go at the intelligence test below.

How clever are you?

Answer the following questions:

1. What were the names of the four Banana Splits?
(a) Fleagle, Bingo, Drooper and Snort
(b) Beagle, Ringo, Scooter and Sport
(c) Eagle, Jingo, Hooter and Cork
(d) Jangle, Bungo, Tottle and Honk

2. What are the surnames of the members of the band The Who?
(a) Daltry, Townsend, Thompson and Moon
(b) Moon, Daniels, Daltry and Hayward
(c) Daltry, Townsend, Duncan and Moon
(d) Entwistle, Daltry, Moon and Townsend

3. What are the names of the four female children in the Ingalls household in the TV programme *Little House on the Prairie*?
(a) Emma, Mary, Grace and Caroline
(b) Mary, Laura, Carrie and Lucy
(c) Laura, Carrie, Mary and Grace
(d) Laura, Mary, Caroline and Grace

4. Which of the two characters below appeared in the children's programme *Pogle's Wood*?
(a) Noggin and Jock
(b) Pippin and Tog
(c) Pipkin and Tod
(d) Tippin and Pop

5. Which of the following is the name of Winston Churchill's mother?
(a) Lady Georgia Randolph Churchill
(b) Lady Mary Randolph Churchill
(c) Lady Jennie Randolph Churchill
(d) Lady Emily Randolph Churchill

6. Ken Barlow in *Coronation Street* is a long-standing character who has had many partners and a number of wives. How did his first wife die?
(a) Car accident
(b) Electrocution by a hairdryer
(c) Suicide by overdose
(d) Heart failure brought on by allergic reaction to Minnie Cauldwell's cat

7. Which one of the following actors never played the Doctor in the long-running BBC series *Doctor Who*?
(a) Peter Davison
(b) Jon Pertwee
(c) Colin Baker
(d) Ian McKellan

8. What are the names of the four original members of the band Queen?
(a) Freddie Mercury, Brian May, Paul Davies and Richard Tyler
(b) Freddie Mercury, Brian May, John Deacon and Roger Taylor
(c) Freddie Mercury, Brian May, John Baron and Roger Tyler
(d) Freddie Mercury, Brian May, John Lord and Richard Taylor

9. In the 1970s TV series *The Sweeney*, what were the two main male characters called?
(a) Jack Owen and Dave Carter
(b) Jack Regan and George Carter
(c) Dave Carter and Phil Owen
(d) Jack Regan and Phil Carter

10. In 1974, a new *Blue Peter* presenter was introduced. What was her name and whom did she replace?
(a) She took over from Victoria Stranks and her name was Laura Johns
(b) She took over from Vicky Standish and her name was Louise Arthur
(c) She took over from Valerie Singleton and her name was Lesley Judd
(d) She took over from Valerie Singleton and her name was Louise Arthur

SCORING

Calculate your mark out of ten.

The answers (in reverse order) are as follows:

10 (c) 9 (b) 8(b) 7(d) 6(b) 5(c) 4(b) 3(c)

2(d) 1(a)

If you have scored 10/10 you are a genius: 8/10 means you are very bright: 6/10 means you are bright: 5/10 means you are of average intelligence; below five and you are a moron.

(NOTE: If you are under 30 years old, you probably didn't score very highly on this test. So can we say all people under 30 are not very bright? Of course not. As you have probably worked out, this test is not fair.)

 FOCUS ON THEMES – biasing factors which affect the validity of psychometric tests

Culture bias (ethnocentric bias) is clearly a problem with the test you have just done. The test is biased in favour of people aged about 40, who had nothing to do but listen to pop records and watch TV in the 1970s. If you weren't there, how on earth could you answer the questions correctly?

Class differences can also affect people's performance on IQ tests. It may be that people from what are considered working-class backgrounds use less formal language and are more involved in practical problem solving, whereas the middle classes use more formal language and abstract problem-solving skills. IQ tests use formal English and more abstract problem-solving questions, which may make them more suitable for people from middle-class environments. This could also result in the tests discriminating against working-class candidates.

What if a test you had to take had been in Portuguese and you had only been learning Portuguese for a short time? Would the test be fair then? Of course not. When someone is not a native speaker of the language the test is written in, and may only have a limited knowledge of the language being used, then the test is not a fair one.

Similarly, we live in a culture where everyone has access to education and the level of literacy is high. However, if you had not been taught to read and write to a very high level, again the test would not be fair. It would not measure your intelligence, just your limited ability to demonstrate it in writing.

If any (or all!) of these factors are present in an intelligence test (or any other psychometric measure), then we have to conclude that the test is not valid and that we are not measuring intelligence at all.

Robert Yerkes (1917) developed a number of what are called 'mass tests', which were developed mainly as screening tests for the US Army, although they ended up being used as a means of selection for refugees from Europe who wanted to enter the US. Gould's (1982) review of the work describes the development of the tests, the problems inherent in their design, and the problems the researchers had when carrying out tests on a massive scale.

He then considers how these tests, which were clearly biased and not valid measures of intelligence, were used to lobby the US government to restrict the immigration of certain groups from Europe in the 1920s and 1930s.

Aim

The aim of Gould's work was to review and evaluate the mass testing of army recruits initiated by Yerkes, and the use, or rather misuse, of these tests to support the hereditarian position that intelligence is innate, and the white supremacists' view that white people are 'naturally' more intelligent than other racial groups.

Method

This article is a review article. It is an edited extract from the book, *The Mismeasure of Man*. It was written by Gould in 1981 and charted the history and problems associated with intelligence testing and documented the efforts by Robert M. Yerkes to establish psychology as a scientific discipline.

Gould describes the psychometric tests designed by Yerkes and his colleagues. He considers problems with both the design and administration of the tests that show that the results of the tests were not valid.

FOCUS ON THEMES AND RESEARCH METHODS –
psychometric tests

Psychometric tests are usually pen-and-paper tests with fixed-response (often multiple choice) items where the respondent answers questions or fills in, for example on intelligence tests, verbal, visuo-spatial or numerical items. For young children and those who cannot read and write, individual tests using, for example, shape matching, can be used as measures of intelligence.

The respondent's calculated score can be compared with the findings from standardisation of the tests on a large sample. This allows us to place people on a scale, e.g. an IQ score of 80 is 'below average', 100 is 'average' and 120 is 'above average', etc.

The measurement of a variable to give one quantitative score is attractive, since it allows us ease of comparison between subjects and means we can group subjects according to their score. However, we must be cautious about this. Is it possible, for example, for a test to measure every aspect of the variable we describe as 'intelligence'? In other words, can we quantify intelligence meaningfully to give each person a score?

Another issue that we have to consider with psychometric measures is culture bias. It is unlikely that we can design a test that will not put one group or another at a disadvantage, due to their language ability (they may have a limited education and their written skills not be fully developed, or they may not be very experienced in the language in which they are being tested if they are not native speakers of the test language) or their cultural background. Psychometric measures need to be both valid (testing what they are claiming to be testing) and reliable (consistent on re-test).

Examples of the use of psychometric measures in the core studies include the use of the Rutter A and Rutter B scales in Hodges and Tizard's study on attachment, the use of the Sally-Anne test in the Baron-Cohen *et al.* study on autism, and the use of memory and IQ tests in Thigpen and Cleckley's study of multiple personality disorder.

Gould's description of how and why the tests were developed and the problems with the design and administration of the tests

Gould begins by telling us about Yerkes and his ambitions for himself and for the development of psychology as a respectable scientific subject. Yerkes was a psychologist at Harvard University. Because psychology was perceived as a 'soft' science, he wanted to improve its status and demonstrate that it could be as objective and quantifiable as other scientific disciplines. Yerkes also believed that intelligence was inherited and therefore could not be changed. He saw an opportunity to give psychology the status it deserved by incorporating his ideas of inherited intelligence and the development of mental testing, which was, at the time, in its earliest stages. If he could show that intelligence tests were reliable and valid, then surely this quantifiable measure would prove his point.

With the outbreak of the First World War, the now Colonel Yerkes developed the idea that it might be possible to use American army recruits as a source of sufficient data to show that intelligence testing was scientific. Previous efforts to do this had been insufficiently coordinated or were simply inadequate. He managed to persuade the government to go along with his idea, and consequently presided over the testing of 1.75 million army recruits in 1917.

The development of the three tests:

From May to July 1917, Yerkes, together with a number of colleagues who shared his views on the hereditary nature of intelligence, wrote the army mental tests.

Together they developed three types of tests. The Alpha and Beta tests were designed to be administered to large numbers of recruits at a time and were supposed to take less than an hour to complete. The Alpha test was for literate recruits. The Beta test was for illiterate recruits. Alpha failures were also to be recalled and retested using the Beta test. The third test was a one-to-one spoken test, and it was intended that all Beta failures be recalled to be tested individually.

The Army Alpha test

Designed for literate recruits, the Alpha test consisted of eight parts. It included items with which we are totally familiar as part of intelligence testing, such as analogies and filling in the next number in a sequence. It required a good basic understanding of language skills and a level of literacy (which must come from education).

The following examples give some idea of the type of questions used in the test:
- Washington is to Adams as first is to...
- Crisco is a: patient medicine, disinfectant, toothpaste, food product?
- The number of Kaffir's legs is: 2, 4, 6, 8?
- Christy Matthewson is famous as a: writer, artist, baseball player, comedian?

Although the tests were considered by Yerkes to measure 'native intellectual ability', in other words, the intelligence you were born with (Gould, p. 349), they were in fact extremely culturally biased. After all, how could someone who was unfamiliar with American culture achieve a decent score? Do you know the number of Kaffir's legs? Do you know who Christy Matthewson was? Only those with a good knowledge of American culture of the time would know this, and so those who were born there or who had lived there longest had the advantage over recent immigrants.

Recent immigrants from non English-speaking countries, were at a double disadvantage: they had a limited command of the language and a limited knowledge of American culture. Even the people who did have a knowledge of English, and therefore sat the Army Alpha tests, were also discriminated against because, unless their knowledge of the language was extremely good, they would still have problems with the questions.

Here are some examples:

1. Finger is to arm as toe is to...
2. Which is the odd one out: pig/badger/bean/elephant/dolphin?
3. Which is the next number in the sequence: 2 5 7 12 19 31?
4. If the hands of a clock seen in a mirror appear to say 4.30, what is the real time?
5. Which of the following is the opposite of small: lots/large/enormous/big?
6. Does the sentence make sense?
   'Mrs Brown has had no children, and I understand that the same was true of her mother.'

Let's look at the answers:

1. Leg – if you chose foot, and you are a native English speaker, imagine how difficult this must be for someone whose native tongue is not English.
2. First of all, we need to understand the meaning of the English words 'odd one out'. The answer could be bean as it's not a mammal, but on the other hand, it could be dolphin because dolphins live in water. Either way, the person could be forgiven for getting the answer wrong.
3. 50 – you simply add the last two numbers together; but what if you don't understand the word 'sequence'?
4. 7.30 – this test of spatial reasoning is not that difficult if you are familiar with the face of a clock.
5. Large would probably be the accepted opposite of small, but enormous and big are not really wrong; but what if you are not that familiar with the language?
6. The sentence is rubbish – language again.

As you can see, lots of items on these 'intelligence tests' assume that you have a good knowledge of cultural objects and a familiarity with the language of the test.

The Army Beta test

This was a pictorial test, designed for people who were illiterate or who failed the Alpha test, consisting of seven parts. It was made up of picture completion tasks. There were also maze tests, counting the number of cubes, finding the next in a series of symbols and translating numerals into symbols given a code to work from.

Here is an example of an item from the Beta test. The task here is to complete the pictures by adding the missing parts.

340

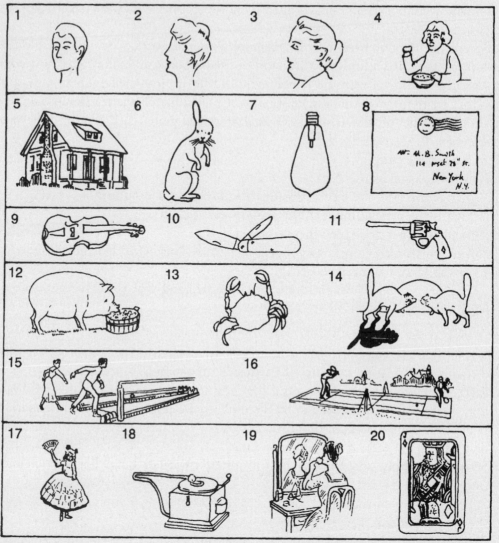

A page of 'picture completion' taken from the Army Beta Test. Note the cultural bias in the pictures

One of the main criticisms of this test was that the pictures which needed completing were extremely culturally biased, and consisted of things that were familiar in American culture but were not relevant to immigrants. If you look at the pictures shown here, you will see that many of them would be alien to people from some other cultures. Supposing you had never used a spoon, or didn't know what one was; picture four would be impossible to complete. What about five, with its missing chimney pot, or seven, without the element from the light bulb, or eight, with its stamp missing? What relevance would this have if you had come from a developing nation? Not everyone has seen a crab or a bowling alley, a tennis court or a phonograph. The pictures, like the questions on the Alpha test, were culturally specific and would be extremely difficult to complete if subjects had no knowledge of some of the items.

In addition to the problems of ethnocentric bias in the items, there was also a major problem in the way the Beta test was presented. Although they were intended to be completed by illiterate recruits, the instructions were written, and in three of the seven parts of the Beta test the answers had to recognise numbers in the questions and form numbers in their answers. Even the 'non-linguistic' items, then, required the recruits to read the instructions, and their responses were recorded by them filling in the test. This was a test intended for illiterates who may never have held a pencil, and so again they were disadvantaged.

To further compound the difficulties inherent in the testing, although the tests were designed to be completed in an hour, most parts could not be completed in the allocated time. If they did not have enough time to finish the test, then their scores, and therefore the average for their group, would be artificially lowered again.

Individual spoken examination:

If recruits failed on the other two tests, they were given an individual spoken examination.

Test:	Intended to be taken by:
Army Alpha, pencil-and-paper test	Literate recruits
Army Beta, pencil-and paper-test	Illiterate recruits
	Alpha failures were to be recalled and tested on the Beta test
Individual Spoken Examination	Recruits who failed the Beta test were to be recalled for one-to-one testing

Table to show the test protocol, that is, the rules for how the tests were to be carried out

As you can imagine, the task of testing 1.75 million army recruits was never going to be an easy one.

Differences in the way the tests were administered occurred between the different army camps. Recruits who were illiterate should have been assigned immediately to the Beta test, or given it if they failed the Alpha test, but this only happened in some of the camps.

The decision about who should take which test also differed from camp to camp. In some camps, the minimum level of schooling was sufficient to warrant sitting the Alpha test, whereas in others the recruits had to have been educated at least to third-grade standard.

A major problem was that Yerkes had understimated the levels of literacy in those to be tested. They had spent less time in school than he had imagined. This meant that the Alpha test was not the best test for most recruits to take. Queues for the Beta test began to build up, however, and this led the test administrators to allocate more men to the Alpha test. In other words, the Alpha test was the test used most often, even though for most recruits it was the least appropriate. This would not have been such an issue had the test protocol been followed, but it was not. Pressed for time (the recruits were, of course, destined for the front in Europe, and those responsible for getting them there were not always sympathetic to the needs of the testers!), the administrators of the test were unable to recall Alpha failures for re-testing on the Beta test. At one camp, the chief tester complained: 'In June it was found impossible to recall a thousand men listed for individual examination. In July Alpha failures among Negroes were not recalled' (Gould, p. 350). This meant that the low Alpha test scores of some disadvantaged groups stood, e.g. recent immigrants and blacks often sat the Alpha test and came out scoring next to nothing.

Also, Beta failures were not recalled for the more time-consuming and costly one-to-one tests. Gould reports that this was particularly the case for black recruits. With racism rife and open in the USA at the time, it is no surprise that Gould tells us that 'the stated protocol scarcely applied to Blacks who, as usual, were treated with less concern and more contempt than everyone'. In fact, only one-fifth of black recruits who failed the Beta test being were retested individually, according to the test protocol.

Results

Despite the problems with the test design and administration, Yerkes seems to have had no compunction in publishing the findings from the tests. The data was analysed by E.G. Boring, Yerkes's lieutenant. Boring selected data from 160,000 recruits. This data was converted to a common standard to look for racial and national averages. The following three 'facts' emerged:

- 'The average mental age of white American adults stood just above the edge of moronity at a shocking and meagre 13. Terman had previously set the standard at 16' (p. 351). This indicated that the country was really 'a nation of morons' (where the title for Gould's article comes from), and as such was taken by the eugenicists to show that the poor, negroes and the feeble-minded had been interbreeding and lowering the overall intelligence of the population.
- The data also showed that European immigrants could be graded by their country of origin, with the darker people of southern Europe and the Slavs of Eastern Europe being less intelligent than the fair people of Western and Northern Europe.

- The black man had an average mental age of 10.41, with results suggesting the lighter the skin colour, the higher the score.

Discussion

Yerkes had achieved his goal. Data had been collected on 1.75 million men and the first mass-produced tests of written intelligence were in use. The tests had a large impact on officer screening. By the end of the war, two-thirds of the men who had been promoted were the ones who had taken the tests and achieved good results. According to Yerkes, there was also a 'steady stream of requests from commercial concerns, educational institutions and individuals for the use of army methods of psychological examining or for the adaptation of such methods to special needs.'

The 'fact' that the average mental age of Americans was 13 was concerning, but this fact seem to be overshadowed by the coup this research offered to the herediatarians. Here was 'scientific evidence' to support the idea that whites were indeed the genetically superior group. Nordic people from Northern Europe had been shown to be the most intelligent.

Bearing in mind that these tests were now accepted measures of innate intelligence, here was 'evidence' that there really was a difference between racial and national groups in their levels of intelligence. This 'evidence' was used by Carl Brigham, Assistant Professor at Princetown University, in a book which was ideal propaganda for any racists. Gould describes Brigham as a 'disciple' of Yerkes, and notes that Yerkes wrote the foreword of the book, praising Brigham for his 'objectivity'. The book dispelled any possible concerns that might be raised about the accuracy of the findings by some very strange reasoning. For example, although some Jews were extremely accomplished as scholars, statesmen and performing artists, these were only noticeable because they were unusual exceptions to the rule. The majority had been assessed as having low levels of intelligence.

Although the tests were supposed to be accurate, irrespective of country of origin or first language, even Yerkes admitted that the results showed that there was a problem for people who weren't familiar with English. The most recent immigrants were Latins and Slavs, who spoke little English, and they had the lowest test scores of all. Also, there was a correlation between the length of time people had been resident in America and their test scores, with people who had been living there the longest having higher scores. This second problem was explained by the fact that the first wave of immigrants had been drawn from the more intelligent groups, and the latest immigrants had consisted of the dregs of Europe in the form of lower-class Latins and Slavs. What an ideal argument to use to restrict immigration!

Gould also shows us that the testing of blacks was far from accurate. Even though half the black recruits scored D on the Beta test and should have been recalled, only one-fifth of them were retested on the individual test. Gould tells us that this led to an artificial lowering of the black average, since the scores of blacks 'increased substantially when the protocol was followed'. For example, at one camp only 14.1% of black Alpha failures didn't get a higher grade when recalled to take the Beta test.

The social and political consequences of Yerkes' work

The fact that blacks failed to be properly assessed, the inherent problems with the test design we considered earlier, and the problems of familiarity with language and culture, are all issues revealed by Gould's review of the testing, clearly challenging the validity of the findings for all groups tested. However, these factors did not seem to have any effect on either Yerkes' or his followers' assertions that the findings from the testing of recruits constituted evidence with which to lobby the US government to introduce more stringent laws of immigration. Their aim was to restrict the numbers of those of 'inferior stock' from taking up residence in the USA.

The Immigration Restriction Act of 1924, passed by the US Congress, was shaped by Yerkes' findings. People from Southern and Eastern Europe, and from the Alpine and Mediterranean nations, who had low scores on the army tests, were not welcome. The way this was controlled was by looking at data from a census of immigrants, which had been conducted in 1890 when immigration from Southern and Eastern Europe was very low. It was decided that the quota of immigrants allowed into American would be 2% of each recorded nation taken from the 1890 figures. This would obviously mean that the numbers of those from 'inferior stock' would be extremely low.

These immigration restrictions were to have horrendous consequences, as the immigration from southern and eastern Europe all but ceased. The persecution of the Jews, which started before the beginning of the Second World War, meant that many Jews tried to escape from their homeland, but there was 'no admittance' to America. In fact, such was the influence of racist views in society that many were turned away even when the quota for that year for their particular group had not been filled.

Calculations suggest that as many as six million people from Southern, Central and Eastern Europe were denied entry into America between 1924 and 1939, when war broke out.

Conclusion

Gould's work clearly shows us that Yerkes' testing, which was subject to a huge amount of experimenter bias, should never have been accepted as a valid test of a supposedly inherited intellectual ability. What makes it worse is that Yerkes' evidence supports the idea that IQ test scores can change over time. The immigrants who had been residents of America had higher test scores than the newly arrived immigrants, which does rather support the idea that the tests were culturally biased.

The racial bias of the testing was also astounding, with many of the black recruits being treated differently to their white counterparts. For no other reason, the nature of the testing situation should have been addressed, but racism was far more acceptable in the early years of this century than it is nowadays. In fact, Yerkes discovered that the relative levels of education between blacks and whites were significantly different, but he explained this by saying that it was because black people were too stupid to realise how important it was to stay on at school. They couldn't win!

Gould concludes his article with the comment that, in relation to the numbers who wanted to emigrate from Europe to America between 1924 and 1939, 'We know what happened to many who wished to leave but had nowhere to go. The paths of destruction are often indirect, but ideas can be agents as sure as guns and bombs' (p. 352).

Commentary

What does the study show us about the validity of pschological findings?

The cultural bias of the tests, the nature of the testing and the situation would have filled the recruits with anxiety. Although a degree of arousal is needed for good performance, if you become too anxious or aroused, the worse your performance becomes. The article notes that many of the recruits were terrified, confused (Gould suggests 'scared shitless'!) and didn't manage to finish the tests in the allocated time, and this would have contributed to their overall level of anxiety. How could such a situation produce a valid measure of intelligence? If we accept that these arguments are fair, surely this points to the injustice of using these tests as a measure of an innate, inherited ability?

Is the study useful?

Gould's work shows us that we have to be cautious in our interpretations of findings and the use to which we put them.

Any psychometric test is open to abuse, and people seem to accept test results blindly, without questioning the nature of the test and the theory on which it has been founded. Tests must be administered in a uniform manner, with identical instructions and conditions for each subject. Unless this degree of rigour is achieved, how can the results from one test be compared with those from another? Even when results are gathered, how those results are interpreted is often very biased. Data that doesn't support the hypothesis can easily be discarded or misinterpreted. To make it worse, the results here were used as a tool of discrimination, which suited the requirements of a political system – a kind of scientific racism, that is, an attempt to use the methods of science to justify racist beliefs and influence racist policies.

Gould's work illustrates the misuse of psychological 'evidence'. His work cautions us to consider carefully how variables have been measured, and under what circumstances, before we accept the findings as a valid explanation of behaviour.

Key questions

1. Why was it so important to Yerkes to develop intelligence testing?
2. Even if the tests had been valid, explain why we would need to be cautious in generalising the findings from the tests to 'people in general'.
3. Yerkes used the findings of his tests as evidence that blacks were genetically inferior in their intelligence to other racial groups. What is a more likely explanation for the finding that blacks scored the lowest in these tests?
4. Can you explain why the white American recruits scored so low in the tests?
5. What do you think Gould meant by: 'The paths of destruction are often indirect, but ideas can be agents as sure as guns and bombs'?

Example Answers are on page 459.

Further reading

- Hinton, P.R. (2000), *Stereotypes, Cognition and Culture*, Hove: Psychology Press.
- Rosenthal and Jacobson in Banyard, P. and Grayson, A. (2000), *Introducing Psychological Research*, Basingstoke: Macmillan Press.

Stereotyping and discrimination

The process of grouping people together and believing that they are all the same is known as stereotyping. The term stereotype was introduced by Walter Lippman in 1922 and was defined as being an oversimplified view of the world that satisfies our need to see the world as more understandable and manageable than it really is. What he actually meant was that if we can attribute a whole set of characteristics to something, we will not have to analyse the thing each time we meet it in order to know about it.

You are walking down the road in the middle of the night on your own. It is dark and damp and the streets are empty. All the houses are in darkness and everyone is in bed. You turn the corner and coming towards you is a group of eight skinheads, wearing boots and turned-up jeans and with shaved heads. What is your immediate reaction?

I would imagine it probably isn't to go up and shake their hands and wish them goodnight. It would probably be something along the lines of 'Oh my God! I'd better get out of here.' Why?

The reason would be something to do with your expectations of this particular group's likely behaviour. You may expect them to be somewhat aggressive or provocative, and would probably perceive that they were not going to be over-friendly and may even by quite dangerous. However, what you don't know is that they are all really Buddhist monks who have just been to a fancy-dress party. Mind you, if you had decided to take the time to try to find out, you may well have been lying in a large heap by the side of the road before you had the opportunity. What you have done is to use the information that was available to you to help you instantly judge the situation in order to predict what was likely to happen. As I am sure you can see, this process serves to maintain our safety, both physical and emotional. If we can estimate the basic characteristics of what we are dealing with, we will know how best to behave.

Stereotyping involves classifying people according to a set of pre-established criteria, such as, if they have shaved heads they may be skinheads; if they walk around in orange robes they are Buddhists; if they are adults wearing a uniform they are members of some kind of authoritative organisation. This kind of classification is usually made on the basis of something as superficial as their appearance. What the person is actually like is totally irrelevant because we simply attribute all sorts of characteristics to them on the basis of the group that we have put them with.

PREJUDICE

Sometimes the attitudes we have towards a group of people are extreme and we call this kind of extreme attitude a prejudice. This prejudice can be either positive or negative, depending on the person holding the views – some men think women drivers are useless (they are negatively prejudiced), but some think women drivers are the best (they are positively prejudiced – and correct!). In this example, our opinions are related to whether we are part of the group – especially as both authors are female! Often these extreme attitudes have virtually no foundation in reality and are based on some minor attribute, like appearance, are influenced by factors such as the media and the way we have been socialised, and tend to ignore the characteristics of the individual and the nature of the situation at the time.

Probably the most obvious form of prejudice is racial prejudice. However, there is also gender prejudice, known as sexism, ageism, or religious prejudice, such as the situation between the Catholics and Protestants in Northern Ireland. None of these prejudices are rational because there are good and bad people in every category, but rationality does not enter the equation here.

One of the most famous studies to have considered the negative aspects of prejudice was a field experiment carried out by a teacher called Jane Elliot, which was reported by Aronson and Osherow (1980). The experiment, known as 'The Eye of the Storm' (but sometimes referred to as the 'blue-eyes brown-eyes' experiment), gives us an insight into how easy it is to create a prejudice.

Jane Elliot was a third-grade teacher in Riceville, Iowa, an area where all the families were white. Because of their environment, these nine-year-olds had no understanding of prejudice and discrimination and the negative effects they can cause, and so she decided to try to teach them what it felt like, as a way of equipping them for later life. She went into the classroom one morning and told the children that she had heard that blue-eyed people had been found to be better than brown-eyed people. They were nicer, more clever and more trustworthy, and so the brown-eyed children were to wear collars which made it obvious, from a distance, that they were the inferior group. She also told the blue-eyed children that they could have a longer playtime, would be allowed second helpings in the dining room and would be given preference over the brown-eyed children in any other activity.

It took just half an hour for the situation in that classroom to deteriorate, with the blue-eyed children turning into prejudiced little individuals. They refused to play with the brown-eyed children, made fun of them, told tales about them to the teacher and discriminated against them at every opportunity. The brown-eyed children responded by becoming depressed and unmotivated. The work they produced was of a poorer standard than normal and they went home tearful and unhappy. The situation had not only caused the blue-eyed children to become prejudiced towards the brown-eyed children, but had also resulted in a kind of self-fulfilling prophecy, whereby the brown-eyed children believed they were useless and responded accordingly.

The following morning, Jane Elliot came into the classroom and confessed to having made a serious mistake. She had got it the wrong way round and it was really the brown-eyed children who were superior and the blue-eyed children would have to wear the collars. The brown-eyed children were elated and responded by being even more unpleasant to the blue-eyed children.

On the third day, she explained that really none of them were superior, and this was simply an exercise to teach them about prejudice and how it feels to be the subject of discrimination as a result of something beyond your control. She likened the situation to skin colour and explained that how they felt was how people who had black skins felt if they were treated as inferior. The children discussed what they had done to each other and how miserable each group had felt. Jane Elliot arranged for the students to attend a reunion when they were in their twenties with children of their own, and even then they remembered the experience and claimed that it had helped them to understand the negative consequences of holding irrational prejudices.

Even when prejudices are irrational, if they are maintained or perpetuated by society they can have very dangerous consequences for the people concerned. The person who is on the receiving end of the prejudice is likely to develop very low self-esteem, seeing themselves as less worthy than the people holding the prejudiced views.

In the 1930s, America was still extremely prejudiced against black people and areas were legally designated as either black or white. The opportunities for betterment for black people were few and far between, and they had little access to education, jobs and state welfare. A study carried out in 1947, by Clark and Clark, showed that African-American children, as young as three years, were already demoralised about their skin colour and felt that to be white was preferable to being black. They were offered the choice of playing with a black or a white doll and most of them chose the white doll because they thought it was better than the black doll. This study was cited by Thurgood Marshall, Chief Counsel for the National Association for the Advancement of Coloured People, when he argued in the Supreme Court that there should be an end to the legalised racial segregation that went on in schools. Clark stated that, 'Human beings... whose daily experience tells them that almost nowhere in society are they respected and granted the ordinary dignity and courtesy accorded to others, will, as a matter of course, begin to doubt their self worth' (K.B. Clark, 1965, p. 64). The result of this case was that the Court ruled that schools should no longer be segregated.

DISCRIMINATION

It should be evident now that if we hold a prejudiced belief, it is likely to lead to some kind of discriminatory behaviour. Discrimination can, therefore, be described as the way we act towards a group of people as a result of our prejudices. The group in question will either be given an advantage or a disadvantage, depending on whether our prejudice is positive or negative.

DOES PREJUDICE HAVE ANY SORT OF FUNCTION?

We mentioned earlier how stereotyping can be seen as having an important function, in that we do not have to go through the process of analysing everyone individually but can make broad generalisations in order to assess the situation quickly. This means that stereotyping and prejudice can be seen as having a survival function. In fact, Ardrey (1966) suggested that people have a basic instinct to defend their territory against all possible invaders and in order to do that we need to identify who is 'one of us' and who is 'one of them'. He said that here people are acting according to what he called a territorial imperative. The problem is that we may not necessarily be defending a territory in terms of a plot of land, but if we consider that our bodies are a kind of territory, then this makes sense.

Richard Dawkins (1976), who wrote the book *The Selfish Gene,* gives an explanation which suggest that nature has a part to play in prejudice, that it is a way of protecting our genes. This xenophobia (which is a fear of strangers and therefore hostility towards them) stems from our desire to protect the purity of our genes, both in ourselves and in those directly related to us.

Other theories are based on the idea that prejudice is really no more than an outlet for our innate aggressions. If you remember, Freud claims that we have innate aggressive tendencies, and Lorenz suggests that aggression is a 'dripping tap', which needs channelling from time to time. Therefore, we vent our aggressions towards people who we believe are responsible for depriving or disadvantaging us. This idea is known as scapegoating and has some evidence to back it up. Hovland and Sears (1940) analysed the number of lynchings that took place in the southern states of the USA and found that they correlated with the price of cotton. What was happening was that the number of lynchings increased whenever the price of cotton went down. The farmers were blaming black people for the poor cotton prices – using them as scapegoats and directing their aggression towards them.

We have already looked at social identity theory, and it would seem that there is a link between prejudice towards groups and that particular theory. If you remember, social identity theory was described by Tajfel and Turner (1986) and stated that we actually get our identity from the group to which we perceive we belong. If we perceive that we belong to a racial group, for example, we will make comparisons between our group and other groups, and will probably see our group as being superior to other groups – we will be positively prejudiced towards our group. Don't forget, if a group believes it is less worthy than other groups, it will be much more likely to accept any discrimination and disadvantage shown towards it without complaint.

CORE STUDY LINK – causes and consequences of prejudice
Both the Tajfel study (p. 77) and the Hraba and Grant study (p. 352) focus on prejudice, with the first linking to causes of prejudice, whilst the other looks at the consequences of prejudice. The Tajfel study considered that in-group preference and out-group prejudice was caused by simply being placed within a group. The Hraba and Grant study looks at the consequences of prejudice when the group perceives itself as different from others. Both these studies have a strong link to social identity theory.

Research such as the study by Sherif described in Chapter 2 (p. 73) has indicated that the way to reduce prejudice and discrimination comes from equal status contact and the pursuit of common goals. Although these techniques are frequently used to reduce tension between groups, we need to ask ourselves whether things are really any different today. The core study in this area, which is a study replicating the Clark and Clark (1947) study, suggests that things are different and that black people, at least, no longer suffer from such low self-esteem. Martin Luther King, the black American Baptist minister, was partly responsible for this change in attitude *towards* black people and *by* black people in America, when he helped found the non-violent civil rights movement against racism and discrimination. This resulted in increased opportunities for black people and, consequently, raised their expectations of achievement. Today black people hold positions of importance in America, although the majority of black people are still likely to be found in the poorest sections of American society.

Authors such as Aronson (1997) point out that racism does still exist in America, although it takes on a different form. He calls it modern racism, and claims that '… it has become more subtle' (Aronson, 1997, p. 511). What he means is that we are now no longer blatantly prejudiced because we are all concerned with and aware of 'political correctness'. We aren't prepared to express our prejudiced views any more for fear of appearing 'racist'. What we do instead is to simply act them out in a very subtle way, by offering less help or charging more to members of different racial groups for the same services or goods.

Jones and Sigall (1971) demonstrated this with something they called the 'bogus pipeline'. This was a machine covered in dials, which participants believed was a kind of lie-detector machine. Jones and Sigall compared the responses of their participants on either a pencil-and-paper questionnaire of prejudice (where they could easily lie) and their responses on the 'bogus pipeline'. They found that participants showed far more racial prejudice and gender prejudice when they were questioned using the 'bogus pipeline' than when they had to fill in the questionnaires.

Perhaps it is fitting that I should end this section on prejudice with an excerpt from the famous speech given by Martin Luther King on 28 August 1963 at the Lincoln Memorial in Washington D.C.

'I have a dream that one day this nation will rise up and live out the true meaning of its creed: "We hold these truths to be self-evident; that all men are created equal."

'I have a dream that one day on the red hills of Georgia the sons of former slaves and the sons of former slaveowners will be able to sit down together at the table of brotherhood.

'I have a dream that my four little children will one day live in a nation where they will not be judged by the colour of their skin but by the content of their character.'

**J. Hraba and G. Grant (1970), 'Black is beautiful:
A re-examination of racial preference and identification',**
Journal of Personality & Social Psychology, 16, 398–402

Background

In 1939, Clark and Clark had carried out a study which was designed to investigate black children's racial preference, racial awareness and racial self-identification, using a set of black and white dolls. The Clarks had found, in a further study in 1947, that black children preferred white dolls: they 'rejected black dolls when asked to choose which were nice, which looked bad, which they would like to play with and which were a nice colour' (p. 398). The conclusion was that this 'doll technique' indicated that the black children had negative attitudes towards their own ethnicity: 'this implies that black is not beautiful' (p. 398).

Subsequent research was mixed. A study by Gregor and McPherson (1966) did not show the same findings as the Clark and Clark study. Instead, it was seen that 7-year-old black children generally preferred a black doll. From this study, Gregor and McPherson theorised that negative attitudes of black children towards their own ethnicity increased depending on the amount of contact they had with white children; the more contact with white children, the more negative black children would be about their own ethnicity. This was supported by the fact that Clark and Clark had found preference for white dolls to be more marked for those in interracial nursery schools than for those in segregated nursery schools. On this point, the work of Morland provided contrary evidence. In a study using pictures rather than dolls, the opposite effect was shown, with black children choosing the black dolls more in an interracial setting.

Aim

The aim of this study was to replicate the work by Clark and Clark (1939), to test the idea that 'for black children interracial contact engenders preference for white'. In other words, given mixed schooling and high contact with whites, would black children demonstrate negative attitudes to their own ethnicity by choosing a white doll?

The study also aimed to investigate whether doll choice corresponds to friendship choices in the real world. Would the children's preference for white or black dolls correspond to whether their friends were white or black?

Method

Design

This study was a quasi-experiment carried out under laboratory conditions.

Subjects

Taking part in this study were 160 children, between the ages of four and eight years, from five primary schools in Lincoln, Nebraska; 89 children were black, which represented 60% of all the black children attending the five schools, the total number of black children being about 150. Lincoln's black population was 1.4%, and the proportion of black children in each school averaged just under 7%. Black children were clearly in the minority, and had a high level of contact with white children, with 70% of the black children reporting that they had white friends. The remaining 71 children were white and came from mixed-race classes.

The black children were classified in three categories, according to skin tone (as the Clark and Clark study had been): 'light' (practically white), 'medium' (light brown to dark brown) and 'dark' (dark brown to black).

Materials

A set of four dolls, two black and two white, which were identical apart from skin colour.

Procedure

In May 1969, the children were interviewed individually, under laboratory conditions, following as closely as possible the procedure used by Clark and Clark in 1939.

They were shown the four dolls and asked the following:

1. Give me the doll that you want to play with
2. Give me the doll that is a nice doll
3. Give me the doll that looks bad
4. Give me the doll that is a nice colour
5. Give me the doll that looks like a white child
6. Give me the doll that looks like a coloured child
7. Give me the doll that looks like a Negro child
8. Give me the doll that looks like you

Although previous work had suggested that it made no difference to results whether the interviewer was white or black, Hraba and Grant nevertheless controlled this variable, varying the race of interviewer for the white and black children.

Variables

The independent variable was the child's skin colour and the dependent variable was the child's racial preference, racial awareness and racial self-identification.

The dependent variable was measured by self-report – the child choosing the doll as their answer to each of the questions. Questions one–four measured 'racial preference'. Questions 5–7 measured 'racial awareness or knowledge'. Question eight measured 'racial self-awareness or racial self-identification'.

The children were then asked to name the race of their best friends, and the children's teachers were asked for the same information. This was to find out if their racial preferences and awareness actually had any behavioural consequences. Would there be any relationship between doll choice and the child's choice of friend?

● **Results**

Table showing comparisons between Clark and Clark's 1939 findings from a sample of black children and the findings from Hraba and Grant's black subjects, and comparisons between the responses of black and white children in the Hraba and Grant 1969 study (adapted from Hraba and Grant, p. 399)

Item	1939 (Clark and Clark)* blacks	1970 (Hraba and Grant) blacks	1970 (Hraba and Grant) whites
1. Play with white doll	67%	30%	83%
Play with black doll	32%	70%	16%
Don't know/no response			1%
2. Nice doll – white	59%	46%	70%
Nice doll – black	38%	54%	30%
3. Looks bad – white doll	17%	61%	34%
Looks bad – black doll	59%	36%	63%
Don't know/no response		3%	3%
4. Nice colour – white doll	60%	31%	48%
Nice colour – black doll	38%	69%	49%
Don't know/no response			3%

*individuals failing to make either choice not included, hence some % add up to less than 100

Clark and Clark (1939) had found that the majority of black children preferred white dolls. They interpreted this to mean that the child 'would rather be white' (Hraba and Grant, p. 399).

Hraba and Grant presented their results in comparison with the findings of Clark and Clark (1939), to consider this interpretation of findings. Would black children again seem to reject their own ethnicity and 'rather be white' in 1969? What would the doll choices of the white children show? Previous studies had suggested that white children would be more likely to choose their own race than black children.

Question one: Give me the doll that you want to play with
In the Lincoln study, both black and white children preferred the doll of their own race, in other words, they made ethnocentric choices in favour of their own ethnic group.

Question two: Give me the doll that is a nice doll
Since 1939 the position had changed, and the black children saw the black doll as being nicer.

Supporting previous studies, Hraba and Grant found that white children were more ethnocentric on both question one and question two.

Question three: Give me the doll that looks bad
Again, a change in the black response to colour was shown in comparison with the 1939 study. In the 1939 study, 59% of black children had chosen a black doll as the one that 'looks bad', compared to 36% in 1969.

There was no significant difference in ethnocentrism on this question between white children and black children.

Question four: Give me the doll that is a nice colour
Black children are much more ethnocentric on this question, whereas the white children are more or less evenly divided.

Questions five–eight obtained answers similar to Clark and Clark. The children made few errors of racial identification or personal identification. Misidentification was more likely for the younger children in the sample.

Clark and Clark had also investigated the effects of skin tone and age on the children's responses, and again Hraba and Grant compared the findings.

The effect of skin tone on children's preferences:
In the Clark and Clark study, the children of light skin colour had a greater preference for the white doll and the dark children the least. This was not found in Hraba and Grant's study.

The effect of age on children's preferences:
The Clarks found that black children of all ages preferred white dolls, with this preference decreasing with age. Hraba and Grant, however, found that black children of all ages preferred the black dolls, with this trend increasing with age.

Two further results related to race were noted:
• The race of the interviewer had no effect on any of the children's responses.
• The children's doll choice was not related to the race of their friends.

Discussion
The findings of this study show that black children were more likely to prefer black dolls, contradicting the findings of Clark and Clark's study, which showed black children preferring white dolls. So it seemed that for the children in the Lincoln study, black was beautiful after all.

Hraba and Grant consider the reasons why their findings differed from the Clark and Clark study, carried out 30 years previously:

- 'Times may be changing' (1969), with black pride increasing in society, and this general increase across the country might explain the findings.
- It might be that black children in Lincoln are atypical of black children generally, and, had Clark and Clark carried out their 1939 study in Lincoln, they may have recorded different results, but as it was carried out elsewhere, we will never know.
- A third reason for the findings may be to do with a greater sense of black pride in Lincoln itself. Hraba and Grant point out that over the two years before the study, a black pride campaign was directed towards the adolescents and young adults in Lincoln, and this may have influenced the feelings of the children who took part in their research, as they may have been modelling the behaviour of older family members and friends.
- The fourth reason that Hraba and Grant give for the difference in findings in their study from Clark and Clark's is that black pride may be increased by interracial contact. The more black children come into contact with and receive acceptance from whites, the higher their pride may be. Hraba and Grant suggest that the fact that 70% of the black children had white friends, and 59% of the white children had black friends, supports this interpretation of their findings.

What interpretations can be made of the fact that doll choice and friendship choices do not correspond with each other?

Previous studies made the assumption that doll choice is a true (valid) measure of racial preference and that it will be matched by children's behaviour in the real world. Hraba and Grant say their findings show that this relationship between doll choice and friendship choices of both white and black children challenge this assumption.

However, Hraba and Grant give three explanations for their findings about the lack of correspondence between doll choice and friendship choices. They consider the possibility that doll choice may not be the same as friendship choice, and also question the assumptions about what 'black is beautiful' really means.

- Their first explanation assumes that doll choice is a valid measure of racial preference and will be matched in the child's behaviour. This explanation interprets the doll choices of black children (who consistently choose black dolls on the preference questions) in a particular way, that 'black is beautiful' and, therefore, that this must lead to a rejection of whites. If these explanations are combined, it would suggest that the black children who preferred black dolls would only have black friends. The problem for the children was that they may only have had white friends because, being in the minority in these Lincoln schools, they had no choice but to make white friends, even though they may have preferred to have black friends. This would explain why the doll choice of black children who consistently preferred black dolls did not correspond to their friendship choices.

- The second explanation makes the same assumption that doll choice and friendship choices correspond. However, it interprets 'black is beautiful' as being a recognition of the acceptance of blacks as being a valued race by whites. Here the expectation would be that the black children who had consistently preferred black dolls would have both black and white friends. This was the case, although trends in the right direction were only approaching significance, so could not be confirmed by this study.

- The third explanation considers that doll choice does not correspond with friendship choices at all. The fact that Hraba and Grant's findings showed that 73% of the children were inconsistent in their doll preferences supports this explanation, as does the fact that children who were consistent (made ethnocentric choices on all four preference questions) had both white and black friends. It may be that where race is the only factor involved in making decisions in the lab about dolls, ethnocentric choices occur. In the real world, however, race may have little to do with the reasons why children make friends with one another, and perhaps there are other criteria, such as personality, that are more important.

Conclusions

The results indicate that black children in interracial settings have little problem with racial identification and are not necessarily oriented to favour whites. The findings also question the validity of the doll technique as a measure of racial preference.

Commentary

Is the study ecologically valid?

Since there is a difference between doll preference and the children's real-life friendship preferences, this suggests that the study is low in ecological validity. The behaviour asked of the subjects in the laboratory, to state their preference for white or black dolls, does not match up with the corresponding behaviour in the real world as to whether they chose white or black friends.

There are always problems when carrying out studies in the laboratory, and this is particularly true when the subjects are children. Being tested in an unusual setting, by someone they are not familiar with, and away from their peers is not a realistic experience for children, so again, we have to question the ecological validity of the study.

Is the study ethical?

Whenever children are being tested there are concerns about informed consent, the right to withdraw and whether debriefing can be given. However, the testing of the children in this study should not have caused undue distress. Being carried out in the schools suggest that someone, at least *in loco parentis* (headteacher or teacher), gave consent for the children to take part, even if parental consent wasn't actually sought.

Problems with using the 'doll technique' to measure racial preference

We have already mentioned that Hraba and Grant questioned whether doll choice is really a valid measure of racial preference. There are also some problems associated with the form of the questions themselves. For example, question three, 'Give me the doll that looks bad', could be interpreted in a number of ways. Does the question mean the doll that looks horrible or the doll that looks naughty? If you have seen so-called 'black dolls', they are often just dolls with white features, cast in brown rather than white plastic. They may well have been judged by the child to look odd, and therefore 'bad'. If *we* have a problem working out what was meant by the question, what do you think the children thought? This raises the question that perhaps some of the results may have been due to the children responding to demand characteristics and trying to work out what the experimenters wanted them to say.

An interesting finding is that in 1939, Clark and Clark recorded only 76% of their sample as giving an answer to question three on the doll that 'looks bad', and in 1969, Hraba and Grant record six children giving no answer or a 'don't know' response to this question. Possibly this was because of the ambiguity of the question.

Another issue is that with whites still dominant in US culture in 1969, and 'white' being used as a description of someone 'with the absence of colour' (a prejudiced view, of course) it may be that the question, 'Give me the doll that is a nice colour' was influenced by the fact that some children may not have seen white as a colour and therefore only picked from between the two 'coloured' dolls. We can't be sure.

The doll technique uses a 'forced choice technique': the child is expected to choose one of the dolls as an answer. The problem is that the questions suggest there is an answer, that is, that one of the dolls does look bad, nice, etc., in comparison to the others. Even if the child doesn't see a difference themselves, they may feel forced to choose one of the dolls as a 'guess', to please the experimenter.

Only choosing one of the dolls means that there are no half measures, and so the attitude that is expressed by the choice of doll may appear to be much more strongly held than it really is. After all, it doesn't give subjects the chance to say, 'I'll choose this one, but I really like that one too and tomorrow I might change my mind'. This method, therefore, doesn't give any indication of the strength of the attitude held.

What if a different sample had been used?

To test the idea that interracial contact would have an effect on black children's racial preferences, the sample used was appropriate. Black children were in the minority, however, and this may explain the fact that they had white friends, even though they preferred black dolls.

What might have been observed if the study had been carried out in schools where the children were mostly black? Or where there was an even mix of white and black children? Do you think this would have affected the results?

● **Key questions**

1. Explain why Hraba and Grant controlled for the race of the interviewer.
2. Question eight measured 'racial self-awareness or racial self-identification'. What would the child's answer to this question tell the researchers?
3. Why did the researchers ask the children about the colour of their best friends?
4. Give two reasons why the study can be considered to be low in ecological validity.
5. Is the study useful?

Example Answers are on page 460.

● **Further reading**

Hinton, P.R. (2000), *Stereotypes, Cognition and Culture*, Hove: Psychology Press.

What is abnormality?

Has it ever worried you how psychiatrists and psychologists determine whether someone is abnormal? After all, most of us, at some time or other, go through stages of being a bit weird, don't we? But where do we draw the line between weird and actually 'abnormal', and if we are abnormal, does that mean we are mentally ill?

One thing that can change our behaviour quite dramatically is the run-up to impending exams. Have you suddenly discovered how housework takes on new meaning? Bedrooms suddenly get tidied, and even the washing-up seems a better prospect than getting your head down to some really serious work. Isn't this sudden fascination with housework some kind of weird, abnormal behaviour? Then, as the exam gets closer, you feel more and more stressed and unhappy, and instead of being your normal, happy-go-lucky self, you become totally antisocial and very quiet. We could say that your behaviour has showed 'substantial change' but does that mean you have actually become 'abnormal'? Well, maybe it is abnormal for you, but there is a reason for it, and surely that makes a difference? It is no more than a kind of temporary abnormality, because as soon as the exams are over, you will revert back to your normal self.

'Simon's gone loopy. Look at him. What on earth is he doing running up and down the high street at ten o'clock on a Saturday night with only a pair of boxers on?'
   'It's the beer, mate!'

Is Simon abnormal? No, he's probably just happy, and that, plus the alcohol, which will have removed some of his inhibitions, has resulted in his decision to run around in his underpants!

You can see that the label abnormal is not quite as clear-cut as it seemed earlier, and cannot simply be assessed by looking at the way someone is behaving. We have to take into account how the person has been over a period of time. We need to consider the situation they are in and whether there is a reason for the way they are behaving. Finally, we ought to take into account whether there is any kind of drug involved, which may have been a cause of their behaviour.

DEFINING ABNORMALITY

There have been a number of attempts to try to find a way of differentiating the normal from the abnormal. The problem is that none of them is really satisfactory.

Statistics

We could begin to look at abnormality by considering some kind of statistical formula, which would help us define who is and who isn't abnormal. If you remember, Galton showed that when we measure large numbers of people the data will fall into a normal distribution curve. Perhaps we could consider the people who, when measured, are statistically rare and fall at either end of the distribution curve as the ones who are abnormal. Take, for example, people who have very low IQs or very high IQs, and who could certainly be considered abnormal. People with very low IQs may actually need some support to help them deal with life and look after themselves, but what about the ones with very high IQs? We are far more likely to see them as lucky rather than abnormal in any way. Other measures of personality or mood state could be used in the same way, but being very happy rather than very miserable, again, could be considered lucky rather than abnormal. Therefore, being statistically rare doesn't actually help when we are trying to work out what we mean by abnormal (in terms of mental illness).

Non-conformity

An alternative way to consider how we define abnormality is to look at whether people's behaviour conforms to what society expects. Have you ever been in the company of someone who has started behaving in a bizarre way (perhaps due to alcohol), or who stands too close to others, or makes personal comments about other people? The chances are you found it quite embarrassing and wanted to remove yourself from the situation. If someone's behaviour makes another person uncomfortable, then perhaps they are abnormal, but it must depend on the audience. After all, not everyone feels uncomfortable about the same things, so it seems the definition here is very much to do with the people watching, rather than the person doing the actions.

Social control

> **FOCUS ON THEMES** – social control
>
> Perhaps abnormality doesn't actually exist, so the concept is no more than a means of social control. When we mentioned Simon's bizarre behaviour on a Saturday night, we realised that he was behaving in only a slightly abnormal way, because it was Saturday and he had been out drinking. What would happen if unusual behaviour wasn't seen in context? Supposing someone behaved in a way that was seen as a weird or unacceptable and this was enough to have him confined and labelled as being mentally ill? How would he convince people that he wasn't actually mad?

The following story was written by a patient at a psychiatric hospital. If you read it, it will make you realise that by labelling someone as abnormal, just because they don't behave in the same way as everyone else, has enormous ethical implications.

Once upon a time, there was a happy man called Joe Odd. He lived in a little hut on the side of a hill with his dog and from his window he could see right into the distance. Around the hut was a beautiful garden where he grew flowers and vegetables and lots of lupins because lupins were his favourite flowers.

On weekdays he went to work in the valley where all the people lived in little boxes all looking just the same, but afterwards he could go home to his little hut and watch the sunset. The people who lived in the boxes thought Joe was very strange because they all watched television. At first they said, 'Why don't you live in a box like us?' So they broke his windows and made up bad stories about him and the police said he was causing a breach of the peace…'Ain't Joe weird – I bet he's queer…or maybe into little boys…yeah, a child molester.'

'And he hates everyone…he's dangerous…let's get him.'

So Joe locked his door and barred his windows and was afraid to go out. The garden became overgrown with weeds. Only his dog stayed by his side. One day a man came to the hut and said, 'Mr Odd, this hut is unhealthy because there is no bathroom, so we are going to pull it down, but we cannot rehouse you because you do not meet the requirements.'

Joe wandered from place to place and stole bottles of milk from doorsteps. One day the police caught him and a social worker came to take his dog to the R.S.P.C.A. Joe was so upset that he hit the social worker…so she said he could not be in his right mind and would have to be assessed. They sent Joe to mental hospital where the doctor examined him and asked him lots of questions about his childhood and his bowel movements…then wrote on some labels and hung them round his neck. Then another social worker wrote a report about how Joe had lived in a hut with the doors and windows barred. So the doctor hung another label round his neck saying 'PERSECUTION COMPLEX'…and gave him some pills to make him feel better. Joe didn't like the pills because they made him feel strange and he wouldn't take them, so the doctor hung an 'UNCO-OPERATIVE' label round his neck and gave him an injection instead.

Every week the doctor asked him lots of questions to find out what was wrong with him, but Joe didn't answer anymore, so he hung an 'UNCOM-MUNICATIVE' label round his neck as well. After a long time they told Joe he was better and they found him a regulation box to live in under the rehabilitation scheme. Joe lived in his little box and from his window he could see lots of other boxes, all looking just the same.

The welfare workers told him he was coping very well, but sometimes Joe still had a feeling he wanted to hit people, only he couldn't remember why he felt like that, because the pills made his head feel sleepy. The social worker looked at Joe's labels and told him that this was all part of his illness and that it might take a long time before he felt really better. One night he thought he heard a voice in his head saying, 'Come with me…I know a beautiful place…come with me.' 'I can't. I am very ill. Can't you see all those labels round my neck?' 'Take them off, Joe,' said the voice again and again and again.

At last Joe lifted the labels from around his neck and threw them away. He was surprised how easy it was, and his head felt so much lighter. He opened the door and followed the voice. He walked for miles and miles and came to a beautiful place with lots of other odd people. He grew some more lupins and played music and painted pictures and flew in balloons, and he brought a cat who followed him everywhere, and everybody there loved Joe. Then one day the people in the boxes found out where he was and said he would have to come back because he was very ill.

A fleet of police cars and ambulances came after him with sirens screaming and Joe ran along the beach into the waves to escape the noise for ever and ever and ever…

Can you see how abnormality is actually quite a frightening concept, because it implies that there is some kind of 'normal' way of behaving, and if we don't fit into that, we can be removed rather than cause our society any sort of discomfort?

Although this is a story, the situation can actually become more serious when people who aren't willing to conform to the behaviour that society expects, like political objectors, are made to conform by being removed and locked up under the pretext that they are abnormal and therefore mentally ill.

This 'social control hypothesis' has been used to help to explain some of the worst cases of psychiatric abuse. In his book *The Gulag Archipelago*, Alexander Solzhenitsyn wrote about the chain of prison camps stretching across the Soviet Union, which were full of people who wouldn't conform to rules and regulations they believed were wrong. The frightening thing is that these situations continue today, for example, in areas where non-democratic governments are trying to maintain control. Another example comes with Japan's drive for industrial success. 'Bins' (as in loony-bins) are used to 'dump' those who are unwilling to conform to the demands of industry. Therefore, in order to instil the appropriate terror, the 'bins' must be sufficiently unattractive. In fact, conditions in Japanese mental hospitals are similar to the old Victorian asylums in the UK, being overcrowded, dirty and often brutal in their discipline. Between 1955 and 1990, the number of in-patients in Japanese mental hospitals increased from 100,000 to around 400,000.

Abnormality as coping

Abnormal behaviour could be seen as no more than a way of coping with life. Gary Craven related the following story when he gave an A level revision lecture in London on relationships. He told the story of a man who found a very bizarre way of coping with a problem he had. Below is a version of the story he told.

Edward wasn't unattractive. In fact, he was quite a good-looking man, but there was something rather strange about him. He explained at a self-help group, when all the students were sitting round in a circle, getting to know each other, that his great interest in life was lifts. He proceeded to fascinate everyone with tales of the lifts he had visited all over the world. Initially he thrilled them with stories of the speed of lifts in New York, which rose 60 storeys in a matter of seconds. He filled them with terror when he related stories of the older lifts in Russia, which creaked and groaned and stopped and started as they slowly slid up the shafts. However, half an hour later, they were all semi-comatose.

Then came the time to talk about his experiences with women. When he began to explain that he had never had much luck with members of the opposite sex, suddenly the people became more interested again. He told them how, every time he started talking to a woman, she seemed to move away from him. Suddenly his eyes lit up. 'But I have noticed that when I am in a lift, it is much better. They seem to talk to me there and I get on so well with them, but then the minute the lift doors open, they disappear.'

Edward had no concept of personal distance, and just stood too close to whoever he was talking to. Most of the time, people made their excuses and left, but in a lift, he had a captive audience – there was nowhere to go!

Edward may well have been raised in another culture where people's need for personal space is very different to that of our culture. He therefore had no idea that there was anything unusual about his behaviour, but he *was* aware that people didn't seem to like him very much. As a way of coping with this situation, he simply adjusted his behaviour until he found a way to make people talk to him. Not understanding the underlying reasons, but having found himself a reasonable solution, his behaviour had become quite abnormal.

A much more simple example of how abnormal behaviour is simply a coping strategy can be seen in people who are fanatical about tidiness, to the extent that every little thing has to be in its place. This fanaticism can become obsessive and can take over their lives. In order to understand the reasons for this we need to look at the rest of the person's life. It may be that they have no confidence in themselves and feel inadequate, so they can only just cope with work and their other responsibilities. Extra problems or burdens would just become too much for them, so in order not to make things more stressful they need to be sure that their home life or office is totally ordered and organised.

The final kind of abnormality I want to mention here is multiple personality disorder. This mechanism of splitting the personality into a number of sub-personalities is really the ultimate form of coping. Here, part of the personality may then deal with specific situations, thereby protecting other parts from harmful situations, such as abuse. You will read about it in the next section, which focuses on multiple personality.

CULTURAL RELATIVITY

By now you will have realised that defining abnormality is going to be extremely difficult, if not impossible. It seems that there is no one thing that allows us to say, without hesitation, this is what we mean by abnormality. If we try to take abnormality as a theoretical concept first and foremost, we should perhaps see if the people who are considered abnormal all share the same features. However, even this doesn't seem to work, because what is considered abnormal in one culture is seen as perfectly normal in another.

At the beginning of the chapter, we mentioned the work of Malinowski and remarked on how the behaviour he described was, to us, very strange and somewhat abnormal. In fact, many practitioners in the Western world assume that the behaviours of the white population are normal and therefore any deviation from this normality by another ethnic group shows some racial or cultural pathology. It should be obvious that what is normal behaviour for that person can only really be judged in relation to the patient's background and culture. The trouble is that because this is not always understood. In Britian, West Indian men are more likely to be admitted to psychiatric hospitals, and psychotic black patients are twice as likely as whites or white immigrants to be in hospital involuntarily. Black patients are more often seen by a junior rather than a senior doctor and, even when they are diagnosed with the same disorder as a white person, are more likely to be given more radical treatments (Littlewood and Lipsedge, 1989). It is also well known that in America, more black people than white are diagnosed as being schizophrenic every year.

THE FEATURES OF ABNORMALITY

Rosenhan and Seligman (1989) tried to get round the problems of identifying what is meant by abnormality. They suggested that if we identify the major features that are more likely to be found in abnormal individuals, we could do a kind of tally – the more you have, the more abnormal you are – and the more abnormal you are, the more likely it is to do with mental illness! They came up with seven features that are based on statistical rarity and social deviance.

1 Suffering

Suffering is often seen amongst people who are mentally ill. The problem here is that some people have no concept of suffering, for example, people with psychopathic personality disorders, and many normal people suffer when they lose someone they love, for example.

2 Maladaptiveness

If someone suffers from maladaptive behaviour, it means that their behaviours are not the sort of behaviours which will allow them to have a fulfilling life because they will probably prevent them from achieving success or happiness. An example of a maladaptive behaviour is when someone has an irrational fear or phobia about something, for example flying, and can't go anywhere or do anything where that behaviour may be necessary.

3 Vividness and unconventionality

This refers to behaviour that is very obviously unusual or unconventional. The trouble is there are always unconventional people who are just eccentric rather than mentally ill.

4 Unpredictability and loss of control

Think back to Simon and his escapade in his boxer shorts. His behaviour was certainly unpredictable. However, most of us are relatively predictable and our behaviour is reasonably well controlled most of the time. Therefore, is this a good measure of abnormality and mental illness?

365

5 Irrationality and Incomprehensibility

Pre-menstrual tension sometimes causes women to behave in an abnormal and incomprehensible way – at least, it probably seems like that to the male members of society. Once the reason for the behaviour is explained however, it no longer seems quite so irrational and incomprehensible. Therefore we have to be careful when judging someone's behaviour as being irrational, because we can never be sure that their behaviour doesn't have a good cause.

6 Observer discomfort

Think of Edward and his lack of understanding of acceptable interpersonal distance. Our social behaviour is governed by a set of rules that we seem to learn but are never actually taught. We learn them as we grow up by monitoring other people's responses to our behaviours. When the rules are broken by another person, we generally become very uncomfortable. This will affect how we feel about that person and whether or not we want to go on associating with them – we find it hard to deal with someone whose behaviour is abnormal, compared with the normal rules of our society.

7 Violation of moral and ideal standards

If a woman works as a prostitute, this is likely to be considered a transgression of the accepted moral standards of our society. The reasons for her decision are not taken into account and she is likely to be judged purely on the basis that earning money in this way is not considered morally acceptable or an ideal method of earning a living.

These seven features do not actually help us a great deal because most of them can be explained in a number of different ways. Although they could be adapted to fit into different cultures, they also involve an element of subjectivity, because it would depend very much on the perception of the person doing the judging. One of us may see behaviour as vivid and unconventional, whereas another person may see it as perfectly normal!

Abnormality as a useful concept

There are times when labelling someone as 'abnormal' can be positive. If we have a person who is extremely distressed and unhappy, and their pattern of behaviour is similar to that of others, then we may well have some idea of the best way of supporting them. Taking a less extreme example, someone who has learning difficulties with literacy, who is diagnosed as dyslexic, may feel a tremendous sense of relief, because that 'label' will have explained their difficulty without suggesting that it is just because they are 'thick'.

It has been recognised that there are lots of different types of abnormality, and each one seems to have a number of common features. Although there is a danger in trying to put people into categories and labelling them accordingly, if they are categorised as carefully and accurately as possible, it means that medical professionals don't have to spend ages trying to work out what is going on for each individual person and can perhaps help them that much more quickly. After all, we know that someone with depression, for example, will have a whole list of symptoms which are likely to follow on, such as problems with sleeping. These problems could be addressed without having to wait to see how the course of the disorder progresses.

What happens when the categorisation is wrong, especially when the person may well have been labelled and treated accordingly by medical professionals. Unfortunately, many of the labels of mental disorders automatically mean that they will be stereotyped, and this will impact on the way they are treated. Take the case of schizophrenia. Many people would describe a schizophrenic as someone who has a split personality, and they would come up with all sorts of behaviours that they might expect to be associated with that categorisation. Well, they would be wrong, because schizophrenia is a kind of *disorganised* personality, not a split personality. Split personality is known as 'multiple personality disorder' (MPD) also know as 'dissociative identity disorder' (DID), which you will read about in the next section. Many diagnosed schizophrenics who are receiving treatment have no symptoms at all. So what is the answer?

CLASSIFICATORY SYSTEMS

There are two classificatory systems which are used to identify mental disorders, but they both owe much to the work of Emil Kraepelin (1856–1926). He suggested that groups of symptoms seem to occur together on a regular basis. This meant that these groups of symptoms (syndromes) could perhaps be classed as diseases. He also believed that they had a biological basis and should be treated in the same way as any other illness. He suggested (1896) that there were two groups of serious mental illness: 'dementia praecox' (later called schizophrenia) and 'manic-depressive psychosis'. If nothing else, he must be acknowledged for recognising that many mental disorders had a biological basis rather than being caused by external factors such as evil spirits or possession by demons.

The International List of Causes of Death was originally compiled by the World Health Organisation as a way of monitoring causes of death throughout the world. In 1939, they added mental disorders to the list, and in 1948, the list expanded further and became known as the International Classification of Diseases (ICD). However, the mental disorders section was not widely accepted and was superseded by the DSM (see below). The current version is the ICD-10, which focuses on descriptions which are grouped according to similarities and differences in signs and symptoms rather than looking at the other aspects of people's functioning in their everyday lives. As some of the signs and symptoms appear in a number of disorders, this makes its use inadequate for psychiatrists.

The Diagnostic and Statistical Manual of Mental Disorders (DSM) was first published in 1952 by the American Psychiatric Association, in response to the ICD. The current version is the DSM IV (1994), and it differs from the ICD because it has a greater number of discrete categories. It also looks at the influence of outside factors on a person as part of the diagnosis. This is obviously much more valid, because the life experiences of a person are very likely to contribute to any kind of disorder.

The DSM consists of five axes or dimensions, which are not only used as a diagnostic tool, but also help with the planning of treatment and prediction of outcomes. Each person is assessed on every axis to give a much broader picture of what is going on in their lives, which is extremely important if we are to give a fair diagnosis.

Clearly, the whole topic of abnormality is one fraught with problems. There are so many issues that need to be considered before we risk planting some kind of label on a person, which may well be with them for the rest of their lives. Schizophrenia, for example, is an incurable illness. If someone is diagnosed, they will only ever become a schizophrenic in remission. Therefore, we can't risk making a mistake.

The key study in this area emphasises just how easy it is to make mistakes when diagnosing mental illness, and how, once someone has been labelled, all their behaviours are seen in a different perspective. If we can't tell the sane from the insane, then it doesn't leave us with much hope. At least the diagnostic criteria used today are far more sophisticated than they were at the time of the key study, which was carried out in 1973. The DSM II was in use at the time, and this second version didn't have the five axes, but much more simplistic diagnostic labels. Therefore, the system we now use for categorisation, we hope, is much less likely to be abused than it was in the past.

D. L. Rosenhan (1973), 'On being sane in insane places',
Science, 179, 250–58

Background

David Rosenhan was one of a number of academics in the 1970s who were concerned about the validity and reliability of psychiatric diagnoses. The system being used by psychiatrists at the time of this study was DSM II. Rosenhan was concerned that the diagnosis was not objective: 'it is commonplace... to read about murder trials where eminent psychiatrists for the defense are contradicted by equally eminent psychiatrists for the prosecution on the matter of the defendant's sanity' (p. 250). In other words, the same symptoms reported by a patient could be interpreted in different ways by different psychiatrists. This, of course, brings the reliability of the diagnostic system into question.

Rosenhan also points out that 'what is viewed as normal in one culture may be seen as quite aberrant in another', and again, this challenges the idea that there is an objective and universal notion of what normality and abnormality actually are.

Rosenhan was not suggesting that odd and deviant behaviour, and the distress it brings to those experiencing it or to those around them, does not exist. He was, however, at issue with the way such behaviour was described and categorised by the system. He wanted to investigate whether the diagnoses given to patients came from symptoms being displayed by the patient themselves or whether their behaviours were being described as abnormal because they were in a psychiatric setting?

CORE STUDY LINK – when we were looking at the prison simulation study by Haney, Banks and Zimbardo (1973) (p. 63), we said that the study was aiming to test the dispositional hypothesis, in other words, to test whether it was the dispositions or character traits of the individuals who were in prison or who worked in prisons, which made prisons brutal places, or whether the brutality was created by the way prisons were organised.

Zimbardo *et al.* came to the conclusion in their study that the best explanation of prison brutality was a situational one, that the brutality was caused by the way prison life was structured, including social roles, and the consequent psychological effects on those working and being held in prisons.

FOCUS ON THEMES – individual versus situational explanations of behaviour

Rosenhan's study considers a similar question to Zimbardo *et al.*'s. Is all the behaviour of patients on psychiatric wards described as abnormal because it is seen a symptom of the individual's illness? Do the hospital staff identify behaviour which is a normal response to being in a psychiatric unit as 'abnormal' and evidence of the person's illness?

He asks, 'do the salient characteristics that lead to diagnoses reside in patients themselves or in the environments in which observers find them?' (p. 251).

In other words, is the diagnosis of mental illness flawed because, once on the ward, the person is seen as abnormal and all their behaviours are judged in this context? Rosenhan's study suggests that the descriptions of patients' behaviour were individual when they should be situational.

This relates to a social psychological concept known as the *fundamental attribution error*. When we are attributing causes to someone's behaviour, we are biased towards the view that they are doing something 'because they are like that', that what we are seeing them do is what they would always do in a similar situation. What we are doing here is making two mistakes. We are ignoring the situational factors which influence behaviour and we are assuming that people are consistent in their behaviour, which often they are not.

Another related attributional bias is the 'actor–observer effect'. This suggests that the fundamental attribution error occurs when we are describing the behaviour of someone else (when we are the observer), but when we are describing our own behaviour (when we are the actor), we tend to describe our behaviour in terms of the situation we were in at the time, rather than in terms of our persistent characteristics. This leads to a further bias, called the self-serving bias. Here we tend to attribute the cause that leads us to being seen in the best light and allows us to preserve our self-esteem. For example, if you got an A in your AS psychology, you may say, 'I am a hard-working and fantastic student and my success is evidence of my brilliance' (an internal attribution), but if you got a U, you might say, 'The textbook was rubbish, so how could I have been expected to pass?' (a situational attribution).

Aim

The aim of Rosenhan's study was twofold. First, he aimed to test the diagnostic system to see if it was valid and reliable. He decided to do this by getting himself and seven others admitted to psychiatric hospitals to see if and how they would be discovered to be 'sane'.

Once on the ward, would the behaviour of these 'pseudopatients' be considered normal, and not lead to a psychiatric diagnosis, or would their behaviour be considered 'abnormal' because of the context they were in? If the former were true, then there would be evidence that the diagnostic system was valid and reliable. If, however, the latter were true, and the pseudopatients were not detected, then given that

• the hospital staff were not incompetent

- the pseudopatient behaved as normally in the hospital as outside it
- it had never previously been suggested that the pseudopatient belonged in a psychiatric hospital

then the fact that the psuedopatients were not detected would 'support the view that psychiatric diagnosis betrays little about the patient but much about the environment in which an observer finds him' (p. 251).

The second aim of the study was to observe and report on the experience of being a patient in a psychiatric hospital. There was little objective evidence on this as doctors did not follow up patients who were discharged, and even if they did, such data might be too subjective (and Rosenhan suggests it might be considered unreliable, as the person was previously considered insane). Researchers had acted as patients in previous studies, but the findings of these may not be valid, since the hospital staff were aware of their presence and may not have treated them like real patients. What would the pseudopatients experience and observe on the psychiatric ward?

Investigating the first aim: could hospital staff identify the pseudopatients as being 'normal'?

Method

Design

The admission of the pseudopatients to the hospitals was studied as a field experiment.

Subjects

The subjects were the hospital staff and patients in 12 hospitals in the USA.

To get a representative sample, the hospitals were in five different states, from the east and west coasts; some were old and shabby, some were quite new; some had good staff-patient ratios, some had not; one was private, the others were federal or state funded, with one university-funded; some carried out research, some did not.

Procedure

The pseudopatients were eight 'normal' people (five men and three women), and Rosenhan himself was one of them, and the first to gain admission to a hospital. Apart from a psychology graduate in his twenties, all were older and 'established' in their jobs/roles: three psychologists, a paediatrician, a psychiatrist, a painter and a housewife. All used fake names to protect their health records in the future, and the subjects who were working in the health service pretended they were in other occupations, to avoid the 'special attentions' that might be given to people from the health professions.

To gain admission, the pseudopatients were to self-present, or self-refer. They phoned the hospitals for an appointment, and on arrival complained that they had been hearing voices which were unfamiliar, of the same sex and said 'empty', 'hollow', and 'thud'. Any other information given by the subjects was completely honest, including details of their family and personal background and recent life experiences. (Note: there had originally been nine pseudopatients, but data from one was omitted from the results because he falsified his personal history.)

These symptoms were chosen because they simulated existential symptoms which come from the realisation that life is really meaningless and so, as moral free agents, we have to create our own values through our actions and accept the responsibility for those actions – we can't blame our lives on anyone else. This 'What's it all for?' experience is often distressing. Also, there are no reports of existential psychosis in any literature on mental illness, and therefore, it was thought that, although auditory hallucinations are a classic feature of schizophrenia, this would make the diagnosis harder to recognise.

(Schizophrenia = a psychiatric disorder which results in the patient suffering from a disorganised personality. They are likely to experience hallucinations, usually auditory, and delusions of grandeur or delusions of persecution.)

As soon as they were admitted to the ward, the pseudopatients ceased simulating any symptoms and aimed to behave as normally as possible, which they were able to do after the 'short-lived nervousness' they had experienced on admission faded away. This nervousness was caused either by the fact that they were admitted so easily and were fearful of being spotted as frauds straightaway and embarrassed, or, for those who had never been on a psychiatric ward, the novelty of the setting.

Results

All the pseudopatients were admitted to the hospitals, where they remained for between seven and 52 days (mean length of stay, 19 days). Of the 12 admissions (some pseudopatients sought admission to more than one hospital), 11 were diagnosed with schizophrenia and one, with identical symptoms, of course, with manic-depressive psychosis. This has a more favourable prognosis (more likely to get better), and it is interesting that this was the diagnosis from the only private hospital in the sample! When those diagnosed as schizophrenic were finally discharged, it was with the diagnosis of schizophrenia in remission. Therefore, none of the pseudopatients was detected as a fake. This was a clear failure in the diagnostic system and it was observed in all 12 hospitals in the sample.

To say they were not detected means that they were not detected by the *staff* in the hospitals. The patients, however, had their suspicions. In the first three hospitalisations, clear records of patient responses were made, with 35 of a total of 118 patients voicing their suspicions. They said things such as, 'You're not crazy. You're a journalist, or a professor [referring to the continual note-taking]. You're checking up on the hospital'. Most patients, however, were reassured by the pseudopatients' claims to have been sick before admission and fine now, but some held the view throughout that the pseudopatients were not 'real' patients. Why did the psychiatrists misdiagnose the pseudopatients? In general medicine, Rosenhan points out, it is better to err on the side of caution and risk diagnosing a healthy person as sick rather than to 'miss' an illness.

This may have been why the pseudopatients were given the misdiagnosis in the study – the doctors were being cautious. In cases where the diagnosis is not clear, this makes sense in general medicine, but in psychiatry this is altogether a different issue. If a healthy person is diagnosed as having a psychiatric disorder, this leaves them permanently stigmatised.

If staff mistook fake patients for real ones, would it also be possible that the opposite would occur, and that they would identify real patients as fake ones? A follow-up study was carried out to test this.

Follow-up study

Rosenhan told the staff at a large hospital, who had heard about the first part of the study and doubted that they would not be able to spot psuedopatients, that some time during the next three months, one or more pseudopatients would attempt to gain admittance to the hospital.

Each member of staff was asked to rate on a ten-point scale the likelihood of the patients who appeared being pseudopatients. Out of 193 patients who attended for psychiatric treatment, 41 were confidently judged to be pseudopatients by at least one member of staff, 23 patients were suspected by at least one psychiatrist and 19 were thought to be acting by one psychiatrist and one other member of staff. In fact, the 193 patients were all genuine patients, as Rosenhan had sent along no pseudopatients. The hospital staff had been judging regular patients.

Rosenhan's conclusions

The fact that the pseudopatients were not detected and were each given a psychiatric diagnosis indicates that psychiatric diagnosis is not always valid. Rosenhan's claim that 'we cannot distinguish the sane from the insane in psychiatric hospitals' is actually given considerable support.

In the follow-up study, the finding that approximately 10% of their normal clients were judged as pseudopatients by two staff members, including a psychiatrist, led Rosenhan to conclude that 'any diagnostic process that lends itself so readily to massive errors of this sort cannot be a very reliable one' (p. 252).

Rosenhan describes what he calls 'the stickiness of psychodiagnostic labels'. He says, 'Having once been labelled schizophrenic, there is nothing the psuedopatient can do to overcome the tag. The tag profoundly colours others' perceptions of him and his behaviour' (p. 253).

In the next section, we shall see how the behaviours demonstrated by and information given by the pseudopatients was interpreted according to their diagnoses.

Investigating the second aim: the experience of psychiatric hospitalisation

Method

Design

Participant observation was used to observe the behaviour of real patients and the hospital staff to record the experiences of psychiatric patients. Pseudopatients also kept a diary and made notes to record their experiences and observations. This was a field study.

Subjects

The subjects were the hospital staff, the real patients and the pseudopatients themselves.

Procedure

Once admitted, the task of the pseudopatients was to behave as normally as they did outside the hospital (where no one had ever suggested they needed to be in a psychiatric hospital!).

The pseudopatients observed and made notes about their experiences, quite openly in front of staff and other patients.

Results

What was the pseudopatients' reaction to their experience?

The pseudopatients found the whole experience extremely unpleasant, not from associating with the patients but because of their experiences with staff. It was found that there were instances of serious physical abuse to patients. Rosenhan reports having watched a patient being beaten by an attendant for going up to him and saying, 'I like you'.

Acts of violence tended to go unchallenged. Verbal abuse was also recorded. Morning attendants would often wake patients with, 'Come on, you m—f—s, out of bed!' (p. 256). Patients' privacy was minimal and the patients suffered loss of power and depersonalisation. They felt as if they were invisible, or unworthy of account, and this threatened their sense of identity.

The pseudopatients' note-taking behaviour

Although they had been concerned that their constant note-taking would be challenged or prevented and had made elaborate arrangements to remove their notes from the wards each day for fear of confiscation, these precautions proved needless.

None of the staff asked them what the notes were, but simply assumed the behaviour was part of their illness. For example, in one case, the comment, 'Patient engages in writing behaviour' was inserted in the daily case notes, as if this were some bizarre and unexplainable symptom of the patient's 'illness'. On another occasion, a patient making notes was told gently by the doctor, 'You needn't write it… If you have trouble remembering, just ask me again.' This shows us how the label given to the patient, their diagnosis, affected the way the doctors and staff perceived their behaviour.

That the note-taking was observably 'normal' for someone studying the hospital was expressed by the real patients, many of whom suspected that the pseudopatients were checking up on the hospital. This did not seem to have occurred to any of the members of staff.

Further examples of how labelling affected the staff's description of the patients and pseudopatients

Anyone who has been in hospital will know that it can be very boring. You soon adapt yourself to getting through the day by moving from one routine activity to another, and mealtimes provide a way to structure the day. You find yourself looking forward to the three o'clock tea trolley for your cup of tea and custard cream. On one occasion, patients waiting outside the cafeteria for lunch were observed by a doctor in the case notes to be displaying the 'oral-acquisitive nature of the syndrome'. Rosenhan comments, 'It seemed not to occur to him [the doctor] that there are very few things to anticipate in a psychiatric hospital besides eating' (p. 253).

Another example of the staff failing to recognise the situational impact on behaviour was noted when one of the pseudopatients was pacing the long hospital corridors. A kindly nurse approached him and asked, 'Nervous, Mr X?' 'No, bored', he said. The nurse assumed that his pacing was a symptom of his disorder rather than his response to the unstimulating and monotonous environment in which she was observing him.

One pseudopatient talked about his upbringing and family, which seemed a typical example of how we experience changes in relationships with our parents as we get older. Sometimes we are closer to one parent at a young age, but when we reach adolescence, we find that we have become closer to the other. This may be due to one of our parents finding it harder to relate to small children, but enjoying a new found closeness as the child matures. Similarly with marital relationships, which do not always run smoothly. Occasionally, minor rows had developed, which were relatively meaningless. He also reported that his children had rarely been spanked. There seems nothing unusual about this history. However, the case notes talked about him having 'a long history of considerable ambivalence in close relationships, which begins in early childhood'. The notes continue by saying that his relationship with his father changes from being distant to 'becoming very intense. Affective stability is absent.' This last sentence means that his feelings have no stability – implying he has emotional swings. The report goes on to describe the fact that his efforts to 'control emotionality with his wife and children are punctuated by angry outbursts and, in the case of the children, spankings'. The report has clearly been distorted by the diagnosis to fit in 'with a popular theory of a schizophrenic reaction' (p. 253).

If a patient went 'berserk' because he had been intentionally or unintentionally mistreated by an attendant, a nurse coming along would not inquire as to what had happened to lead to the outburst. It seemed not to be an option that the behaviour was a result of immediate environmental factors impacting on the patient, or anything to do with the staff or the hospital. Instead, his behaviour was seen as being due to his illness or perhaps his having been upset by a family visit (especially if they had visited recently).

Medication

Rosenhan reports that 2,100 pills were handed out to the pseudopatients during their stays in the hospitals, although all but two were pocketed or flushed down the toilet. The pseudopatients often found the medication of other patients down the toilet before flushing their own. As long as the behaviour of the patients was acceptable whilst on the wards, such actions were not noticed.

Staff contact

The staff tended to keep themselves away from the patients except for administrative or practical duties. The doctors were even more remote than the nurses, and seemed to maintain the greatest distance, only seen by patients when they came onto the ward to start their shift and again when they departed, with the time they were on duty being spent in the 'staff cage' or in their offices. Patients spent on average, under seven minutes a day with senior members of staff over the course of their stay. Surely it should have been the other way round, with these senior members of staff who wield the most power being the most familiar with the patients' case histories and behaviours?

The physicians acted as models for those lower down the staff hierarchy. The attendants were the staff on the ward who had least power and were the ones likely to spend most time with the patients. However, they tended to take their lead from the physicians, and avoided contact with patients by spending most of their time in the staff cage.

Two key psychological factors were observed to be affecting the patients (and the pseudopatients): powerlessness and depersonalisation

The pseudopatients reported on the patients' complete lack of power in the psychiatric wards. Their movements were watched and restricted, they had virtually no contact with staff and their medical files were available to all members of staff, even volunteers.

Acts of violence against patients were observed by other patients, some of whom were pseudopatients writing it all down. The abusive behaviour immediately stopped when another member of staff appeared. The fact that staff were considered credible witnesses and patients were not is an indication of the patients' lack of power.

We have already noted that those with the most power (the physicians) spent least time with the patients, and that attendants spent most of their time in the cage, where the power within the ward was based. The fact that staff went about their business as if the patients were not there, and that the ward staff spent as little time on the ward with the patients as possible, added to the invisibility felt by the pseudopatients.

The patients also suffered from a minimum of personal privacy. For example, physical examinations carried out prior to admission were conducted in semi-public rooms where 'staff went about their own business as if we were not there' (p. 256). Once on the ward it was not unusual for toilet cubicles to have no doors and for the 'personal hygiene and waste evacuation' of the patient to be 'monitored' (p. 256).

Evidence from the study shows that patients could not initiate contact with staff, that they were expected to be passive and to respond only to any overtures initated by staff members. Rosenhan illustrates this point clearly with the findings of a study on responses to patient-initiated contact carried out at four of the hospitals. The nature of this study involved recording responses by staff to a courteous and relevant request made by the pseudopatient. This was adapted to fit the target person and the setting, but followed along the lines of, 'Pardon, me, Mr [or Dr or Mrs] X, could you tell me when I will be eligible for grounds privileges?' (or 'when will I be presented at the staff meeting?'). The request was never asked of the same staff member on any one day, to avoid irritating them or raising their suspicions, and it was neither bizarre nor disruptive. It was the initiation of a perfectly reasonable conversation.

Contact	Psychiatrists in Rosenhan's study	Nurses and attendants in Rosenhan's study
Moves on, head averted	71%	88%
Makes eye contact	23%	10%
Pauses and chats	2%	2%
Stops and talks	4%	0.5%
Number of respondents	13	47
Number of attempts	185	1283

Table showing the responses to patient-initiated contact (adapted from Rosenhan, p. 255).

As you can see from the table, the patients were pretty ineffective when it came to initiating a conversation with a staff member with a polite and relevant question. The response rate for psychiatrists was only about 7%, with the other staff being even worse, responding only about 4% of the time.

As Rosenhan points out, the time a person spends with you can be a measure of your importance to him. Lack of eye contact and lack of verbal contact indicate avoidance and depersonalisation. Given this fact, it is not surprising that the pseudopatients felt de-individuated and unworthy of account. The fact that the majority of reactions was in the 'moves on, head averted' category shows how they may have come to believe that they were 'invisible' to staff.

Rosenhan compared these findings with a similar study carried out at Stanford University. A female student asked six similar questions (for directions, about college admission and if there was financial aid) of tutors in the university faculty and the university medical centre. In the university medical centre she added a comment after her first question. To some respondents she said, 'I'm looking for an internist', and to others she said, 'I'm looking for a psychiatrist', and to yet a third group she made no additional comment; otherwise the questioning was the same. The results were as follows:

Contact	'Looking for a psychiatrist' Medical centre	'Looking for an internist' Medical centre	No additional comment Medical centre
Moves on, head averted	0%	0%	0%
Makes eye contact	11%	0%	0%
Pauses and chats	11%	0%	0%
Stops and talks	78%	100%	90%
Mean number of questions answered (out of six)	3.8	4.8	4.5
Number of respondents	18	15	10
Number of attempts	18	15	10

Table showing reponses to questions asked by a female student in the university medical centre (adapted from Rosenhan, p. 255)

The response rate was generally much higher in the university medical centre than it was for the pseudopatients on the ward. It is interesting that when the female student indicated she was 'looking for a psychiatrist', the percentage response decreased to 78%. This may indicate that people find mental illness quite hard to deal with, and were reluctant to help someone 'looking for a psychiatrist' because of the social stigma associated with mental illness.

What were the consequences of depersonalisation for the pseudopatients?

Rosenhan reports that the pseudopatients were sufficiently distressed by their experience of depersonalisation to instigate a number of attempts to re-establish and assert their identity. A graduate student in psychology asked his wife to bring in his books so he could catch up on his studies, even though this was likely to give away his true profession. Another pseudopatient tried to initiate a romantic involvement with a nurse. He then told staff he was applying to be a psychology graduate and then engaged in psychotherapy with other patients. It is clear from these examples that the pseudopatients were greatly affected by their experience, and these could be seen as attempts to reassert their individuality.

What were the sources of depersonalisation?

Rosenhan considers two sources of depersonalisation in psychiatric hospitals. First, he sees depersonalisation as a product of generally held prejudices toward the mentally ill. 'The mentally ill,' he tells us, 'are society's lepers'. We avoid contact with them at all costs. This is ingrained in the history of institutionalised care for the mentally ill, who were often locked up indefinitely and subjected to brutal treatment. Society's response was not only out of sight, out of mind, but 'if you are out of your mind it is best if you are out of our sight'. Rosenhan points out that the staff in psychiatric wards are not immune from this prejudice, and that it influences them in the hospital setting, just as it does outside the hospital on people in society at large.

The second source of depersonalisation was, according to Rosenhan, a result of the hierarchical structure where, as we have seen, doctors have all the power, patients have none, and those staff in between follow the doctors' model of avoidance of contact with patients. Rosenhan says that this does not mean that the staff were uncaring, in fact, he states, 'our overwhelming impression of them was of people who really cared, who were committed and who were uncommonly intelligent.' However, 'where they failed, as they sometimes did painfully, it would be more accurate to attribute those failures to the environment in which they, too, found themselves than to personal callousness'. In other words, the behaviour of both the staff and the patients can be attributed to situational rather than individual factors.

Other sources of depersonalisation may also be at work; where money is tight, patient contact may be first to suffer. This is facilitated by the extensive use of psychotropic drugs, which control the patients and keep them passive.

Rosenhan's conclusions

Rosenhan describes how psychiatric hospitals create environments where behaviour gets easily distorted to fit in with diagnostic labels and social prejudices.

Consequently, patients are treated in such a way as to perpetuate any problems they may have. Rosenhan suggests the need for further research into social psychology of institutions both to facilitate treatment and deepen understanding. After all, wouldn't it be better to work at changing the way we think about people in distress and try to provide the kind of social environment which would help and support them?

If patients were powerful rather than powerless, if they were viewed as interesting individuals rather than diagnostic entities, if they were socially significant rather than social lepers, if their anguish truly and wholly compelled our sympathies and concerns, would we not *seek* contact with them, despite the availability of medications?

Rosenhan, p. 257

Commentary

Is the study ecologically valid?

To the extent that the real behaviour of real patients and real staff was observed, the study is high in ecological validity. However, can we consider the reports of the pseudopatients' own feelings and responses as being the same as those of real patients? For example, the experience of the pseudopatients was different from the real patients' experience in that the pseudopatients knew that their diagnosis was false and that they were not really mentally ill. Their experience was comparable to real patients' experience in that staff were unaware of the false diagnosis of the pseudopatients and treated them the same way as they treated the other patients, and in this way their experience is a valid one.

As to whether the conclusion that there were problems with diagnosis are genuine, there are some concerns that need to be addressed. Although the pseudopatients, once they had been admitted, believed they had stopped showing any signs of abnormality, we cannot be sure that this was the case. If they were anxious and nervous, this might well have influenced their behaviour, both prior to diagnosis and after they had been admitted to the wards. This, and the novel experience of being institutionalised, or being separated from loved ones, may have meant that their behaviour appeared more unusual than they might have thought.

The study highlights the ease with which the pseudopatients were misdiagnosed. However, the doctors were not completely wrong in their diagnoses, because after a period of observation they did diagnose the pseudopatients as having schizophrenia in remission, in other words, their absence of symptoms was noted and they were discharged. Nonetheless, this does not account for their misdiagnosis in the first place.

Is the study ethical?

The ethical considerations of the study involve deception, whereby the medical practitioners were deceived by the pseudopatients in the symptoms they claimed to be experiencing. The follow-up study also raises some ethical concerns. It involved real patients being treated with undue suspicion and perhaps not receiving the care they felt they needed. This could have added to the anguish they were already experiencing, as they would not, presumably, have self-referred for psychatric care if they were not experiencing a considerable amount of distress.

The covert observation of staff and patients on the wards raises the issue that informed consent was not obtained from the subjects. They were not given the right to withdraw and they could not be debriefed. Rosenhan justifies this by pointing out that without concealment of the identities of the pseudopatients, the findings would not be valid. He says that to counteract any effects of this concealment, he ensured that the anonymity of particular hospitals and their staff would be maintained.

What about the ethics surrounding the safety of the pseudopatients? At the outset, Rosenhan says he did not realise how difficult it was to get discharged at short notice from a psychiatric ward. However, with legal advice, a writ of habeus corpus was prepared for each of the pseudopatients on entry and an attorney was kept on call. (Although usually used to compel the police to justify the continued detention of a suspect, a writ of habeus corpus, issued by a judge, would require that a person who is detaining another present the detainee in court.)

The pseudopatients reported that they did not like the experience and wanted to be discharged straightaway on admission. However, they did as they had been instructed and Rosenhan was able to report back their findings.

At least the pseudopatients had the advantage of knowing that they were not mentally ill and, unlike the real patients, would leave the powerlessness and depersonalisation of the institution behind when they left the hospital. For the real patients, who needed care, however, powerlessness and depersonalisation were part of the package. Even if they did get well enough to be discharged, the stigma of mental illness would be with them for ever.

Is the study useful?

At the time it was reported, the study highlighted problems with the diagnosis of mental illness that needed to be addressed. The current diagnostic criteria, DSM IV, is a great deal more reliable and valid than DSM II, although there is probably still room for improvement.

To gain admission to an institution now in the US is much more difficult than at the time of this study. Now the patient must:

1. be diagnosed as having a mental disorder (and diagnosis now takes longer to confirm, e.g. continuous symptoms for one–six months for schizophrenia)

2. be suffering from a disorder which could not be treated in a less restrictive environment
3. be a danger either to themselves or to others.

Because of this, Rosenhan's study would not be possible to replicate. This is, of course, a strength and not a weakness and demonstrates the impact of studies such as this one on the diagnostic system.

The study also provided evidence of the powerlessness and depersonalisation that was experienced by the patients, the lack of contact with staff, the abusive behaviour that went unchecked and the reliance on medication rather than contact with caring and supportive staff in the treatment of psychiatric patients. Nowadays, the 'total institution' approach to the care of psychiatric patients is considered the exception rather than the norm. Where possible, people are cared for in the community. However, this does not mean that there are not problems associated with such provision. Financial pressures mean that the care that is needed may not be provided. Staff may be overstretched and serve large geographical areas.

Most depressing is that the social stigma associated with psychiatric illness is no less in evidence now than it was in 1973, and integrating people with mental illness into a community that both fears and shuns them can be difficult. Education is a key factor in successful integration. If you want to know more, contact the Zito Trust. You can visit their website at: http://www.zitotrust.co.uk/

Key questions

1. How did the pseudopatients get themselves admitted to the hospitals?
2. Give two examples of how labelling distorted the interpretations staff made of the pseudopatients' behaviour.
3. Describe the sample used in the study and explain how Rosenhan tried to make it a representative sample.
4. The researchers used a covert observation technique. How else could they have investigated what the experience of being in a psychiatric ward was like? How might using this different method affect their findings?
5. What ethical issues does this study raise?

Example Answers are on page 460.

Further reading

Cave, S. (2002), *Classification and Diagnosis of Psychological Abnormality*, Routledge: London.
Stirling, J. D. and Hellewell, J.S.E. (1999), *Psychopathology*, Routledge: London.

Multiple personality

Like intelligence, personality is a concept which varies according to the theorist although we all have a pretty good idea what the concept means to us. Therefore, it is virtually impossible to give the ultimate definition of personality – suffice to say, we know that each one of us has something unique about us which separates us from others, and we tend to refer to that as our personality.

Personality can be defined as 'the distinctive and characteristic patterns of thought, emotion and behaviour that define an individual's personal style and influence his or her interactions with the environment' (Atkinson *et al.*, 1993, p. 525). This definition really captures the fact that each of us has distinctive patterns of thought, emotion and behaviour, and it is how these patterns interact that makes us what we are. It also suggests that if each one of us has these patterns, the component parts of each can be compared to those of other people.

The personality traits with which people are most familiar are those traits of introversion and extroversion. Eysenck (1947) describes an extrovert as very outgoing, liking lots of company, someone who seeks excitement and doesn't mind taking chances. On the other hand, the introvert is quiet and reserved, tends to keep his feelings to himself, prefers his own company or the company of small groups of other people and is often believed to be shy. We all fall somewhere on a continuum between the two extremes, and we could therefore use a measure of extroversion as a means to compare ourselves with others. However, even if we found someone with very similar measures on a number of different traits, it does not mean that they will be like the next person. Some of us achieve great things, while others achieve a very modest amount in our lives, and these differences seem to be as much to do with our genetic inheritance, our socio-economic class, our family experiences, our life chances and our culture as they are with the type of person we seem to be. The whole package is too closely linked to be able to extract one aspect and leave all the others behind.

Lawrence Pervin (1984) made the point that:

Personality research is not the study of perception but rather of how individuals differ in their perceptions and how these differences relate to their total functioning. The study of personality focuses not only on a particular psychological process, but also on the relationships of different processes. Understanding how these processes act together to form an integrated whole often involves more than understanding each of them separately. People function as organised wholes, and it is in the light of such organisation that we must understand them.

Pervin, 1984, p. 3

The point that Pervin is making is that we really need to look at all the processes that make up personality and how these processes fit together to make an individual. Each one of us has a childlike part of us that makes us react in an egocentric or irrational way. We all have a logical and analytical part which allows us to assess situations and make decisions. We have parts which make us sociable or insular, parts which make us jealous, parts which make us frightened, parts which make us resentful, inquisitive, compassionate and so on. Many of these parts fit in with Freud's theory of personality, whereby the id, the ego and the superego all have a role to play. Other parts don't fit so well with his theory but, nevertheless, still exist. Each one of us, therefore, is made up of lots of different characteristics in lesser or greater amounts, which, put together, make us the individuals we are. But what happens when these parts don't fit together to make a unified whole?

One of the most fascinating mental disorders is multiple personality disorder or dissociative identity disorder (DID), as it is now known. It is fascinating, partly because it is so rare and causes such bizarre behaviour, and partly because it is a disorder which has a purely psychological basis. It is not the same as schizophrenia, although the terms tend to be used interchangeably by people who don't know the difference. People who suffer from DID seem to have all the different aspects of their personality, but each part is contained in a separate unit. Pervin suggested that in a 'normal' person all these processes act together to form an integrated whole, which is what our personalities are, but it seems that in DID they don't form an integrated whole. Instead they stay as individual units, each one taking on the aspects of an individual personality, so it is as if one body contains lots and lots of different people.

Someone who suffers from DID can therefore have any number of different personalities and each split is locked into its own personal role. Each personality has its own characteristics and likes and dislikes. Each may even live its own life alongside the others, while being contained within one body. Therefore, we will have the childlike part, the sensible part, the jealous part, the fun-loving part and so on, all as individual units, which are often given different names.

In order to be diagnosed as having dissociative identity disorder, the DSM IV says the person must have at least two separate 'personalities', which they call ego states or alters, and each one must have its own way of feeling and acting that is totally independent from any of the other alters. Each one of these alters has to come forward and take control at different times. Their existence can't be temporary either – they must exist for some time and should cause the person quite a lot of disruption, rather than simply being the result for example of taking drugs or drinking too much.

People who suffer with DID are extremely likely to have gaps in their memories. If they are aware of one alter, but there are for example three, they will not know what is going on when the other two take turns of being in control. It will be as if they keep having blackouts or lapses in memory, which must be really frightening. What must be even worse is if one unrecognised alter does something and the person is unaware of it. When the second alter arrives, it will have to deal with the consequences. In fact, it could be quite embarrassing.

'Hi Jude. How do you feel after your exploits last night?'

'My exploits – what do you mean?' said Jude, looking puzzled.

'You know – after we left the pub last night.' Kathy chuckled.

'I don't know what you are talking about,' said Jude, feeling angry.

'Yeah, right. So how do you explain the garden gnomes that are sitting in your front garden?'

Jude felt a sort of icy shiver. When she went out to get in her car this morning, she wondered why there were hundreds of garden gnomes sitting on her lawn. Her mum was out, and she didn't remember seeing them the night before.

'And what about Kevin?'

'Who's Kevin?' asked Jude, still trying to work out where the gnomes had come from.

'Who's Kevin? You're joking. He's the one that ran off with your bra and put it on the statue in the High Street – you must have been well gone.'

'I er, I um, I don't know what you mean. No, I mean I *really* don't know what you are talking about.'

'So I suppose you don't remember moving that bench from outside Boots into the middle of the High Street and dancing on it with three balloons and not a lot else to cover your modesty! We were thinking of putting out a hat and collecting money from passers-by.'

Jude at this point removed herself from the conversation.

If each alter has its own memories and patterns of behaviour and relationships, then each one will act in the way it feels is appropriate. Some alters may know about others, but not all of them, and some may be unaware of the existence of any other personality. There are often primary alters and subordinate alters. The primary alters are the main personalities, which manifest most often. The subordinate alters have lesser relevance and are rarely present, or may even be undetected for some time after the disorder is recognised. Often the subordinate alters may hear the voices of the others but not be aware of who they belong to; in other instances, some of the alters may even talk to each other. Each alter will usually be very different, possibly even of the opposite sex. Some may be older than others, some may be extrovert and some introvert. Each one will have its own patterns of behaviour, its own experiences, its own memories and its own relationships with other people. It is literally like having a number of different people living in the same body, each one making their own decisions and acting out their own roles. They may even have different physical characteristics, for example, one may be left-handed, another right-handed. One may even like one type of food whilst the next may find it disgusting.

SYMPTOMS AND CAUSES OF DID

In order to understand what the disorder actually is and how it develops, we have to return to Zimbardo's study of prisoners and guards. The most influential factor on their behaviour was the role they believed they were playing. If we consider ourselves, we know our lives are made up of a number of roles and each one is played out according to the situation we find ourselves in. Supposing one of those situations is really horrific; if we can keep that role separated from the rest of our lives, it is a way of protecting us from damage. In effect, it's an abnormality which has been 'produced' as a coping mechanism.

There are, in fact, four kinds of dissociative disorders which affect the person's sense of identity, and each one may well have a very similar cause. They all result in the person becoming dissociated (or disconnected) from who they were before they developed the condition. This may be caused by 'simple amnesia' (dissociative amnesia), or the amnesia may be so dense that the person takes on a new life without realising they can't remember the past (dissociative fugue). It may be that they lose their sense of self and take on an almost robotic role (depersonalisation disorder), or it may be due to the fragmenting of the personality (dissociative identity disorder). However, DID is considered more chronic and serious than other dissociative disorders and the chances of a full recovery are considerably lower.

Although DID was recognised in the nineteenth century, it seems that there was a fall in reported cases between 1920 and 1970, but then it increased again. This may well have been due to the popularity of schizophrenia as a diagnosis in the intervening years. One thing that was quite interesting was that there was a rise in the number of alters of diagnosed patients that seemed to coincide with the publication of a book called *Sybil* (Schreiber, 1973), which told the story of a woman with 16 personalities. Before Sybil, the number of alters was two or three, but after the book the average rose to ten.

The condition usually starts in early childhood but may well be unrecognised as it is quite rare and is less likely to be the first diagnosis the practitioner arrives at. In fact, there are a number of theories to explain the cause of DID, but it is recognised today that it is often associated with some kind of traumatic childhood event, such as sexual abuse, although the event is not always sexual in nature. Putnam *et al.* (1983) surveyed therapists who work with DID clients and found that 80 per cent of their clients had suffered physical abuse in their childhood and 70 per cent had been incest victims. Other research has indicated an even higher incidence.

According to Freud, DID develops as a result of repression of wishes or desires. If you remember, Freud claims that children have sensual desires which focus on their opposite-sex parent when they pass through the Oedipal stage. They manage to curb the desires, but if they re-emerge in adulthood, the person may do something rash and impulsive of a sexual nature. If this happens, a way of dealing with it would be to repress the memory into the unconscious (motivated forgetting). If this does not work, another way of dealing with the problem would be to actually split that part of the personality from conscious awareness (Buss, 1966) or, alternatively, cope with the memory by giving the 'part of them' that carried out the act a new independent identity.

Probably the most accepted theory is that DID occurs in early childhood as a way of coping with traumatic or disturbing events. Learning theorists suggest that the child learns how to deal with the stressful memories by adopting an avoidance technique. The child 'hypnotises' or fools itself into believing that the events haven't happened to them, but to someone else, and this someone else becomes another alter. Bliss (1983) discovered that people suffering from DID are easier to hypnotise than controls and suggested that this might support the idea.

Not surprisingly, women are more likely to develop DID than men. This may well be affected by the fact that the instances of girls becoming victims of sexual abuse are higher than boys. A study of 796 college students found that 19 per cent of the women and 8.6 per cent of the men had been sexually abused as children (Finkelhor 1979). The women often present other symptoms, such as depression or headaches, before the DID is acknowledged. It seems that DID is frequently accompanied by substance abuse, self-abuse or suicide attempts – all of which go along with low self-esteem or guilt arising from abuse.

It's not surprising then, that children who have been through such traumatic relationships find it hard to deal with what has happened. Of course, they would need to protect themselves from any further hurt and perhaps this fragmentation would be a way of doing so. If this is the case, the treatment must involve trying to convince the person that it is not necessary to split their personality in order to deal with their earlier traumas and to help them to reintegrate. However, before this can happen, they have to acknowledge the actual split. It seems that hypnosis is a good technique to use as it gives the person access to hidden portions of the personality. But as you will see, it may actually result in the belief that there are other alters – even when there aren't!

DIAGNOSIS OF DID

It's essential that there are very stringent criteria for the diagnosis of DID, because it has been used as a legal defence in a number of court cases. An example is the case of the serial killer known as the 'Hillside Strangler', who was brought to trial in California in the 1980s. Ken Bianchi pleaded not guilty by reason of insanity, because he claimed he was suffering from DID. A number of researchers were very sceptical about his defence and, as a result of this, decided to conduct some research to find out if it was possible to fake the disorder by using the same method as Bianchi's interviewer had done.

Spanos, Weekes and Bertrand (1985) conducted research on a group of under-graduate students, which showed that they were able to give an account of a second personality within them, simply by receiving a session of hypnosis which suggested that they either had a second personality or that they had simply blocked off parts of themselves. This evidence casts quite a lot of doubt on the existence of DID, but nevertheless, there are still a large number of professionals who accept DID as a real disorder, even if it is extremely rare.

The final criteria which is used in diagnosis is the amount of difference between the alters. Sometimes physiological measures such as EEGs are used because of their lack of subjectivity, and these have been found to produce significant differences between the personalities in DID sufferers compared with controls. The problem lies in the fact that there is no ultimate test which can confirm the existence of DID.

One of the implications of DID is to do with the status of different alters and the law. Elyn Saks (1992), from the University of Southern California Law Centre, argued that the body should only be considered a container for the person. It is therefore the person who should be to blame and not the body. Obviously in a 'normal' person, they are the same thing, but not in a situation where the body contains a number of different 'people'. The problem comes when one 'alter' knows what the other one is doing – does that make them both to blame? An alternative to this is if one alter knows what the other one has done but can't actually stop it – by law, the alter who hasn't actually committed the act isn't guilty. Surely the one who didn't commit the act *is* guilty because it should have reported the act of the other? Confusing, isn't it?

One case where DID was accepted was the case of Eve White. This was the most carefully documented report of dissociative identity disorder at the time and, as such, deserves a place with the core studies. It is interesting to note that the whole idea behind the therapy was to try to reintegrate the alters into a whole person. This method of treatment recognises the significance of each part of our personality as components of a whole, and acknowledges that we *really* are complex beings with many different facets.

Corbett H. Thigpen and Hervey Cleckley (1954), 'A case of multiple personality',

Journal of Abnormal & Social Psychology, 49, 135–51

Background

Is the diagnosis of dual personality or multiple personality disorder (the precursors of the diagnosis DID) a valid one? Is it really possible for more than one 'personality' to reside in one body, each with experiences, memories and wills separate and distinct from each other?

Thigpen and Cleckley described the scepticism with which psychiatry regarded such a diagnosis; that the MPD sufferer was to psychiatry what the unicorn or centaur was to natural history, simply a myth. Although cases had been reported in the past, notably the case of Mrs Beauchamp, reported by Morton Prince in 1909, modern psychiatry in the 1950s tended to gloss over or ignore MPD. The authors suggest that this is probably because of a lack of contemporary and objective evidence. The diagnosis relies heavily on the patient's subjective reporting of experience, and may therefore be the product of the patient's deceit or the observer's wishful thinking, and was (and still is) treated with a great deal of scepticism.

Thigpen and Cleckley, however, believed they may have discovered such a case, and this study is a report of their findings. They, too, had viewed MPD with scepticism, but now reported that, 'our direct experience with a patient has forced us to review the subject of multiple personality. It has also provoked in us the reaction of wonder, sometimes of awe' (p. 136).

Had the psychiatrists really encountered the psychiatric equivalent in myth and rarity to the unicorn? Was this a true case of MPD?

Aim

The aim of this case study was to document the psychotherapeutic treatment of a 25-year-old woman, with a history of severe headaches and blackouts, whom therapy revealed appeared to have multiple personality disorder. The purpose was to review the evidence and consider the validity of the diagnosis.

Method

The case study method was used, with the subject (patient) attending for regular therapeutic sessions over a 14-month period. Using notes from over 100 hours of therapy, the researchers documented the evidence for the diagnosis of MPD.

The data was, therefore, heavily reliant on the patient's self-report of her subjective experiences. The therapists also interviewed the patient's husband and family.

As well as the evidence from interviews, tests were carried out in an attempt to distinguish the personalities from each other. Psychometric measures were taken of memory function and IQ, the Rorschach ink-blot test was used and EEG patterns were recorded and compared. A handwriting expert also compared the handwriting of the personalities.

The subject and the beginnings of the evidence of MPD

The patient in the study, given the name Eve White by the researchers to protect her identity, was, on referral, a fairly run-of-the-mill case. She had been referred because of 'severe and blinding headaches'.

At the first interview she told of 'blackouts' following the headaches, where she suffered memory loss.

Eve White's marriage was disintegrating and this caused her a great deal of concern and distress. She had a four-year-old daughter, to whom she was devoted, and this compounded her distress about her failing marriage. At first she was only able to attend for consultation irregularly as she was travelling quite a distance. After some months of therapy, the authors noted that 'encouraging symptomatic improvement occurred, but it was plain that this girl's major problem had not been settled'.

Her case seemed ordinary, with Eve White being described at that time as a client presenting with 'commonplace symptoms and a relatively complex but familiar constellation of marital conflicts and personal frustrations'.

The loss of memory for a recent trip puzzled the psychiatrists. They hypnotised her and this seemed to be cleared up, however, it was at this point in her treatment that an event occurred which was to be a key factor in the emergence of 'another' personality in the therapy room. They received a letter from Eve White that appeared to have been finished off by someone else, described as a 'child-like hand'.

Questioned on her next visit, Eve White denied sending the letter, but did remember starting one. She was then agitated and distressed and asked whether it meant she was insane if she was hearing an imaginary voice. This question surprised the therapists, because Eve White had shown no other symptoms of 'schizoid' behaviour, and also because she was able to report the voice with a concern about the experience which was atypical of those patients experiencing auditory hallucinations.

Before the therapist could reply, however:

…as if seized by a sudden pain she put both hands to her head. After a tense moment of silence, her hands dropped. There was a quick restless smile, and in a bright voice that sparkled she said 'Hi there, Doc…'

p. 137

She then crossed her legs and the therapist noticed for the first time that they were attractive. It seemed as if someone else, someone other than Eve White was now present in Eve White's body:

Instead of that retiring and gently conventional figure, there was in the newcomer a childishly daredevil air, an erotically mischievous glance, a face marvellously free from the habitual signs of care, seriousness and underlying distress, so long familiar in her predecessor. This new and apparently carefree girl spoke casually of Eve White and her problems, always using *she* or *her* in every sentence, always respecting the strict bounds of a separate identity. When asked her own name she immediately replied 'Oh, I'm Eve Black'.

p. 137

The therapists were so convinced that this was a 'newcomer', different from Eve White in every respect, that they believed that this might be a case of MPD, a major 'find' in the world of psychiatry.

From this point on, their interest in and therapy with this client increased.

Differences between and experiences of Eve White and Eve Black

Over the 14 months of therapy, the therapists found out a lot about the personality they called Eve Black (EB):

- EB had 'enjoyed an independent life since Mrs White's early childhood', so had appeared long ago in Mrs White's life.
- Eve White (EW) was not consciously aware of EB, and although told of the existence of EB in therapy she remained unable to access EB or her memories or experiences. EW was 'in abeyance' or 'unconscious' when EB was 'out' (one 'personality' at a time is supposedly dominant in such cases, and the dominance of the other personality was described as her coming 'out').
- EB, on the other hand, was aware of EW and was able to follow the thoughts and actions of EW as a 'spectator'. Although an onlooker in EW's home life and aware of EW's feelings, EB did not participate in or share them. She dismissed as 'silly' EW's concerns about her failing marriage and spoke of the devotion of EW to her four-year-old daughter as 'something pretty corny'.
- EB could at first only be 'brought out' by the therapists while EW was under hypnosis. She could, however, 'pop out' at any time in EW's life. The therapists didn't know how she did this, but she would not come out at their request without hypnotising EW. However, after a few sessions using hypnosis it was possible to study the two personalities simply by asking the one to allow the other to come out to speak to the therapists. This helped the therapists, but made life difficult for EW as now EB found she could get out more and take over. EB being in control often made for unpleasant consequences for EW.
- EB was neither compassionate nor cruel to EW, she seemed unaffected by

human emotions. EB was 'shallowly hedonistic', intent only on pleasure-seeking and fun in the present moment. Unfortunately for EW, 'fun' for EB had often meant 'mischief' as a child, and she reported having got EW into trouble with her parents at six years old. They had forbidden her from walking through the woods to play with children who lived on the other side, as they felt it wasn't safe. EB had done this, however, and only let EW 'come out' to receive the 'whipping' for disobeying her parents.

- EB was, it soon became clear, prone to lying. Her 'evidence' in therapy was therefore considered by the authors to be less reliable than that given by EW, who seemed honest and open. EW could, however, substantiate some of EB's stories, agreeing there were times when as a child she had received punishments from her parents without knowing the reason why. Some of EB's claims about her adult behaviour were substantiated by EW's husband and family.

- Until she agreed to being 'introduced' to them by the therapists, EB had managed to conceal herself from EW's family when she was out. She had done this by pretending to be Eve White (imitating her voice and mannerisms and behaviours). When EB's true character had been shown, EW's family considered the 'wayward behaviour, ill will, harshness and occasional acts of violence' as being 'unaccountable fits of temper in a woman [EW] habitually gentle and considerate' (p. 139).

- On one occasion EB 'recklessly bought several expensive and unneeded new dresses and two luxurious coats'. This caused EW's husband to go into a rage for 'wantonly plunging him into debt'. EW tried to protest her innocence, but of course, her husband did not accept this. He did calm down, however, when she agreed it would be a disaster for them to be in such debt and took the clothes back to the shop. EW told the therapists she thought her husband had planted the clothes to make her look as if she had gone mad. This fitted in with the problems they were having with their marriage. EB had not only been extravagant in her shopping, but also 'revels in cheap night clubs, flirting with men on the make'. She also told the therapists, 'When I go out and get drunk ... *she* wakes up with the hangover. She wonders what in the hell's made her so sick'. Although EB had not been the cause of the marital problems between EW and her husband, it was clear that her behaviours when she was out did little to help overcome them, if such reconciliation were possible.

- Although usually indifferent to EW's four-year-old daughter, EB did once hurt her, although she denied this (even though there was evidence to the contrary from EW's husband). She did confess to it later, saying flippantly, 'The little brat got on my nerves'.

With all this evidence, the therapists came to believe that EW and EB were indeed two separate personalities, taking turns in the same body. However, they recognised that it was difficult for them to explain to anyone else exactly *what* it was that made them believe that EB was different from EW, drawing the parallel that a man could pick out his wife from 100 other women looking and dressing similarly, but could not give the instructions to a stranger to do the same. They did, however, draw up a comparison between the two to try to catalogue the qualitative differences between them that, for Thigpen and Cleckley, marked out EW and EB as distinctly separate from each other.

FEATURE	EVE WHITE	EVE BLACK
Summary of character	Demure, 'almost saintly'.	Party girl, childishly vain, egocentric.
Face	Sweet and sad.	Pixie-like eyes dance with mischief.
Dress and behaviour	Dresses sensibly (conservatively). Has a stooped posture, is dignified. Reads poetry. Is well-liked, industrious and capable.	Dresses provocatively (sexily), is witty, coarse and rowdy. Likes to play pranks: her intent is fun, but the consequences often cruel for others.
Attitude	Serious and distressed by her current problems, didn't blame her husband, loved her daughter deeply.	Never serious, unaffected by human emotions, grief and tragedy.
Allergy to nylon	Reported no such allergy.	Claimed to be allergic to nylon and didn't wear stockings when she was out for long periods.

Summary of differences between Eve White and Eve Black (adapted from pp. 141–2)

Of course, this evidence is subjective, and in order to try to satisfy the scientific readers, Thigpen and Cleckley arranged for tests to be done to try to establish the two personalities as distinct from one another. Two types of tests were used, psychometric tests, where IQ and memory function were tested, and two projective tests, the Rorschach ink-blot test and a test drawing human figures.

> ## FOCUS ON RESEARCH METHODS – projective tests
>
> In a projective test, the subject is asked to draw something or look at something. The way they draw the figure or what they 'see in' the ink blot is supposed to reveal their personalities, in other words, they 'project' themselves onto the test and this can supposedly be summarised by a person trained in administering the tests.
>
> Whether such tests provide a valid description of the person is affected by the fact the respondent may lie, manipulating their responses to try to give a good (or perhaps, bad) account of themselves. The test interpretation will also be affected by the prevailing beliefs of the psychiatric profession at the time of testing, or indeed the personal beliefs held by the tester.

These tests were carried out by a well-qualified expert. The findings are summarised in the table below.

TEST	EVE WHITE	EVE BLACK
Wechsler intelligence test (IQ)	110	104
Wechsler memory test	Superior	Inferior
Projective tests (human figure drawing and Rorschach test)	Indication of • Repression • Conflict and anxiety in her role as mother • Hostility to her mother	Indication of • Regression (the name she used was in fact the patient's maiden name) indicating a desire to return to an earlier period of life, before marriage

The findings from the tests are not conclusive and do not provide evidence that the two are separate from each other.

Attempts at therapy and the emergence of a third personality, Jane

Although a fascinating case for both the therapists and the reader, the purpose for the patient of being in consultation with the therapists was to get relief from her difficulties and distress. The therapists noted that in previously reported cases, the secondary personality 'helped' the other. There appeared to be no evidence of EB helping EW, in fact, all the evidence appeared to the contrary; EB's behaviour when she was out simply made matters worse for EW.

As a therapeutic intervention, Thigpen and Cleckley tried to encourage EB to help. She would, however, only help if it interested her to so do. She would lie and pretend to be helping when she was not, when in fact she was doing the opposite and 'her behaviour was particularly detrimental to Eve White's progress' (p. 142). They did, however, manage to encourage her to cooperate by bargaining with her. It became clear that now she was aware of her existence, EW could block EB out and prevent her from taking over (although EW was still not wholly successful at this). The therapists bargained with EB for good behaviour in return for more time out.

Further revelations came from EB at this point. She could influence EW even when she was not out. It was she, she claimed, who had been the voice EW had heard and she who was responsible for giving EW headaches. She also claimed to be able to wipe out memories from Eve White, and she used this as an explanation for EW having no memories of beatings she was made to receive at the hands of a man with whom EB had cohabited prior to EW's own marriage. Whilst there were no records of the 'marriage' a distant relative had described to the therapists, there was good evidence that she had lived with a man at this time, although EW denied this ever happened.

After about eight months, it appeared that EW was indeed getting better. She was no longer with her husband and her daughter was living with her parents. This latter point caused her great distress, but she was comforted by the fact that she was able to hold down a job and provide for her daughter. She was doing well in her job and hopeful of a reunion with her husband. EB had been causing less trouble, and rarely 'came out' at work, which she found boring, because she did not want to interfere with the 'breadwinner' when she was earning her keep. However, in leisure hours she often 'got in bad company, picked up dates, and indulged in cheap and idle flirtations', but EW, unaware of this, was spared the embarrassment of this conduct.

However, at this point, when things seemed to have been going so well, EW took a turn for the worse. The headaches and blackouts returned, and this time a room-mate found her unconscious twice as a result of the blackouts. What was different was that EB claimed not to be causing the headaches and, although she did not get headaches, she was also experiencing the blackouts this time. She told the therapists, 'I don't know where we go, but go we do'.

EW found it hard to work and her new-found confidence waned. It looked as if she would have to be hospitalised, as the therapists thought 'a psychosis was impending'. Although they kept this from EW, they told EB about it by way of warning her off mischief: if EW was put in an institution so would she be, and this would greatly curtail her activities!

Thigpen and Cleckley also attempted to fuse the two personalities together, on the assumption that they had somehow started off as integrated and later fractured apart. They did this by trying to call both personalities out at the same time, but this caused the patient more distress and they stopped attempting it.

They then approached this by trying to work back into childhood with the two personalities, presumably to take them back to the point where EB emerged. They were able to do this with EW through hypnosis, but never managed to hypnotise EB.

Soon after the headaches and blackouts had returned, EW was in such a session, and recalling a painful experience, when she had been scalded by hot water as a child when:

396

As she spoke her eyes shut sleepily. Her head dropped back on the chair. After remaining in this sleep or trance perhaps two minutes her eyes opened. Blankly she stared about the room, looking at the furniture and the pictures as if trying to orient herself. Continuing their apparently bewildered survey, her eyes finally met those of the therapist, and stopped. Slowly, with an unknown husky voice, and with immeasurable poise, she spoke. 'Who are you?'

p. 144

Thigpen and Cleckley say that it was apparent that this was neither EB nor EW. A third personality had 'come out', and the therapists called her Jane. They studied this 'other woman' and described her as follows:

she apparently lacks EB's obvious faults and inadequacies. She also impresses us as far more mature, more vivid, more boldly capable and more interesting than EW … in her [Jane] are indications of initiative and powerful resources never shown by the other [EW]

p. 145

The differences between Eve White, Eve Black and Jane

By their descriptions, it is clear that Thigpen and Cleckley could identify EW, EB and Jane by their demeanour and behaviour. But again, this is subjective evidence.

Two more experts were brought in to study the now three personalities for evidence of observable distinctions between them that would support the diagnosis of multiple personality disorder.

The handwriting of each was analysed by an expert who concluded that 'beyond any doubt they have been written by one and the same individual'. An EEG was used to record and compare their brainwave activity. The results were as follows:

Eve White	Eve Black	Jane
11 cycles per second (normal)	12.5 cycles per second, a slightly fast EEG reading that is sometimes associated with psychopathic personality	11 cycles per second (normal)

Jane and EW could not be distinguished from each other; they were both described as 'normal'. EB, however, was borderline-normal and was distinguishable from Jane and EW.

The way forward for the patient?
Having studied the three personalities for some time, the therapists came to see Jane taking over as a possible answer to EW's problems:

As time passes, Jane stays 'out' more and more. She emerges only through EW, never yet having found a way to displace EB or to communicate through her.

p. 146

They describe Jane as compassionate for EW's distress and able to come out and help EW at work. They say:

Could Jane remain in full possession of that integrated human functioning we call personality our patient would probably, we believe, regain full health, eventually adjust satisfactorily, perhaps at a distinctly superior level and find her way to a happy life.

p. 146

However, they claim that it was neither their intent, nor in their power, to bring about such an outcome. They ask, 'Would any physician order euthanasia of the heedlessly merry and amoral but nevertheless unique EB?'

Although Jane would be a good mother to EW's daughter and probably would not return to EW's husband and the problems of the marriage, would 'killing off' EW, or allowing her to 'leave forever' for her child's sake be the right answer? Jane thought not. She wrote to the therapists, having 'seen' EW apparently saving a child from being knocked down in the street: 'She [EW] must not die yet. There is so much I must know, and so very much I must learn from her...' and on the saving of the child, 'I have never been thus affected by anything in my four months of life'.

Jane had shared knowledge of both Eves' behaviours after her own emergence, but no access to experiences or memories of either Eve before she had first emerged, knowing only what she had been told. EW was conscious of neither Jane nor EB, although was aware of their existence through the reports of the therapists. EB was aware of EW but not of Jane.

Discussion

Thigpen and Cleckley consider that they may not have observed a true case of MPD, but may have been 'thoroughly hoodwinked by a skilful actress' (p. 147). However, given that the therapy went on for an extended period of time in which they noted nothing which would suggest that the patient was faking, 'we do not think that any person could over months avoid even one tell-tale error or imperfection'.

Was Eve White's disintegration of personality due to schizophrenia? Thigpen and Cleckley considered this to be unlikely, since none of the personalities showed any symptoms of that disorder.

In moving towards the diagnosis of MPD, Thigpen and Cleckley concede that they may have lost their objectivity because of their involvement with the patient, and therefore their judgement was affected by their relationship with her. They point out that whilst the three personalities appeared distinct and separate to the therapists, the evidence from objective testing was 'not particularly impressive', and could not provide clear evidence of distinctions between EW, EB and Jane.

The therapists were careful not to make the claim that the case was indeed one of MPD, but suggest that the experiences of their client raised a number of important questions for both psychology and psychiatry. What do we mean by 'personality'? How are we to describe it?

They discuss the case of Mrs Beauchamp, presented by Morton Deutsch in 1909, and suggest that both a review of his work and further study of patients with MPD in the future might give psychiatrists the necessary insight to explain that which could not be scientifically explained at the time of writing up the case of Eve White.

Commentary

Is the study ethical?

The study was governed by medical ethics at the time rather than the ethical guidelines for research with human participants in use today. The use of a pseudonym was an ethical consideration to protect the patient and her family on publication of the case. The researchers also raise the point of whether it is ethical to 'kill off' one of the personalities (if the disappearance of one of them was akin to their 'death') in therapy.

Is the study useful?

As it presented an intriguing case and asks thought-provoking questions about our use of the term 'personality', the study is useful in encouraging us to further our understanding of human behaviour and experience. However, whether the findings in this unique case can be useful, even to a particular client group, is questionable. The number of people with such a disorder is very small, and it is possible that their differences would so greatly outweigh their similarities as to make the experience of one such case bear little resemblance to any other.

Is the study valid?

If Eve White was just a 'skilful actress' then the study is not valid. The dependence of the diagnosis on self-report of the patient's experiences contributes still to the debate surrounding DID.

What are the strengths and weaknesses of the case study method illustrated in this study?

The strengths include the large amount of detailed and qualitative data gathered about the patient in over 100 hours of therapy. The longitudinal nature of the study made it harder for the patient, if she was faking, to keep up any pretence.

The weaknesses include the possibility that the researcher's relationship with the patient may have affected their judgement of the case and led to them being unwittingly 'fooled' by the patient, or indeed overlooking any evidence that might have suggested she was 'play-acting' or evidence of any other explanation for the behaviour they observed.

Key questions

1. Explain what is meant by the term 'multiple personality disorder'.
2. Describe the outcome of the projective tests used to assess Eve White and Eve Black.
3. Why did Thigpen and Cleckley have EEG measures taken of Eve White, Eve Black and Jane?
4. Is there any way other than by the patient's self-report that it could have been established whether there really were three personalities living in the same body?
5. Why do you think Thigpen and Cleckley were reluctant to claim that their study described a true case of MPD?

Example Answers are on page 461.

Further reading

• Cave, S. (2002), *Classification and Diagnosis of Psychological Abnormality*. Routledge: London.
• Davison, G. and Neale, J. (1996), *Abnormal Psychology*. New York: Wiley, 6th edition.

- Schreiber, F.R. (1973), *Sybil*. Harmondsworth: Penguin.
- Sizemore, C.C. (1978), *I'm Eve*. New York: Berkley Publishing Group.
- Stirling, J.D. and Hellewell, J.S.E. (1999), *Psychopathology*. Routledge: London.
- Thigpen, Corbett, H. and Cleckley, Harvey M. (1957), *The Three Faces of Eve*. London: Secker & Warburg.

Postscript

The real name of the subject for this key study was Chris Sizemore. She wrote a book called *I'm Eve* (Sizemore and Pittillo, 1977), where she maintained that Thigpen and Cleckley's case study was really the tip of the iceberg. She reported that her personality continued to fragment after the end of the therapy, until 21 separate alters inhabited her body. She stated that there were nine before the time of her therapy and that Thigpen and Cleckley never managed to make contact with them. There were a number of traumatic events in her childhood which may have caused this fragmentation, although none of them were sexual in nature. She had seen a man drown when she was about two years of age, and had witnessed another cut into pieces by a saw at a timberyard. One event which left her traumatised, and may well have been the core of the fragmentation, was when she was held high off the floor by her mother and made to touch the face of her dead grandmother. She was five years old at the time, but even as an adult could remember the clammy cold cheek. Sizemore believes that the reason she developed these separate personalities was as a way of coping with the harshness of life.

Perhaps this is a fitting final study because it emphasises that, despite what we know about people, they still continue to confuse us. Perhaps this book has given you some insight into human behaviour and thought and has made you realise how amazing and complex we humans really are. Each year we achieve a greater understanding of ourselves, but with each possible answer comes a series of new questions.

You will probably have found already, that when you tell people that you are studying psychology, they will instantaneously assume that you are psycho-analysing them, and you are now in a position to put them straight. Doesn't it make you want to shout at them that it is not that easy! Even when you know as much as you do now, all you can do is to pick up patterns and trends in behaviour when you first meet someone. It takes a long time to really get to know people and fully understand what makes them tick, because we are all individuals and what motivates one person may have no influence on the next. But part of the fun is getting to know them, and the other part of the fun is trying to work it all out. Even then, you may well get some of it wrong, but if it makes you more tolerant of human weaknesses, then we have done our job.

We are all different and yet we all have so much in common. At least the majority of us have only got ourselves to deal with. Imagine having numerous versions of yourself inside your body and having to cope with all of them... the mind boggles!

The core studies exams

Exams? Nothing to it! All you have to do is know what you *need* to know, then learn it, then reproduce it under examination conditions. Easy?

Well, no, it's not easy, but it is something that any student can do once they learn the relevant techniques. The trouble is, we don't always think and behave as rationally as we might – this is something we have to train ourselves to do. Let's take an example. When you buy a new phone or a new computer, are you one of those people that shoves the instruction book, plastic cover intact, into your sock drawer, turns on your new toy and begins pressing those buttons? I'm inclined to do this. My parents bought me Monopoly when I was 10. I never read the rules. I played my older sister a million times and, uncannily, she always won…

This method of learning can be seen in two ways, either as the 'trial and error' approach, thinking you'll get the hang of it as you go along, or as a result of an illogical belief that we all seem to have that we can just 'do things'. Well, you have never taken AS level exams before, so why is it you hold the belief that once you are sitting behind the desk in the exam room it will all be all right? Unlike me, I hope you will not be casting aside the instruction book, but, instead, that you will learn from my mistakes and read on. This chapter is your OCR AS instruction manual.

The purpose of this chapter is to tell you what you need to learn, give you some insight into ways you can learn and ways to test your learning, and also to put to good use in the exam room what you have learned.

Knowing what you need to know for Core Studies 1 (CS1)

You have to remember one very important factor. The examiners are your friends in this game. They are on your side. There is plenty of information to help you, and what you haven't been given in the specification, your teachers have been given in the Guidance Notes for Teachers.

By now you have probably gleaned that there are 20 core studies and that two-thirds of the examinations, Core Studies one and Core Studies two, will require you to know these inside out and backwards.

DETAILS OF CORE STUDIES ONE, UNIT NUMBER 2540

This unit:
- tests students' knowledge and understanding of the 20 core studies
- tests their ability to make evaluative points about the studies
- tests their ability to see the studies in the wider perspective of psychological concepts and methods.

Students answer 20 compulsory short questions, one on each study.

What should students be prepared to answer questions about on the CS1 paper?
- the information in the studies
- the methods used in the studies
- the way the results are analysed and presented
- the conclusions that can be drawn from the studies
- the context of the studies
- the general psychological issues illustrated by the studies.

LEARNING WHAT YOU NEED TO KNOW – REVISING THE CORE STUDIES

Getting ready

Some things we need to remember, some things we don't. If we are going to remember something, then we will probably write it down and keep a record of it. Organisation is the key word here. You need a system.

First, you will need to organise your folder(s), to make sure you have notes on all the things you need to know. These are best sorted according to the perspectives: cognitive, social, individual differences, developmental and biological, as in the specification, with each approach separated by file dividers. It will probably make most sense if you store them in the order that your teacher taught them to you. You may also have a section on research methods, and the work you have done in the psychological investigations folder can be useful to you in the core studies too.

The next step is to read your folder and look for gaps. Have you got studies – or bits of studies – missing from your folder? Are there concepts in there that you don't understand or haven't an explanation for? Well, use this book to look them up, or talk to your teacher. It's important to work out what's missing and plug the gaps – you can't start to revise if you don't have the complete picture.

You are now ready to begin your revision, but you *must* remember that you are not revising if you are not writing stuff down! Learning/revising is an active process! You will need to equip yourself with notepaper and pens for revision, with an option on coloured pens and index cards. Having organised your folder(s) and got your equipment ready, you have everything you need organised in one place and now you are ready to start learning the studies.

Revision activities

You need know the stories of the studies. How research papers are presented can help you here, as you get a structure for your story: background, aims and hypotheses, method (design, subjects, procedure, materials, variables), results (are findings qualitative or quantitative? are they gathered by self-report, observation or biomedical measures?), discussion and conclusion.

Making summary sheets

You can make summary sheets for each of the 20 studies: keep these sheets at the front of your file to read and work from later. You may have done this after you covered the study in class, when it was fresh in your memory, but it is also a useful activity for refreshing your memory of the studies towards the end of the course.

Researcher(s) and date study was published
Title of study
Aim
Method (design, sample, location, procedure)
Results (include how any variables were measured)
Discussion points/conclusions

Evaluation points
    You can use the questions we have used in our commentaries of the studies to help you with your evaluation:
    Is the study ecologically valid?
    Is the study useful?
    Can we generalise the findings from the study to a broader population?
    What are the strengths and weaknesses of the research methods and data-gathering methods that have been used in the study?
    Is the study ethical?
    The OCR Teachers' Guide suggests the following questions will also help you with your evaluation points:
    What if the sample was different?
    What if the location was different?
    What if the measurement was different?
    What if the procedure was different?
    What if the procedure was ethical?

Condensing your notes

To begin with, your summary sheets may be fairly dense and you may have difficulty squeezing all the points from the study on one side of A4. This is normal, so don't worry. The next stage in the revision process is to work with your notes and condense them. The idea now is to reduce your notes, and the reason you will be able to write less and still remember the details of the study is because you will be learning the details as you go along. Once you can write the study on one side of A4 it is time to turn to index cards. Index cards are very useful for revision; once you have condensed your notes, the cards act as 'cues' for your memory and are therefore a good revision aid. Using cards gives you a portable set of revision notes, which you can put in your pocket and take with you anywhere.

We have a lot of 'dead time' in our daily lives, such as time we spend waiting for or travelling on a bus or train, and index cards can be whipped out and that time used effectively. This gives you more 'real time' for relaxing and enjoying yourself!

Testing your learning

Use past papers to test your learning. These will give you an idea of the kinds of questions that can be asked about the studies.

You can use index cards to test your memory too, for example, you might make up a set of cards of 'samples' in the study, as follows:

Side one
The sample in Milgram's study on obedience to authority…

Side two
– A volunteer sample drawn from those answering an advert in a local newspaper to take part in a study on learning and punishment
– the sample size was 40
– all subjects were male, aged 20–50
– subjects were drawn from a range of professions.

You can make sets on the aims of the studies, the findings of the studies, the IV and DV in the studies, controls used in the studies, etc. They are particularly helpful if you are trying to learn definitions or key concepts for a study, for example:

Side one
Study: Piliavin et al. (subway Samaritan)
Key concept = DIFFUSION OF RESPONSIBILITY

Side two
Diffusion of responsibility means that the more people present, the less responsible each individual feels (because the responsibility is 'shared out') so the less likely someone is to receive help.
This was what happened in laboratory studies of helping, but not in the Piliavin et al. study in the field.

You don't want to spend all your time making these, though – get yourself a study buddy, share out the card-making tasks and then swap! If you can cajole your mum or dad into helping you revise, they can use the cards to test your knowledge, or study buddies can test each other.

Knowing what you need to know for Core Studies 2 (CS2)

Revising for CS1 is a relatively straightforward task as you can focus on each study in turn, learning the narrative of the study and details of how it was carried out. Core Studies two (CS2) is a much harder exam, both in its structure and its content. Instead of the short-answer questions, you have to write structured essays. Instead of considering the studies in terms of their linear storyline, you have to consider what the studies have or don't have in common related to the methods used and the themes and approaches the study raises. There will be help on how to structure your essays later. First, let's focus on the content for Core Studies two.

DETAILS OF CORE STUDIES 2, UNIT NUMBER 2541

This unit tests how well students can draw out and apply methods, themes and perspectives in the core studies.

Students answer two structured essay questions in one hour, one from section A and one from section B.

In order to answer the questions on this exam paper you must know about research methodology, themes and perspectives. You must be able to recognise these and apply them to the core studies. In order to help you prepare for this paper, first we shall look at some methodological issues, and then at the themes and perspectives. There will be revision activities along the way, so keep your pen and paper handy.

METHODOLOGICAL ISSUES IN THE CORE STUDIES

You need to know about the strengths and weaknesses of the experimental method and apply these to the core studies.

In a true experiment:
- the experimenter manipulates one variable, the independent variable (IV) to see if it causes a change in another variable (the DV)
- all other variables (extraneous variables) are controlled or kept constant to prevent them from confounding the study – we can therefore demonstrate cause and effect, the IV causes the DV to change
- subjects are randomly allocated to conditions
- a control or comparison group is used.

Experiments where these criteria are not met are known as natural experiments or quasi-experiments. We have come across examples of these where the IV occurs naturally and cannot be manipulated by the experimenter, such as Baron-Cohen *et al.*'s study of autism and Sperry's study of split-brain patients.

Experiments can be carried out in the laboratory, or in a natural setting, which is described as being 'in the field'.

Revision activity

Using your knowledge of the core studies and the evaluative issues in the tables given below, draw up and complete the tables entitled 'Laboratory experiments in the core studies' and 'Field experiments in the core studies'.

Evaluation of laboratory experiments

Strengths	Weaknesses
• High level of control over extraneous variables • IV can be manipulated and isolated as a causal factor, establishing cause and effect between the IV and the DV • Allows the use of sensitive technical equipment (EEG, PET scan) or complicated apparatus (see Sperry)	• Lack ecological validity – lab behaviour is artificial behaviour • Internal validity may be low because of possible biasing factors, such as subject reactivity (responding to demand characteristics) or experimenter bias • Deception may be necessary as to the true purpose of the study in order to avoid Ss responding to demand characteristics – this raises ethical issues • Restricted samples used mean it is difficult to generalise the findings to people in general • If the study is quasi-experimental in design, this means the researcher does not have full control over the IV

Evaluation of field experiments

Strengths	Weaknesses
• High ecological validity – 'real' behaviour can be studied • IV can manipulated and isolated as a causal factor, establishing cause and effect between the IV and the DV	• Low control over extraneous variables, so we cannot be entirely sure that there is a causal relationship between the IV and the DV • Often covert observation is used to gather data and this raises ethical issues (deception, invasion of privacy, lack of informed consent, etc.) • If the study is quasi-experimental in design, this means the researcher does not have full control over the IV

Laboratory experiments in the core studies

Study	IV/DV	Subjects	Strengths of lab expt in this study	Weaknesses of lab expt in this study
Tajfel (intergroup discrimination)	Study 1: Study 2:			
Loftus and Palmer (eyewitness testimony)	Study 1: Study 2:			
Baron-Cohen et al. (autism)				
Samuel and Bryant (conservation)				
Bandura et al. (aggression)				
Raine et al. (murderers' brains)				

407

Sperry (split brains)				
Schachter and Singer (emotion)				
Hraba and Grant (doll choice)				

Field experiments in the core studies

Study	IV/DV	Subjects	Strengths of field expt in this study	Weaknesses of field expt in this study
Piliavin *et al.* (subway Samaritan)				
Rosenhan (sane in insane places)				

You may be asked about the strengths and weaknesses of repeated measures and independent groups designs in the CS2 exam. You will have definitions of these in your work on the Psychological Investigations exam. Draw up a table to give definitions of these designs and to show the strengths and weaknesses associated with them, and then work out which of the core studies use which design. Why do you think the researchers chose this design? You can do a similar set of tables for longitudinal and cross-sectional designs. Again, work out which studies use which design. Why do you think the researchers chose this design?

You need to know about the strengths and weaknesses of the non-experimental methods as used in the core studies:
In particular you should consider the use of the case study and psychometrics (see Themes below) in the core studies.

A case study is an in-depth study of one individual or small group. Often a case study is carried out longitudinally, allowing development or changes to be observed over time. This method allows a great deal of qualitative data, rich in detail and high in validity, to be gathered. Techniques used in case studies include interviews and psychometrics, and these methods bring their related strengths and weaknesses to the case. For instance, if the researchers have developed a long-standing and close relationship with the subject, their objectivity may be reduced and therefore they may be biased in their reporting of the interview. Psychometric tests are usually self-report pen-and-paper tests and are open to falsification or manipulation by a clever subject. Replication of case studies is very difficult, especially as they are often of atypical or unusual cases (e.g. Little Hans, Eve White), and this means we have to be cautious in generalising the findings to others. This, in turn, reduces the usefulness of the findings.

Revision activity

Draw out and complete the following table on case studies in the core studies:

Study	Strengths of using the case study method in this study	Weaknesses of using the case study method in this study
Freud's case study of Little Hans		
Thigpen and Cleckley's case study of Eve White		
Gardner and Gardner's study of Washoe		

You need to know about measurement issues, e.g. what are the strengths and weaknesses of observational and self-report methods of data gathering?

Using observational methods to gather data

Strengths include	Weaknesses include
• Where covert observation is used, studies can be high in ecological validity as 'real' behaviour is being observed (NB ecological validity is reduced if the lab is the setting for the study).	• Ethical concerns in covert observations. • Reductionism where quantitative methods and codings/ratings are used • Observer bias – consciously or unconsciously affecting the results so that they fit in with the hypothesis. • Reliability – if only one observer is used, we have to question the reliability/ objectivity of the results.

- In participant observations the observer can get a real insight into the situation being observed as they experience it first-hand.

- In overt observations (or participant observations) the presence of the researcher may influence the behaviour of Ss and this will mean results are not valid.
- In participant observations the observer may lose their objectivity as they are influenced by their experience of the situation.

Using self-report methods to gather data: questions, questionnaires, interviews

Strengths include	Weaknesses include
• Cost- and time-effective – can gather large amounts of data in a short time. • Can measure attitudes /beliefs/cognitive abilities that cannot be otherwise measured. • Closed questions/ rating scales on questions can provide quantitative data for analysis.	• May be falsifiable. Ss lie; perhaps responding to demand characteristics, or due to evaluation apprehension, they give socially desirable answers, etc. If data is falsifiable, we have to question its validity. • Closed questions (forced response questions) may frustrate the S who may then lose interest and not answer carefully, again reducing the validity of the study. • Questions used can be leading questions – suggesting the answer that ought to be given, thus the researcher is influencing the S's responses. Children may be particularly susceptible to leading questions.

Revision activity

Using your knowledge of the core studies and the information given above about data-gathering methods, draw out and fill in the following tables:

Using observational methods in the core studies

Studies using observational techniques	What was observed and how?	Strengths of observational measures in this study	Weaknesses of observational measures in this study
Milgram (obedience)			
Zimbardo (prison simulation)			
Piliavin *et al.* (subway Samaritan)			
Bandura *et al.* (aggression)			
Gardner and Gardner (Washoe)			
Rosenhan (sane in insane places)			

Using self-report methods in the core studies

Studies using observational techniques	How was self-report used?	Strengths of self-report measures in this study	Weaknesses of self-report measures in this study
Hraba and Grant (doll choice)			
Samuel and Bryant (conservation)			
Baron-Cohen *et al.* (autism)			
Loftus and Palmer (eyewitness testimony)			
Schachter and Singer (emotion)			

Dement and Kleitman (dreaming)			
Gould (IQ tests)			
Thigpen and Cleckley (MPD)			
Freud (Little Hans)			
Hodges and Tizard (attachment)			

You need to know about sampling and generalisability issues.
You need to be able to describe and evaluate the samples used in the core studies. You should learn what we mean by a volunteer (self-selected) sample, an opportunity sample, an unsolicited sample (imposed sample) and a random sample. You need to identify the type of sample used in each of the core studies and discuss their strengths and weaknesses. Your index cards will help you to sort the samples according to type. For example, which of the core studies studied children? Which had volunteer samples? Which studied students? Which used unsolicited samples?

Index cards can also help you draw out other comparisons and contrasts between studies, including whether the studies were lab- or field-based, used self-report or observational measures. They will help you to see, literally by laying them out in front of you, the patterns of methods and themes emerging across the studies.

THEMES IN THE CORE STUDIES

Throughout this book you will have come across boxes of text headed 'Focus on themes'. In the CS2 examination you will be asked to consider how themes and perspectives relate to the core studies and to compare and/or contrast these across studies.

The themes and perspectives are:
- Applications of psychology to everyday life
- Determinism
- Ecological validity
- Ethics
- Ethnocentric bias
- Individual and situational explanations
- Nature and nurture

- Psychometrics
- Qualitative and quantitative measures
- Reductionism
- Reinforcement
- Social control
- Usefulness of psychological research
- Validity and reliability.

Approaches in psychology, or perspectives as they are also known, are themes too:
- The social approach
- The cognitive approach
- The developmental approach
- The physiological approach
- The individual differences approach.

In order to help you with the exam, what follows are descriptions of the themes and examples of how these relate to the core studies.

Theme: Applications of psychology to everday life – usefulness of psychological research

Are the studies any use in helping to solve problems for people in the real world?

The questions are, helpful to whom, and for what? (See the notes on Usefulness at the end of this section on Themes.)

Examples of the applications of the findings of the core studies

Study	Usefulness of findings
Zimbardo	Helps us understand what creates brutality in prisons and could be used to inform prison reform.
Hodges and Tizard	Confirms for us that fostering/adoption is a good option for children – early fostering/adoption may prevent early privation experiences and the negative effects they cause later on.
Samuel and Bryant/Piaget	Understanding cognitive development in children can inform teachers about what is appropriate to teach at what stage in a child's development, and how to teach it (interactive learning environment that enables child to move from stage to stage when they are ready).
Baron-Cohen *et al.*	Understanding how autistic children think can help those who care for such children to have an under standing of the child's perspective – perhaps helping the carer put the child's bizarre behaviours and rages

	into perspective, making it easier to meet the child's needs.
Loftus and Palmer	If memory is reconstructive in nature and can be altered by the use of leading questions, then we must take great care about how we question people on whose memory we rely, most importantly witnesses to crimes whose testimony in a court of law may be important evidence.
Raine *et al.*	Helps us to explain the biological influence on violent behaviour. Controversially, should we be identifying children with low pre-frontal brain activity (e.g. with ADHD) and trying to affect this with, for example, Ritalin and behaviour-modification techniques?
Gould	Shows us we should be careful to consider the validity and reliability of psychometric tests, particularly in terms of their culture bias. It also cautions that such tests in the wrong hands can be used as agents of social control.

Theme: Determinism

How much of our behaviour is controlled by us? To what extent do we exercise free will? What is the cause of our behaviour, and do we have any control over it? If we have little or no control, then our behaviour is determined and we lose our free will. This raises a number of questions:

- If we do not freely choose our behaviour, how far should we be held responsible for it?
- If our behaviour can be controlled by outside forces, who should we trust to make the decisions?

The free will–determinism argument is one from philosophy, but one that also has implications for psychology. Hard determinism suggests that our behaviour is entirely determined by factors outside our control. This is an interesting philosophical argument, for if our behaviours are determined by external or internal influences beyond our control, can we be held responsible for our actions? Soft determinism, meanwhile, sits in the middle of the free will–determinism continuum, suggesting that a person makes choices which are influenced by other factors, so both free will and determinism play a part.

Examples of determinism in the core studies

In psychology, there are a number of different types of determinism:
- Environmental determinism – the environment or situational factors cause

behaviour. For example, the social psychological core studies by Milgram and Zimbardo *et al.* demonstrate that environmental factors, such as the role we are given to play or the relationship we have to an authority figure, can impact on the person so much that he may act cruelly towards others against conscience. The study by Hraba and Grant on doll choice in black children shows how the environment can lead to a reduced pride in your group identity (Clark and Clark, 1939) and how changes in the way your group sees itself and is valued by society can lead to increases in racial preference and pride in your ethnicity (Hraba and Grant, 1970).

- Unconscious determinism – behaviour is caused by the unconscious to satisfy unconscious drives. The example of this in the core studies is Freud's study of Little Hans. Freud sees Hans' behaviour as being governed by his unconscious progression through the stages of psychosexual development, and describes the boy's behaviours in terms of unconscious desires and motivations. These motivations could be uncovered through analysis of Hans' dreams and fantasies. Freud describes Hans' fear of horses, for example, as being symbolic of castration fear, a fear which Freud saw as residing in the boy's unconscious mind but impacting on his behaviour in the form of a phobic reaction.

- Biological determinism – behaviour is caused by biology, e.g. brain structure. An example from the core studies is Raine *et al.*'s study on the influence of brain structure and activity on the behaviour of murderers pleading not guilty by reason of insanity. Another biological determinant of behaviour is the maturation process. Hodges and Tizard aimed to find out if there is a critical period for the development of attachment beyond which environmental enrichment will have no effect on social/family relationships. Their work seemed to show that in the case of social relationships early negative experiences determined problems for all the ex-institutionalised children.

Theme: Ecological validity

Ecological validity is a type of 'external validity'. This means the extent to which generalisations can be made from the test environment to other situations.

A study is high in ecological validity if the behaviour subjects are asked to perform resembles a behaviour they, or people similar to them, perform in real life. Laboratory studies tend to be low in ecological validity, since the setting is artificial and therefore unlikely to represent 'real-life' behaviour. This is especially true when children are tested individually in the laboratory, isolated from their usual social environment and tested by people they don't know. Some researchers argue that the only method that has high ecological validity is covert observation in a natural setting, as this studies people's freely chosen and normal behaviour without the biasing factor of their knowledge that they are being observed.

High or low ecological validity in the core studies?

Study	Low ✗	High ✓
Milgram	✗ lab study, untypical task	
Zimbardo *et al.*	✗ simulated prison, unlike real prison	
Piliavin *et al.*		✓ covert observation of behaviour in natural setting
Tajfel	✗ laboratory experiment	
Loftus and Palmer	✗ laboratory experiment	
Baron-Cohen *et al.*	✗ laboratory experiment, kids tested alone	
Gardner and Gardner	✗ Washoe was out of her natural environment and encouraged to perform behaviours chimps don't naturally perform (sign, brush her teeth, use a potty chair!)	
Samuel and Bryant	✗ laboratory experiment, kids tested alone	
Bandura *et al.*	✗ laboratory experiment, kids tested alone	
Freud		✓ covert observation of behaviour in natural setting (question is, how was this behaviour interpreted?)

Dement and Kleitman	✗ laboratory study (we don't sleep in a lab or wired up to an EEG machine!)	
Sperry	✗ laboratory experiment, Ss restricted (no talking, for example)	
Schachter and Singer	✗ laboratory experiment	
Raine	✗ laboratory study, CPT task lacks comparison with aggressive behaviour	
Rosenhan	✗ 'normal people' don't usually seek diagnosis of mental illness or hospitalisation	✓ covert observation of behaviour in natural setting
Thigpen and Cleckley	✗ therapeutic setting, using retrospective data	
Hraba and Grant	✗ laboratory experiment, kids tested alone	

Theme: Ethics

Because the participants in psychological studies are people, we should treat them with care and respect, protecting them from both psychological and physical harm. Psychologists have membership of professional organisations, the American Psychological Association (APA) in the USA, and here in Britain the British Psychological Society (BPS). These professional bodies oversee the work of psychologists and provide ethical guidelines to be followed when carrying out research on human subjects.

The guidelines include the following:

• Participants should be informed of the nature and procedures of the study prior to taking part so that they can make an informed choice to take part, and give their informed consent to participate in the investigation.

- Deception should be used only if necessary, and as little as necessary. For example, to avoid demand characteristics, it may be necessary to use a cover story to conceal the true purpose of the study. Where deception has been used, debriefing is needed.
- Thorough debriefing should be given, explaining the nature and findings of the study and providing further support e.g. counselling, if required or requested.
- Participants should be protected from both physical and psychological harm, including undue stress, whilst taking part in the study. They should be protected from self-knowledge or experiences that negatively impact on their self-esteem and dignity.
- Confidentiality/anonymity should be assured and maintained for all those taking part in the study.
- The participants' privacy should not be invaded.
- Participants should be informed of their right to withdraw at any time, or to withdraw their data at the end of the study.
- Participants should not be coerced into taking part or continuing with a study, whether by directly refusing to allow them to stop when they want to or by implicitly engaging their commitment to continue with payment.

The guidelines represent what psychologists should be aiming for in their studies, but in reality it is difficult to carry out work that doesn't at least bend, if not blatantly flout, one or more of these 'rules'.

In deciding whether or not a study which breaches ethical guidelines should be (or should have been) carried out, we need to consider the following:

1. Does the aim of the study justify it being carried out? Is it a worthwhile study? Will it explore areas which have not been explored before? Will the results help us understand behaviour better?
2. If the ethical code was broken, are the findings important enough to justify this?

The salient question we have to ask when considering the ethics of a study involving human participants is: does the end justify the means?

Examples of ethical issues raised by the core studies

An important note here is that some of the core studies were carried out a long time ago. The ethical guidelines that relate to current psychological practice have been amended and refined since some of these studies were carried out, and, in some cases, as a result of these studies being carried out. Some of the studies would probably not be allowed to be carried out in the way that they were if we wanted to replicate them today.

STUDY	Informed consent	Deception (e.g. cover story)	Debriefing (adequate care after the study?)	Coercion	Confidentiality/ anonymity /invasion of privacy	Right to withdraw	Harm/ embarrassment/ pain
Schachter and Singer (emotion)	No – true purpose of study was concealed.	Yes – cover story about the effects of Suproxin on vision was used. Ss were deceived into thinking the stooge was a fellow subject.	Yes – Ss were debriefed afterwards.		Yes - anonymity of Ss was maintained.		
Bandura, Ross and Ross (imitation)	No – true purpose of study was concealed. Also there is an issue here about who gives consent for minors (Ss = 3 to 5-year-olds). No evidence of parental consent.		No – Ss were not debriefed, and in any case, even if the study were to be explained to a 3 to 5-year-old, they would not be able to understand.	Yes – the children were encouraged (forced?) to remain in room 3, the E went in with them to ensure they did stay for the full 20 minutes.	Yes – anonymity of Ss was maintained.	No – some children had to be accompanied into the third room because they didn't want to enter it, or would not stay for the allotted time. The child clearly wanted to withdraw, but the researchers ensured that they did not.	Yes – in stage 2 the child was deliberately upset. We might guess that some of the children were also perturbed or upset by their experience with the aggressive adult and their antics with Bobo in stage 1. In the long term, might the children in the aggressive condition have been harmed by their experience of the aggressive adult?

STUDY	Informed consent	Deception (e.g. cover story)	Debriefing (adequate care after the study?)	Coercion	Confidentiality/ anonymity /invasion of privacy	Right to withdraw	Harm/ embarrassment/ pain
Piliavin, Piliavin and Rodin	No – Ss were observed covertly, without their knowledge and consent.	Yes – Ss were led to believe the victim really was in trouble when he was acting and that other team members were just ordinary passengers.	No – Ss were observed in a public setting without their consent. It was not possible to identify them all and follow up the study with a debriefing.		Yes – anonymity of Ss was maintained. And No – we might argue that there was an invasion of privacy. Shouldn't people be able to go about their lives without being studied?	No – Ss were unaware they were in a study so were given neither the opportunity to consent or to withdraw from the study.	Possibly Ss felt uncomfortable at their inaction, if they did not help. This is unpleasant self-knowledge that they experienced as a result of the study. The situation could have been stressful for all observers and helpers.
Tajfel	No – true purpose of study was concealed. Also there is an issue here about who gives consent for minors (Ss = 14 to 15-year-olds).	Yes – cover story about tests of vision was used. Ss were deceived into thinking the matrices were not part of the study.			Yes – anonymity of Ss was maintained.		

SUDY	Informed consent	Deception (e.g. cover story)	Debriefing (adequate care after the study?)	Coercion	Confidentiality/ anonymity /invasion of privacy	Right to withdraw	Harm/ embarrassment/ pain
Milgram	No – true purpose of study was concealed.	Yes – Ss were deceived into thinking that the allocation of the role of 'learner' was by chance and that the 'learner' was really receiving painful (and possibly harmful) electric shocks. The E and the learner were stooges, too.	Yes – Milgram followed up his work with immediate debriefing and, a year later, with assessment by a psychiatrist, who found no evidence of harm caused by the study.		Yes – anonymity of Ss was maintained.	No – some subjects said afterwards that they felt that they could not withdraw and felt they had to continue (but this is exactly what Milgram was trying to investigate!). When Ss protested or questioned the procedure, the E told them they must continue.	Critics, notably Baumrind, argued that the procedure in Milgram's study put Ss under extreme stress. Milgram disagreed, even though he had to discontinue one trial as the 'teacher' had a convulsive seizure! In the long term, the self-knowledge gained by Ss who went all the way to 450v may also have been damaging to their self-esteem.

You also need to note that there are separate guidelines for animal studies. So the comparative study in the core studies (the Gardner and Gardner study on teaching sign language to Washoe) is not governed by the same ethical guidelines. For ethical concerns raised in this study, see the commentary at the end of the write-up of the core study in this book.

Theme: Ethnocentrism/ethnocentric bias

Ethnocentrism means seeing one's own group as better than other groups, or only seeing the world from your own point of view, or the point of view of your group or culture.

In psychology we often study one group or culture (usually American, male, middle-class and white) and use the findings to describe 'people in general'. However, because cultures, regions, towns, villages and groups of all kinds have different values, customs and norms, to try to generalise findings from studies carried out only in one culture (e.g. only the Western culture) is to be guilty of ethnocentric bias.

Examples of ethnocentric bias in the core studies

If studies were carried out on a specific group (eg age group, gender, all from one region, all students, all from one school, all from one culture) then we cannot generalise the findings to other groups/cultures or to people in general. In other words, there is an ethnocentric bias in the sample. Examples from the core studies include:
- student samples, e.g. Schachter and Singer, Zimbardo
- subjects from the same school, e.g. Tajfel, Bandura
- subjects from a particular region/country, e.g. Milgram, Zimbardo, Tajfel, Schachter and Singer
- gender bias in the sample, e.g. Milgram, Zimbardo, Tajfel, Schachter and Singer, Freud (all males) and Dement and Kleitman (mostly males).

Examples of ethnocentrism in the core studies: choosing your group over another; seeing your group as superior

- Tajfel shows how 'mere belonging to one group and knowledge of another' leads people to make ethnocentric choices in favour of their in-group. We call this discrimination.
- Hraba and Grant show how culture change in the US from 1939–69 influenced black children's doll choices: in 1969 they made ethnocentric choices, chose the black doll when asked which was nice and which they wanted to play with (showing racial preference), whereas in 1939 they had chosen white dolls (in 1969 white children also made ethnocentric choices, that is, chose the white doll).
- Gould shows how culture bias in Yerkes' tests enabled him to provide evidence

for his racist, white supremacist views, which are in themselves illustrative of extreme attitudes developed from an ethnocentric bias. The tests had an ethnocentric bias, favouring people with a good command of English; those who had been in America the longest and were familiar with the culture were more able to answer questions about 'Crisco' and suchlike.

- Does Deregowski show ethnocentrism/racism in the inclusion of anecdotal evidence by early missionaries, such as Mrs Donald Fraser, which presents the tribespeople as being 'silly' to be tricked by a slide on a sheet into thinking it was a real elephant?

Theme: Individual and situational explanations

How far is behaviour caused by individual factors (biology and genetics/maturation/personality) and how far by factors in the environment (social context, culture)?

This theme raises issues that overlap with two other themes, determinism (see above) and the nature–nurture debate (see below).

Examples of individual and situational explanations of behaviour from the core studies

Individual (internal) explanations:

- Raine *et al.*'s study on murderers' brains shows how brain structure may influence violent behaviour, and this shows that the individual's behaviour can be influenced by their biology, an internal factor.
- Freud's case study of Little Hans demonstrates Freud's assumptions that all behaviour is driven by internal (individual) factors. Freud saw all behaviour as being in response to the demands of unconscious drives, and therefore internally motivated.
- Another motivation for behaviour is illustrated by Tajfel's study and his Social Identity Theory. The purpose of in-group affiliation is to boost self-esteem. The motivation is to satisfy an underpinning human need for self-esteem, and this is an internal factor.
- Behaviour is also influenced by developmental factors, such as the stage of maturation the individual has reached or the impact of critical periods of development on their behaviour. Hodges and Tizard aimed to find out if there is a critical period for the development of attachment beyond which environmental enrichment will have no effect on social/family relationships, and it seemed that the negative early experiences of the ex-institutional adolescents had an impact on their relationships at 16.

Situational (external) explanations:

- A number of the core studies illustrate the impact of culture, an external factor, on behaviour. Hraba and Grant showed how cultural change in the way black people viewed themselves and an increase in black pride affected the doll preference of the black children in 1969. Tajfel showed how 14-year-old boys were 'programmed' by society to compete and discriminate, but also to consider 'fairness' in their choices. Rosenhan showed how staff interpretations of behaviour were biased to assume all the behaviours of inmates were due to their pathology and not caused by the setting (the culture of institutionalisation) in which the behaviour was observed.

- Zimbardo *et al.* demonstrated how social roles, the situation in which a person was placed and their perception of what was required of them affected the behaviour of both the guards and the prisoners in their study.
- Milgram's study illustrates how social pressure, particularly from an authority figure, influences people's behaviour.
- Bandura *et al.* showed how children learn through observation, and this clearly demonstrates the impact of the environment on their behaviour. A factor that may affect the performance of the learned behaviour is reinforcement, further evidence from the study of the influence of external factors, in this case external reinforcers, on behaviour (see Reinforcement below).

Theme: The nature–nurture debate

Banyard describes the nature–nurture debates as 'fairly pointless theoretical debates, popular in the 1950s, concerning whether a given psychological ability was inherited or whether it was learned through experience'. The question was, is behaviour inborn (genetic, inherited, innate) or is it learned (affected by cultural and environmental influence)?

Whilst early on there were two clear camps on this issue, with the Nativists to the one extreme, claiming all behaviour was innate (for example, Yerkes and his hereditarian colleagues) and, on the other hand, empiricists (such as Skinner and the behaviourists) claiming that all behaviour was learned. Currently the question is not whether behaviour is innate or learned, but rather how much of a behaviour (if any) is genetically determined. The debate has been taken over by the human genome project (for a review, see Karon Oliver's *Applying Skills to Psychology*, chapter 3).

Examples of the nature–nurture debate from the core studies

Deregowski	Considers whether the perception of line drawings is innate or learned. His work shows how cross-cultural studies can be useful in establishing whether behaviour is learned or innate. If a behaviour is not culturally universal, that is people in different cultures behave in different ways, then we can assume that this behaviour is as a result of nurture rather than nature.

His findings show that the perception of depth (3D) in drawings is learned, as Africans were generally 2D perceivers and Westerners 3D perceivers.

Hodges and Tizard	Considers whether there is an innately programmed 'critical period' by which if a child hasn't developed an emotional bond with a significant caregiver, they will have long-term problems in their social/family relationships. The study shows that there does seem to be a long-term effect of early privation, especially in social relationships in the ex-institutionalised adolescents.
	The study also shows the effect of nurture. The adopted children had an enriched environment and this was able to counteract the negative effects of privation on family relationships of the adopted 16-year-olds.
Hraba and Grant	Shows that nurture (cultural influence) can have an impact on a child's self-esteem, in terms of their racial preferences and pride in their ethnicity.
Gould	Yerkes tried to claim that there was such a thing as 'native intellectual ability' – an intelligence that was set at birth and inherited. He went on to use his misinterpretation of his findings to 'prove' that whites were innately more intelligent than darker-skinned people – not true!
Raine et al.	Shows that biology influences aggressive behaviour, but this is not the sole cause. Biology interacts with other variables in order to lead to aggression (nature and nurture interacting).

Theme: Psychometrics

Psychometric tests are instruments (e.g. pen-and-paper tests, one-to-one tests) that have been developed to measure mental characteristics, e.g. intelligence tests (IQ tests), brain damage/brain function (STM capabilities), creativity, personality, job attitudes, aptitude and skills. Although they often provide quantitative measurements that are attractive to psychologists, as this makes comparison between subjects and analysis of data possible, there are some problems associated with psychometric tests. They are often completed as self-reports, so data may be falsified. This affects their internal validity.

425

Validity is a problem in general for these tests. Are they really testing what they say they are testing? It is very difficult to design a test that does not contain cultural biases and can be used for people in general.

Reliability is also important. If Ss do not score significantly similar results on an equivalent test, then the tests are not reliable (and if they are not reliable, they are not valid). Psychometric tests need to be administered and assessed by trained individuals. In the wrong hands they can be misinterpreted, for example, low IQ scores used to 'label' someone as stupid, and treating them accordingly!

Examples of psychometric tests used in the core studies

Study	Use of psychometrics in the study
Gould (IQ testing)	Gould describes Yerkes' 'intelligence tests' and shows how the tests can be affected by culture bias. The Ss' command of the English affected their scores, and the questions favoured Americans or those immigrants who had been in America the longest.
Hodges and Tizard (attachment)	Hodges and Tizard asked teachers to complete the Rutter B scale for the ex-institutional children. This comprises 26 items and is used for psychiatric screening (it is a psychometric measure of mental health).
Thigpen and Cleckley (three faces of Eve)	Eve White and Eve Black 'both' did IQ tests and memory tests to see if they were different, the intention of testing was to objectively assess whether there were really two personalities in one woman. Although the testing was useful as it provided quantitative data so that the two Eves could be compared, the tests were inconclusive. For example, their IQ scores were 110 and 104, hardly different at all, and both 'average'.
Baron-Cohen *et al.* (autism)	Baron-Cohen *et al.* tested all the children on a standardised test, 'The Sally-Anne Test', designed to measure whether or not they had a theory of mind. This would be established if they could answer the belief question correctly.

Themes: Reductionism

Reductionism is the tendency to explain complex phenomena by reference to only one factor, such as learning or biology. For example, physiological reductionism is a problem where studies focus on a purely biological explanation of behaviour, e.g. biomedical explanations of illness. Laboratory-based studies are reductionist as they reduce people to the sum of their behaviour in the lab, and this is not realistic since this is only a sample of their total behaviours. This is known as experimental reductionism. Data-gathering techniques that quantify behaviour can also be reductionist, e.g. describing someone using just an IQ score, when they are clearly much more than that one numerical assessment. Focusing on one psychological approach or explanation is reductionist, so any study that looks at behaviour from just the cognitive or just the social point of view, for example, is reductionist. Trying to explain complex social behaviours in simple terms is also reductionist. For example, prejudice is a complex behaviour which has many causes, e.g. scapegoating, classical conditioning, operant conditioning, modelling, socio-economic inequalities, political oppression, and Tajfel reduces it to the Ss' 'mere belonging to one group and knowledge of another group'.

Another source of information for you is the chief examiner's report on the way exams have gone for each exam series. These can have useful snippets of information in them as well as helping you to understand what the examiners are looking for and avoid the mistakes of previous students. For example, your chief examiner points out that reductionism is often seen as a 'problem' in research, and this is because 'an extreme reductionist approach tends to miss the wood by looking at the trees'. Whilst focusing on this negative aspect of the approach, students tend to miss the fact that a reductionist approach can also be useful to researchers. This is because it allows scientists to focus on particular variables and identify their effect, thus increasing our understanding of behaviour.

Themes: Reinforcement

Reinforcement is a concept from behaviourism. The behaviourists, notably Skinner, thought direct reinforcement was essential in the acquisition of behaviour, or learning. Reinforcers increase the probability that a behaviour will recur in similar circumstances. Reinforcers can be both positive and negative. For example, if you wash your mum's car and she gives you money in return, this is an example of positive reinforcement. You will be likely to perform the behaviour again (wash the car) to experience the positive reinforcer (receiving money). However, if you borrow your mum's car without her permission, and your mum then bans you from borrowing it again for a month, this is an example of negative reinforcement. The behaviour your mum is trying to reinforce here is 'not taking the car without permission', and the negative reinforcer is the period of the ban. So you will be more likely to perform the behaviour (not take the car without permission) to avoid the negative reinforcer (being banned for a month). This is clearly an important part of cultural transmission from parent to child and is very useful when training the family pet (though sadly I have yet to find the reinforcer that will get my cat to wash my car).

Examples of reinforcement in the core studies

Bandura, Ross and Ross:

Being directly reinforced is not the only way we learn: Bandura *et al.* considered the role of imitation and vicarious reinforcement in their study on the learning of aggression. They demonstrated that direct reinforcement was not essential for learning to have taken place and that we can learn by observing and imitating. The child did not need to be externally reinforced to carry out the behaviour. This showed that reinforcement could be internal, too. Boys feel good about being aggressive because they've been positively reinforced for it before; girls feel bad about it or inhibit their aggressive behaviour because they have been negatively reinforced for it before. This feeling good or bad acts as a reinforcer and either encourages or inhibits displays of aggressive behaviour. Bandura *et al.* conclude that although reinforcement is not essential for learning a behaviour, it may play a big part in whether or not someone decides to perform that learned behaviour.

Gardner and Gardner:

In training Washoe, the Gardners used instrumental conditioning, 'shaping' her behaviour by rewarding (reinforcing) her for sign-like gestures, then rewarding only well-formed signs and those made in the right context. She therefore acquired signs by being positively reinforced.

Of course, this highlights one difference between children's language learning and Washoe's: children do not need to be reinforced for language – they acquire it spontaneously.

Themes: Social control

Social control refers to the attempt to influence the behaviour of people and so encourage them to behave in a passive way or in socially desirable ways: how are people 'kept in their place'?

Examples of social control from the core studies

- Milgram illustrates how we are obedient to authority figures: if we accept a figure as an authority figure we find it difficult to withdraw from the situation or question the person's judgement. We lose our sense of personal agency and see the authority figure as 'responsible'.
- Zimbardo shows how when we take on social roles we again lose our sense of personal agency and act according to what we think the role requires. The role therefore 'controls' our behaviour.
- Hraba and Grant show how the structure of the dominant culture (white

supremacists in charge, segregation of blacks and whites) affected the racial preference of the black children. They were taught by their experience that it was bad to be black and they consequently had little pride in their ethnicity. This kept them in their place as the out-group in society.

- Gould shows how Yerkes and his colleagues used scientific racism (they interpreted the data from the tests to support their own dogma) to support the heredetarian argument. The hereditarians were able to successfully lobby for legislation to restrict the immigration of darker-skinned Eastern and Southern Europeans in the '20s and '30s. Their biased interpretations of the findings led to the policies that left millions of Europeans unable to escape the holocaust.

- The diagnosis of abnormality ('mental illness' in Rosenhan's day, now called 'mental disorder') can also be seen as an agent of social control. People who were diagnosed and admitted to institutions suffered a loss of freedom. Is this for the good of the patient, the good of society, or controlling 'undesirables', getting rid of embarrassing family members, etc.?

Themes: Validity and reliability

A test or measure is valid if it tests what it is supposed to test. Ecological validity is a form of external validity, and we have discussed this already as a separate theme. In the Deregowski study we also came across a type of validity called concurrent validity. What this means is that two studies measuring the same variable have come up with similar findings. Hudson's pictures task and the tridents task both seemed to suggest that some of the Zambian schoolchildren were 2D perceivers and some were 3D perceivers. The two tasks were, therefore, concurrently valid, each supporting the validity of the other.

Internal validity is determined by the extent to which a study is free of design faults which may affect the result, meaning that the test is not a true test of what it intended to measure.

Factors which reduce the validity (internal validity) of findings include the following:

- Low generalisability of findings, e.g. sample biases, ethnocentric bias, difficulty extrapolating to other groups of people/settings. If the findings are not generalisable then they are not valid.
- Demand characteristics. If Ss are taking part in a study they will try to work out what the study is about. Demand characteristics are the cues/clues present, given away by the procedure/questions/tasks, or given unconsciously by those carrying out the test, which suggest to the S what the hypothesis is. There are two responses Ss may make to having worked out what they think the study is about:
  1. to try to please the experimenter and get the experiment to 'work' – out of a desire to be 'right', they modify their behaviour/answers to fit in with how they think the experimenter expects them to behave
  2. the 'sabbotage' effect – here the aim is to spoil the experiment by not acting in the way they think is expected of them (this may be just for the sake of it,

or because they want to make the statement, 'I am not typical').

Of course, both these responses to demand characteristics mean Ss are falsifying their responses, and this means that the validity of the findings comes into question where Ss responding to demand characteristics is a possibility in a study.

- If it is possible that a confounding variable has operated systematically alongside the IV then this may affect the validity of the findings. For instance, in independent groups designs and matched Ss designs it is difficult to control subject variables. In other words, there may be differences between the two groups other than that one has the IV introduced, and this means it is possible that subject variables have confounded the study, and therefore we have to question the validity of the findings.

Reliability refers to the consistency of a measurement. A test or measure is reliable if it gives similar results when carried out again in similar circumstances. In other words, if the findings prove to be replicable, which is a key element in scientific study, then the test or measure is reliable. Correlational analysis is used to test for both reliability and validity, and this is a common use of correlations in psychological investigations. We are most able to carry out the study again and establish the reliability of studies where quantitative analysis has been used, for example, in laboratory-based experiments. We are least able to establish the reliability of case studies that gather qualitative data. Low reliability brings the validity of findings into question. If the study is not replicable, it is unlikely to be valid. If a study is low in validity, this in turn reduces its usefulness.

Examples of validity and reliability issues in the core studies: revision activity

- Which core studies have low ecological validity?
- Which core studies use self-report data-gathering methods that can be falsified, leading us to question the validity of the findings?
- Which studies have sample biases that restrict the generalisability of the studies and mean they are not valid measures of people in general?
- Why might brain-imaging techniques, such as the PET scan used by Raine *et al.*, not give valid results?
- Why are Yerkes' tests not valid measures of 'native intellectual ability'?
- Identify two studies from the core studies where it would be relatively easy to establish the reliability of the findings, and two core studies where it would be difficult to establish the reliability of the findings.

Themes: Qualitative and quantitative data

Quantitative data is numerical data, such as categories and frequencies, percentages, etc. It is attractive to gather quantitative data because of the ease with which people's performances on a test or task can be compared. The data is also easy to summarise and present, and statistical analysis is possible. It is also easier to establish the reliability of findings that are numerical, as this can be done by re-testing and correlating the results of the first and second tests to see if there is a significant positive correlation. The trouble is, quantitative data gives a narrow view of the person, one that is both reductionist and lacking in validity. The alternative is to gather qualitative data which usually takes the form of verbal descriptions, such as reports of what has been observed or written reports of interviews. Whilst it is more difficult to compare, analyse and draw conclusions from qualitative data, or to replicate it to tests for reliability, what you gain is an increase in the depth and detail of the findings, and, therefore, increasing validity.

Scientific study usually implies the gathering and analysis of quantitative data, using inferential statistics to establish cause and effect or correlation between variables. Psychological investigations have, therefore, historically tended to focus on quantitative methods of analysis. However, qualitative research methods, such as discourse analysis, are now appearing more frequently in psychological literature. As you might imagine, many researchers try to incorporate the strengths of both qualitative and quantitative data in their work, and there are examples of this in the core studies.

Examples of qualitative and quantitative data in the core studies

Study	Qualitative data	Quantitative data
Milgram	Nervous laughter and sweating was observed	65% went up to 450v, 100% went to 300v
Zimbardo *et al.*	Guards made prisoners do humiliating things, made up arbitrary punishments (especially during counts)	
Piliavin *et al.*	Comments elicited from passengers by observers e.g. 'it's for a man to help him'	In cane (ill) condition, victim was helped spontaneously on 62/65 trials (drunk = 19/38)
Tajfel		Inferential analysis of the numbers of points awarded was carried out
Loftus and Palmer		Study 1 – speed estimate was measured as an average per condition

		Study 2 – 16/50 Ss in 'smashed' condition reported seeing broken glass, compared with 6/50 in the control condition
Baron-Cohen *et al.*		85% of 'normal', 86% of Down's and 20% of autistic children got the belief question right
Deregowski	Anecdotal evidence of Mrs Donald Fraser (elephant slide on sheet)	Inferential statistics showed 3D Zambian schoolchildren took longer to draw the impossible trident
Gardner and Gardner	Washoe was observed to show creativity in her signing – combining words to increase meaning e.g. ('go sweet' to be carried to the raspberry bush	By 22nd month, she had 30 signs that met the strict criteria set by the Gardners for the acquisition of a sign
Hodges and Tizard	Interviews and questionnaires gathered qualitative data	Interviews and questionnaires gathered quantitative data, also Ss were given a score on the Rutter B scale
Samuel and Bryant		DV was measured as an average number of errors out of 12 per condition.
Bandura *et al.*		Children's aggressive behaviour was recorded using categories recording at 5-second intervals for 20 minutes in stage 3
Freud	Study is largely qualitative – an example is the description of Hans' fantasy of the two giraffes	

Dement and Kleitman		Out of 191 awakenings in REM sleep, 152 dream recalls were recorded. Out of 160 NREM awakenings, only 11 dream recalls were recorded
Sperry	Ss could not name an object placed in their left hand out of their view	
Schachter and Singer		DV measured on a rating scale −4 to +4 (happiness answer minus anger answer on questionnaire)
Raine et al.		PET scan provides quantitative data about brain activity
Rosenhan	The behaviour of patients was judged to be due to their 'pathology' rather than considered normal given the environment, e.g. 'patient engages in writing behaviour' was recorded about the diary keeping as if it were an abnormal behaviour	In the follow-up study, 10% of the research hospital's normal intake were suspected of being pseudopatients by two members of the hospital staff
Gould	Gould points out that tests were not carried out according to the protocol and this meant that results were not valid	Gould reports Yerkes' 'facts' from the testing: average American male was a moron (mental age = 13), and blacks were worst of all (average mental age = 10.4)

Thigpen and Cleckley	As this is a case report of therapeutic sessions, any episode described by the researchers is going to give qualitative data	Psychometric test scores, memory function scores, EEG scores
Hraba and Grant		Number of children picking each doll was recorded and analysed, e.g. white children picked the white doll more on questions 1 and two than black children picked the black doll (white children were more these questions)

Themes: Usefulness

Are the findings of a study useful? Well, the questions are: useful for what and to whom? Findings may be useful to psychologists in that they help to explain or predict behaviour, or generally useful for helping to explain behaviours and solve problems in the real world.

On the one hand, then, studies can be considered useful to psychology itself: a study or theory may be highly generative, that is, it leads to a great deal of further research, both testing and refining the conclusions drawn in a particular area of study. Examples of work which was highly generative include Freud's theory of psychosexual development, Piaget's theory of cognitive development and Bowlby's theory of attachment. It follows that studies which contribute to the debate in a particular area are also useful to psychology, e.g. Hodges and Tizard's work considers and provides some evidence of a 'critical period' in children's social and emotional development (an idea suggested by Bowlby but wrongly attributed by him to maternal deprivation as it is privation that seems to be a problem). Another example is that Samuel and Bryant's work contributes to the debate concerning children's cognitive development by providing support for the sequence of Piaget's stages, but also suggesting refinements to the timing of the stages as their work suggests he underestimated young children's abilities.

On the other hand, usefulness can be assessed by asking: are the conclusions/findings from the study any use in helping solve problems in the real world? This takes us back up to the beginning of this section on themes in the core studies, and the Applications of Psychology to Everyday Life (see p. 413).

Usefulness can be assessed in relation to both the methods and themes in the core studies. The usefulness of a study will be reduced if:

- the study is low in ecological validity and therefore findings cannot be easily generalised to a real-life setting,
- the study is reductionist and ignores other important factors or variables which affect behaviour
- the findings of the study are not valid, e.g. if demand characteristics could have affected the findings
- sample biases mean the findings are not generalisable to a broad population.

Revision activity

Using index cards, write the theme on one side and a definition of it on the other. Learn these and and test yourself!

APPROACHES/PERSPECTIVES

The 20 core studies are presented in the specification under 5 approaches or perspectives. These are the social approach, the cognitive approach, the developmental approach, the physiological approach and the individual differences approach. However, it is important for you to recognise that these categories are artificial, and that some of the studies straddle one, two or even three of the approaches. For example, the Baron-Cohen *et al.* study of autism is presented here as a cognitive study, as it looks at theory of mind as a cognitive process. However, it could just as easily be considered a study of individual differences, given that the target population is an atypical group – children with autism. It might also be seen as a developmental study, looking at the role of development in the acquisition of theory of mind. Samuel and Bryant's conservation study might sit as well in cognitive psychology as it does in developmental, where the AS places it. Freud's study of Little Hans is also a developmental one here, but could just as well be placed in the individual differences approach, as it deals with Hans' phobia, which is an abnormal behaviour. Bandura, Ross and Ross's work is in the developmental approach here, as we focus on what it shows about learning and imitation, but you will find it is referred to in many social psychology tests as an example of how we learn from our social surroundings, and indeed, Bandura called his theory, Social Learning Theory. We shall look at each of the approaches in turn, consider their strengths and weaknesses and apply these to the core studies.

Approaches: The social psychological approach

This approach aims to investigate our social behaviour. In particular, researchers have looked at social influence, that is, how our actions can be affected by others, or by the context in which we find ourselves. When we are trying to understand why someone has done or said something, do we look to the person or do we look to society for the causes of the behaviour?

Researcher(s)	Focus of study
Milgram	Obedience to a malevolent authority
Haney, Banks and Zimbardo	Prison simulation to consider the cause of brutality in real prisons
Piliavin, Piliavin and Rodin	Helping behaviour in the New York subway and factors that influence helping
Tajfel	Intergroup discrimination

Strengths and weaknesses of this approach include:
- The social approach helps us to consider factors in the social environment which determine our behaviour. For example, it is useful to recognise that authority figures have control over us, because armed with this information we should be able to work out that we have to be very careful to whom we give such authority. Milgram's work can, on the one hand, be seen as dark and depressing, revealing something negative about humanity. On the other hand, however, Milgram said that although it seems we are 'puppets' of our social environments, we are in fact 'puppets with power'. In a democracy we have power to choose those in authority, and Milgram's work cautions us we should treat that power with respect and use it wisely.
- Zimbardo *et al.*'s work shows us that if we had the inclination and resources to do so we could reform the prison service and perhaps solve the humanitarian issues surrounding how we treat those who have wronged us and those who watch over them. Unfortunately, this remains a fantasy in most cultures, where the emphasis of the penal service is on revenge and punishment and the outcome is high recidivism by prisoners on release and, consequently, more misery.
- Two of the studies in the specification show that we are more influenced by others than we might like to think (Milgram, Zimbardo *et al.*) and these challenge our belief that we act autonomously (according to our own free will).
- On a more positive note, the study by Piliavin *et al.* showed that, contrary to the case of Kitty Genovese and the depressing levels of help demonstrated in laboratory studies, the people on the New York subway did come forward to help a fellow passenger in need. This shows us the problems with laboratory studies of social behaviour, which lack ecological validity and aren't good predictors of real-life behaviour.
- It is useful to study the causes of social ills such as prejudice. If we are to reduce discrimination it is helpful to understand the factors which bring it about.

Tajfel's work contributes to such understanding, although his explanation that in-group discrimination occurs because of a need to raise self-esteem does not really lead us to an obvious solution if we are to reduce discrimination either in an individual or in society at large.

- Demand characteristics may be a problem. In laboratory studies especially, findings may not be valid because Ss are simply responding to the demand characteristics present in the study. Orne suggests that this was what was happening in Milgram's study.

- There are difficulties applying controls to people so it is hard to establish that the IV is a causal factor. This is especially true in field experiments, such as the one carried out by Piliavin *et al.* on the New York subway.

- There are difficulties with measurement of variables and so it is hard to achieve validity. For example, Tajfel had to rely on self-report data and it could be that the boys were responding to demand characteristics and favouring their group because that is what they were supposed to do.

- Hraba and Grant's work shows that social psychology is a product of its time. Changes in culture lead to changes in behaviour. This makes us question the value of research carried out a long time ago, and given that all the social psychological core studies were carried out before 1973, this means we must be cautious in generalising the findings from those studies to people today.

- Cultural differences in behaviour are often overlooked when generalising results, and this leads to findings being used to describe people in general when in fact the research carries an ethnocentric bias. For example, can the social psychological studies in the core studies which were carried out in New York, Yale University, Stanford University and Bristol be used to generalise to other non-Western cultures?

Approaches: The cognitive approach

Cognitive psychology is concerned with the study of mental processes, e.g. memory, language production and comprehension, thinking and reasoning, paying attention and perception. Cognitive psychology considers the brain to be an information processor, based on a computer analogy. The brain inputs, stores and outputs information. Of course, it is much more complicated than this, but this mechanistic model of the brain provides a plausible framework for the study of cognitive processes which is our current best explanation of what is going on in our heads. Cognitive neuroscience is a discipline that aims to study scientifically the cognitive processes. This approach favours the scientific method. Three of the four cognitive core studies present laboratory-based investigations of mental processes (Baron-Cohen *et al.*, Loftus and Palmer and the work by Hudson described in the Deregowski study).

Researcher(s)	Focus of study
Baron-Cohen *et al.*	Does the autistic child lack a theory of mind?
Loftus and Palmer	Can questioning (language) lead people to reconstruct their memory of an accident they witnessed on film?
Deregowski	Is the perception of pictures innate or learned?
Gardner and Gardner	Can a chimpanzee learn sign language?

Strengths and weaknesses of this approach include:

- The emphasis on controlled scientific study in cognitive psychology provides objective evidence in which we can have confidence. It is also easier to test such studies for reliability. For example, the Baron-Cohen *et al.* study could be quite quickly and easily repeated to see if its findings are replicable.
- Understanding the problems of children with autism can be useful to those who care for them at home or at school. Understanding their unusual and perplexing behaviours may make the care of the child more manageable.
- Loftus and Palmer demonstrate the frailty of human memory and its reconstructive nature. If we are to rely on human memory in a court of law, then it is a strength of cognitive psychology that we are able to present a coherent explanation of the strengths and failings of eyewitness testimony.
- Whilst rigorous and controlled studies in the lab are useful, the predominance of this method in the study of cognitive processes means that ecological validity is low. On the other hand, if you sacrifice rigour and control in the pursuit of higher ecological validity, as Bartlett did in his work on the 'War of the Ghosts' study, you end up with qualitative data that is difficult to draw conclusions from.
- The 'machine analogy' is reductionist. The human brain is more than just a machine. The cognitive approach often takes a narrow focus on behaviour and ignores important social and emotional factors that may impact on behaviour. For example, would the findings of the Loftus and Palmer study be different if Ss had seen a real-life accident, with all the emotional and physiological changes that witnessing such an event might bring with it?
- Cognitive processes can only be studied by inference, that is, we cannot study them directly, we can only gather what is going on in someone's head by recording what they can or can't tell us or can or can't do. Thus cognitive psychology relies a great deal on self-report and observational methods to gather data, and the biases present in each type of measurement may mean that the findings are not valid.

- To study the development of cognitive processes you have to study children. This means that you have the problem of making sure that the child's answers are not contaminated by others. This usually means bringing the child into a laboratory setting and testing them individually, as was done with the Sally-Anne test in the Baron-Cohen *et al.* study, and the Samuel and Bryant study on cognitive development and the conservation tasks. This way of testing children outside their normal social setting lacks ecological validity.
- There are ethical concerns with the study of children which relate to informed consent. This is a problem for both Baron-Cohen *et al.* and Deregowski (Hudson's work with Zambian and other African children).
- Cross-cultural studies are useful in ascertaining whether or not cognitive processes are innate or learned. However, these studies are expensive and can be influenced by the ethnocentric bias of the researcher (e.g. the Deregowski study).

Approaches: The developmental approach

This approach looks at the development of behaviours. Development is a lifelong process, but the core studies focus particularly on child development.

The core studies consider emotional development (Hodges and Tizard), Freud's theory of psychosexual development, which is a personality theory, the acquisition of behaviours through imitation (observational learning – Bandura *et al.*) and cognitive development (Samuel and Bryant).

Researcher(s)	Focus of study
Freud	The treatment, through analysis, of Little Hans' phobia – is this evidence for the Oedipus complex?
Bandura, Ross and Ross	Can we learn by imitation?
Samuel and Bryant	Do younger children than Piaget suggested conserve if only one question is asked in the conservation experiment?
Hodges and Tizard	Do early privation experiences have negative long-term effects on social and family relationships? Are these effects reversible?

Strengths and weaknesses of this approach include:
- Longitudinal studies are a feature of developmental psychology. They follow the development of Ss over a period of time and allow us to infer cause and effect

between variables. For example, the work by Hodges and Tizard shows the effects of early privation experiences before the age of two on social and family relationships in adolescents of 16.

- Longitudinal studies bring their weaknesses, however, and a common one is subject attrition. As the study progresses, subjects lose contact or decide to withdraw, and this leaves a volunteer bias in the sample at the later stages of the investigation. For example, of the 65 children studies at age four, Hodges and Tizard were able to study 51 at age eight, and at age 16, only 39 were available for study. This makes us question the validity of the findings.
- Longitudinal studies are, however, costly, in terms of the researcher's time and money. The alternative is to carry out a cross-sectional study, sampling children of different ages and comparing their performance to get a picture of development. Such an approach was taken by Samuel and Bryant, who used an independent groups design, studying five-, six-, seven- and eight-year-olds' performances on the conservation tasks. Using this method they were able to show that the ability to conserve improves with age, as Piaget had suggested.
- Developmental research can demonstrate the role of both internal factors and environmental factors on behaviour. For example, Hodges and Tizard show how an environmental factor, the children's early privation experience, impacted on their later relationships. Samuel and Bryant show the role of maturation in the development of cognitive abilities as they demonstrated that children's ability to conserve improved with age.
- Studying children brings ethical concerns, including whether or not children can give their informed consent to take part. For example, Bandura *et al.* make no reference to obtaining parental consent for a study in which they exposed impressionable youngsters to an adult model behaving in an aggressive way in the aggression condition. All children were subject to being deliberately upset in stage two, and some children were coerced into staying in room three for the required 20 minutes when they clearly did not want to. It is also possible that the questioning of 16-year-olds on their 'social difficulties', as Hodges and Tizard did in their study may also have caused distress to participants.
- There are problems with studying children under laboratory conditions, especially where they are tested by strangers in strange environments, and are isolated from their peers. This means that studies which are carried out in this way lack ecological validity. Examples of this are the studies by Bandura *et al.* and Samuel and Bryant.
- Whilst the use of the case study method in the study by Freud gives a great deal of qualitative data and studies Hans over a period of time to get a full picture of his experiences, it is affected by researcher bias. Both Freud and Hans' father, who carried out most of the interviews and observations of the boy, believed in fraud's psychosexual theory of development and saw Hans as a 'Little Oedipus'. This affected the way in which they reported and interpreted the boy's

experiences. The relationship between the boy and his father may also mean that the boy was susceptible to leading questions and this reduces the quality of the evidence. For example, when Hans' father asked, 'When the horse fell over, did you think of your daddy?' Hans' response, 'Yes. Perhaps. It is possible', may have been to please his father rather than to truly express what he thought at the time.

Approaches: The physiological approach

This approach considers the impact of biology (e.g. brain, nervous system, endocrine system, genetics) on behaviour. The advances in this field have been assisted by the development of technology (such as PET scanners) which allows us to study the living brain, and the ability to isolate the effects of specific genes should also mean that this field will continue to improve our understanding of the influence of biology on behaviour.

Study	Physiological process
Schachter and Singer	Emotion – is it a mix of arousal and context?
Raine *et al.*	Are some people aggressive because they have abnormal brain function? (e.g. low pre-frontal activity)
Dement and Kleitman	Does REM sleep correlate with dream recall?
Sperry	Lateralisation of brain function – what do the left and right hemispheres do?

Strengths and weaknesses of this approach include:
- This approach can help us to map brain activity and lead to greater under-standing of the physiognomy of the brain, for example, Sperry's work on the lat-eralisation of brain function.
- Physiological studies can lead to treatments for those with problem behaviours, e.g. treating low theta-wave activity with biofeedback to counteract low stimulation in the pre-frontal cortex that may be linked to impulsive or aggressive behaviours.
- The approach is very scientific, grounded in biology.
- Problems arise when studying abnormal subjects, e.g. brain damaged or split-brain patients (Sperry, Raine *et al.*) and murderers (Raine *et al.*). It is hard to make generalisations from studies of atypical subjects.
- Brain-imaging techniques rely on relatively new technology. There can be errors in the images caused when the information is made into an image by the

machine or by the interpretation of the person viewing the image. Imaging techniques allow us to see that the brain is active, but active doing what?

- This approach can explain biological influences on behaviour, but researchers must be careful to avoid reductionist explanations of behaviour, that is, seeing the behaviour as being solely caused by biology. For example, Raine *et al.* are very careful to caution against this and are at pains to point out that aggression is not solely caused by biology, only that biology may influence aggression.

- Studies carried out in the laboratory are low in ecological validity, for example, Dement and Kleitman had Ss sleep in their sleep laboratory. We sleep differently when we are not in our own bed, and this must have been more true where Ss were not only in a strange bed but also being observed, wired up to an EEG machine and awoken by a doorbell at intervals through the night.

- Even though the approach tries to be scientific, our limited ability to study brain processes directly and objectively means we have to rely on self-report data, and here demand characteristics may be a problem. For example, in Dement and Kleitman's study, Ss could have falsified reports about whether they were dreaming or not, or about the content of their dreams.

- Ethical issues arise where researchers try to avoid demand characteristics, e.g. deception of Ss (the cover story to do with testing the effects of 'Suproxin' on vision) is an issue in Schachter and Singer's study.

Approaches: *The individual differences approach*

The study of individual differences does just that, it studies the differences between individuals on certain variables. A great deal of work has been done on personality and intelligence, considering, for example, the nature–nurture debate in relation to these. Psychometric tests play a big role in the study of personality and intelligence, and the core study by Gould shows how such tests can be used, and abused, by scientists and politicians alike.

Another factor that can be considered an individual difference is the impact of culture on our behaviour. Cultural differences can be those that occur on a grand scale between countries, or small-scale cultural differences such as those between families and households. Cultural differences also occur with the passage of time and the changes, within one country, for example, in norms, values and customs. Hraba and Grant compare the cultural impact in the USA in 1939 on black children's racial preferences with those of black children in the USA in 1969.

In psychology the focus of scientific research is to study representative samples and establish general rules about human behaviour. This is known as the nomothetic approach. An alternative to this is to study those people who do not 'fit the mould', those who are atypical or even unique. This is known as the idiographic approach. For example, Sperry's split-brain patients represent a tiny number of people, but because of their fascinating medical condition (being commissurotomy patients) they are more than worthy of scientific study.

The study of atypical behaviours can benefit the individual(s) being studied and can also give us insight into the complexity of human experience and behaviour. Two of the core studies focus on abnormal psychology, considering the diagnosis of mental illness.

Researcher(s)	Focus of study
Gould	Research review of the development of IQ tests in WW1 in the USA and the misuse of tests, which clearly had an ethnocentric bias, to lobby the US government to restrict immigration.
Hraba and Grant	Replication of an earlier study by Clark and Clark (1939) to report the changes in racial self-identity and preference in black children 30 years after the original study.
Rosenhan	To investigate the reliability of psychiatric diagnosis by seeing if 'sane' people would be diagnosed as mentally ill. Also to observe and report the experience of being a patient in a psychiatric hospital.
Thigpen and Cleckley	To report on a possible case of multiple personality disorder and consider the validity of this rare diagnosis.

Strengths and weaknesses of this approach include:
- Gould's work illustrates clearly that we have to be careful in both the development and administration of psychometric tests on a large scale. The fact that tests such as the one developed by Yerkes and his colleagues are fundamentally culture-biased illustrates just how difficult it is to establish measures that can apply universally and allow cross-cultural comparisons to be made in any meaningful way.
- The use of the psychometric measures in the Thigpen and Cleckley study makes for ease of comparison between the two Eves. The fact that they scored very similarly on the IQ test, however, is inconclusive; since they both obtained 'average' scores, this neither confirms nor refutes their separate identities.
- Focusing on an individual, such as Eve White, may improve our understanding of her experience and help suggest treatments that may help her and anyone else presenting similar symptoms in the future. The other side of this coin, however, is that the rarity of such cases may lead to intrusive investigations and excessive study and testing, which may not help the individual and could in fact distress them. There is also the question of whether generalisations from case studies are

possible, and it may be that the findings of the Thigpen and Cleckley study would not help other people who may be experiencing the same symptoms.

• Rosenhan's work contributed to the debate over the diagnosis of mental illness. This study, and others investigating the diagnostic process, led to revisions in the diagnostic system. The use of biochemical treatments and revisions leading to the development of DSM IV mean that the kinds of diagnostic error made in Rosenhan's study should not be made today.

• Rosenhan's work demonstrates the strength of using covert observation to gather data in a natural setting. The reported experiences of the pseudopatients and their observations of the staff and real patients must have made for difficult reading for health professionals working in psychiatric hospitals.

• There are problems with the research methods used in the study of individual differences. Gould highlights the problems associated with the development of psychometric tests. Thigpen and Cleckley's work shows how difficult it is to provide qualitative data that is objective or convincing, especially in the controversial case of MPD. Rosenhan's work relies on the reports by participant observers, and it may be that they lacked objectivity in reporting what was for them a negative personal experience.

Doing the exams

Remember, the examiner is your friend, and to make the exams user-friendly examiners make it very clear how the exams will be structured and give you tips on how to organise your answers in order to do your best. This is a very important part of your instruction manual.

There are three exams and you have an hour for each one:
• Core Studies one – one hour
• Core Studies two – one hour
• Psychological Investigations – one hour

CORE STUDIES 1 – THE STRUCTURE OF THE EXAM

This paper consists of 20 compulsory questions, one per study. These are short answer questions, and your answers need not be in full sentences, as long as you give enough information to get the marks available.

CORE STUDIES 2 – THE STRUCTURE OF THE EXAM AND EXAM TIPS

Candidates are required to answer two out of four questions, one question from section A and one from section B.

Tip: for each section there is a choice; you CHOOSE ONE question out of the two in section A and CHOOSE ONE question out of the two in section B. Do not answer all four questions!

In section A you are asked to write about ONE STUDY you choose from a given selection in relation to some aspect of methods, themes and perspectives.

In section B you are given four studies and asked to write about ALL FOUR STUDIES in relation to the issue in the question (methods/themes/perspectives).

You have *half an hour* for each section, and should not spend more than half an hour on each section.

Example section A questions – from the OCR specimen papers

1. Psychological research is often carried out on a limited number of people. The sample chosen will have an effect on the results of the research.

Choose ONE of the core studies listed below and answer the following questions.

- Haney, Banks and Zimbardo (prison simulation)
- Milgram (obedience)
- Tajfel (intergroup discrimination)

(a) Describe how participants were selected in your chosen study. [6]
(b) Using examples, give TWO strengths and TWO weaknesses of the sample used in your chosen study. [12]
(c) Suggest ONE other sample for your chosen study and say how you think this might affect the results. [8]

2. One way in which psychologists carry out research is by gathering a great deal of data about one individual. This method is known as a case study.

Choose ONE of the core studies listed below and answer the following questions.

- Freud (Little Hans)
- Thigpen and Cleckley (MPD)
- Gardner and Gardner (Project Washoe)

(a) Describe how the case study method was used in your chosen study. [6]
(b) Using examples, give TWO strengths and TWO weaknesses of the case study as used in your chosen study. [12]
(c) Suggest ONE alternative way your chosen study could have been investigated and say how you think this might affect the results. [8]

Section A part (c)

Exam tips

In section A part (c) you will either be asked to:

- suggest a change that could be made to your chosen study and comment on the effect this would have on the findings (here you get four marks for the change and four marks for describing how the findings might differ), or
- suggest two changes to your chosen study (here you get four marks for each suggested change).

To prepare for section A part (c), it would be useful to consider the following questions in relation to each of the core studies:

- What if the sample were different? (Can you suggest a different sample for the study? How might this affect the results?)
- What if the location were different? (Can you suggest a different location for the study? If it were in a lab, could it be taken into the field? How might this affect the results?)
- What if the measurement were different? (Can you suggest a different method of measurement for the study? If not, why not? How might this affect the results?)
- What if the procedure were different? (Can you suggest changes to the procedure of the study? How might this affect the results?)
- What if the procedure were ethical? (Could the study be carried out ethically? Would gaining informed consent, for example, spoil the study? Is a cover story necessary?)

Section B questions

These questions are in two parts. Part (a) requires you to apply the given question to *ALL FOUR of the studies named*. Part (b) requires you to consider four problems (e.g. those psychologists have to overcome in their studies), giving an example of a study that illustrates each problem, *OR* to consider two strengths and two weaknesses of a method or approach, again using *studies to support the points made, and commenting on it.*

Exam tip: how do you answer the part (b) questions to get 12/12?

In both section A and section B questions on the Core Studies two exam, the model for presenting part (b) is as follows:

1. *Identify AND describe the problem/strength/advantage/disadvantage* e.g. 'one problem with the use of deception is that if the informed consent of Ss is not obtained then this raises ethical concerns.'
2. *Illustrate the problem/strength advantage/disadvantage with a study* e.g. 'for example, in the obedience study, if Milgram had told his subjects they would be encouraged to deliver electric shocks in the study, they may not have volunteered in the first place. They may also not have wanted to take part in a study of "obedience" as they consented to a study on "learning and punishment".'
3. *Finish off with a comment that develops an argument or makes a conclusion* e.g. 'So what this means is that deception as used in this study leads us to question whether the study was carried out ethically, as the Ss may not have consented if they were aware of the full procedural details or if they knew the true purpose of the study.'

You get one mark for each of the three numbered points above, so doing this four times for four different issues accounts for the 12 available marks.

In answering section B part (b) questions it is not necessary to refer to all four named studies, as the same study can be used to illustrate more than one problem (or strength/weakness or advantage/disadvantage).

Revision activity

Here are some examples of the kinds of question you might have to answer in section B of the Core Studies two exam. You should use these to practice writing structured essays.

1. *Usefulness/application of psychology to everyday life:*
It is sometimes argued that psychological research should have some use for ordinary people engaged in their everyday lives. Use the studies listed below to answer the following questions:
- Milgram (obedience)
- Piliavin, Piliavin and Rodin (subway Samaritan)
- Bandura, Ross and Ross (aggression)
- Freud (Little Hans)

(a) What do these studies tell us about human behaviour and experience? [12]
(b) Using examples, explain 4 problems we have when we try to apply findings from psychological studies to everyday life. [12]

2. *Determinism/individual & situational explanations of behaviour*
'Why do I behave the way that I do? Do I have the freedom to choose, or is my behaviour determined by forces beyond my control, such as the environment in which I live, my family or my culture?' Using the core studies listed below, answer the following questions:
- Hodges and Tizard (social relationships)
- Haney, Banks and Zimbardo (prison simulation)
- Deregowski (perception)
- Bandura, Ross and Ross (aggression)

(a) Describe what each study tells us about the factors that influence our behaviour. [12]
(b) Using examples, identify four problems psychologists have when they try to investigate factors that influence our behaviour. [12]

3. *Validity:*
In general terms, validity refers to whether a measure actually measures what it claims to measure. Using the core studies listed below, answer the following questions:
- Hraba and Grant (doll choice)
- Baron-Cohen, Leslie and Frith (autism)

- Hodges and Tizard (social relationships)
- Raine, Buchsbaum and La Casse (brain scanning)

(a) Describe the behaviour measured in each of the named studies, explaining how it was measured. [12]
(b) Comment on the validity of the measurement of variables using examples from the four named studies. [12]

4. *Ethnocentric bias:*
Ethnocentrism refers to the tendency to overestimate the worth of people in the same group as you and to undervalue people who are not in the same group as you. Psychology itself is sometimes said to be ethnocentric because it undervalues, or gives less attention to, the behaviour and experience of certain groups of people in our society. Use the studies listed below to answer the following questions:
- Tajfel (intergroup discrimination)
- Hraba and Grant (doll choice)
- Gould (IQ testing)
- Deregowski (perception)

(a) What do these studies tell us about ethnocentrism and prejudice? [12]
(b) Using examples, consider the advantages and difficulties of studying diverse groups of people in psychology. [12]

5. *The cognitive approach:*
Some of the core studies take a cognitive approach to human behaviour and experience. This approach considers how we think, perceive, use language and how our memory works. Using the core studies listed below, answer the questions which follow:
- Loftus and Palmer (eyewitness testimony)
- Baron-Cohen, Leslie and Frith (autism)
- Deregowski (perception)
- Gardner and Gardner (Project Washoe)

(a) Describe how cognitive processes were studied in each of the four named studies. [12]
(b) Using examples, identify two strengths and three weaknesses of the cognitive approach. [12]

DOING EXAMS CAN BE LOVING EXAMS...

Now you have worked your way through this chapter, you should have a good idea of what it is you need to know for Core Studies one and two and have some ideas about how you can learn the studies and revise for the exams. You also have guidelines on how to structure your answers so the examiners will be able to give you credit for all your hard work.

Being organised and prepared can take the stress out of exams and leave you with just enough of a buzz of arousal to really enjoy it and do your best on the day. We hope you found this book useful. Good luck!

Answers to key questions

Warning! These will not give you all the possible right answers, and they won't do all the work for you either!

MILGRAM, p. 38

1. A quantitative finding is that 65% of all subjects went to 450 volts on the shock generator. A qualitative finding is that the subjects who continued were observed to show signs of stress and tension; sweating and nervous laughter, for example.
2. No. The guidelines would need to be broken to include deception and visiting some level of stress upon the participants. (Do you think a replication of this study would be useful? Could it be ethically justified?)
3. Orne suggests that Ss worked out that they were not really giving electric shocks and that the high level of obedience was as a result of Ss 'playing along' with the study and acting in a way they believed the E expected them to.
4. Milgram in fact carried out a similar experiment with female subjects and came up with similar results. Commonly, A level students in psychology classes claim that they would not continue on the shock generator, but perhaps this is because they, like those questioned by Milgram before the lab study was carried out, are not able to predict accurately their performance in such a situation. It is possible that the gender and age of subjects in this study doesn't matter, and the results would be the same regardless of who was tested.
5. Over to you.

PILIAVIN, RODIN AND PILIAVIN, p. 59

1. (i) One advantage of covert observation techniques is that you are observing 'real-life' behaviour, so your data may be highly valid. One disadvantage of covert observation techniques is that, when observing Ss without their consent and perhaps invading their privacy this method of data-gathering raises ethical concerns. (ii) HINT: what did each of the observers have to do? How long did they have to do it in? Do you think it would be easy to observe and record

the other passengers without them knowing they were being observed?

2. An independent variable is the variable the E manipulates or observes to see if it causes a change in another variable (the dependent variable). In this study, the three independent variables were whether the victim appeared to be drunk or ill, the race of the victim and the behaviour of the model.

3. Examples of quantitative findings include the fact that the 'drunk' victim was helped spontaneously (before 70 seconds had passed after the victim collapsed) in 19/38 trials and the 'ill' victim was helped spontaneously in 62/65 trials.

   Qualitative evidence includes the comments the observers elicited from the other passengers, such as, 'It's for men to help him'.

4. HINT: in the train, passengers were a captive audience. What is different about being in a big shopping centre and how might this affect the results?

HANEY, BANKS AND ZIMBARDO, p. 70

1. This study could not be carried out in a real prison for both ethical and practical reasons. 'Innocent' subjects could not be put in what had been established as brutal prison environments for ethical reasons. For practical reasons, the study would not have been possible in a real prison setting, since the aim of the study was to see whether it was the inmates'

brutality or the brutality of the environment that made the prisons so brutal. In a real prison, both of these variables are present and the one would confound the other.

2. The uniforms were intended to have the following psychological effects: Guards: intended to give a sense of power, control, machismo, status and anonymity.
   Prisoners: intended to emasculate and give a sense of powerlessness and oppression, and a loss of identity.

3. Zimbardo *et al.* drew up a contract to fully inform Ss of the loss of civil rights for those in the role of prisoner. No physical violence was permitted, to protect participants from harm. Some Ss were allowed to withdraw. The study was brought to an early close as a result of its negative impact on the behaviour of the guards, the prisoners and the researchers themselves.

4. The study lacks ecological validity and so does not tell us exactly why real prisons are brutal places. The guards may have been play-acting the role of what they thought a guard should be like, rather than how they might really behave in the job of guard in a real prison. The prisoners were unlike the real inmates of prisons as they were volunteers, not convicted of any crime, and therefore their reactions cannot be seen as typical of those of real prisoners.

5. HINT: look up the problems of using student samples in psychological research to help you decide if a different type of sample would have affected the results.

TAJFEL, pp. 85-86

1. *In-group and out-group:* in-group = a group you see yourself as belonging to, and 'out-group' = a group you see yourself as not belonging to.

   Maximum joint profit: this is a strategy for selecting the pair of points on a matrix which sees the boys as a whole group. The pair selected is the one which, when added together, gives the largest possible amount of points.

   Maximum in-group profit: this is a strategy of choosing the pair of points which gives the biggest possible reward to the in-group member, regardless of whether this means giving more or less to the 'other' group.

   Maximising the difference in favour of the in-group: this strategy ensures that the in-group member gets more than the out-group member, even if this means the in-group getting less than the maximum available. This shows discrimination occurring.

2. If both fairness and maximising the difference were influencing his choices, the pair the boy would choose would be 11,9 or 10,7. Here, the in-group still gets more, but the out-group doesn't get as little as they would if the choice 7,1 were made. So the choice is made 'fairer' by making the difference smaller.

3. Over to you.

4. Reductionism can be a positive issue in Tajfel's study as the approach of isolating one variable to see its effect shows that 'mere belonging to one group and knowledge of another group' does indeed trigger discrimination. However, reductionism can also be a criticism here, as prejudice and discrimination are far more complex than the theory of in-group preference suggests.

LOFTUS AND PALMER, p. 114

1. 'Reconstructive memory' is a psychological theory of memory in which we remember events or experiences in a way that we think makes sense. Instead of remembering exactly what happened in an objective way, our memory is distorted by what we think could or should have happened. Our attitudes and beliefs will have an impact on this.

2. A leading question is a question which, by its form or content, suggests the answer that should be given. They are of special interest in the study of eyewitness testimony because they can introduce new information which can alter a witness's memory of events. In other words, they lead the witness to reconstruct their memory of events to fit in with what the question suggests.

3. In real life, everyone would see the accident from a different viewpoint, and so may have different accounts of what happened. In real life, witnesses are called in order to establish whose fault an accident was, and so, on witnessing a real-life accident, people may focus on trying to work this out. In real life,

concerns for the safety of those in the cars, or even themselves, may affect the witnesses. They may experience heightened arousal (see Piliavin study), which may affect their memory.

4. DV for experiment one = average speed the cars were travelling for each condition.

DV for experiment two = the number of subjects in each condition who reported seeing broken glass.

Both DVs were measured by self-report.

The advantages in this study of quantitative measurement include the easy comparison between conditions (e.g. in experiment two, 16/50 Ss in the smashed condition reported seeing broken glass, compared with 6/50 in the control condition). The use of inferential statistics is also possible where quantitative data is gathered, and the inferential analysis of the findings allowed the authors to establish causal relationships between the IVs and the DVs in their two experiments.

4. Why does the student sample give us problems? Who else could be tested? Would this increase or decrease the generalisability of the sample? Why? Remember, if the generalisability of the findings is increased, this may increase the validity of the study.

DEREGOWSKI, p. 136

1. Is the perception of depth in line drawings learned or innate?

2. The problem with this type of anecdotal evidence is that it gives a subjective (and unscientific) account of events. There may also be some ethnocentric bias in the way the Westerners described the behaviour of the Africans.

3. The validity of the pictures task was established by testing a group of Zambian schoolchildren who had been classified as either 2D or 3D perceivers on the pictures task. Hudson theorised that 3D perceivers would take longer trying to reproduce a picture of the impossible trident (an image that looks like it is one of a 3D object, but is in fact an illusion of an object that could not exist as 3D in the real world). They would take longer as they would try to see depth in the picture and be confused by it, whereas 2D perceivers would just see it as a line drawing and would not have difficulties reproducing it. The 3D perceivers did in fact take longer to draw the object, and this supports the fact that they really were attempting to see 3D in the drawing, supporting the validity of the findings from the pictures task.

4. The advantage of a split-style drawing is that you can see all aspects of the object or animal it depicts at once. Deregowski also suggests that split-style drawings are more aesthetically pleasing than 'realistic' or 'perspectival' drawings.

5. Over to you.

453

SAMUEL AND BRYANT, p. 189

1. Child is egocentric, can't conserve.
2. The control group shows how the children use witnessing the of the objects to help them answer the questions correctly. Children who did not see the transformation, those in the fixed-array condition, were least able to get the right answers.
3. The replicability of results is a key feature in scientific research. Establishing the reliability of findings can increase our confidence in their validity. Certainly if a test is not reliable, it is not likely to be valid.
4. In support of Piaget, Samuel and Bryant showed that conservation is an ability that improves with age. Their major criticism was that using two questions confused the younger children and forced them to give the wrong answer. Because of this, Piaget had underestimated the cognitive abilities of younger children.
5. Can you?

BARON-COHEN, LESLIE AND FRITH, p. 150

1. To have a theory of mind is to be able to understand that other people have minds, and that others have thoughts and beliefs in the same way as you have thoughts and beliefs, and that the thoughts and beliefs of others can differ from your own. Lacking a theory of mind is also known as 'mind-blindness'.
2. In the Sally-Anne test a child is tested individually. The E has two dolls, Sally and Anne. Sally has a basket into which she puts her marble. Anne has a box. Sally 'goes out' and while she is 'away', Anne 'takes' the marble from the basket and puts it in her box. When Sally 'returns' the child is asked, 'Where will Sally look for her marble?' (the belief question). The child is asked three control questions, the naming, memory and reality questions.
3. The majority of the autistic children could not answer the belief question correctly.
4. Mind-blindness (lacking a theory of mind) explains the odd use of language by people with autism. It also explains why people with autism don't understand emotions, such as embarrassment, which rely on social understanding.
5. Understanding how autistic children think can help us understand why they behave the way they do, and this understanding can help those around them to make sense of and perhaps be more tolerant towards the often bizarre and challenging behaviours which autistic children present.

GARDNER AND GARDNER, p. 168

1. Experimenter bias occurs when an E consciously or unconsciously influences the outcome of their study so that the findings support their hypothesis. This bias can also occur in the experimenter's interpretation of findings. For example, did the Gardners interpret Washoe's arm

waving as manual babbling because this is what they wanted it to be?

2. Hint: can you find out what the ethical guidelines for the study of animals are?

3. Washoe learned single signs to begin with and her use of signs to stand for a concept can be compared with children's holophrastic speech. Another comparison is Washoe's creativity in combining signs to increase the meaning of her utterances, and this could be compared with the two-word stage in children's language development. Washoe, however, needed to be conditioned to learn signs, whereas children acquire language spontaneously. Children also acquire grammar, including structure dependence, spontaneously. Washoe was not very concerned about word order and so did not demonstrate structure dependence in her signing.

4. What do *you* think?

BANDURA, ROSS AND ROSS, p. 208

1. One strength of covert observation techniques in this study is that the child was being observed without them knowing, so the data may be highly valid. One disadvantage of covert observation techniques is that when observing Ss without their consent, or in this case without parental consent, this method of data-gathering raises ethical concerns.

2. Reliability refers to the consistency of a measure or test. Where two or more observers, raters or scorers are using the same measure, they should give consistent results when assessing the same subject or event. This is known as inter-rater (or inter-scorer or inter-observer) reliability. In this study, a female researcher and the child's teacher assessed the children's level of aggression before the test. To ensure their assessments were accurate, they were tested for inter-rater reliability, and a good agreement between them in the children's usual level of aggression was observed.

3. Step two was where children were exposed to 'mild aggression arousal'.

• The children in the aggressive model condition might have had their aggressive tendencies inhibited by observing the aggression of the adult, so for them, step two was designed to counteract this.

• The children in the non-aggressive model condition were *supposed* to have had their aggression inhibited by their experience of observing the passive adult. For them, step two was to provide them with a reason to be aggressive, and see if they would then be less aggressive having seen the model than the control group.

• The control group experienced step two to ensure the only difference between them and the other two groups of children was their experience of observing either model. They would then provide a baseline of aggression against which the other two groups could be compared.

4. The Bobo doll in room three was only three foot high as the children

were, naturally, much smaller than the adult, so they needed a child-size version of Bobo they could easily throw in the air and such.

5. No evidence of parental consent; the children were deliberately upset in step two; they were encouraged (coerced?) to remain in the third room when some of them were upset and didn't want to (the E stayed in the room with them to make sure they stayed too).

HODGES AND TIZARD, p. 228

1. Control group one = matched controls from the London area, matched for sex, position in family, etc. The purpose of this group was to provide a comparison to show what 'normal' (non-institutionalised) adolescents' relationships were like.

   Control group two = same-sex classmate, closest to them in age. This control group provided the teachers of the ex-institutionalised children with a 'normal' comparison with the ex-institutionalised adolescent in their class when completing the questionnaires.

2. When subjects drop out of a longitudinal study, or when they decide to withdraw from the study, this means that the sample reduces in size. It may be that those left behind are not typical of the original sample and this means that the findings may not be valid. It may be that those left behind in this study are those that felt they didn't mind discussing their family/relationship problems, wheras those who declined to take part might have been faring worse and were unwilling to reveal this as part of a study.

3. The resources available to adopted children were probably higher. Adoptive parents tend to be financially secure, and want to have a child to whom they can dedicate time and attention, so their emotional needs were met in the family setting. For the restored children, the problems that led to them being put into care in the first place may not have been completely resolved. The parents were ambivalent about the child's return and the child might have come to resent its parent(s) for what it saw as abandonment or rejection when it was sent away from home.

4. It seems that there is a link between early privation experience and attention-seeking with adults in the ex-institutional adolescents. It could be that they are seeking to have their unfulfilled early needs met by the adults they encounter. It could be that, as infants, they sought the attention of available adults in order to find one with whom they could bond, and this pattern of attention-seeking in adolescence may be a result of a learned behaviour pattern.

5. It is the findings from such research that has affected current policy in the UK, which does not place babies and infants in institutional care, but instead aims to provide foster homes for them, providing them with substitute parent(s) who can try to ensure that their emotional needs are met.

FREUD, p. 248

1. A case study is usually carried out over an extended period of time, and therefore samples the S's behaviour more than a snapshot study might. A case study gathers a great deal of qualitative evidence about the subject, and this is unlikely to be true of a snapshot study. This means a more valid description of the S's behaviour can be drawn from a case study. A case study can also track development of the S over time, and this is not possible in a snapshot study.

2. Hans' father was a biased observer. He was a supporter of Freud's theories and his observations of the boy and interpretations of the boy's behaviour were not objective. His relationship with his son might also mean the boy would say things to please his father, perhaps in response to leading questions, so this makes us question the validity of the evidence.

3. Freud interpreted Hans' fear of being bitten by a horse as symbolic of his unconscious fear of castration by his father as punishment for focusing his libido on his mother. The horse represented the father and the biting represented the castration.

4. No. Even when his mother threatened to have the doctor to come and cut off his widdler (if he continued to masturbate) he wasn't perturbed, and when asked what he would widdle with then, he simply replied 'with my bottom'.

5. Hans had seen a bus-horse fall over and this may have been an upsetting event that triggered his fear of horses, which developed into a phobia. It could be that the huge horses of the type that pulled buses at the time of the study were simply very terrifying to a tiny boy, and again, this may have triggered his fear.

SCHACHTER AND SINGER, p. 274

1. Without a baseline measure there is no evidence that the study had any impact on the subjects' mood state at all.

2. Emotions are an important part of human experience and this is why it is useful to study them. If emotions influence our behaviour or attitudes, then it is both interesting and useful for us to understand how.

3. The all-male US student sample in this study fails to represent 'people in general'. The biases in the sample mean we should be cautious about generalising the findings to a broader population.

4. Hint: what if the sample were all female?

5. Strength = high level of control over variables enables cause and effect to be established to show the interplay of cognition and arousal in our experience of emotion.

Weakness = the laboratory setting lacks ecological validity. The arousal was artificially induced and we have to question whether this arousal is the same as when we experience a 'real' emotion.

DEMENT AND KLEITMAN, p. 290

1. An objective measure of dreaming would improve the validity of dream studies which had, up to this point, relied wholly on Ss' self-reports of dreams. This was further limiting the investigation of dreaming, as the S needed to be woken up to establish whether they were dreaming or not. Establishing an objective measure would extend the work that could be done on dream activity.

2. To prevent the presence of the E from influencing the response of subjects.

3. The sample in this study is gender-biased and was also carried out in the USA. This means we must be cautious in generalising the findings to a broader population. Also, the sample was very small, with only five subjects being studied thoroughly and this cannot be representative of people in general.

4. The major weakness of the correlational design is that cause and effect between variables cannot be established. We can only infer that REM and dream recall co-occur, not that one causes the other.

5. Hint: people sleep differently when not in their own bed. Could the study be done outside the lab in a natural setting? What problems might the researchers face if they took their study into people's homes?

SPERRY, p. 303

1. They have not had their corpus callosum surgically cut and so both sides of the brain communicate with the other internally.

2. To prevent the S's eye movements from affecting which side of the visual field was being targeted.

3. If they saw their hands, then the dominant side of the brain would inhibit the hand governed by the minor hemisphere.

4.
- Cup, as this image is going to the linguistic left hemisphere.
- Monkey, as this is what the right hemisphere saw and the right hemisphere governs the left hand.
- He will say he doesn't know why he drew the monkey and has no recollection of doing so. This is because the side of the brain that is 'talking' in response to the experimenter's question (the left hemisphere) did not see the monkey and did not not draw it. This was all done by the minor (right) hemisphere, without the knowledge of the left.
- No. He will not remember this particular image of a monkey, as the left side of the brain has not seen it and has no memory of it.

5. Over to you.

RAINE, BUCHSBAUM AND LACASSE, p. 320

1. The matched control group was used to control extraneous subject variables, such as brain injury,

epilepsy or schizophrenia, to prevent them from confounding the study.

2. Medication could have interfered with the brain chemistry of Ss so they were kept free from medication, again, to prevent confounding variables.

3.

- PET = positron emission tomography
- FDG = fluorodeoxyglucose
- CPT = continuous performance task
- NGRI = not guilty by reason of insanity

4. The lab setting and test procedure are not ecologically valid. The CPT could be criticised as lacking ecological validity. As the CPT was not an aggressive behaviour, and was only a target-setting task, we should be cautious in assuming that NGRIs' brain activity would differ from normal on any other type of behaviour, including acts of aggression.

GOULD, p. 346

1. Objective measurement is a key feature of scientific investigation. If psychology was to gain scientific credibility, objective measurement was required. Yerkes saw the establishment of objective measures of intelligence as a way to put psychology, and himself, firmly on the scientific map.

2. The sample had a number of ethnocentric biases, including the fact that it was all male and all of a certain age. This means the findings would not have been representative of people in general, even if the tests had been valid.

3. Blacks were openly discriminated against and had less access to education than whites, so would not do well on the written tests. During, the testing, blacks were, as Gould tells us 'treated with... more contempt' than the other recruits. Those blacks who failed the Alpha and Beta tests were not recalled for individual testing, and this artificially reduced their average as a group.

4. The test protocol was not followed, so Alpha and Beta failures were not recalled, and again, the failure to test recruits on the individual test may have artificially reduced the average for the group. It could, of course, be that Yerkes' scale was too ambitious and that he had overestimated what the 'average' score on his test should be.

5. The ideas that were generated by the work of Yerkes and his colleagues had a damaging effect. They were used as arguments for the restriction of immigration in the 1920s and 1930s, a time when those wanting to escape the oncoming persecution, by the Nazis, for example, were refused entry to the USA. According to Gould, the US immigration policies condemned many, who had sought to leave Europe, to suffer destruction at the hands of their persecutors.

HRABA AND GRANT, p. 359

1. This was done to ensure that whether the interviewer was black or white did not confound the results.
2. This would tell the researchers whether the child knew to which racial group it belonged.
3. To see if there was a relationship between doll choice (racial preference) and their choice of friends.
4. Doll choice is not an ecologically valid measure of racial preference. Testing a child individually in a laboratory is not an ecologically valid setting.
5. Hint: Useful to whom? For what?

ROSENHAN, p. 382

1. They phoned the hospital admissions and complained of hearing a voice saying 'thud', 'hollow' and 'empty'. They were given an appointment, at which they were admitted to the hospital.
2. The staff recorded in the case notes of one pseudopatient, 'patient engages in writing behaviour', as if this were some symptom of their 'illness' rather than normal behaviour for someone investigating the hospital! The patient was never asked about his note-taking or why he was doing it. Also, a patient pacing up and down out, of boredom, was assumed by a member of staff to be 'nervous', so the interpretation of the pacing was again that it was symptomatic of the person's 'illness'. Once labelled 'mentally ill' all the person's behaviours were interpreted as being related to their 'illness' rather than caused by the hospital environment.
3. Rosenhan selected 12 hospitals in the USA. The staff and patients in these hospitals would be the sample. He sought to make these representative by having a range of hospitals, old and shabby and new, research oriented and not, state or federally funded, private or public, and from both coasts and different states.
4. Rosenhan could have carried out the observation overtly with the permission of staff, as had been done in previous studies. However, Rosenhan did not do this as he believed that the findings would not be valid if staff were aware of the presence of the pseudopatients.
5. The study uses covert observation, and there are therefore ethical concerns raised by the invasion of privacy (especially of vulnerable patients on the wards) and of consent. Staff and patients were deceived by the pseudopatients.

THIGPEN AND CLECKLEY, p. 399

1. Multiple personality disorder is a term that was used to describe the coexistence of more than one personality in one body, each being dominant at different times.
2. The findings from the projective tests carried out on Eve White and Eve Black:

Eve White

Projective tests (human figure drawing and Rorschach test) indicated:

- Repression
- Conflict and anxiety in her role as mother
- Hostility to her mother

Eve Black

Projective tests (human figure drawing and Rorschach test) indicated:

- Regression (the name she used was in fact the patient's maiden name) indicating a desire to return to an earlier period of life, before marriage

3. The EEG tests were carried out to try to provide objective evidence for the existence of the three separate personalities.

4. Given that the tests of the three personalities failed to conclusively confirm their separate existence, perhaps the alternative might be to observe the S. With filming equipment installed in her home without her knowledge, and/or covert observation of her behaviours outside the home it might be established whether or not the S was just a very good actress playing out a role for the researchers.

5. MPD, if it existed at all, was very rare. The psychiatric profession, researchers included, viewed it with scepticism. The objective tests had not provided evidence that the three separate personalities existed, and so the only evidence they had was that from interviews with the S herself. They recognised that, although unlikely, since she made no errors over an extended period, they could be being 'hoodwinked by a consummate actress'. These are the reasons why the researchers were reluctant to claim Eve as a true case of MPD.

461

Bibliography

Ahrens, S.R. (1954), 'Beiträge zur Entwicklung des Physiolgnoimie und Mimikerkenntnisse' (Contributions on the development of physiognomy and mimicry recognition), *Seitschrift für Experimentelle und Angewandte Psychologie*, 2, 412–54.

Aitchison, J. (1983), *The Articulate Mammal*, London: Hutchinson, 2nd edition.

Alexander, P.C. and Lupfer, S.L. (1987), 'Family characteristics and long-term consequences associated with sexual abuse', *Archives of Sexual Behaviour*, 16, 235–45.

Allen, V.L. and Levine, J.M. (1971), 'Social pressures and personal influence', *Journal of Experimental Social Psychology*, 7, 122–4.

Allport, F.H. (1955), *Theories of Perception and the Concept of Structure*. New York: Wiley.

Allport, G.W. (1954), *The Nature of Prejudice*, Wokingham: Addison-Wesley.

Ardrey, R. (1966), *The Territorial Imperative*, New York: Dell.

Arendt, H. (1965), *Eichmann in Jerusalem: A report on the banality of evil*, New York: Viking.

Aronson, E. (1976), *The Social Animal*, San Francisco: W.H. Freeman & Co.

Aronson, E. (1994), *The Social Animal*, New York: W.H. Freeman & Co., 7th edition.

Aronson, E. and Osherow, N. (1980), 'Co-operation, prosocial behaviour and academic performance: Experiments in the desegregated classroom' in L. Bickman (ed.), *Applied Social Psychology Annual, Vol. 1*, Beverley Hills, CA: Sage Publications.

Aronson, E., Wilson, T.D. and Akert, R.M. (1997), *Social Psychology*, New York: Longman, 3rd edition.

Asch, S.E. (1951), 'Effect of group pressure upon the modification and distortion of judgements' in H. Guetzkow (ed.), *Groups, Leadership and Men*, Pittsburg, PA: Carnegie Press.

Aschoff, J. (1979), 'Circadian rhythms: General features and endocrinological aspects' in *Endocrine Rhythms*, edited by D.T. Krieger, New York: Raven Press.

Atkinson, R.C., and Shiffrin, R.M. (1968), 'Human memory: a proposed system and its control processes' in K.W. Spence and J.T. Spence (eds), *The Psychology of Learning and Motivation, 2*, London: Academic Press.

Atkinson, R.C. and Shiffrin, R.M. (1971), 'The control of short-term memory', *Scientific American*, 224, 82–90.

Atkinson, R.L., Atkinson, R.C., Smith, E.E. and Bem, D.J. (1993), *Introduction to Psychology*, New York: Harcourt Brace Jovanovich, 11th edition.

Ax, A.F. (1953), 'The physiological differentiation between fear and anger in humans', *Psychosomatic Medicine*, 15, 433–42.

Ayers, I. (1991), Rair driving: Gender and race discrimination in retail car negotiations, *Harvard Law Review*, 104.

Bandura, A., Ross, D. and Ross, S.A. (1961) *Transmission of Aggression through Imitation of Aggressive Models*.

Bandura, A. (1977), 'Self-efficacy: toward a unifying theory of behavioural change', *Psychological Review*, 84, 191–215.

Bandura, A. (1977), *Social Learning Theory*, Englewood Cliffs, NJ: Prentice Hall.

Banyard, P. and Grayson, A. (1996), *Introducing Psychological Research*, Basingstoke: Macmillan Press.

Bard, B. and Sachs, J. (1977), 'Language Acquisition Patterns in Two Normal Children of Deaf Parents', paper presented to the 2nd Annual Boston University Conference on Language Acquistion, October 1977, cited in J.G. de Villiers and P.A. de Villiers (1978), *Early Language*, London: Fontana.

Baron-Cohen, S. and Bolton, P. (1993), *Autism: the facts,* Oxford: Oxford University Press.

Baron-Cohen, S., Cosmides, L. and Tooby, J. (1997), *Mindblindness: An Essay on Autism and Theory of Mind*, Cambridge, MA: MIT Press.

Barrett, M.D. (1986), 'Early semantic representations and early word usage', in S.A. Kuczaj and M.D. Barrett (eds), *The Development of Word Meaning*, New York: Springer Verlag.

Bates, E., Bretherton, I. and Snyder, L. (1988), *From First Words to Grammar: Individual differences and dissociable mechanisms*, Cambridge: Cambridge University Press.

Bee, H. (1992), *The Developing Child*, New York: Harper Collins.

Bee, H. (1995), *The Growing Child*, New York: Harper Collins.

Berne, E. (1964), *Games People Play*, London: Penguin.

Blakemore, C. (1988), *The Mind Machine*, London: BBC Books.

Bliss, E.L. (1983), 'Multiple personalities, related disorders, and hypnosis', *American Journal of Clinical Hypnosis*, 26, 114–23.

Bowlby, J. (1951), *Maternal Care and Mental Health*, Geneva: World Health Organisation.

Bowlby, J. (1953), *Childcare and the Growth of Love*, London: Penguin.

Brown, G.L., Goodwin, F.K., Ballenger, J.C., Goyer, P.F. and Major, L.F. (1979), 'Aggression in human correlates with cerebrospinal fluid amine metabolites', *Psychiatry Research*, 1, 131–9.

Brown, R. (1973), *A First Language*, Cambridge, MA: Harvard University Press.

Brown, R. (1986), *Social Psychology*, New York: The Free Press, 2nd edition.

Brown, R. (1995), *Prejudice: Its Social Psychology*, Oxford: Blackwell.

Bruner, J.S. and Goodman, C.C. (1947), 'Value and need as organising factors in perception', *Journal of Abnormal and Social Psychology*, 42, 33–44.

Burnstein, E., Crandall, C. and Kitayama, S. (1994), 'Some neoDarwinian decision rules for altruism: Weighing cues for inclusive fitness as a function of the biological importance of the decision', *Journal of Personality and Social Psychology*, 67, 773–89.

Burt, C. (1912), 'The evidence for the concept of intelligence', *British Journal of Educational Psychology*, 25 158–77.

Burt, C. (1966), 'The examination at eleven plus', *British Journal of Educational Studies*, 7, 99–117.

Buss, A.H. (1966), *Psychopathology*, New York: Wiley.

Buss, A.H. (1966), 'Instrumentality of aggression, feedback and frustration as determinants of physical aggression', *Journal of Personality and Social Psychology*, 3, 153–62.

Butterworth, G. and Harris, M. (1994), *Principles of Developmental Psychology*, Lawrence Erlbaum Associates Ltd.

Cannon, W.B. (1927), 'The James-Lange theory of emotions: A critical examination and an alternative', *American Journal of Psychology*, 39, 106–24.

Cannon, W.B. (1929), *Bodily Changes in Pain, Hunger, Fear and Rage*, New York: Appleton-Century-Crofts.

Carey, S. (1978), 'The child as word learner', in M. Halle, J. Bresnan and G. Miller (eds), *Linguistic Theory and Psychological Reality*. Cambridge, MA: MIT Press.

Carlson, N.R. (1986), *Physiology of Behaviour*, London: Allyn and Bacon, 3rd edition.

Carter, R. (1998), *Mapping the Mind*, London: Weidenfeld & Nicolson.

Cave, S. (2002), *Classification and Diagnosis of Psychological Abnormality*, London: Routledge.

Chomsky, N. (1965), *Aspects of the Theory of Syntax*, Cambridge, MA: MIT Press.

Chomsky, N. (1968), *Language and Mind*, New York: Harcourt Brace Jovanovich.

Clark, K. and Clark, M. (1947), 'Racial identification and preference in Negro children', in T.M. Newcombe and E.L. Hartley (eds), *Readings in Social Psychology*, New York: Holt, 169–78.

Clarke, A.M. and Clarke, A.D.B. (1976), *Early Experience: Myth and Evidence*. London: Open Books.

Craik, F. and Lockhart, R. (1972), 'Levels of processing', *Journal of Verbal Learning and Verbal Behaviour*, 11, 671–84.

Crutchfield, R.S. (1962), cited in R. Gross (1992), *Psychology: The Science of Mind and Behaviour*, London: Hodder and Stoughton, 2nd edition.

Curtiss, S. (1977), *Genie: A psycholinguistic study of a modern-day 'wild child'*, London: Academic Press.

Dabbs, J.M, Carr, T.S. Frady, R.L. and Riad, J.K. (1995), 'Testosterone, crime and misbehaviour among 692 male prison inmates', *Personality and Individual Differences*, 18, 627–33.

Damasio, A.R., Tranel, D. and Damasio, H. (1990), 'Individuals with sociopathic behaviour caused by frontal damage fail to respond autonomically to social stimuli', *Behavioural Brain Research*, 41, 81–94.

Darley, J.M. and Batson, C.D. (1973), 'From Jerusalem to Jericho: A study of situational and dispositional variables in helping behaviour', *Journal of Personality and Social Psychology*, 27, 100–8.

Darley, J.M. and Latané, B. (1968), 'Bystander intervention in emergencies: Diffusion of responsibility', *Journal of Personality and Social Psychology*, 8, 377–83.

Darley, J.M. and Latané, B. (1970), 'Norms and normative behaviour: field studies of social interdependence' in J. Macauley and L. Berkowitz (eds), *Altruism and Helping Behaviour*, New York: Academic Press.

Davison, G. and Neale, J. (1996), *Abnormal Psychology*, New York: Wiley, 6th edition.

Dawkins, R. (1976), *The Selfish Gene*, Oxford: Oxford University Press.

Dement, W. (1960), 'The effect of dream deprivation', *Science*, 131, 1705–7.

Diamond, S., Baldwin, R. and Diamond, R. (1963), *Inhibition and Choice*. New York: Harper & Row.

Diener, E. (1979), 'Deindividuation, self-awareness and disinhibition', *Journal of Personality and Social Psychology*, 37, 1160–71.

Diener, E. (1980), 'Deindividuation: The absence of self-awareness and self-regulation in group members' in P.B. Paulus (ed.), *Psychology of Group Influence*. Hillsdale, NJ: Lawrence Erlbaum.

Diener, E., Fraser, S.C., Beaman, A.L. and Kelem, R.T. (1976), 'Effects of deindividuation variables on stealing among Halloween trick-or-treaters', *Journal of Personality and Social Psychology*, 33, 178–83.

Dobson, C.B., Hardy, M., Heyes, S., Humphreys, A. and Humphreys, P. (1993), *Understanding Psychology*, London: Weidenfeld and Nicolson.

Dollard J., Doob, L., Miller, N., Mowrer, O.H. and Sears, R.R. (1939), *Frustration and Aggression*, New Haven, CT: Yale University Press.

Donaldson, M. (1978), *Children's Minds*, London: Fontana.

Dunn, J. and Kendrick, C. (1979), 'Interaction between young siblings in the context of family relationships' in M. Lewis and L.A. Rosenblum (eds), *The Child and its Family*, New York: Plenum Press.

Dunn, J. (1988), *The Beginnings of Social Understanding*, Oxford: Blackwell.

Dunn, J. and Munn, P. (1985), 'Becoming a family member: family conflict and the development of social understanding in the first year', *Child Development*, 50, 306–18.

Dunn, J. and Plomin, R. (1990), *Separate Lives: Why siblings are so different*, New York: Basic Books.

Dunn, J., Kendrick, C. and MacNamee, R. (1981), 'The reaction of first-born children to the birth of a sibling: mother's reports', *Journal of Child Psychology and Psychiatry*, 22, 1–18.

Dutton, D.C. and Aron, A.P. (1974) Some evidence for heightened sexual attraction under conditions of high anxiety. *Journal of Personality & Social Psychology*, 30, 510–17.

Eagly, A.H. (1987), *Sex Differences in Social Behaviour: A social-role interpretation*, Hillsdale, NJ: Erlbaum.

Eagly, A.H. and Crowley, M. (1986), 'Gender and helping behaviour: A meta-analytic review of the social psychological literature', *Psychological Bulletin*, 100, 283–308.

Eichelman, B. (1993), 'Bridges from the animal laboratory to the study of violent or criminal individuals', in S. Hodgins (ed.), *Mental Disorder and Crime*, Newbury Park, CA: Sage, 194–207.

Eysenck, H.J. (1947), *Dimensions of Personality*, London: Routledge and Kegan Paul.

Eysenck, H.J. (1952), 'The effects of psychotherapy: An evaluation', *Journal of Consulting Psychology*, 16, 319–24.

Eysenck, H.J. (1970), *Crime and Personality*, London: Paladin.

Eysenck, H.J. (1973), *The Inequality of Man*, London: Temple Smith.

Eysenck, H.J. and Gudjoinsson, G.H. (1989), *The Causes and Cures of Criminality*, New York: Plenum.

Fantz, R.L. (1961), 'The origin of form perception', *Scientific American*, 204, 66–72.

Finkelhor, D. (1979), *Sexually Victimised Children*, New York: Free Press.

Fiske, S.T. and Taylor, S.E. (1991), *Social Cognition*, New York: McGraw-Hill, 2nd edition.

Flavell, J.H. (1985), *Cognitive Development*, London: Prentice Hall.

Freud, S. (1909), *Analysis of a Phobia in a Five-year-old Boy*, in *The Pelican Freud Library* (1977), Vol. 8, Case Histories 1.

Freud A. and Dann, S. (1951), 'An experiment in group upbringing', *Psychoanalytic Study of the Child*, 6, 127–68.

Freud, S. (1930), *Civilisation and its Discontents*, London: Hogarth Press.

Frith, U. (1990), *Autism*, Oxford: Blackwell.

Frith, U. (2002), *Autism: Explaining the Enigma*, Oxford: Blackwell.

Gazzaniga, M.S., LeDoux, J.E. and Wilson, D.H. (1977), 'Language, praxis and the right hemisphere: Clues to some mechanisms of consciousness', *Neurology*, 27, 1144–7.

Gerard, H. and Miller, N. (1975), *School Desegregation*, cited in R. Brown (1986), *Social Psychology*, New York: The Free Press, 2nd edition.

Gergen, K.J., Gergen, M.M. and Barton, W. (1973), 'Deviance in the dark', *Psychology Today*, 7, 129–30.

Geschwind, N. and Levitsky, W. (1968), 'Human brain: left-right asymmetries in temporal speech region', *Science*, 161, 186–7.

Gilbert, G.M. (1951), 'Stereotype persistence and change among college students', *Journal of Abnormal and Social Psychology*, 46, 245–54.

Gluhbegovic, N. and Williams, T.H. (1980), *The Human Brain: A Photographic Atlas*, Hagerstown, MD: Harper & Row.

Goldfarb, W. (1943), 'The effects of early institutional care on adolescent personality', *Journal of Experimental Education*, 12, 106–29.

Gregory, R. (1977), *Eye and Brain*, London: Weidenfeld and Nicolson.

Gross, R. (1992), *Psychology: Science of Mind and Behaviour*, London: Hodder & Stoughton, 2nd edition.

Gross, R. (1999), *Key Studies in Psychology*, London: Hodder and Stoughton, 3rd edition.

Gunter, B. and McAleer, J. (1990), *Children and Television*, London: Routledge.

Gwinner, E. (1986), 'Circannual rhythms in the control of avian rhythms', *Advances in the Study of Behaviour*, 16, 191–228.

Harris, M., Jones, D., Brookes, S. and Grant, J. (1986), 'Relations between the non-verbal context of maternal speech and rate of language development', *British Journal of Developmental Psychology*, 4, 261–8.

Harris, P.L. (1988), *Children and Emotion: the Development of Psychological Understanding*, Oxford: Blackwell.

Harris, P.L. and Muncer, A. (1988), 'Autistic Children's Understanding of Beliefs and Desires', paper presented at the British Psychological Society Developmental Section Conference, Coleg Harlech, Wales.

Harris, J. (1990), *Early Language Development*, London: Routledge, part two.

Hartmann, E. (1973), *The Functions of Sleep*, New Haven: Yale University.

Hartmann, E. (1984), *The Nightmare*, New York: Basic Books.

Hauri, P. (1979), 'What can insomniacs teach us about the functions of sleep?' in R. Drucker-Colin, M. Shkurovich and M.B. Sterman (eds), *The Functions of Sleep*, New York: Academic, 251–71.

Hawkes, N., *The Times*, London, 27 January 1999, reported in *Psychology Review*, Vol. 6 no. 3, February 2000.

Hayes, K.H. and Hayes, C. (1951), 'Intellectual development of a house-raised chimpanzee', *Proceedings of the American Philosophical Society*, 95, 105–9.

Hayes, N. (1993), *Principles of Social Psychology*. Hove: Psychology Press.

Heim, A. (1970), *Intelligence and Personality*, Harmondsworth: Penguin.

Hetherington, E.M. and Parke, R.D. (1987), *Child Psychology: A Contemporary Viewpoint*, New York: McGraw-Hill.

Hicks, R.E. (1975), 'Intrahemispheric response competition between vocal and unimanual performance in normal adult human males', *Journal of Comparative and Physiological Psychology*, 89, 50–60.

Hinde, R.A. (1987), *Individuals, Relationships and Culture: Links between Ethology and the Social Sciences*, Cambridge: Cambridge University Press.

Hinton, P.R. (2000), *Stereotypes, Cognition and Culture*, Hove: Psychology Press.

Hobbes, T. (1986), *Leviathan*, Harmondsworth: Penguin Press (original work published in 1651).

Hockett, C.F. (1959), 'Animal "languages" and human language', *Human Biology*, 31, 32–9.

Hodges, J. and Tizard, B. (1989), *Social and family relationships of ex-institutional adolescents*.

Hofling, K.C., Brotzman, E., Dalrymple, S., Graves, N. and Pieces, C.M. (1966), 'An experimental study in the nurse–physician relationship', *Journal of Nervous and Mental Disorders*, 143, 171–80.

Hohmann, G.W. (1966), 'Some effects of spinal cord lesions on experienced emotional feelings', *Psychophysiology*, 3, 143–56.

Horn, J.M. (1983), 'The Texas adoption project: Adopted children and their intellectual resemblance to biological and adoptive parents', *Child Development*, 54, 268–75.

Horne, J. (1988), *Why We Sleep: The functions of sleep in humans and other mammals*,

Oxford: Oxford University Press.

Horne, J.A. and Minard, A. (1985), 'Sleep and sleepiness following a behaviourally "active" day', *Ergonomics*, 28, 567–75.

Hovland, C.I. and Sears, R.R. (1940), 'Minor studies in aggression: 6. Correlation of lynchings with economic indices', *Journal of Psychology*, 9, 301–10.

Hubel, D.H. and Wiesel, T.N. (1979), 'Brain mechanisms of vision', *Scientific American* 241 (3), 150–62.

Huesmann, L.R. and Eron, L.D. (1984), 'Cognitive processes and the persistence of aggressive behaviour', *Aggressive Behaviour*, 10, 243–51.

Huesmann, L.R. and Eron, L.D. (1986), *Television and the Aggressive Child: A cross-national comparison*, Hillsdale, NJ: Erlbaum.

Hughes, M. (1975), *Egocentrism in Preschool Children*, unpublished Ph.D. thesis, University of Edinburgh.

Huston, T.L., Ruggiero, M., Conner, R. and Geis, G. (1981), 'Bystander intervention into crime: A study based on naturally-occurring episodes', *Social Psychology Quarterly*, 44, 14–23.

Ineichen, B., Harrison, G. and Morgan, H.G. (1984), 'Psychiatric hospital admissions in Briton: 1. Geographical and ethnic factors', *British Journal of Psychiatry*, 145, 600–4.

Jackson, J.L., Calhoun, K.S., Amick, A.E., Maddever, H.M. and Habif, V.L. (1990), 'Young adult women who report childhood intrafamilial sexual abuse: Subsequent adjustment', *Archives of Sexual Behaviour*, 19, 211–21.

Jackson, P. (1995), *Dear Uncle Go: Male Homosexuality in Thailand*, Bangkok: Bua Luang Books.

Jacobs, P.A., Brunton, M. and Melville, M.M. (1965), 'Aggressive behaviour, mental abnormality and the XXY male', *Nature*, 208, 1351–2.

James, W. (1884), 'What is an emotion?', *Mind*, 19; 188–205.

Jensen, A.R. (1969), 'How much can we boost IQ and scholastic achievement?', *Harvard Educational Review*, 39, 1–123.

Jones, E. (1953–7), *Sigmund Freud: Life and Work*, New York: Basic Books, 3 vols.

Jones, E.E. and Sigall, H. (1971), 'The bogus pipeline: A new paradigm for measuring affect and attitude', *Psychological Bulletin*, 76, 349–64.

Jones, R.K. (1966), 'Observations on stammering after localized cerebral injury', *Journal of Neurology, Neurosurgery and Psychiatry*, 29, 192–5.

Kalat, J.W. (1988), *Biological Psychology*, Belmont: Wadsworth.

Kamin, L. (1974), *The Science and Politics of IQ*, Harmondsworth: Penguin.

Kanner, L. (1943), 'Autistic Disturbances of Affective Contact', *Nervous Child*, 2, 217–50.

Kanner, L. and Eisenberg, L. (1955), 'Notes of the follow-up studies of autistic children' in P. Hoch and J. Zubin (eds), *Psychopathology of Childhood*, New York: Grune and Stratton.

Karau, S.J. and Williams, K.D. (1993), 'Social loafing: A meta-analytic review and theoretical integration', *Journal of Personality and Social Psychology*, 65, 681–706.

Karlins, M., Coffman, T.L. and Walters, G. (1969), 'On the fading of social stereotypes: Studies in three generations of college students', *Journal of Personality and Social Psychology*, 13, 1–16.

Katz, D. and Braly, K.W. (1933), 'Racial stereotypes of 100 college students', *Journal of Abnormal and Social Psychology*, 28, 280–90.

Kaufman, L. and Rock, I. (1962), ' The moon illusion', *Science*, 136, 1023–31.

Kelley, H.H. (1973), 'The process of causal attribution', *American Psychologist*, 28, 107–28.

Kellogg, W.N. and Kellogg, L.A. (1933), *The Ape and the Child*, New York: McGraw Hill.

Kelman, H.C. (1958), 'Compliance, identification and internalisation: Three processes of attitude change', *Journal of Conflict Resolution*, 2, 51–60.

Kelman, H.C. and Hovland, C.I. (1953), 'Reinstatement of the communication in delayed measurement of opinion change', *Journal of Abnormal and Social Psychology*, 48, 327–35.

Kilham, W. and Mann, L. (1974), 'Levels of destructive obedience as a function of transmitter and executant roles in the Milgram obedience paradigm', *Journal of Personality and Social Psychology*, 29: 696–702.

Kimura, D. (1973a), 'Manual activity during speaking – I. Right handers', *Neuropsychologia*, 11, 45–50.

Kimura, D. (1973b), 'Manual activity during speaking – II. Left handers', *Neuropsychologia*, 11, 51–5.

Kinsborne, M. (1972), 'Eye and head turning indicates cerebral lateralisation', *Science*, 176, 539–41.

Kolb, B. and Wishaw, I.Q. (1990), *Fundamentals of Neuropsychology*, New York: W.H. Freeman, 3rd edition.

La Piere, R.T. (1934), 'Attitudes vs Actions', *Social Forces*, 13, 230–7.

Lahey, B.B. (1983), *Psychology: An introduction*, Dubuque, IA, William C. Brown & Co.

Latané, B. and Darley, J.M. (1968), 'Group inhibition of bystander intervention', *Journal of Personality and Social Psychology*, 10, 215–21.

Latané, B. and Darley, J.M. (1970), *The Unresponsive Bystander: Why doesn't he help?*, Englewood Cliffs, NJ: Prentice Hall.

Latané, B. and Rodin, J. (1969), 'A lady in distress: Inhibiting effects of friends and strangers on bystander intervention', *Journal of Experimental Social Psychology*, 5, 189–202.

Le Bon, G. (1895), *The Crowd: a study of the popular mind*, London: T. Fisher Unwin.

LeDoux, J., Wilson, D.H. and Gazzaniga, M. (1977), 'A divided mind', *Annals of Neurology*, 2, 417–21.

Lenneberg, E. (1967), *Biological Foundations of Language*, New York: Wiley.

Lewis, D.O., Pincus, J.H., Bard, B. *et al.* (1988), 'Neuropsychiatric, psycho-educational, and family characteristics of 14 juveniles condemned to death in the United States', *American Journal of Psychiatry*, 154, 584–9.

Liebert, R.M. and Baron, R.A. (1972), 'Some immediate effects of televised violence on children's behaviour', *Developmental Psychology*, 6, 469–75.

Lintern, F., Williams, L. and Hill, A. (2003), *Psychology AS for OCR*, Oxford: Heinemann.

Littlewood, R. and Lipsedge, M. (1989), *Aliens and Alienists: Ethnic Minorities and Psychiatry*, London: Unwin Hyman.

Loew, C.A. (1967), 'Acquisition of a hostile attitude and its relationship to aggressive behaviour', *Journal of Personality and Social Psychology*, 5, 335–41.

Loftus, E.F. and Burns, H.J. (1982), 'Mental shock can produce retrograde amnesia', *Memory and Cognition*, 10, 318–23.

Loftus, Elizabeth F. (1996), *Eyewitness Testimony*, Cambridge, MA: Harvard University Press.

Lorenz, K. (1950), 'The comparative method in studying innate behaviour patterns', *Symposium of the Society of Experimental Biology*, 4, 221–68.

Lucas, A., Morley, R., Cole, T.J., Lister, G. and Leeson-Payne, C. (1992). 'Breast milk and subsequent intelligence quotient in children born pre-term', *The Lancet*, 399, 261–4.

Maccoby, E.E. and Jacklin, C.N. (1974), *The Psychology of Sex Differences*, Stanford, CA: Stanford University Press.

Malinowski, B. (1927), *Sex and Repression in Savage Society*, New York: Harcourt Brace Jovanovitch.

Mantell (1971), cited in R. Gross (1992), *Psychology: Science of Mind and Behaviour*, London: Hodder & Stoughton, 2nd edition.

Maranon, G. (1924), 'Contribution à l'étude de l'action émotive de l'adrénaline', *Revue Française d'Endocrinologie*, 2, 301–25.

McGarrigle, J. and Donaldson, M. (1974), 'Conservation accidents', *Cognition*, 3, 341–50.

McGovern, D. and Cope, R. (1987), 'The compulsory detention of males of different ethnic groups, with special reference to offender patients', *British Journal of Psychiatry*, 150, 505–12.

Mead, M. (1928), *Coming of Age in Samoa*, Harmondsworth: Penguin.

Meadows, S. (1993), *The Child as a Thinker*, London: Routledge.

Meeus, W.H.J. and Raaijmakers, Q.A.W. (1986), 'Administrative obedience: Carrying out orders to use psychological-administrative violence', *European Journal of Social Psychology*, 16, 311–24.

Milgram, S. (1963), 'Behavioural Study of Obedience', *Journal of Abnormal & Social Psychology*, 67, 371–378

Milgram, S. (1974), *Obedience to Authority*, New York: Harper Torchbooks.

Miller, G. (1956), 'The magical number seven, plus or minus two: some limits on our capacity for processing information', *Psychological Review* 63: 81–97.

Moghaddam, F.M., Taylor, D.M. and Wright, S.C. (1993), *Social Psychology in Cross-Cultural Perspective*, New York: W.H. Freeman and Co.

Moffitt, T.E. (1988), 'Neuropsychology and self-reported early delinquency in an unselected birth cohort', in Moffitt, T.E., Mednick, S.A. (eds), *Biological Contributions to Crime Causation*, New York: Martinus Nijhoff, 93–120.

Morris, R. (1994), 'Three Sexes and Four Sexualities: Redressing the Discourses on Gender and Sexuality in Contemporary Thailand', *Positions*, 2 (1), 15–43.

Mullen, B. (1986), 'Atrocity as a function of lynch mob composition: A self-attention perspective', *Personality and Social Psychology Bulletin*, 12: 187–97.

Murdock, B.B. (1962), 'The serial position effect of free recall', *Journal of Experimental Psychology*, 64, 482–88.

Needleman, H.L., Schell, A., Bellinger, D., Leviton, A. and Allred, E. (1990), 'Lead-associated intellectual deficit', *New England Journal of Medicine*, 322, 83–8.

Nelson, K. (1973), 'Structure and strategy in learning to talk', *Monographs of the Society for Research in Child Development*, 38 (one and two).

Oliver, K. (2001), *Applying Skills to Psychology*, London: Hodder & Stoughton.

Olweus, D. (1980), 'Familial and temperamental determinants of aggressive behaviour in adolescent boys. A causal analysis', *Developmental Psychology*, 16, 644–66.

Orne, M.T. (1962), 'On the social psychology of the psychological experiment, with particular reference to demand characteristics and their implications', *American Psychologist*, 17, 776–83.

Ornstein, R. (1986), *The Physiology of Consciousness*, Harmondsworth: Penguin, (2nd edition).

Pavlov, I.P. (1927), *Conditioned Reflexes*, London: Oxford University Press.

Perner, J. (1991), *Understanding the Representational Mind*, Cambridge, MA: Bradford Books/MIT Press.

Perner, J., Leekam, S. and Wimmer, H. (1987), 'Three year olds' difficulty in understanding false belief: cognitive limitation, lack of knowledge or pragmatic misunderstanding?' *British Journal of Developmental Psychology*, 5, 125–37.

Pervin, L.A. (1984), *Personality*, New York: John Wiley, 4th edition.

Piaget, J. and Inhelder, B. (1956), *The Child's Conception of Space*, London: RKP.

Piliavin, I.M., Rodin, J.A. and Piliavin, J.A. (1969), *Good Samaritanism, an Underground Phenomenon?*

Piliavin, I.M. Piliavin, J.A. and Rodin, J. (1975), 'Costs, diffusion and the stigmatised victim', *Journal of Personality and Social Psychology*, 32, 429–38.

Piliavin, J.A., Dovidio, J.F., Gaertner, S. and Clark III, R.D. (1981), *Emergency Intervention*, New York: Academic Press.

Putnam, F.W., Post, R.M. and Guroff, J.J. (1983), '100 cases of multiple personality disorder', paper presented at the annual meeting of the American Psychiatric Association. New York.

Rasmussen, T. and Milner, B. (1977), 'The role of early left-brain injury in determining lateralisation of cerebral speech functions', *Annals of the New York Academy of Sciences*, 299, 355–69.

Rehm, J., Steinleitner, M. and Lilli, W. (1987), 'Wearing uniforms and aggression. A field experiment', *European Journal of Social Psychology* 17, 357–60.

Richter, C.P. (1922), 'A behaviouristic study of the activity of the rat', *Comparative Psychology Monographs*, 1, 1–55.

Ringelmann, M. (1913), 'Recherches sur les moteurs animés: Travail de l'homme', *Annales de l'Institut National Argonomique*, 2e série, tome 12, 1–40.

Rivers, W.H.R. (1901), 'Vision' in A.C. Haddon (ed.), *Reports of the Cambridge Anthropological Expedition to the Torres Straits*, vol. two, part 1, Cambridge: Cambridge University Press.

Rose, S.A. and Blank, M. (1974), 'The potency of context in children's cognition: an illustration through conservation', *Child Development*, 45: 499–502.

Rosenhan, D.L. and Seligman, M.E.P. (1989), *Abnormal Psychology*, New York: Norton, 2nd edition.

Rosenzweig, M.R. (1984), 'Experience, memory and the brain', *American Psychologist*, 39: 365–76.

Ross, L. and Nisbett, R.E. (1991), *The Person and the Situation*, New York: McGraw Hill.

Russell, J. and Roberts, C. (2001), *Angles on Psychological Research*, Cheltenham: Nelson Thornes.

Rutter, M. (1981), *Maternal Deprivation Reassessed*, Harmondsworth: Penguin, 2nd edition.

Sacks, O. (1985), 'The twins' in *The Man Who Mistook his Wife for a Hat and Other Clinical Tales*, New York: Harper & Row.

Sacks, O. (1995), *An Anthropologist on Mars*, London: Picador.

Samuel, J. and Bryant, P. (1984). *Asking Only One question in the Conservation Experiment.*

Sapir, E. (1929), 'The status of linguistics as a science', *Language*, 5, 207–14.

Savage-Rumbaugh, S. (1988), 'A new look at ape language: comprehension of vocal speech and syntax', *Nebraska Symposium on Motivation*, 35, 201–55.

Schachter, S. (1964), 'The interaction of cognitive and physiological determinants of emotional state', in L. Berkowitz (ed.), *Advances in Experimental Social Psychology*. vol. 1, New York: Academic Press.

Schaffer, H.R. (1971), *The Growth of Sociability*, Harmondsworth: Penguin.

Schaffer, H.R. and Emmerson, P.E. (1964), 'The development of social attachments in infancy', *Monographs of Social Research in Child Development*, 29, no. 94.

Schreiber, F.R. (1973), *Sybil*. Harmondsworth: Penguin.

Searle, A. (1999), *Introducing Research and Data in Psychology*, London: Routledge.

Sears, D.O. (1988), 'Symbolic racism' in P. Katz and D. Taylor (eds), *Eliminating Racism. Profiles in Controversy*, New York: Plenum, 53–84.

Seashore, R.H. and Eckerson, L.D. (1940), 'The measurement of individual differences in general English vocabularies', *Journal of Educational Psychology*, 31, 14–38.

Segall, M.H., Campbell, D.T. and Herskovits, M.J. (1963), 'Cultural differences in the perception of geometric illusions', *Science*, 139, 769–71.

Seligman, M.E.P. (1975), *Helplessness: on Depression, Development and Death*. San Francisco: W. H. Freeman & Co.

Shallice, T. and Warrington, E.K. (1970), 'Independent functioning of verbal memory stores: a neuropsychological study', *Quarterly Journal of Experimental Psychology*, 22, 261–73.

Sheridan, C.L. and King, K.G. (1972), 'Obedience to authority with an authentic victim', *Proceedings of the 80th Annual Convention of the American Psychological Association*, 7, 165–6.

Sherif, M. (1966), *Group Conflict and Co-operation: Their social psychology*, London: RKP.

Shields, J. (1962), *Monozygotic Twins Brought Up Apart and Brought Together*, London: Oxford University Press.

Shotland, R.L. and Straw, M.K. (1976), 'Bystander response to an assault: When a man attacks a woman', *Journal of Personality and Social Psychology*, 34, 990–9.

Sigman, M., Mundy, P., Sherman, T. and Ungerer, J.A. (1986), 'Social interaction of autistic, mentally retarded and normal children and their caregivers', *Journal of Child Psychology and Psychiatry*, 27, 647–55.

Sime, J.D. (1983), 'Affiliative behaviour during escape to building exits', *Journal of Environmental Psychology*, 3, 21–41.

Sizemore, C.C. (1978), *I'm Eve*, n.p.: Berkely Publishing Group.

Skinner, B.F. (1938), *The Behaviour of Organisms*, New York: Appleton-Century-Crofts.

Skinner, B.F. (1957), *Verbal Behaviour*, New York: Appleton-Century-Crofts.

Slobin, D.I. (1975), 'On the nature of talk to children' in E.H. Lenneberg & E. Lennenerg (eds), *Infant Development*, Hove: Lawrence Erlbaum Associates Ltd.

Smith, P. and Cowie, H. (1988), *Understanding Children's Development*, Oxford: Blackwell.

Spanos, N.P., Weekes, J.R. and Bertrand, L.D. (1985), 'Multiple personality: A social psychological persepctive', *Journal of Abnormal Psychology*, 94, 362–76.

Spearman, C. (1904), 'General intelligence, objectively determined and measured', *American Journal of Psychology*, 15, 201–93.

Springer S.P. and Deutsch, G. (eds), (1993), *Left Brain/Right Brain*, New York: W.H. Freeman & Co., 4th edition.

Stang, D.J. (1973), 'Conformity, ability and self-esteem', *Representative Research in Social Psychology*, 3, 97–103.

Stern, D. (1977), *The First Relationship: Infant and Mother*, London: Fontana.

Stirling J.D. and Hellewell, J.S.E. (1999), *Psychopathology*, London: Routledge.

Storr, A. (1989), *Freud*, Oxford: Oxford University Press.

Szasz, T.S. (1960), 'The myth of mental illness', *American Psychologist*, 15, 113–18.

Tajfel, H. (1970), 'Experiments in intergroup discrimination', *Scientific American*, 223, 96–102.

Tajfel, H. (1982), *Social Identity and Intergroup Relations*, Cambridge: Cambridge University Press.

Terman, L.M. (1916), *The Measurement of Intelligence*, Boston: Houghton Mifflin.

Thibaut, J.W. and Kelley, H.H. (1959), *The Social Psychology of Groups*, New York: Wiley.

Thigpen, Corbett, H. and Cleckley, Harvey M. (1957), *The Three Faces of Eve*, n.p.: Secker & Warburg.

Tizard, B. and Hodges, J. (1978), 'The effects of early institutional rearing on the development of eight-year-old children', *Journal of Child Psychology and Psychiatry*, 19, 99–118.

Tizard, B. and Rees, J. (1974), 'A comparison of the effects of adoption, restoration to the natural mother and continued institutionalisation on the cognitive development of four-year-old children', *Child Development*, 45, 92–9.

Tulving E. (1972), 'Episodic and semantic memory' in E. Tulving and W. Donaldson (eds), *Organisation of Memory*, London: Academic Press.

Turnbull, C.M. (1961), *The Forest People*, New York: Simon and Schuster.

Valins, S. (1966), 'Cognitive effects of false heart-rate feedback', *Journal of Personality and Social Psychology*, 4, 400–8.

Watson, J.B. and Rayner, R. (1920), 'Conditioned emotional reactions', *Journal of Experimental Psychology*, 3, 1–14.

Watson, R.I. (1973), 'Investigation into deindividuation using a cross- cultural survey technique', *Journal of Personality and Social Psychology*, 25, 342–5.

Wechsler, D. (1958), *The Measurement and Appraisal of Adult Intelligence*, Baltimore: Williams and Wilkins, 4th edition.

Weiner, B. (1992), *Human Motivation: Metaphors, theories and research*, Newbury Park, CA: Sage.

Whyte, W.F. (1943), *Street Corner Society*, Chicago: University of Chicago Press.

Wicker, A.W. (1969), 'Attitudes versus actions: The relationship between verbal and overt behavioural responses to attitude objects', *Journal of Social Issues*, 25, 41–78.

Wilde Astington, J. (1994), *The Child's Discovery of the Mind*, London: Fontana Press.

Williams, K., Harkins, S. and Latané, B. (1981), 'Identifiability as a deterrent to social loafing: Two cheering experiments', *Journal of Personality and Social Psychology*, 40, 303–11.

Williams, T.M. (ed.) (1986), *The Impact of Television: A national experiment in three communities*, New York: Academic Press.

Wimmer, H. and Perner, J. (1983), 'Beliefs about beliefs: representation and constraining function of wrong beliefs in young children's understanding of deception', *Cognition*, 13: 103–28.

Witkin, H.A., Mednick, S.A., Schulsinger, F., Bakkestrom, E., Christansen, K.O., Goodenough, D.R., Hirschhorn, K., Lundsteen, C., Owen, D.R., Philips, J., Rubin, D.B. and Stocking, M. (1976), 'Criminality in XYY and XXY men: the elevated crime rate of XYY males is not related to aggression', *Science,* 193, 547–55.

Zimbardo, P.G. (1969/1970), 'The human choice: Individuation, reason and order versus deindividuation, impulse and chaos', in W.J. Arnold and D. Levine (eds), *Nebraska Symposium on Motivation*, Lincoln: University of Nebraska Press.

Index